COVID-19 and Schools

This book features contributions from leading experts who present peer-reviewed research on how the unprecedented COVID-19 pandemic affected U.S. teachers, students, parents, teaching practices, enrolments, and institutional innovations, offering the first empirical findings exploring educational impacts likely to last for decades.

The COVID-19 pandemic presented the greatest crisis in the history of U.S. schooling, with America's 50 states, thousands of school systems, and tens of thousands of private and charter schools responding in myriad ways. This book brings together peer-reviewed, empirical research on how U.S. schools responded and on the educational and health impacts likely to persist for many years. Contributors explore how the U.S. responses differed from those in other countries, with slower reopening, and both reopening and modes of instruction varying widely across states and school sectors. Compared to European countries, U.S. responses to reopening schools reflected political influences more than health or educational needs, though this was less true in market-based private and charter schools. The pandemic was a catalyst for school choice movements across the U.S. Many parents reacted to school closings by exploring alternatives to traditional public schools, including an important and likely permanent innovation, small, parent-created, or "pod" schools. As the papers here detail, long-term student learning loss and health and socioemotional impacts of COVID-19 closings may well last for decades. This volume concludes by exploring teacher experiences across different sectors following the pandemic.

COVID-19 and Schools will be a key resource for academics, researchers, and advanced students of education, education policy and leadership, educational research, research methods, economics, sociology, and psychology. The chapters included in this book were originally published as a special issue of the *Journal of School Choice*.

Robert Maranto holds the 21st-Century Chair in Leadership in the Department of Education Reform at the University of Arkansas, Fayetteville, Arkansas, USA. He has produced 15 books including *Educating Believers: Religion and School Choice* (2021) and *President Obama and Education Reform* (2012), while serving on his local school board.

David T. Marshall is an Associate Professor in the College of Education at Auburn University, Auburn, Alabama, USA. His research focuses on the COVID-19 pandemic and K-12 education, as well as charter schools and school choice. Dr. Marshall is a former teacher and previously served as a Chair of the Alabama Public Charter School Commission.

COVID-19 and Schools
Policy, Stakeholders, and School Choice

Edited by
Robert Maranto and David T. Marshall

LONDON AND NEW YORK

First published 2024
by Routledge
4 Park Square, Milton Park, Abingdon, Oxon, OX14 4RN

and by Routledge
605 Third Avenue, New York, NY 10158

Routledge is an imprint of the Taylor & Francis Group, an informa business

Introduction © 2024 David T. Marshall and Robert Maranto
Chapters 1–12 © 2024 Taylor & Francis

All rights reserved. No part of this book may be reprinted or reproduced or utilised in any form or by any electronic, mechanical, or other means, now known or hereafter invented, including photocopying and recording, or in any information storage or retrieval system, without permission in writing from the publishers.

Trademark notice: Product or corporate names may be trademarks or registered trademarks, and are used only for identification and explanation without intent to infringe.

British Library Cataloguing-in-Publication Data
A catalogue record for this book is available from the British Library

ISBN13: 978-1-032-54686-5 (hbk)
ISBN13: 978-1-032-54687-2 (pbk)
ISBN13: 978-1-003-42615-8 (ebk)

DOI: 10.4324/9781003426158

Typeset in Minion Pro
by codeMantra

Publisher's Note
The publisher accepts responsibility for any inconsistencies that may have arisen during the conversion of this book from journal articles to book chapters, namely the inclusion of journal terminology.

Disclaimer
Every effort has been made to contact copyright holders for their permission to reprint material in this book. The publishers would be grateful to hear from any copyright holder who is not here acknowledged and will undertake to rectify any errors or omissions in future editions of this book.

Contents

Citation Information		vii
Notes on Contributors		ix
	Introduction *David T. Marshall and Robert Maranto*	1
1	COVID-19 and Schooling in the U.S.: Disruption, Continuity, Quality, and Equity *Robert Maranto, Rodrigo Queiroz e Melo, and Charles Glenn*	6
2	We're All Teachers Now: Remote Learning During COVID-19 *Dick Carpenter and Joshua Dunn*	13
3	Parent-Created "Schools" in the U.S. *Angela R. Watson*	41
4	Reopening America's Schools: A Descriptive Look at How States and Large School Districts Navigated Fall 2020 *David T. Marshall and Martha Bradley-Dorsey*	50
5	Are School Reopening Decisions Related to Funding? Evidence from over 12,000 Districts During the COVID-19 Pandemic *Corey A. DeAngelis and Christos A. Makridis*	83
6	The Longer Students were Out of School, the Less They Learned *Harry Anthony Patrinos*	106
7	COVID-19 and School Closures: A Narrative Review of Pediatric Mental Health Impacts *David T. Marshall*	121
8	The Pre-Pandemic Growth in Online Public Education and the Factors that Predict It *Trevor Gratz, Dan Goldhaber, and Nate Brown*	131

vi   CONTENTS

9 This Time Really Is Different: The Effect of COVID-19 on Independent K-12
   School Enrollments   163
   Benjamin Scafidi, Roger Tutterow, and Damian Kavanagh

10 Opting Out: Enrollment Trends in Response to Continued Public School
   Shutdowns   189
   Will Flanders

11 COVID-19 Safety Concerns, School Governance Models, and Instructional
   Modes: An Exploration of School Quality Perspectives During the Pandemic   202
   Jason Jabbari, Takeshi Terada, Ethan Greenstein, and Evan Rhinesmith

12 Teacher Morale, Job Satisfaction, and Burnout in Schools of Choice Following
   the COVID-19 Pandemic   238
   David T. Marshall, Natalie M. Neugebauer, Tim Pressley, and Katrina Brown-Aliffi

   Index   259

Citation Information

The following chapters were originally published in the various volumes and issues of the *Journal of School Choice*. When citing this material, please use the original page numbering for each article, as follows:

Chapter 1
Introduction to a Special Section on COVID-19 and Schooling in the U.S.: Disruption, Continuity, Quality, and Equity
Robert Maranto, Rodrigo Queiroz e Melo, and Charles Glenn
Journal of School Choice, volume 14, issue 4 (2020) pp. 527–533

Chapter 2
We're All Teachers Now: Remote Learning During COVID-19
Dick Carpenter and Joshua Dunn
Journal of School Choice, volume 14, issue 4 (2020) pp. 567–594

Chapter 3
Parent-Created "Schools" in the U.S
Angela R. Watson
Journal of School Choice, volume 14, issue 4 (2020) pp. 595–603

Chapter 4
Reopening America's Schools: A Descriptive Look at How States and Large School Districts are Navigating Fall 2020
David T. Marshall and Martha Bradley-Dorsey
Journal of School Choice, volume 14, issue 4 (2020) pp. 534–566

Chapter 5
Are School Reopening Decisions Related to Funding? Evidence from over 12,000 Districts During the COVID-19 Pandemic
Corey A. DeAngelis and Christos A. Makridis
Journal of School Choice, volume 16, issue 3 (2022) pp. 454–476

Chapter 6
The Longer Students Were Out of School, the Less They Learned
Harry Anthony Patrinos
Journal of School Choice, volume 17, issue 2 (2023) pp. 161–175

Chapter 7

COVID-19 and School Closures: A Narrative Review of Pediatric Mental Health Impacts
David T. Marshall
Journal of School Choice (2023), DOI:10.1080/15582159.2023.2201734

Chapter 8

The Pre-Pandemic Growth in Online Public Education and the Factors that Predict It
Trevor Gratz, Dan Goldhaber, and Nate Brown
Journal of School Choice, volume 16, issue 3 (2022) pp. 497–528

Chapter 9

This Time Really Is Different: The Effect of COVID-19 on Independent K-12 School Enrollments
Benjamin Scafidi, Roger Tutterow, and Damian Kavanagh
Journal of School Choice, volume 15, issue 3 (2021) pp. 305–330

Chapter 10

Opting Out: Enrollment Trends in Response to Continued Public School Shutdowns
Will Flanders
Journal of School Choice, volume 15, issue 3 (2021) pp. 331–343

Chapter 11

COVID-19 Safety Concerns, School Governance Models, and Instructional Modes: An Exploration of School Quality Perspectives during the Pandemic
Jason Jabbari, Takeshi Terada, Ethan Greenstein, and Evan Rhinesmith
Journal of School Choice, volume 17, issue 2 (2023) pp. 254–289

Chapter 12

Teacher Morale, Job Satisfaction, and Burnout in Schools of Choice Following the COVID-19 Pandemic
David T. Marshall, Natalie M. Neugebauer, Tim Pressley, and Katrina Brown-Aliffi
Journal of School Choice (2023), DOI: 10.1080/15582159.2023.2201737

For any permission-related enquiries please visit:
http://www.tandfonline.com/page/help/permissions

Notes on Contributors

Martha Bradley-Dorsey, Department of Education Reform, University of Arkansas, Fayetteville, AR, USA.

Nate Brown, School of Social Work, University of Washington Seattle, WA, USA.

Katrina Brown-Aliffi, Arts & Humanities, Teachers College of Columbia University, New York, NY, USA.

Dick Carpenter, College of Education, University of Colorado at Colorado Springs, CO, USA.

Corey A. DeAngelis, American Federation for Children, Cato Institute, Reason Foundation, Washington DC, USA.

Joshua Dunn, Department of Political Science, University of Colorado at Colorado Springs, CO, USA.

Will Flanders, Wisconsin Institute for Law & Liberty, Milwaukee, WI, USA.

Charles Glenn, Department of Educational Leadership, Boston University, MA, USA.

Dan Goldhaber, School of Social Work, University of Washington Seattle, WA, USA.

Trevor Gratz, School of Social Work, University of Washington Seattle, WA, USA.

Ethan Greenstein, Social Policy Institute, Washington University in St. Louis, USA.

Jason Jabbari, Social Policy Institute, Washington University in St. Louis, MO, USA.

Damian Kavanagh, Mid-South Independent School Business Officers (MISBO), Georgia, USA

Christos A. Makridis, Digital Economy Lab, Stanford University, USA; Chazen Institute, Columbia University, New York City, NY, USA.

Robert Maranto, Department of Education Reform, University of Arkansas, Fayetteville, AR, USA.

David T. Marshall, Department of Educational Foundations, Leadership, and Technology, Auburn University, Auburn, AL, USA.

Rodrigo Queiroz e Melo, School of Law, Portuguese Catholic University, Lisbon, Portugal.

Natalie M. Neugebauer, Department of Educational Foundations, Leadership, and Technology, Auburn University, Auburn, AL, USA.

NOTES ON CONTRIBUTORS

Harry Anthony Patrinos, Office of the Chief Economist, Europe and Central Asia, World Bank, Washington DC, USA.

Tim Pressley, Department of Psychology, Christopher Newport University, Newport News, VA, USA.

Evan Rhinesmith, School of Education, Saint Louis University, St. Louis, MO, USA.

Benjamin Scafidi, Kennesaw State University, Kennesaw, GA, USA.

Takeshi Terada, Social Policy Institute, Washington University, St. Louis, MO, USA.

Roger Tutterow, Kennesaw State University, Kennesaw, GA, USA.

Angela R. Watson, Johns Hopkins Institute for Education Policy, Baltimore, MD, USA.

Introduction

David T. Marshall and Robert Maranto

The SARS-CoV-2 (COVID-19) pandemic disrupted most facets of life in early 2020, and schooling was no exception. In the United States, schools closed for in-person instruction in all 50 states, and remote learning occurred for the balance of the 2019–2020 school year. This edited volume shares social science research conducted throughout the COVID-19 pandemic. The *Journal of School Choice* published a special section on COVID-19, and the impact the policy response to it was having in late 2020, of which the first four chapters of this volume were included. The first chapter was the introduction for the special section. In it, Robert Maranto, Rodrigo Queiroz e Melo, and Charles Glenn share their international survey findings and introduce the next three chapters. In the intervening months and years, the journal has published eight additional pieces exploring the impact that the pandemic has had on K-12 education in the United States. This collection of articles focuses primarily on three themes: (1) school closure and reopening policy during the pandemic; (2) how various constituencies experienced the pandemic and its aftermath; and (3) the rise of school choice movements during the crisis.

The decision to close schools was quite radical, though likely prudent given what little information existed about the nature of the virus at the start of the pandemic. This was part of a larger mitigation strategy to slow the spread of COVID-19. According to research Katherine Auger and her colleagues (2020), published in *JAMA*, states that closed schools earlier experienced significantly fewer deaths and hospitalizations due to COVID-19. In other words, the decision to close schools on March 12, 2020, as Michigan did, was associated with fewer detrimental health outcomes than the decision to close schools on March 23, 2020, when Texas closed schools. However, research conducted since the initial surge of COVID-19 has suggested otherwise. For example, Jay Varma and colleagues (2020) studied COVID-19 cases in New York City among K-12 school employees and students between October and December 2020 and compared them to the community at large. For each of the weeks they studied, public school employees and students who were physically in schools had lower rates of infection than the rest of the city's population – and indication that schools were not vectors of transmission. Ample research conducted in the United States has emerged that suggests students suffered academically, socially, and emotionally during the lockdowns and school closures (e.g., Duckworth et al., 2021; Halloran et al., 2021).

It is against this backdrop with which school closure policy must be judged. The evidence on student learning loss has caused even some of the most ardent proponents of school closures to change their minds. Karl Lauterbach, Germany's pro-lockdown public health minister, called the lengthy school closures "a big mistake" and "unnecessary" in a February 2023 German public broadcasting interview, when, as recent as April 2022, he was still warning against removing COVID-19-related restrictions too quickly (Luyken, 2023). Public policy always features trade-offs, and in the case of COVID-19 school closures, the public health benefit of closing schools did not outweigh the academic losses suffered by students.

Five chapters in this volume explore school closure and reopening policy. In Chapter 1, Robert Maranto and his colleagues share survey findings from 21 countries collected in the summer of 2020. Overall, they found that all of the 15 European school systems represented in their sample either had already reopened their schools by the summer of 2020 or planned to do so by September 2020. In Chapter 4, David Marshall and Martha Bradley-Dorsey present descriptive research that explored state and large school district reopening policy in August 2020. The pair reviewed school reopening plans for all 50 states and tallied how large school districts were planning to open by learning modality (i.e., fully in-person, remote only, or hybrid). Compared to the European countries described in Chapter 1, American schools were much less likely to reopen in person for Fall 2020. Marshall and Bradley-Dorsey found that two-thirds of large school districts planned to reopen remotely as of August 21, 2020. The number actually jumped to 74% by the start of the school year (Marshall & Bradley-Dorsey, 2022). They also found that school districts whose student bodies were 85% or more non-White were statistically and substantially less likely to reopen for in-person instruction in the fall of 2020, raising equity concerns. In Chapter 5, Corey DeAngelis and Christos Makridis analyzed data from more than 12,000 school districts to explore whether Fall 2020 reopening decisions were related to funding. One might assume that districts with more money might be more likely to reopen if having resources was a primary factor in these decisions. Conversely, they found a positive relationship between remote learning and revenue per student. Despite public assertions to the contrary, the evidence suggests that schools did not fail to reopen schools due to a lack of the resources to do so. In Chapter 6, World Bank economist Harry Patrinos shares findings from his work comparing pandemic learning loss across 41 countries. He finds that the longer the schools were closed, the more learning loss there was in a country. On average, countries closed their schools for 21 weeks, and this was associated with about a year's worth of learning loss. Students in Sweden, which never closed its schools, experienced no learning loss. In Chapter 7, David Marshall reviews the literature exploring student's mental health impacts related to school closures. Though schools initially closed as part of an effort to keep students safe from COVID-19, the closures led to disastrous mental health outcomes for children and adolescents including increased anxiety, stress, and depression, as well as increases in suicidal ideation and incidence. Overall, the evidence suggests that future decisions about school closures should take into account the overall health impacts on students and not myopically focus on one threat (in this case, COVID-19).

Three of the chapters included in this volume discuss the experience of stakeholders in K-12 education, namely of parents and teachers. In the second chapter, Dick Carpenter and Joshua Dunn share findings from survey research conducted with parents during the summer of 2020, exploring their perceptions of remote learning. Overall, they found that parents were generally positive about the experience during the early weeks of the pandemic. Parents who enrolled their children in private and charter schools were more positive about the experience than those who enrolled their children in traditional public schools. Carpenter and Dunn found that more than a third of parents indicated that they would elect to enroll their children in school remotely for the fall of 2020 – an educational option that all families were privy to for the 2020–2021 school year. In Chapter 11, Jason Jabbari, Takeshi Terada, Ethan Greenstein, and Evan Rhinesmith also explore parent perceptions of instructional quality during the pandemic. Using two waves of survey data, Jabbari and his colleagues found that parents perceived private and charter schools to be of greater school quality; however, they did not find differences in parent perceptions of quality across learning modalities. Charter school parents associated hybrid instruction with lower school quality, while private school parents did not see hybrid learning modalities the same. In Chapter 12, David Marshall, Natalie Neugebauer, Tim Pressley, and Katrina Brown-Aliffi explored teacher perspectives at the end of the 2021–2022 school year – a point in time when COVID-19 mitigation protocols had been removed throughout the United States, except for mask wearing in a few areas. They found that private school teachers reported greater levels of job satisfaction than teachers in traditional public schools and that private and charter school teachers reported greater levels of morale than their traditional public school peers. Teachers across sectors experienced similar levels of burnout. Private and charter school teachers reported having more autonomy in the classroom than teachers in traditional systems.

The remaining four chapters explored a range of school choice movements that were evident during the pandemic. Although school choice programs such as private school vouchers and charter schools have been in existence for decades now, most families still enrolled their children in traditional public schools run by traditional publicly funded and operated school districts prior to the pandemic. However, since schools closed in March 2020, trend lines have decidedly moved in the direction of more choice. During the pandemic, parents "voted with their feet" and indicated that they wanted additional educational options for their children. Between Spring 2021 and Spring 2022, traditional public school enrollments saw a nine percent decrease, which translates to roughly 4 million students (Jacobson, 2022). Meanwhile, charter school enrollments increased by seven percent during the 2020–2021 school year (Veney & Jacobs, 2021), and private school enrollment and homeschooling increased (Jacobson, 2022). Private Christian schools have seen their enrollments increase 35% since the start of the pandemic (Lee & Swaner, 2023). In short, the COVID-19 pandemic and subsequent policy decisions made by traditional school systems created an opening for more parents to desire additional educational options for their children.

In Chapter 3, Angela Watson explores learning pods – commonly referred to as "pandemic pods" during the summer of 2020 and during the 2020–2021 academic year. As parents began to see that traditional public schools in some areas were hesitant to open their doors, they began to form learning pods as an alternative that would allow their children to learn in person and not exclusively through devices. This was especially attractive for parents with younger children. In Chapter 8, Trevor Gratz, Dan Goldhaber, and Nate Brown explored pre-pandemic trends in online public education. They found that zip codes with greater levels of wealth, as well as those with slower internet speed, had lower rates of online enrollment. They also found that higher standardized test scores in the neighboring traditional public schools were negatively associated with online enrollment. These trends are important to consider as a backdrop to the greatest experiment in large-scale online learning that has ever been attempted in the United States. In Chapter 9, Benjamin Scafidi, Roger Tutterow, and Damian Kavanagh examine private school enrollment trends during the pandemic. There was an initial spate of closures at the start of the pandemic (McCluskey, 2022), and economic downturns have historically been associated with downward private school enrollment trends. However, Scafidi and his colleagues report that 70% of independent schools saw their enrollments increase during the 2020–2021 school year. The main determinant of these increases was whether neighboring traditional public schools were offering an in-person learning option. In Chapter 10, Will Flanders shares similar findings. He explored data from Wisconsin that suggests that school districts that only offered remote learning during the 2020–2021 school year faced the largest enrollment declines, with enrollment increases found in private schools and in school districts with established (pre-pandemic) virtual learning options.

Each of the articles featured in this edited volume contributes to our larger understanding of what happened to K-12 education during the COVID-19 pandemic. Understanding how major school policy decisions – including the decision to close schools – impact students is important for navigating future crises. It is equally important to understand how stakeholders like teachers and parents experienced the pandemic. Finally, the COVID-19 pandemic potentially marked the beginning of a new era of school choice policy. During the pandemic, parents sought additional educational options for their children and policy is beginning to catch up. Between the summer of 2022 and the first few months of 2023, Arizona, Arkansas, Florida, Indiana, Iowa, Utah, and West Virginia have all passed universal school choice legislation, and there is legislation pending in several other states. Scholars who wish to study these school choice initiatives would be wise to revisit the catalyst that created this opening. The articles included in this volume that discuss pandemic-era alternatives to traditional public schooling would be a good place to start.

References

Auger, K. A., Shah, S. S., Richardson, T., Hartley, D., Hall, M., Warniment, A., Timmons, K., et al. (2020). Associations between statewide school closures and COVID-19 incidence and mortality in the US. *JAMA, 324*(9), 859–870. https://doi.org/10.1001/jama/2020.14348

Duckworth, A. L., Kautz, T., Defnt, A., Satlof-Bedrick, E., Talamas, S., Lira, B., & Steinberg, L. (2021). Students attending school remotely suffer socially, emotionally, and academically. *Educational Researcher, 50*(7), 479–482. https://doi.org/10.3102/0013189X211031551

Halloran, C., Jack, R., Okun, J. C., & Oster, E. (2021). *Pandemic schooling mode and student test scores: Evidence from US states.* (No. w29497). National Bureau of Economic Research. http://www.nber.org/papers/w29497

Jacobson, L. (2022, September 20). 'Wake-up calls': New parent survey shows 9% enrollment drop in district schools. *The 74.* https://www.the74million.org/article/wake-up-calls-new-parent-survey-shows-9-enrollment-drop-in-district-schools/#:~:text=Conducted%20by%20Tyton%20Partners%2C%20a,into%20over%204%20million%20students

Lee, M., & Swaner, L. (2023, January 11). *Public schools have lost over a million students. Here's where they're going.* National Review. https://www.nationalreview.com/2023/01/public-schools-have-lost-over-a-million-students-heres-where-theyre-going

Luyken, J. (2023, February 10). We went too far with Covid restrictions, says Germany's pro-lockdown minister. *The Telegraph.* https://www.telegraph.co.uk/world-news/2023/02/10/went-far-covid-restrictions-says-germanys-pro-lockdown-minister

Marshall, D. T., & Bradley-Dorsey, M. (2022). Reopening schools in the United States. In D. T. Marshall (Ed.), *COVID-19 and the classroom: How schools navigated the great disruption* (pp. 147–164). Lexington Books.

McCluskey, N. (2022). Assessing the pandemic's toll on private schools. In D. T. Marshall (Ed.), *COVID-19 and the classroom: How schools navigated the great disruption* (pp. 183–196). Lexington Books.

Varma, J. K., Thamkittikasem, J., Whittemore, K., Alexander, M., Stephens, D. H., Arslanian, K., Bray, J., & Long, T. G. (2021). COVID-19 infections among students and staff in New York City public schools. *Pediatrics, 147*(5), e2021050605. https://doi.org/10.1542/peds.2021-050605

Veney, D., & Jacobs, D. (2021, September). *Voting with their feet: A state-level analysis of public charter school and district public school trends.* Washington, DC: National Alliance for Public Charter Schools. https://www.publiccharters.org/sites/default/files/documents/2021-09/napcs_voting_feet_rd6.pdf

COVID-19 and Schooling in the U.S.: Disruption, Continuity, Quality, and Equity

Robert Maranto, Rodrigo Queiroz e Melo, and Charles Glenn

ABSTRACT

Globalization brings benefits such as economic growth and exposure to new products and people. Yet it also brings risks, as shown most recently by the COVID-19 pandemic. Here, we introduce a special section on how American k-12 schooling is responding to that pandemic. While media coverage has arguably overstated the dangers of COVID-19, this introduction and the three papers in this special section offer more empirical takes, which together suggest more pragmatism than partisanship in public responses. In the introduction, we compare U.S. and international schooling responses to the pandemic, in part using a survey of informants in 21 nation-states. Generally, the U.S. is taking a more cautious approach than most other developed countries regarding school reopening. Second, in a short white paper, Angela Watson of Johns Hopkins University offers a summary of the extant knowledge of learning pods in the U.S., a fascinating innovation flourishing during the pandemic. Third, in "Reopening America's Schools: A Descriptive Look at How States and Large School Districts are Navigating Fall 2020," David Marshall of Auburn University and Martha Bradley-Dorsey of the University of Arkansas discuss how the 50 U.S. states and 120 largest school districts are reopening, largely online. Finally, in "We're All Teachers Now: Remote Learning During COVID-19," Dick Carpenter and Joshua Dunn of the University of Colorado/Colorado Springs report results from a national survey of parents, including comparisons of public, charter, and private schools.

Fear and anger are the most reliable drivers of engagement; scary tales of young victims of the pandemic, intimating that we are all at risk of dying, quickly go viral; so do stories that blame everything on your political adversaries. Both social and traditional media have been churning out both types of narratives in order to generate more clicks and increase their audience.

Sonal Desai (2020)

The crisis

COVID-19 may be the worst global pandemic since the four waves of the 1918–20 flu pandemic. Fortunately, nearly all societies are now far better prepared regarding nutrition, sanitation, and health care. Since 1900, human life expectancy globally has nearly doubled to roughly 70, higher in post-industrial nations. In every respect save (possibly) psychologically people are in far better shape than in 1918, and thus far more likely to survive sickness (Deaton, 2013). At this writing COVID-19 is estimated to have killed under a million people globally, a large toll sure to rise, but orders of magnitude fewer than the estimated 50 million killed in the earlier pandemic, which struck when the global population was about a quarter of today's total (currently about 1 in 1,500 Americans are thought to have died from the effects of COVID-19). Healthier populations are less vulnerable to everything, including coronavirus. In contrast to the earlier pandemic, the vast majority of COVID-19 fatalities are the old and the ill. The first 15,596 COVID-19 deaths in California included only *three* school age children, fewer than in some flu seasons. Just 1.5% of California's fatalities were under age 35; 64% aged 70 or older (California Department of Public Health, 2020). COVID-19 will thus rob relatively fewer years of life than many other causes. Generally, this illness kills and incapacitates those institutionalized in nursing homes, not schools, suggesting the need to protect vulnerable staff and the families of students more than students.

Further, societies are materially far better off than in 1918, reducing the dangers of pandemic. People in developed and many developing countries have more living space, so they can socially distance, decreasing contagion. Information technology allows many to work from home, limiting exposure for "nonessential" workers. Large welfare states and private sector supply chains for food and other essential items have kept people in developed and developing countries from dire material distress, even if some are unemployed, isolated, depressed, and fearful (Deaton, 2013; Maranto, 2020). In the U.S., at least, young people in particular dramatically overestimate the personal danger of the pandemic, in part due to social media's constant repetition of rare cases of deaths among the relatively young, and in part due to partisan divisions in a presidential election year (Desai, 2020). No doubt fears were exacerbated by the Trump administration's questionable handling of the crisis and the President's near daily misstatements and provocations, not to mention more prevarications than most presidents tell. In fairness, social media lends itself to repeating disinformation of all types and is uniquely suited to spreading panic rather than perspective (Lukianoff & Haidt, 2018; Twenge, 2017). This makes it difficult for even the most competent and honest leadership to manage crises.

An additional factor is public ignorance, perhaps particularly in the U.S. and here particularly among the young, including widespread absence of basic knowledge about mathematics and statistics (Bauerlein, 2009). This reflects not just the recent development of social media but more than a century of American public schools emphasizing social skills, custodial care of the young, and vocational skills rather than knowledge (Hirsch, 1996; Maranto & Wai, 2020). Public ignorance may force public officials including U.S. school boards and educational leaders to overreact to coronavirus in ways jeopardizing both academic achievement and equity. Given widespread fear, it is not surprising that Americans erred on the side of closing physical schools in spring and keeping physical schools closed in fall, even though this will mean both less and less equitable learning. As the survey reported later in this section by Carpenter and Dunn shows, large majorities of public and private school parents agreed that under online learning in spring 2020, their children fell behind academically. As Opalka and Talkington (2020) report, charter schools were much more likely than traditional public schools to continue some semblance of testing and grading policies.

Generally, as Frederick M. Hess (2020) recently summarized, the spring experience with online schooling reduced academic learning:

> Researchers at NWEA, Brown, and the University of Virginia have estimated that students will begin the coming school year already woefully behind, with just two-thirds the learning gains in reading and as little as half of the gains in math that we would normally expect. This is hardly a surprise, given that nearly a quarter of students were truant and that, even as the spring semester ground to an end, only a fifth of school districts expected teachers to provide real-time instruction ... the evidence is pretty clear that, for most learners, virtual learning today is significantly less effective than classroom instruction. Research suggests that is likely to be particularly true for disadvantaged students.

Hess adds that initial evidence suggests that school districts have learned far too little from poor online performance in the spring.

Ironically, at a time when American thought leaders constantly talk about educational equity, online learning is increasing achievement gaps, with upper-income parents far more likely than others to supplement schooling with home lessons. In contrast to the U.S., most European countries may have arrived at school reopening policies striking a better balance between health and academic achievement and equity.

Non-American responses to COVID-19

In early August 2020 we surveyed a convenience sample of informants in the U.S., 15 European countries, two Asian countries (Kazakhstan and Malaysia), and three developing countries (Columbia, Kenya, and South Africa), for an n of 21. (A total of 58 deliverable requests were sent.) Given the initial uncertainties of COVID-19 mortality rates in spring 2020, with some predicting tens of millions of deaths worldwide, both the U.S. and nearly every other country closed schools in March or shortly thereafter. (Kazakhstan waited until May 22.) Schools then reopened online, usually after 2 weeks, though for certain large American school districts this took far longer. Since few U.S. teachers had online teaching experience, this did not go well (Hess, 2020; Marshall, Shannon, & Lee, 2020). Most other countries also closed physical schools in March and reopened online shortly thereafter.

In contrast to the U.S., numerous countries (the United Kingdom, Northern Ireland, Malaysia, Turkey, Hungary, Italy, Kazakhstan, Spain, Albania), some of which had high COVID-19 caseloads, reopened physical schools in July, August, or September, some earlier or with variations by type of school or student age, given the relative immunity of younger students. Other countries prioritized earlier physical reopenings, at least for some students. Sweden closed physical schools only for students aged 16 or older, while keeping schools open for younger students, who are less vulnerable to COVID-19 and more dependent on adult supervision, albeit with certain precautions. The Netherlands reopened elementary schools in June and secondary schools in September, with the expectation that higher education would remain closed until February. Israel closed physical schools on April 1 but reopened them on May 30. Germany closed physical schools on March 12, reopening June 1. Slovenia and Greece closed most schools on or about March 12 and reopened May 18. Portugal also closed schools on May 12, reopening kindergarten and secondary senior year on March 18, with full reopening in the fall. Albania closed schools in March, and reopened in late May, but only for end of year examinations for certain grades; essentially its schools closed until fall.

As will be noted by the Marshall and Bradley-Dorsey article that follows, many U.S. school districts urged schools to attempt to protect physically vulnerable staff, perhaps by assigning online teaching or limiting in-person duties. Informants in 12 of the 20 other nations surveyed indicated this was a common practice (the U.K., Israel, Netherlands, Germany, Turkey, Sweden, Slovenia, Portugal, Greece, Italy, South Africa, Columbia). As noted, many U.S. traditional public schools stopped teaching new material, and ended formal assessments, in effect giving up on academic growth and measurement. Informants in only three other countries (Northern Ireland, Israel, Italy) reported that their schools stopped teaching new material. Informants in these countries, the U.S., and seven other countries indicated that formal assessments were ended as a result of COVID-19, at least for spring 2020 (the U.K., Albania, Malaysia, Sweden, Portugal, Greece, and Turkey).

Resembling the U.S., just over one-third of our non-U.S. informants indicated that their countries allowed local and regional variations regarding physical closing and opening of state-run schools, about two-thirds reported such variation in curricula. (We suspect the real figures are higher.) Yet certain commonalities remained. In the U.S., and elsewhere, nearly all schools required staff and students (save for the very young) to wear masks and practice some degree of social distancing. About two-thirds of informants report social distancing norms of 1.5 meters or more, but one-third indicate norms of 1 meter or less, or that such norms are "hardly ever practiced." Many reported such basic precautions as opening windows, to discourage spread of Coronavirus. What is different, however, is that schools in certain European systems reopened in Spring 2020 or left it up to individual schools or regions. At the time of our survey, all European countries where we had informants planned or already had reopened physical schools for fall 2020, without calendar changes, though typically with masks and social distancing.

The situation is more complex in the few developing countries in the sample, not surprisingly given the more difficult tradeoffs low-income countries may face between education and health, where health-care infrastructure is less developed and multiple generations often share the same household. In Columbia, Kenya, and South Africa physical schools closed in March to be replaced by online schools and lessons by radio. Columbia has allowed leeway for regions and for private schools, though with equity concerns given digital divide related issues. Equity concerns may be even greater in the two African nations. A Kenyan respondent wrote:

The State ordered the closure of all schools, determining the re-opening dates, and have now written off the 2020 academic year, directing all schools to reopen in 2021. However, independent schools have challenged this in court, wishing to be permitted to re-open sooner when they meet safety standards. The case is still on going.

Similarly, a South African respondent observed:

The opening of the schools were phased in – different grades at different times. The grade 12 (last year of schooling) was the first grade to start and is on-going. Parents were given the option to do online schooling or register for homeschooling. However, currently all government (public) schools are closed for a month as they expect the peak in August. Private schools were given the option to choose. The Congress of South African Students have opposed this and has called for the closure of all schools – again citing anger at the two tier approach that they see as providing an advantage and believe that all schools should follow the same rules … The glaring difference between rich and poor became increasingly stark as a huge number of school going children have no access to resources (computers, data etc) to be able to continue with online schooling … Recently, schools have been asked to open in some communities so that they can continue with the feeding scheme to children who rely on the school meal for the day.

Perhaps the biggest takeaway is that all 15 European school systems where we had informants reported that they had already or would reopen physical schools at least by September, though typically with masks and social distancing save for the very young. In this, relative to Americans, the Europeans seem to have prioritized academic achievement and equity.

What follows

The short white paper and two peer reviewed articles which follow will cover other aspects of the COVID-19 pandemic and American schooling. In her short, invited essay on parent-created schools, often referred to as "learning pods," Angela Watson describes what we know about these innovative small "schools," often with 10–15 students and one or two teachers. These have grown quickly under COVID-19, providing more academic content and socializing than online schools, but less contagion than physical schools. State regulations may affect how much this innovation can spread.

In "Reopening America's Schools: A Descriptive Look at how States and Large School Districts Navigated Fall 2020," David Marshall and Martha Bradley-Dorsey outline how the 50 U.S. states and 120 largest school districts are reopening. As noted, to a much greater degree than in Europe, American schools are opening online only – this is the case for more than two-thirds of the large districts. This is particularly true in high poverty and high minority areas, perhaps reflecting greater distrust of the government or the greater toll COVID-19 has taken in these communities. Most states allow local school districts and charter schools considerable autonomy. Some condition reopening in a region on the number of active cases. Some states urge or require that school districts reopen physically, for reasons related to educational equity. As noted, low-income children, in particular, usually do better in physical schools. Despite recent political polarization, the authors find much pragmatism and relatively little partisanship in reopening policies, with one noted exception: more democratic states are more likely to suspend athletics, which play a vital role in U.S. public schools.

Finally, in "We're All Teachers Now: Remote Learning During COVID-19," Dick Carpenter and Joshua Dunn present results from a national survey of 1,743 parents conducted in the first 2 weeks of August. About 8 in 10 parents report that their schools eventually provided remote learning support after closing in March, and most reported that they felt adequately prepared, and assisted by schools. Private and charter schools were more likely to require online attendance, grade assignments and far more likely to offer direct communication with teachers. Having their children at home led many parents to have greater appreciation for the work teachers do. Reflecting this, only a small percentage of respondents said they were going to homeschool in fall 2020, but more than a third planned to send their child to a virtual school out of concern about their child's health.

Of course, this is just the start of what will likely be continuing research on schooling under COVID-19, a pandemic which like its 1918–20 predecessor, in one form or another may continue for some time.

Disclosure statement

No potential conflict of interest was reported by the authors.

References

Bauerlein, M. (2009). *The Dumbest Generation: How the digital age stupefies young Americans and jeopardizes our future*. New York, NY: Penguin Press.

California Department of Public Health. (2020, September 6). Cases and deaths associated with COVID-19 by age group in California. Retrieved from https://www.cdph.ca.gov/Programs/CID/DCDC/Pages/COVID-19/COVID-19-Cases-by-Age-Group.aspx

Deaton, A. (2013). *The great escape: Health, wealth, and the origins of inequality*. Princeton: Princeton University Press.

Desai, S. (2020, July 29). On my mind: They blinded us from science. *Franklin Templeton*. Retrieved from https://www.franklintempletonnordic.com/investor/article?contentPath=html%2Ffthinks%2Fcommon%2Fcio-views%2Fon-my-mind-they-blinded-us-from-science.html&fbclid=IwAR15y57eU0nS9LVqgjvhbfsd1zz46Ac1dbnT_t9LXBZiZDpkzHLlR29wa8E

Hess, F. M. (2020, August 20). The hard truth about remote learning this fall. *National Review*. Retrieved from //www.aei.org/op-eds/the-hard-truth-about-remote-learning-this-fall/

Hirsch, E. D. (1996). *The schools we need and why we don't have them*. New York, NY: Doubleday.

Lukianoff, G., & Haidt, J. (2018). *The coddling of the American mind*. New York, NY: Penguin Press.

Maranto, R. (2020, June 13). Has Coronavirus made America *The Village*? Shyamalan's classic horror movie captures political mood. *National Review*. Retrieved from https://www.natio nalreview.com/2020/06/coronavirus-the-village-shyamalan-movie-captures-current-political-mood/

Maranto, R., & Wai, J. (2020, January). Why intelligence is missing from American education policy and practice, and what can be done about it. *Journal of Intelligence*, 8(1). Retrieved from https://www.mdpi.com/2079-3200/8/1/2

Marshall, D. T., Shannon, D. M., & Lee, S. M. (2020, September 2). How teachers experienced the COVID-19 transition to remote instruction. *Phi Delta Kappan*.

Opalka, A., & Talkington, B. (2020, May 12). Avoiding long-term harm from "Do No Harm" grading policies. Seattle, WA: Center for Reinventing Public Education. Retrieved from //www.crpe.org/thelens/avoiding-long-term-harm-do-no-harm-grading-policies

Twenge, J. M. (2017). *iGen: Why today's superconnected kids are growing up less rebellious, more tolerant, less happy, and completely unprepared for adulthood—and what that means for the rest of us*. New York, NY: Atria books.

We're All Teachers Now: Remote Learning During COVID-19

Dick Carpenter and Joshua Dunn

ABSTRACT
This study examined educational experiences of families under COVID and their schooling decisions in the 2021 school year. Results from a survey of 1743 parents indicate most schools provided educational resources ranging from hardcopy packets to live online instruction. Parents were generally positive about the experience. Parents in private and charter schools reported a more positive experience than those in traditional public schools. Only a small percentage of respondents said they were going to homeschool in fall 2020, but more than a third planned to send their child to a virtual school out of concern about their child's health.

This study examines the experiences and perspectives of parents and families with remote learning in spring 2020 during COVID-19 closures. For the latter part of the 2020 school year, parents had the primary responsibility of teaching their children at home. This presented parents with the opportunity to observe and evaluate (a) what their children were learning, (b) the ability and willingness of schools to provide educational resources to families, and (c) other educational options.

This experience at remote learning may have confirmed parents' reliance on the neighborhood school, while for others it may have compelled them to consider other options. Since we are writing in August 2020, this is one of the first studies to systematically examine the educational experiences of families under COVID and what that may mean for schooling decisions in the 2020–2021 school year and beyond.

Background

How schools responded

When schools began closing in mid-March, teachers and administrators rushed to create educational content through hundreds of thousands of paper packets and online lessons (Blume, Kohli, Xia, & Esquivel, 2020; Crain, 2020; Keane,

2020). One common, although not exclusive, approach was sending students weekly assignments at the beginning of each week. Students would then work independently or with a parent, seeking help from teachers during office hours if they had questions (Koh, 2020). Teachers became "advisers" and maintained contact through video chats or over the telephone (Keane, 2020; Koh, 2020).

The implementation of such initiatives was uneven, as illustrated by two adjacent districts in Milwaukee (Richards, 2020). Nicolet High School, a single-school district with about 1,000 students, created an online learning system in a matter of days and worked to secure necessary hot spots for students and staff. Next door the Whitefish Bay School District, which enrolls around 3,000 students, took a month to create a virtual learning plan drawing numerous complaints from parents.

Inconsistent possession of or access to technology was a part of the uneven implementation (Crutchfield & Londberg, 2020). Moving to online instruction often required schools to ensure families had devices – laptops or tablets – and even internet access. Duval County Public Schools in Florida, for example, distributed 3,500 hotspots and 37,000 laptops (Bloch, 2020). The Jacksonville, Florida, school district estimated more than 27,000 students needed laptops (Bloch, 2020), and the Miami school district provided students 90,000 devices and 11,000 hotspots (Richards, 2020). Los Angeles Unified, purchased 200,000 computers for students and contracted with Verizon to connect households to the internet for free. A California state partnership with Google provided free Wi-Fi to 100,000 households (Blume et al., 2020).

Nevertheless, acquiring technology and internet access reportedly proved difficult for many parents. Some estimated, for example, 200,000 California households lacked devices to participate in virtual instruction (Koh, 2020). States provided funds for internet hot spots, but extreme demand left store shelves empty and families waiting weeks to get online. Even if technology was available, some families struggled to gain permission from their landlords to install the necessary equipment (Blume et al., 2020). Students unable to access internet at home sat outside businesses with free wifi to do homework (Bloch, 2020). And some districts reportedly failed to deliver needed devices out of fear the mere distribution would facilitate spread of the virus (Crutchfield & Londberg, 2020).

The uneven implementation of at-home learning extended beyond technology. One survey of parents found only around a third of families received resources from their schools, such as lessons or curricular materials (Park & Winchester, 2020). Some schools required students to sign into learning platforms daily and graded students' work, while others checked in with students only periodically and gave all students As on their assignments (Richards, 2020). Still others elected not to provide any online classes but provided families with resources at the district website (Needles, 2020).

For schools providing organized instruction, the offerings took many forms: live video lessons, recorded lectures, one-on-one support over the phone, or feedback delivered through an online platform (Gross & Opalka, 2020; Richards, 2020). In a study of school district responses to COVID-19, Malkus, Christensen, and Schurz (2020) found one in five schools were in districts that offered rigorous remote instruction. Perfunctory remote instruction was more common, with 40% of schools falling into this category. The remaining schools offered moderate packages of remote instruction.

Some districts offered synchronous, online classes mimicking the classroom experience, but most students saw their teachers only for a few minutes a day or a week, and some not at all (Cavanagh, 2020; Davis, 2020). Many districts explicitly encouraged or expected teachers to make direct contact with their students. The most common method was e-mail communication. Other forms included web-based platforms, scheduled office hours, phone calls, and homework hotlines (Malkus et al., 2020). One survey of parents found less than half (47%) reported receiving "a lot" of information from their child's school about resources and support available to them. More than 80% said they received information from their child's school at least once a week, and more than half (54%) received information three times a week or more.

Much of the preceding came from contemporaneous reporting during the COVID school closures, but two research teams tracked school responses from March to May, with summary results available at the end of the school year. The first (Gross & Opalka, 2020) found the large majority of public districts tracked – 85% – made sure their students received some form of grade- and subject-specific curriculum in packets, assignments posted online, or guidance to complete segments of online learning software. Yet, just one in three districts expected teachers to provide instruction, track student engagement, or monitor academic progress for all students, leaving learning largely to chance or the diligence of parents.

The second (Malkus et al., 2020) found across most measures in the study, public schools ended the year by providing core educational services. Ninety-five percent provided meals to students, 66% provided devices, and 70% provided internet access to students at home. Almost all schools (97%) provided some form of remote instruction, most commonly asynchronous web-based platforms, followed by hardcopy instructional packets and then synchronous web-based classes. Many schools (67%) announced assignments were being graded, although the plurality graded only on completion. Finally, although almost two-thirds of schools expected student participation, less than a third established any mechanism for taking "attendance."

What learning looked like at home

Had school districts monitored student engagement, they would have found children spent an average of 4.2 hours per weekday on school work, with 22%

of parents reporting their child spending less than one hour per weekday on school work (Park & Winchester, 2020). For their part, parents – mostly mothers – spent approximately 2.5 hours per weekday helping their children with school (Park & Winchester, 2020; Watson, 2020). For parents regularly at home, some structured the time, with daily schedules that included not only school work, but also chores, exercise, meals, and free time (Carter, 2020; Needles, 2020; Watson, 2020). Nonetheless, many media reports told of parents being overwhelmed. This was particularly so in families with multiple children spread widely across grades. One Pennsylvania mother of three children described the challenge of keeping track of four different school e-mail accounts and 12 Google livestreams, all while transitioning her job to home (Flaccus & Gecker, 2020).

Many parents, however, were not home during the day, which meant in families with siblings, older children cared for younger ones, making school-work difficult (AP, 2020a). In such circumstances, schoolwork was pushed to weekends or late in the evenings (AP, 2020a). In other cases, parents tapped informal networks of friends and family to create study groups of classmates doing remote learning together (Ovide, 2020). For students without adults at home and no peer support group, remote learning reportedly grew increasingly difficult (Blume et al., 2020; Crutchfield & Londberg, 2020).

Early on, some school districts appeared to exacerbate the situation by attempting to continue the curricula on the same pace as in school (Davis, 2020). Some students reported the workload was even greater than they had been used to in school (Bloch, 2020). Although 90% of families said they used school-provided resources (Park & Winchester, 2020), reports occasionally surfaced of schools assigning science experiments and art projects that required parents to go to stores in search of materials not commonly kept in homes (Davis, 2020).

Not surprisingly, some frustrated and exhausted parents chose to disconnect entirely for the remainder of the school year (Flaccus & Gecker, 2020), including teachers and college professors (Cavanagh & Fox, 2020; Weiner, 2020). Instead of schooling at home, their children watched TV, played video and board games, cooked and baked, cleaned and sewed, read, and pursued their own interests (AP, 2020a; Carter, 2020; Cavanagh & Fox, 2020; Koh, 2020; Weiner, 2020). One enterprising father even taught his son how to short stocks (Das, 2020).

These are, of course, general, anecdotal descriptions. The most significant differences appeared to be based on the type of school families attended. Many private schools, freed from red tape and populated with digitally savvy families, pivoted more easily to remote learning (Richards, 2020). In Tacoma, Washington, for example, public schools chose not to provide active remote learning, instead posting and distributing resources that included activity packets and links to additional learning tools (Needles, 2020).

Meanwhile, Charles Wright Academy, a private school in Tacoma, shifted to a remote learning platform that included both asynchronous work and synchronous classes.

One study (Common Sense Media/SurveyMonkey, 2020) compared the remote learning activities of teens in public versus private schools and found stark differences illustrated in Table 1. Private school students more often were in contact with teachers, attended online classes, and used technology to connect with the school. In a different study, when asked about class attendance, 47% of public school students said they had not attended a class, compared with just 18% of private school students (Kamenetz, 2020a).

Assessing the experience

In the final assessment, remote learning in spring 2020 received decidedly mixed reviews (Hamilton, 2020). Although large percentages of parents professed to feeling prepared to help their children (EdChoice, 2020; Education Trust-West, 2020), 52% agreed the experience was harder than they expected (Park & Winchester, 2020). Moreover, a large majority expressed concern about providing productive learning at home (Baldassare, Bonner, Dykman, & Lawler, 2020). Media anecdotes frequently reported parents feeling overwhelmed and inadequate (Bloch, 2020), including university professors (AP, 2020a), college presidents (Strauss, 2020), and Hollywood celebrities (Newcomb, 2020).

According to some, schools performed poorly (Henderson, 2020), with remote learning declared an "utter failure" (DeMarche, 2020). By mid-May, many school districts ended early, "giving up" on "cumbersome" remote learning (Strassel, 2020). As the spring months wore on, student participation declined (Bloch, 2020) as students struggled with technology and found home environments not optimal for learning (Blume et al., 2020; Davis, 2020; Koh, 2020). One survey taken in May reported more than two-thirds of parents

Table 1. Differences in learning activities between public and private school students.

	Public	Private
Connecting with their teacher		
... once a day or more	31%	66%
... a few times a day	15%	33%
... once an hour or more	2%	14%
... less than once a week	28%	4%
Having a dedicated space where they can do schoolwork at home	71%	67%
Attended an online or virtual class	53%	82%
Using e-mail to stay connected to school	68%	78%
Using a learning management system to stay connected to school	50%	65%
Using video chat or videoconferencing to stay connected to school	39%	88%
Using texts to stay connected to school	33%	33%
Using social media to stay connected to school	26%	23%
Using messenger apps to stay connected to school	21%	24%
Using phone calls to stay connected to school	19%	15%

were concerned about their children falling behind, and almost the same percentage feared it would affect their educational success for longer than a year (Koh, 2020). "A lot of parents were disillusioned with what they saw over the last 120 days," said Luis Huerta, a professor of education and public policy at Teachers College at Columbia University. "They felt the level of instruction was not up to par and that schools dropped the ball during the transition" (Ali, 2020).

Conversely, other evidence suggested parents were satisfied with their schools' performance. One survey found 57% of parents agreed their child's remote schooling worked better than expected (Park & Winchester, 2020). Another reported more than 90% of parents approved of how schools handled closures (Baldassare et al., 2020), and still another found more than 80% of parents believed their schools were doing a good or excellent job (Education Trust-West, 2020). In a *USA Today*/Ipsos poll (Education Trust-West, 2020), more than 70% of parents approved of their schools' efforts, and more than 60% believed their schools prepared their children well for remote learning.

Of course, the most revealing assessment may be what parents elected to do for fall 2020. Some authors predicted the schooling at home experience would compel parents to choose different options for their children. McDonald (2020) asserted, "we may be on the brink of a massive educational reset." Henderson (2020) opined, "Get ready. A school renaissance is coming." By that Henderson meant increased school choice, specifically more homeschooling and lower enrollment in public schools.

Yet, signals from parents did not clearly point to a "renaissance." Some polls showed most parents were going to send their children back to their neighborhood schools (Chua, DeJonckheere, Reeves, Tribble, & Prosser, 2020). Only small percentages planned to hold their children out, mostly due to concern for the health of someone in their homes (Chua et al., 2020; Gallegos, 2020). Other sources suggested the number of students not returning to neighborhood schools was going to be greater. School officials in Alabama, for example, expressed belief that 15% to 20% of parents would not send their children to traditional schools (Crain, 2020). After surveys from parents showed greater preferences for virtual learning, some school officials around the country began preparing fully online options (Belsha, 2020). At the end of May, Crain (2020) reported seven states were already planning to offer full-time virtual school, and school districts with pre-existing virtual schools were seeing a surge of enrollment.

Interest in homeschooling also appeared to spike. Homeschooling organizations reported unprecedented numbers of contacts from parents seeking advice and resources (Ali, 2020; Bethencourt, 2020; Goree, 2020; Kamenetz, 2020b). Estimates of families that would homeschool during in 2020–2021 ranged from 40% to 60% (Lardieri, 2020; Schultz, 2020; USA Today/Ipsos, 2020), and some predicted 1% to 2% of those would continue homeschooling even after the pandemic (Ali, 2020).

Throughout summer 2020, homeschool pods emerged as an option. Based on micro-schools or homeschool coops, pods would operate with a small group of children consistently schooling together in a home (Picchi, 2020). Parents would lead instruction in some (Lisickis, 2020), while in others teachers or tutors hired by participating families would lead (Courtney, 2020; Kamenetz, 2020b; Picchi, 2020). Although critics pointed to inequities created by such pods (Bastian, 2020) – more affluent families can afford such schooling – parents concerned about their children's education and health and their own employment longevity appeared unmoved by such concerns (Picchi, 2020).

Of course, these projections were largely published in early summer 2020. Results from our research are based on a survey of parents administered in August 2020, making them a bit more accurate. Moreover, aside from a few exceptions (Gross & Opalka, 2020; Malkus et al., 2020; Park & Winchester, 2020), much of the narrative above came from contemporaneous media reporting throughout spring 2020, not systematic research. Thus, our findings are among the first to systematically examine families' experiences and assessments during COVID remote learning. Much more research on the educational implications of COVID-19 will be forthcoming. Studies like ours will help provide the context necessary to understand and interpret that future research.

Methods

Our study was guided by five primary questions:

(1) What access did parents and students have to resources provided by the school?
(2) What forms did remote learning take?
(3) What was the engagement of parents and students with remote learning?
(4) What were parent perceptions of the effectiveness of their at-home schooling experience?
(5) What were parents planning to do for schooling options in 2020–2021?

Data

Answers to these questions were based on survey data we collected from a sample of 1743 parents (representing 3,414 children) across the United States. A professional polling firm (Technometrica) administered the survey, which we created, online during the first two weeks of August 2020. The survey included 44 mostly closed-ended questions about the resources families had during at-home schooling, how children spent their day, how much time was spent on schoolwork, communication with school, assessment of the experience, plans for the 2021 school year, and basic demographics.

To ensure a representative sample by school type, we stratified based on traditional public school (TPS; 84%), private school (10%), and charter school (6%) using a quota system built into the survey. Throughout, respondents were prompted to answer substantive questions while focusing on their youngest child in a given school type. That child was used to fill school type quotas. For example, if a parent reported having three children in charter schools, the parent was asked to focus on the youngest of those. So the unit of analysis was a parent/guardian answering on behalf or thinking of a specific child. Similar to other research in which parents are asked to think about a particular child when answering survey questions (Carpenter & Winters, 2015), the "youngest child" approach was used to focus respondents' attention on a particular school and child when answering questions. Many of the questions asked about school responses and resources, amount of time a child spent on schoolwork, and the like. Without focusing on a specific child, respondents with multiple children would answer questions by trying to "average" across schools and children, struggle to know how to answer, or simply skip questions. Prompting respondents to think of a particular child, therefore, reduces "noisy" and/or missing data.

Table 2 presents the sex, race/ethnicity, education levels, and household incomes of respondents. The majority were white females. More than 50% held at least a college degree. Slightly more than 60% reported household incomes of greater than 50,000 USD. Additionally, respondents' mean age was 39 (sd = 9), and the mean number of children per respondent was two (sd = 1.2). Almost 76% of respondents were married.

When compared to national population statistics (U.S. Bureau of the Census, 2018, 2020, n.d.), the sample composition is similar in some respects but different in others. Substantially more of the respondents were women, and education levels were somewhat higher in the sample. A greater percentage of the sample was White, but differences in income between the sample and the national population were small.

Disaggregated by school type, there were differences among these characteristics. As Table 2 illustrates, TPS respondents were more often female than those responding about charters and private schools. Charter and private school respondents reported higher education levels and higher household incomes. Differences in respondent age were trivial, but those in charters (mean = 3.0, SD = 1.6) reported having more children than those in TPS (mean = 1.9, SD = 1.1) and private schools (mean = 2.0, SD = 1.4). A greater percentage of private school respondents (96%) also reported being married, as compared to those in charters (84%) and TPS (73%).

Table 3 includes the employment status of respondents and their spouses. A little more than half of respondents were working full time when data were collected. The next largest percentage (18%) classified themselves as homemakers. A little more than 60% of their spouses were working full time. Equal percentages of respondents and spouses were working part-time (10%).

Table 2. Sex, race/ethnicity, education levels, and household income of respondents by school type.

	Charter	Private	TPS	Total	National Population
Sex					
Male	59%	66%	23%	29%	49%
Female	41%	34%	77%	71%	51%
Race/Ethnicity					
White	68%	82%	75%	75%	60%
Black	6%	4%	8%	7%	13%
Asian	6%	6%	5%	5%	6%
Native American	1%	0%	1%	1%	1%
Other	0%	0%	1%	1%	1%
Hispanic	20%	8%	11%	11%	19%
Education Level					
Some high school	2%	0%	3%	3%	7%
High school graduate	10%	5%	21%	19%	28%
Some college	9%	8%	25%	23%	28%
College graduate	26%	16%	28%	26%	21%
Some graduate courses	5%	2%	3%	3%	NA
Graduate/Professional degree	50%	69%	20%	27%	12%
Household Income					
Under $20,000	9%	1%	13%	11%	15%
Between $20,000 and $30,000	8%	2%	13%	11%	9%
Between $30,000 and $40,000	3%	5%	10%	9%	9%
Between $40,000 and $50,000	5%	3%	8%	7%	8%
Between $50,000 and $75,000	13%	12%	19%	18%	17%
Between $75,000 and $100,000	12%	11%	14%	14%	13%
Between $100,000 and $200,000	34%	48%	18%	22%	22%
Between $200,000 and $250,000	8%	12%	3%	5%	9%
Over $250,000	8%	6%	2%	3%	
Not sure	1%	1%	1%	1%	NA

Table 3. Respondent and spouse employment status.

	Respondent	Spouse
Employed full-time	54	64
Employed part-time	10	10
Unemployed and currently looking for work	6	4
Unemployed and not currently looking for work	2	3
Student	1	0
Retired	2	3
Homemaker	18	9
Self-employed	4	3
Unable to work	3	2

Analysis

We analyzed data with descriptive statistics (e.g., means and frequencies) using sample weights so the sample reflected the population based on respondent race/ethnicity and region of the country. We did not apply inferential statistical tests, instead choosing only a descriptive approach for this article. In subsequent products we will be applying statistical testing in more sophisticated analyses to examine differences across a number of community and respondent characteristics. For some questions we disaggregated results by school type and by parental work status. As discussed above, contemporaneous reports often showed differences in remote learning by school type.

Media stories also commonly highlighted the struggles of working parents in coordinating remote learning with work responsibilities. Therefore, we explored whether systematic differences existed consistent with the media reporting from spring 2020.

Limitations

Like any study, ours is not without limitations. First, as Table 2 illustrates, the sample may skew more toward women and people who have higher education levels. Moreover, the percentages of personal characteristics are not always equal based on school type. Sample weights applied during analyses address some but not all these differences. Second, by necessity, parents were instructed to answer questions thinking of their youngest child in a certain school type. This may result in responses more representative of children in younger grade levels.

Results

We begin by describing the experiences of families with at-home schooling. This is followed by an assessment by parents and finally results on what families planned for the 2020–2021 school year.

The experiences of parents and students

After schools closed in March, 82% of participants reported their schools eventually developed some type of remote learning (see Figure 1). Ten percent reported schools canceled classes and provided no remote learning, with the remainder resuming or continuing classes until the end of the school year. For families in schools canceling classes and providing no resources, most students (49%) spent their time primarily watching TV and playing games. Only 28% engaged in a learning program created by parents. The remainder worked around the house, worked for pay, or pursued other interests.

The responses of schools by type of school were not, however, consistent. Charter schools compared to the other school types were less likely to provide remote learning and more likely to cancel in-person classes and provide no at-home learning. Charters compared to the other school types were also somewhat more likely to continue in-person classes. Although this pattern in charter schools may seem inconsistent, Figure 1 illustrates the distributions by school type. Greater than 90% of TPS and private school families either did remote learning or no formal learning at all. That left only small percentages that continued in person. Among charter parents, however, a smaller percentage participated in remote learning, leaving a comparatively greater number

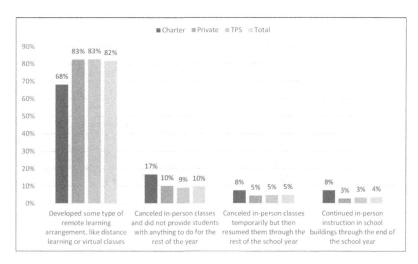

Figure 1. How schools responded to COVID-19.

of families distributed across the other options of no remote learning or continuing in person.

The remote learning schools provided took the form of instructors teaching live through a video platform (59.8%) and/or providing students software or pre-recoded videos (59.2%). Half of parents also reported receiving paper packets, worksheets, or books. Among schools providing remote learning, it varied by school type (see Figure 2). Private schools more often provided real-time, online learning and were least likely to provide hardcopy materials. Charters more than TPS also provided real-time and video learning.

Given how much remote learning depended on technology, access to devices (laptops/tablets) was particularly important. As it turns out, such access was nearly ubiquitous, with 94% of families reporting access (TPS = 93%, private = 98%, charter = 100%). For almost a third of those families, however, their schools provided the devices, with TPS most often distributing devices (TPS = 34%, private = 16%, charter = 29%). Relatedly, 84% of families described their internet access as reliable or very reliable (TPS = 81%, private = 96%, charter = 96%). Most families (95%) paid for their own internet, but when schools provided internet, charter schools more frequently did so than the other school types (TPS = 3%, private = 5%, charter = 18%).

Remote learning was most often semi-structured, with weekly assignments and occasional communication with the school (see Figure 3). A quarter of respondents said remote learning was highly structured with daily assignments, and somewhat less than that said it was mostly unstructured. The structure of remote learning differed by school type, with private and charter schools more often than TPS requiring daily assignments and frequent communication with teachers. Conversely, families in TPS more often worked in semi- or unstructured environments.

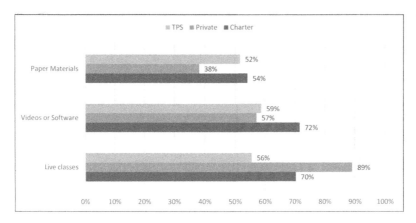

Figure 2. Types of remote learning by school type.

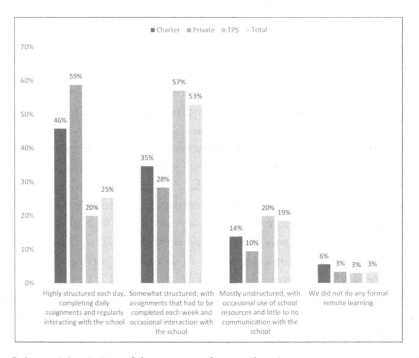

Figure 3. Parents' descriptions of the structure of remote learning.

Communication between teachers and students most often occurred at least a few times per week, and for almost 30% of families, it happened daily (see Figure 4). Given the differences by school type in the format of remote learning, it is not surprising that differences in communication were large, with charter and private schools communicating more frequently with students than TPS. Notably, 14% of TPS participants reported communication occurred less than once a week or rarely.

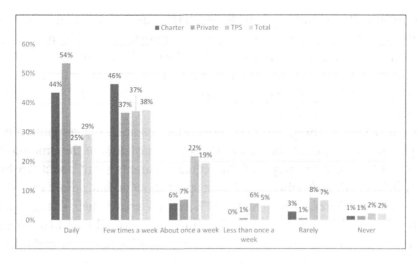

Figure 4. Frequency of communications between teachers and students.

During remote learning, schools also had varying expectations of students. Overall, a little more than one-third of parents reported assignments were graded and played an important role in the final grade for the year (see Figure 5). That differed substantially, however, by school type. Seventy-seven percent and 65% of charter and private school parents respectively reported that expectation, compared to 32% of TPS parents. Conversely, only small percentages of charter and private school parents said assignments were not graded, but more than one fifth of TPS parents said that was the case in their schools.

Participation or "attendance" in remote learning also varied by school type. Overall, 79% of parents said schools required their child's

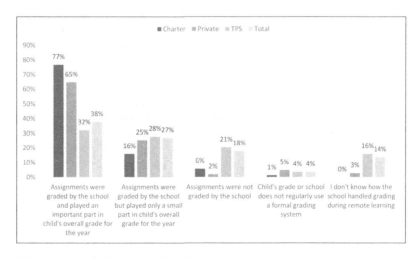

Figure 5. Expectations during remote learning.

participation. By school type, 93% of charter and 91% of private-school parents reported mandatory participation compared to 77% of TPS parents. Although required, schools did not always closely monitor participation. Sixty-one percent of parents said their school actively tracked participation, with charters (87%) and private schools (85%) actively tracking more than TPS (57%).

During remote learning, mothers most often assumed the responsibility for managing or helping their children (59%), but almost 30% of the time mothers and fathers managed the responsibility equally. Parents spent about 2.5 hours per day helping with schoolwork; children spent about an hour more each day in remote learning. Parents most often (67%) characterized their engagement as heavily involved daily (see Figure 6). For those less involved than that, 45% said work responsibilities consumed their attention, but 43% said their child did not want help.

When parental involvement was disaggregated by work status, the results were predictable (see Figure 7). More parents who were not working more often reported heavy, daily involvement as compared to those working. The difference between those working part time and those working full time, however, was marginal.

Part of parental involvement included communicating with schools. That communication most often occurred through e-mail, particularly for TPS and private schools (see Figure 8). Charter and private school parents also frequently communicated with schools through video conferencing, but TPS parents did so significantly less often. Charter schools also appeared to use online methods such as school websites, mobile apps, and online portals more often than the other school types.

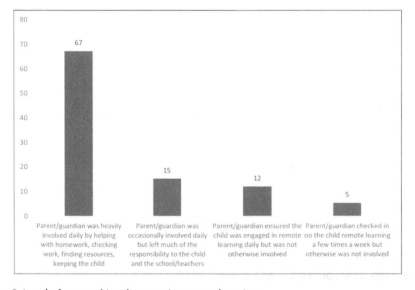

Figure 6. Level of parental involvement in remote learning.

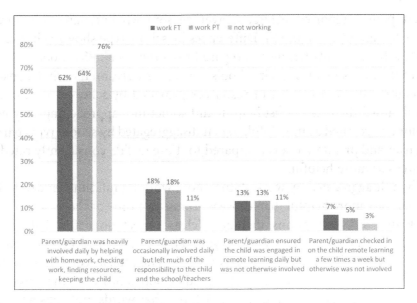

Figure 7. Level of parental involvement in remote learning by parent work status.

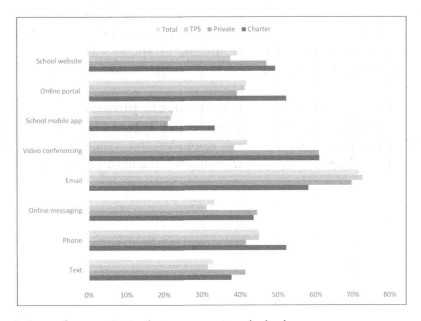

Figure 8. Types of communication between parents and schools.

Parents' assessment of the experience

Two common themes in media reporting in spring 2020 were (a) how difficult parents found at-home schooling and (b) the chaotic and inconsistent response by schools. Our survey results, however, tell a different story.

First, parents reported feeling, on average, somewhat prepared to help with remote learning (see Figure 9). Differences by school type showed charter and private school parents felt more prepared than those in TPS schools.

Parental assessments of their schools' responses were, on the whole, positive (see Figure 10). Across a list of resources provided by schools, parents consistently rated them as at least helpful and sometimes approaching very helpful. None were rated as unhelpful. When disaggregated by school type, parents in charter and private schools compared to those in TPS consistently rated the resources as more helpful.

When disaggregated by work status, those working full time tended to find the resources more helpful than those working part time or those not working (see Figure 11). Exceptions included "clear expectations for daily/weekly schoolwork" and "regular access to your child's teachers." For both items, those working full time found the resources less helpful, as compared to those working part time or not working. It should be noted, however, the range of all these differences was between 4.8 and 5.4, in other words, not substantial.

Similarly, when parents rated the effectiveness of communications between the school and them, the various methods were rated as effective and sometimes approaching very effective (see Figure 12). For almost all methods of communication, charter schools were perceived as most effective, followed by private schools and then TPS. One notable exception was the use of texts, where charter schools were not perceived as effective as the other two school types.

In response to a series of summary statements, parents likewise appeared sanguine, although with some exceptions (see Figure 13). Overall, parents agreed their children had sufficient resources and materials and believed they and their children were connected to their teachers. They also somewhat

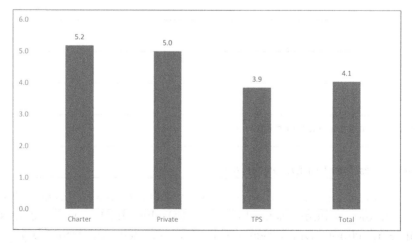

Figure 9. How prepared parents felt to help with remote learning. Scale: 1 = very unprepared, 2 = unprepared, 3 = somewhat unprepared, 4 = somewhat prepared, 5 = prepared, 6 = very prepared

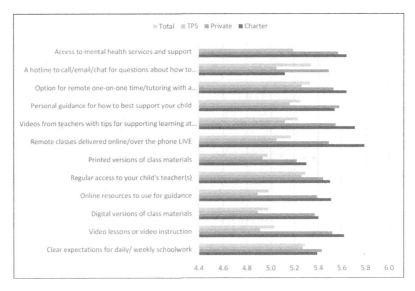

Figure 10. How helpful parents found resources provided by schools. Scale: 1 = useless, 2 = barely helpful, 3 = somewhat unhelpful, 4 = somewhat helpful, 5 = helpful, 6 = very helpful

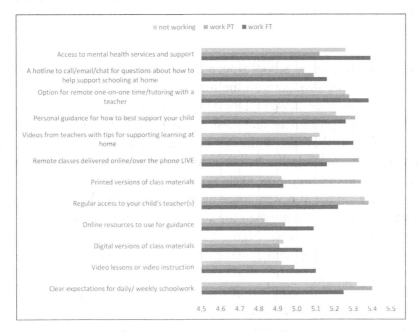

Figure 11. How helpful parents found resources provided by schools disaggregated by respondent work status. Scale: 1 = useless, 2 = barely helpful, 3 = somewhat unhelpful, 4 = somewhat helpful, 5 = helpful, 6 = very helpful

agreed children were able to use the technology easily and the schools provided effective remote learning. At the same time, parents agreed remote learning required too much of them and their children and were concerned the experience caused their children to fall behind.

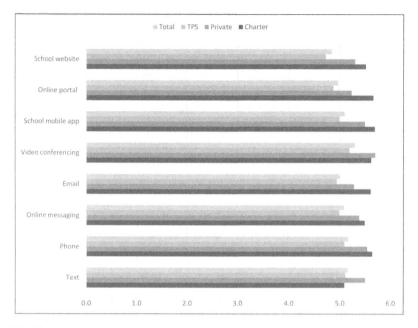

Figure 12. Effectiveness of communication between schools and parents by school type. Scale: 1 = very ineffective, 2 = ineffective, 3 = somewhat ineffective, 4 = somewhat effective, 5 = effective, 6 = very effective

When disaggregated by school type, a clear trend is evident, wherein charter parents agreed more strongly with the summary statements followed by private school parents and then those in TPS. This means, for example, charter parents expressed stronger agreement that their children possessed sufficient resources and materials, but they also more strongly believed the experience left their children behind academically. In other words, charter parent responses were more polarized in that they more likely agreed with positive summary statements listed in Figure 13, but also were more likely to agree with the negative ones.

A similar trend is evident when the summary statements are disaggregated by respondent work status (see Figure 14). Those working full time were more likely to express stronger agreement across all the statements – positive and negative – as compared to those working part time or not working. Conversely, those not working often, although not always, reported less agreement across the statements.

In an overall assessment, we asked parents how satisfied they were with the remote learning experience. On average, parents said they were somewhat satisfied (Scale: 1 = very satisfied 2 = satisfied, 3 = somewhat satisfied, 4 = somewhat unsatisfied, 5 = unsatisfied, 6 = very unsatisfied), although response varied by school type. Those in charter schools expressed greater satisfaction, followed by private-school parents and then those in TPS. When disaggregated by respondent work status, those working full time reported

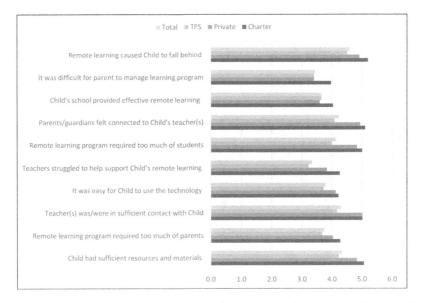

Figure 13. Summary statements about remote learning by school type. Scale: 1 = disagree strongly, 2 = disagree, 3 = disagree somewhat, 4 = agree somewhat, 5 = agree, 6 = strongly agree

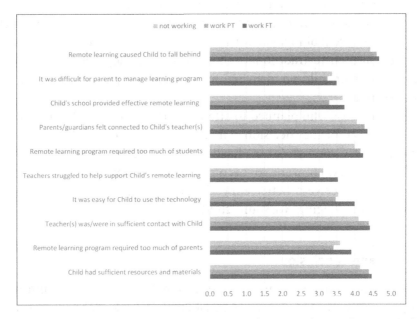

Figure 14. Summary statements about remote learning by respondent work status. Scale: 1 = disagree strongly, 2 = disagree, 3 = disagree somewhat, 4 = agree somewhat, 5 = agree, 6 = strongly agree

the greatest satisfaction, followed by those working part time and then those not working.

Yet, when asked about their plans for the 2020–2021 school year, charter parents appeared less committed to remain in a charter school (see Figure 15).

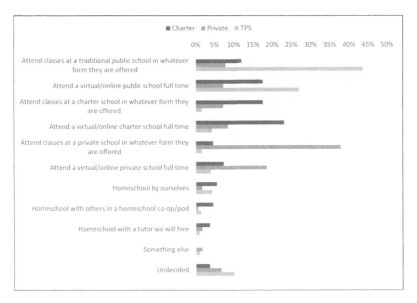

Figure 15. School plans for the 2020–2021 school year.

Instead, TPS parents seemed to express a stronger preference to remain in the same sector. Charter school parents more than those in the other two sectors planned to homeschool in some form. On average, 47% of parents planned to send their children to traditional schools however they operated, 36% were going to send their children to virtual schools, and 7% planned to homeschool in some fashion.

Finally, for those who planned to attend a virtual school or homeschool, we asked the reason for that decision. The results were predictable. Eighty-seven percent expressed concern for the health of their children or someone in their homes if the children were to become infected. Seven percent said their children would receive a better education that way, and only 5% expressed concern about managing work and childcare.

Discussion and conclusion

This study surveyed 1,743 parents in traditional public, charter, and private schools across the United States in August 2020. We asked about what schooling at home looked like for their families, what educational resources schools offered, parents' assessment of the experience, and their plans for the 2020–2021 school year.

We found the vast majority of schools provided educational resources ranging from hardcopy packets and worksheets to live online instruction. Schools sometimes provided laptops and even internet service for those who needed it. For their part, students and parents – mostly mothers – spent an average of 3.5 and 2.5 hours a day, respectively, working through assignments and materials provided by schools. Teachers maintained frequent contact with families through various methods including e-mail, texting, video meetings, web portals, and phone calls. Despite the grim real-time descriptions of schooling at home that dominated the media in spring 2020, parents we surveyed were generally positive about the experience.

Although as of this writing schools and parents were still deciding about enrollment for the 2020–2021 school year, only a small percentage of respondents to our survey said they were going to homeschool, but more than a third planned to send their child to a virtual school. Of those who were going to homeschool or choose a virtual school, concern about their child's health was naturally the dominant motivation. Most respondents said they were going to send their children to their traditional public/charter/private school in whatever form the school opened – in person, hybrid, or completely online.

The positive opinions expressed by parents could reflect the sample composition. Those of greater means, two-parent households, and higher education levels may not have experienced the burdens of remote learning as profoundly as those in more challenging circumstances. We note, however, many of the survey questions focused on the actions and resources of the schools themselves. Parents were not simply evaluating their efficacy at remote learning; they were also reflecting on how their schools responded, and parents with children in private and charter schools report a more positive experience than those in traditional public schools. Those opinions are in no small part a measure of what schools did or did not do.

Additionally, given the circumstances, parents may have given schools the benefit of the doubt in the quality of the schools' responses. Indeed, this may help explain what appears to be contradictory findings – parents generally expressing satisfaction with their remote learning experience but also worry their children may have fallen behind academically. Recall other surveys indicated 57% of parents found remote learning worked better than expected (Park & Winchester, 2020). Thus, remote learning may have been better than anticipated, leading to a sense of satisfaction (i.e., relief), but not effective enough to allay concerns about their child's academic growth.

This may also explain differences by work status. Those working full time were consistently more sanguine about the resources provided by schools and the remote learning experience. Given the pressures on full time workers to manage work and home responsibilities, a better-than-anticipated experience may have produced higher satisfaction. Of course, these results may also interact with school type, where full time workers – who tend to report greater household incomes – may also send their children to private schools at greater rates. In future research, we intend to explore such relationships in greater detail.

What, then, is to be learned from these results? First, they suggest large scale change to schooling in the United States is technically possible. As Keane (2020) described, prior to the COVID-19 closures, the quantity and quality of online instruction and even technology use in classrooms was uneven and mostly ad hoc. Questions persisted about whether widespread virtual education was possible (Horn & Staker, 2011). These results suggest it is. The circumstances were not optimal, with schools rushing to create remote learning programs in a matter of days and weeks, and the quality of the programming certainly would have been greater with more preparation time. But these results show that despite little time to prepare, inadequate resources, and no training, schools created programs with which parents were at least somewhat satisfied overall and elements of which they rated as helpful and effective. Indeed, given the circumstances, it is surprising schools did so well. If they could do so under these conditions, what more is possible under better circumstances?

Yet, possible and probable are not the same thing. To put it plainly, our data indicate the "educational renaissance" some soothsayers predicted will not occur (Henderson, 2020). When asked their plans for fall 2020, the percentage of parents choosing homeschooling was small, nothing close to the 40% to 60% predicted by some (Lardieri, 2020; Schultz, 2020; USA Today/Ipsos, 2020). Yes, a non-trivial percentage chose virtual schools, but primarily for health concerns, not for a better education. This strongly suggests when the pandemic wanes, many of those in virtual schools will return to their brick-and-mortar schools as before. In other words, the percentage of families choosing virtual schools for the 2020–2021 school year is comparably large but likely temporary. Moreover, popular articles throughout summer 2020 frequently announced "Interest in homeschooling has 'exploded amid pandemic'" (AP, 2020b), provided homeschooling resources (Kenniston, 2020; Remadna, 2020), and featured stories about homeschool pods (Basu, 2020), but our results suggest this reflects a small minority of families.

To the extent parents will school at home, our results indicate they want someone else to lead it, hence the percentages of parents choosing virtual rather than homeschool. Recall, when schools canceled classes and provided no resources, most students spent their time on things other than schooling. Moreover, the results in Figure 15 show most TPS parents are remaining in a TPS.

Wholesale change to homeschooling and even virtual schooling in the long term is unlikely for one simple reason: Parents cannot or will not do it. As Horn and Staker (2011) observed,

> Home and full-time virtual schooling requires significant parental involvement ....The majority of students in America need school – or a supervised place to learn. Various societal stakeholders "hire" schools to do many things for their children, just one of which is learning. A custodial job – keeping children safe – is equally important for many.

They conclude, "home schooling and full-time virtual schooling will not substitute for mainstream schooling." Our data suggest the same.

Of course, plans on the part of schools and parents were exceptionally fluid as the 2020–2021 school year began. Moreover, widespread coverage of possible teacher sick-outs (Cassell, Gaudiano, & Mays, 2020) and reports of positive COVID cases in schools accompanied by quarantines (deBruijn, 2020; Muller, 2020) likely exacerbated the unsettled circumstances. Parents could make last-minute flights to homeschooling to create a greater sense of certainty and stability for their children. Even if that happens, our data still suggest it will be a short-term move rather than a "massive educational reset" (McDonald, 2020). This assumes, of course, the pandemic and closure decisions do not continue indefinitely, and no other similar event transpires.

Second, the results likely illustrate the influence of markets on school performance. Throughout the results, and consistent with findings from earlier research (Common Sense Media/SurveyMonkey, 2020), private schools frequently appeared to be the most responsive, engaged, and innovative, followed by charters and then TPS. In the school choice literature, much ink has been spent debating the outcomes of public versus private schools (Krueger & Zhu, 2004; Miller & Moore, 1991), with choice opponents attributing superior private school outcomes to student differences (Pianta & Ansari, 2018). Here, however, there are no student outcomes. Differences are manifest in the schools themselves. Private schools more often chose to communicate with students, create real-time, online programs, and set higher expectations.

One may assert private schools were able to do so because of greater resources. Yet, most private schools in the United States are modest enterprises. The average student body is 150 students. Two-thirds are religious schools (Broughman, Kincel, & Peterson, 2019). The average tuition is 11,000 USD (National Center for Education Statistics, 2013), a figure almost identical to (i.e., slightly less than) average per pupil expenditures in public schools (National Center for Education Statistics, 2019). Private schools operate with less bureaucracy than public schools, but the most relevant difference is that private schools operate in a market and TPS largely do not. Because enrollment is the lifeblood of private schools, they worked during COVID closures to retain students by operating more responsively and resourcefully than TPS, whose funding streams, although reduced, continued throughout the COVID-19 closures. When it comes to student outcomes, some of the differences between private and TPS do reflect differences in student populations, but these results suggest differences also likely reflect how the schools operate and the influence of markets on those operations.

TPS are not completely immune from competition. Reporting from late May, for example, described concerns among some Alabama district superintendents about losing students in fall 2020 to already-operational virtual schools in other districts (Crain, 2020). Concern was so acute, the state department of education pursued a statewide virtual school that would enroll children from any district but – critically – allow the home districts to retain funding attached to the students (Crain, 2020; Sell, 2020). Of course, Alabama's private schools will not be similarly relieved of market pressure, meaning they will continue to have to operate responsively and innovatively to retain students.

During spring 2020, the predictions of educational pundits became an echo chamber: "Teaching will never be the same" (Bolton, 2020), "Why schools will never be the same" (Keierleber, 2020), or "Homeschooling during the coronavirus pandemic could change education forever" (Broom, 2020). Whether the pandemic would be a watershed moment for educational change depended at least in part on the experiences and attitudes of parents. Our results suggest little permanent change will result from those experiences. The inertia of TPS appears able to withstand even a worldwide pandemic.

Disclosure statement

No potential conflict of interest was reported by the authors.

Funding

This work was supported by the Searle Freedom Trust [na].

References

Ali, S. S. (2020). *Parents are opting to home school their children because of COVID-19, but experts say it might not be for everyone.* Retrieved from https://www.nbcnews.com/news/us-news/parents-are-opting-home-school-their-children-due-covid-19-n1232739

AP. (2020a). *'I just can't do this.' Frustrated parents giving up on home school.* Retrieved from https://www.fox5ny.com/news/i-just-cant-do-this-frustrated-parents-giving-up-on-home-school

AP. (2020b). *Interest in homeschooling has 'exploded' amid pandemic.* Retrieved from https://www.mprnews.org/story/2020/08/12/interest-in-homeschooling-has-exploded-amid-pandemic

Baldassare, M., Bonner, D., Dykman, A., & Lawler, R. (2020). *Californians & education.* Retrieved from https://www.ppic.org/wp-content/uploads/ppic-statewide-survey-californians-and-education-april-2020.pdf

Bastian, R. (2020). *How educational inequality In America could be impacted by the home-schooling pod frenzy.* Retrieved from https://www.forbes.com/sites/rebekahbastian/2020/07/19/how-educational-inequality-in-america-could-be-impacted-by-the-homeschooling-pod-frenzy/#9b03a872cbaf

Basu, T. (2020). *American parents are setting up homeschool "pandemic pods".* Retrieved from https://www.technologyreview.com/2020/07/30/1005810/american-parents-are-setting-up-homeschool-pandemic-pods-microschool/

Belsha, K. (2020). *Some students will stay home in the fall. School districts have to figure out how to teach them.* Retrieved from https://ctmirror.org/2020/06/28/some-students-will-stay-home-in-the-fall-school-districts-have-to-figure-out-how-to-teach-them/

Bethencourt, A. (2020). *Parents consider homeschooling next school year, worry classrooms won't be safe from virus.* Retrieved from https://kfoxtv.com/newsletter-daily/parents-consider-homeschooling-next-school-year-worry-classrooms-wont-be-safe-from-virus

Bloch, E. (2020). *'Mama is tired': After school closures, some families burn out on online classes, others thrive.* Retrieved from https://www.usatoday.com/story/news/education/2020/05/05/coronavirus-online-classes-school-closures-homeschool-burnout/3055101001/

Blume, H., Kohli, S., Xia, R., & Esquivel, P. (2020). Tough realities as students struggle with home learning. *Los Angeles Times,* Retrieved from https://enewspaper.latimes.com/infinity/article_share.aspx?guid=a0189d0116-0180c0189b-4563-b0128d-c6036c0181d0116e0182.

Bolton, R. (2020). *Teaching will never be the same again.* Retrieved from https://www.afr.com/work-and-careers/education/teaching-will-never-be-the-same-again-20200320-p54cc2

Broom, D. (2020). *Homeschooling during the coronavirus pandemic could change education forever, says the OECD.* Retrieved from https://www.weforum.org/agenda/2020/04/coronavirus-homeschooling-technology-oecd/

Broughman, S. P., Kincel, B., & Peterson, J. (2019). *Characteristics of private schools in the United States: Results from the 2017–18 private school universe survey first look* (NCES 2019-071).

Carpenter, D. M., & Winters, M. (2015). Who chooses and why in a universal choice scholarship program: Evidence from Douglas County, Colorado. *Journal of School Leadership, 25* (5), 899–939. doi:10.1177/105268461502500505

Carter, M. (2020). *Some parents considering making home school permanent after schools reopen.* Retrieved from https://www.wkbw.com/rebound/coronavirus-stress/some-parents-considering-making-home-school-permanent-after-schools-reopen

Cassell, M., Gaudiano, N., & Mays, M. (2020). *Teachers unions test goodwill with strike threats, hardball negotiations.* Retrieved from https://www.politico.com/news/2020/08/18/teachers-unions-school-reopening-coronavirus-397997

Cavanagh, E. (2020). *An award-winning teacher with 12 years of experience explains why she isn't homeschooling her kids during the coronavirus pandemic.* Retrieved from https://www.insider.com/a-teacher-says-she-isnt-homeschooling-during-the-coronavirus-pandemic-2020-3

Cavanagh, E., & Fox, E. G. (2020). *Some parents say they're not homeschooling during the coronavirus pandemic because it's too stressful.* Retrieved from https://www.insider.com/parents-wont-homeschool-in-coronavirus-pandemic-because-of-stress-2020-3

Chua, K.-P., DeJonckheere, M., Reeves, S. L., Tribble, A. C., & Prosser, L. A. (2020). *Plans for school attendance and support for COVID-19 risk mitigation measures.* Retrieved from https://ihpi.umich.edu/sites/default/files/2020-06/plans%20for%20school%20attendance%20and%20support%20for%20risk%20mitigation%20measures%20among%20parents%20and%20guardians_final.pdf

Common Sense Media/SurveyMonkey. (2020). *How teens are coping and connecting in the time of the coronavirus.* Retrieved from https://www.commonsensemedia.org/sites/default/files/uploads/pdfs/2020_surveymonkey-key-findings-toplines-teens-and-coronavirus.pdf

Courtney, N. J. (2020). *Parents are spending $125,000 a year on at-home education pods to protect kids from coronavirus risks at school.* Retrieved from https://www.insider.com/parents-spending-125000-private-tutors-to-teach-kids-at-home-2020-7

Crain, T. P. (2020). *Alabama prepares for more students to choose online school next year.* Retrieved from https://www.al.com/news/2020/05/alabama-prepares-for-more-students-to-choose-online-school-next-year.html

Crutchfield, A., & Londberg, M. (2020). *'I'm really struggling': In 6 home classrooms, families keep learning alive in a pandemic.* Retrieved from https://www.wvxu.org/post/im-really-struggling-6-home-classrooms-families-keep-learning-alive-pandemic#stream/0

Das, U. I. (2020, April 15). Generation zoom makes do. *Wall Street Journal*, p. A15.

Davis, L. S. (2020). *It's time to accept that the point of school has changed*. CNN. Retrieved from https://www.cnn.com/2020/04/28/opinions/time-to-accept-covid-19-has-changed-education-selin-davis/index.html

deBruijn, E. (2020). *Student at Plano ISD tests positive. Here are all the COVID-19 cases at local schools*. Retrieved from https://www.wfaa.com/article/news/education/covid-19-coronavirus-cases-dallas-fort-worth-schools/287-6f175d53-b031-4219-8501-7de74e8c3f30

DeMarche, E. (2020). *Orange County school Board of Education wants schools to reopen, no social distancing: Report*. Retrieved from https://www.foxnews.com/us/orange-county-school-board-of-education-wants-schools-to-reopen-no-social-distancing-report

EdChoice. (2020). *Public opinion tracker*. Retrieved from https://edchoice.morningconsultintelligence.com/assets/31705.pdf

Education Trust-West. (2020). *California parent poll: COVID-19 and school closures*. Retrieved from https://west.edtrust.org/ca-parent-poll-covid-19-and-school-closures/

Flaccus, G., & Gecker, J. (2020). *'I just can't do this.' Some overwhelmed parents are opting to abandon pandemic homeschooling*. Retrieved from https://time.com/5824855/parents-overwhelmed-homeschooling-coronavirus/

Gallegos, M. (2020). *Parents considering homeschooling instead of sending their children back to the classroom*. Retrieved from https://www.kiiitv.com/article/news/education/parents-considering-homeschooling-instead-of-sending-their-children-back-to-the-classroom/503-3ef586c8-3d5f-40df-9b92-f3826147389a

Goree, A. (2020). *'They're not alone out there:' CCSD parents seek homeschooling option for upcoming year*. Retrieved from https://news3lv.com/news/local/theyre-not-alone-out-there-ccsd-parents-seek-homeschooling-option-for-upcoming-year

Gross, B., & Opalka, A. (2020). *Too many schools leave learning to chance during the pandemic*. Retrieved from https://www.crpe.org/thelens/too-many-schools-leave-learning-chance-during-pandemic

Hamilton, R. C. (2020, May 19). Let children go to summer school. *Wall Street Journal*, p. A17.

Henderson, D. R. (2020, July 30). The virus may strike teachers unions. *Wall Street Journal*, p. A15.

Horn, M. B., & Staker, H. (2011). *The rise of K–12 blended learning*. Retrieved from https://aurora-institute.org/wp-content/uploads/The-Rise-of-K-12-Blended-Learning.pdf

Kamenetz, A. (2020a). *4 In 10 U.S. teens say they haven't done online learning since schools closed*. Retrieved from https://www.npr.org/sections/coronavirus-live-updates/2020/04/08/829618124/4-in-10-u-s-teens-say-they-havent-done-online-learning-since-schools-closed

Kamenetz, A. (2020b). *5 radical schooling ideas for an uncertain fall and beyond*. Retrieved from https://www.npr.org/2020/06/17/878205853/5-radical-schooling-ideas-for-an-uncertain-fall-and-beyond

Keane, R. (2020, May 2). Coronavirus forces teachers to learn a different tune. *Wall Street Journal*, p. A11.

Keierleber, M. (2020). *Top education leaders discuss how they've navigated the coronavirus so far — And why schools will never be the same*. Retrieved from https://www.the74million.org/top-education-leaders-discuss-how-theyve-navigated-the-coronavirus-so-far-and-why-schools-will-never-be-the-same/

Kenniston, E. F. (2020). *Thinking of homeschooling? Local parents share their resources*. Retrieved from https://berksweekly.com/education/thinking-of-homeschooling-local-parents-share-their-resources/

Koh, Y. (2020, May 7). Schools try to stem 'Covid slide' learning loss. *Wall Street Journal*, Retrieved from https://www.wsj.com/articles/schools-try-to-stem-covid-slide-learning-loss-11588857722.

Krueger, A. B., & Zhu, P. (2004). Inefficiency, subsample selection bias, and nonrobustness: A response to Paul E. Peterson and William G. Howell. *American Behavioral Scientist, 47*(5), 718–728.

Lardieri, A. (2020). *1-in-5 teachers unlikely to return to schools if reopened in the fall, poll finds.* Retrieved from https://www.usnews.com/news/education-news/articles/2020-05-26/1-in-5-teachers-unlikely-to-return-to-schools-if-reopened-in-the-fall-poll-finds

Lisickis, R. (2020). *Neighborhood decides to do co-op homeschooling, retired Marine takes up teaching PE and kids love it.* Retrieved from https://www.boredpanda.com/coop-schooling-lockdown-retired-marine/?utm_source=google&utm_medium=organic&utm_campaign=organic

Malkus, N., Christensen, C., & Schurz, J. (2020). *School district responses to the COVID-19 pandemic: Round 6, ending the year of school closures.* Retrieved from https://www.aei.org/wp-content/uploads/2020/06/School-district-responses-to-the-COVID-19-Pandemic-Round-6.pdf

McDonald, K. (2020). *Homeschooling during the COVID-19 pandemic.* Retrieved from https://www.cato.org/blog/homeschooling-during-covid-19-pandemic

Miller, M. D., & Moore, W. P. (1991). Private-public school differences in the United States: Findings from the second international mathematics study. *International Journal of Educational Research, 15*(5), 433–444. doi:10.1016/0883-0355(91)90023-L

Muller, B. (2020). *37 students in quarantine after Glynn County school reports positive case of COVID-19.* Retrieved from https://www.news4jax.com/news/local/2020/08/22/37-students-in-quarantine-after-glynn-county-schools-reports-one-positive-case-of-covid-19/

National Center for Education Statistics. (2013). *Table 205.50.* Retrieved from https://nces.ed.gov/programs/digest/d13/tables/dt13_205.50.asp

National Center for Education Statistics. (2019). *Public school expenditures.* Retrieved from https://nces.ed.gov/fastfacts/display.asp?id=66

Needles, A. (2020). *Homeschooling? You're not alone. Tacoma parents share plans, resources as schools close.* Retrieved from https://www.thenewstribune.com/news/coronavirus/article241236086.html

Newcomb, A. (2020). *Charlize Theron calls home-schooling her two daughters 'incredibly stressful'.* https://www.today.com/parents/charlize-theron-calls-home-chooling-her-two-daughters-incredibly-stressful-t185835

Ovide, S. (2020). When home becomes a classroom. *New York Times*, p. A2.

Park, D., & Winchester, H. (2020). *COVID-19 closures a redefining moment for students, parents & schools.* Retrieved from https://assets.documentcloud.org/documents/6895624/Learning-Heroes-Survey-Results.pdf

Pianta, R. C., & Ansari, A. (2018). Does attendance in private schools predict student outcomes at age 15? Evidence from a longitudinal study. *Educational Researcher, 47*(7), 419–434. doi:10.3102/0013189X18785632

Picchi, A. (2020). *Homeschool pods are gaining traction amid worries about school reopening; here's how parents are getting the finances to work.* Retrieved from https://www.usatoday.com/story/money/2020/07/28/parents-working-home-due-coronavirus work-home-requirements-has-parents-pooling-resources-hire-tutor/5498620002/

Remadna, N. (2020). *Planning to homeschool? Here are some tips.* Retrieved from https://www.kxan.com/news/education/texas-parents-consider-homeschooling-as-covid-19-concerns-linger/

Richards, E. (2020). *'Historic academic regression': Why homeschooling is so hard amid school closures.* Retrieved from https://www.usatoday.com/story/news/education/2020/04/13/coronavirus-online-school-homeschool-betsy-devos/5122539002/

Schultz, T. (2020). *National poll: 40% of families more likely to homeschool after lockdowns end.* Retrieved from https://www.federationforchildren.org/national-poll-40-of-families-more-likely-to-homeschool-after-lockdowns-end/

Sell, M. (2020). *Statewide virtual school provider selected, broadband access 'inequities' remain.* Retrieved from https://www.wbrc.com/2020/07/02/statewide-virtual-school-provider-selected-broadband-access-inequities-remain/

Strassel, K. A. (2020, May 16). One of America's remotest states makes remote learning work. *Wall Street Journal*, p. A13.

Strauss, V. (2020, May 4). She's a college president and a cognitive scientist. But her 9-year-old daughter isn't impressed with her home schooling. *Washington Post*, Retrieved from https://www.washingtonpost.com/education/2020/2005/2004/shes-college-president-cognitive-scientist-her-2029-year-old-daughter-isnt-impressed-with-her-homeschooling/.

U.S. Bureau of the Census. (2018). *HINC-01. Selected characteristics of households by total money income.* Retrieved from https://www2.census.gov/programs-surveys/cps/tables/hinc-01/2019/hinc01_1.xls

U.S. Bureau of the Census. (2020). *Educational attainment in the United States: 2019.* Retrieved from https://www2.census.gov/programs-surveys/demo/tables/educational-attainment/2019/cps-detailed-tables/table-1-1.xlsx

U.S. Bureau of the Census. (n.d.). *QuickFacts: United States.* Retrieved from https://www.census.gov/quickfacts/fact/table/US/LFE046218

USA Today/Ipsos. (2020). *Nearly half of Americans support reopening schools before there is a coronavirus vaccine.* Retrieved from https://www.ipsos.com/sites/default/files/ct/news/documents/2020-05/topline_usa_today_gen_pop_covid_education_052620.pdf

Watson, B. (2020). *Moms adjust to homeschooling during COVID-19 outbreak.* Retrieved from https://www.pressrepublican.com/news/coronavirus/moms-adjust-to-homeschooling-during-covid-19-outbreak/article_991fa9ad-4d86-5efe-8a0e-1f7af6bd588e.html

Weiner, J. (2020). I refuse to run a home school. *New York Times*, p. A29.

Parent-Created "Schools" in the U.S.

Angela R. Watson

ABSTRACT
After a turbulent spring of COVID induced virtual learning, some traditional public schools in the U.S. are hesitant to reopen with face-to-face instruction in fall 2020. In response to this uncertainty, many parents are taking their childrens' education into their own hands. Some are banding together to create their own kind of school, with small groups of students limiting contagion, referred to as learning pods. Many wonder what exactly these pods are and how they work. Even more pressing are concerns of equity and strategies ensuring that all families have access to this homegrown education option. Here, I define learning pods, examine what we know about the likely efficacy of learning pods, given current evidence, and discuss policy strategies that savvy innovators are trying across the country that could serve as quality guardrails and to expand access.

After a turbulent spring of COVID induced virtual learning, some traditional public schools are understandably hesitant to reopen with face-to-face instruction. While some public schools plan to open in the fall of 2020, many are opting for some form of blended or virtual learning (Horn, 2020). In response to this uncertainty, many parents are taking their childrens' education into their own hands (Maxouris, 2020). Some are choosing to send their children to private schools that are offering in-person instruction, for a price (Blad, 2020). Others are banding together to create their own kind of school, with small groups of students, colloquially referred to as learning pods. Media stories of these "pods" abound, but many people wonder what exactly they are and how they work. Even more pressing are concerns of equity and strategies that might be leveraged to ensure that all families have access to this homegrown education option.

The saying that necessity is the mother of invention describes the creation of these pods. Learning pods, also called pandemic pods (Fox, 2020) and nano-schools, are a grassroots education innovation. Parents, seeking a safe but rigorous learning environment for their child, and whose needs are not met by current education options, are creating their own "school." In this memo, I define learning pods as they stand today with the understanding that they will continue to morph in the coming weeks and months. I examine what we know about the likely efficacy of learning pods, given current evidence, and discuss policy strategies that savvy innovators are trying across the country that could serve as quality guardrails and to expand access.

A variation of microschools (Horn, 2015; Vander Ark, 2017), think one room school house, learning pods can take many forms. While there is no exact definition for learning pods, they are generally very small nonpublic schools with a few mixed age students, often from a few families. Media reports highlight learning pods created in suburban backyards complete with a certified teacher. Others are created and run by parents who take turns educating their own children (Fox, 2020). Still others use churches or other available community space and hire tutors, or find volunteers. Some use their public-school virtual curriculum and instruction with an adult supervisor. Others may purchase a curriculum, or create their own. There seems no end to parents' creativity and resourcefulness (Horn, 2020).

The legality of learning pods varies by state. Depending on the location, a learning group may be classified as a homeschool or nonpublic school depending on state laws around compulsory education, as well as local laws such as those for city, county, even neighborhood property owners' associations. For example, students are considered homeschooled if they receive instruction at home by a parent in Washington and Michigan. However, if these same parents hire a tutor to handle instruction, they are no longer considered a "homeschool." Similarly, if children from another family join a home-based learning pod, they would become a nonpublic school, and would have to meet an additional set of legal requirements. In some states, two families can join to homeschool their children, but three families schooling together is defined as a private school. Hiring a teacher or tutors to instruct children at home could come with additional regulations. Some states require certification for private tutors. For example, in New York, a non-parent can teach a child at home if the parent assumes ultimate responsibility. However, this only applies to a single family; more than that and it is a private school (Jones, 2020).

While setting up a school at the kitchen table may seem relatively straightforward, owning a "business" that involves other people's children can be complicated. As soon as a home school is legally considered a nonpublic or private school, certain legal requirements that help ensure basic safety and serve as gateways to entry may become applicable. These requirements could include school zoning laws and childcare laws aimed at ensuring child safety. A business may be required to meet basic fire safety regulations that, depending on occupancy, could require full sprinkler systems. Then, there are compensation laws and tax implications if the school organizer is paying a teacher and/or charging "tuition" to member parents. School organizers must consider teacher qualifications and curricular requirements. Some states require instruction in certain subjects, such as state history, or even certain hours for instruction during the day. Of course, there are also background checks, both for child safety and financial history. If the school is legally considered a business, then licensing and permits may be required at the local level. The need for additional insurance, such as liability insurance in case anyone is injured, may be required and is certainly prudent. Schools may also need to meet immunization requirements. The list goes on (Jones, 2020).

Parents looking for support in navigating the legal requirements of setting up their own learning pod can turn to a burgeoning industry that supports learning pods, for a fee, such as Bubbles by Swing Education, School House, Learning Pods, and others. These businesses will assist with legal concerns, curriculum acquisition, and even match parents with certified teachers in their area. With the legal and safety concerns addressed, I turn to concerns of efficacy.

Empirical research on learning pods, participation rates, demographics, and efficacy are nonexistent. They are simply too new for empirical research to exist. For hints at how learning pods are organized, and evidence of participation, I turn to recent media reports, of which, luckily, there are many. Media outlets like *The New York Times, The Washington Post, Education Week*, and *Education Next*, all ran stories on learning pods in August of 2020 before most public schools started. Without a body of research, the next reasonable strategy is to consider the research on the nearest relative to learning pods, the microschool. Unfortunately, the literature on micro-schools is likewise scarce (Squire, King, & Trinidad, 2019). Fortunately, research evidence does exist on more established predecessors to learning pods, such as homeschooling, hybrid or cooperative learning models, virtual schooling, tutoring, and private schools. For additional information, I also turn to the literature on positive academic outcomes attained through classroom size reduction, and individualized learning. Facilitating these and other high-impact strategies could easy occur in these tiny, nimble, and innovative schools.

States control education and therefore definitions, policies, and requirements can vary widely by location. This is particularly true with homeschooling. Despite these variations, homeschooling is generally defined as parent-led education that occurs in the home. Homeschool has grown for decades (McQuiggan, Megra, & Grady, 2017), with explosive growth reported during COVID school closures and safety concerns (Hollingsworth, 2020; McDonald, 2020). But some ask if homeschool is effective. While rigorous research evidence if difficult to obtain, a recent review of the literature on homeschooling found that homeschoolers outperform their traditionally schooled peers in nearly two-thirds of the studies reviewed. Another third of studies found neutral or mixed outcomes, while only 5% of homeschool studies found negative academic outcomes (Burke, 2019). While homeschooling is slightly different from learning pods, they are both oftentimes parent-led and instruction usually occurs at home. A common criticism of homeschooling is that children may lack needed social interaction and are isolated at home. Learning pods, as an alternative to homeschooling, add social interaction with other adults and children, as well as opportunities for cooperative learning that may be an improvement over some homeschool situations. Another important criticism of homeschooling is that it could be used to hide abuse (Bartholet, 2019; Dwyer & Peters, 2019). Learning pods offer an opportunity for adults from outside the family to interact with children and possibly abate some of these concerns.

Hybrid schooling, or cooperatives, serve as an alternative to home-only schooling. In this model, students are either officially homeschooled, or classified as attending a private school. The student attends, either in person or virtually, classes taught by someone else, part of the time. Sometimes this teacher is another parent, but in many cases, these are hired teachers with subject expertise (Johnson, 2020). The co-op model is similar to learning pods in that students are schooled at home in many cases, and are taught by an assortment of parents and hired instructors.

Virtual schooling is similar to what most American students received during the spring of 2020. Student receive a mix of synchronous and asynchronous instruction, via the internet, at home. While some studies have found that virtual charter schools are not as effective as traditional schooling (Woodworth et al., 2015), there are questions about structural differences, such as testing policies, that may disadvantage virtual students (Beck, Watson, & Maranto, 2019). Some learning pods may use virtual instruction. However, they can provide in-person instruction and peer interaction, improving on traditional virtual learning models.

Hiring a tutor with subject expertise to teach students has a long history in the US and abroad. Tutoring has been part of the teaching system in Oxford and Cambridge Universities since the 15th century. Tutors are meant to serve not only as an instructor, but also mentor students. Robert Slavin, of the Johns Hopkins School of Education, concludes that tutoring is one of the most powerful education interventions (Slavin & Steiner, 2020). Tutoring may be particularly effective for students at-risk. A study of at-risk college students found that tutoring was positively associated with student retention and academic performance (Rheinheimer, Grace-Odeleye, Francois, & Kusorgbor, 2010). High-dose tutoring is also effective (Ander, Guryan, & Ludwig, 2016; Sawchuk, 2020). The link from research on tutoring to learning pods is obvious; both involve a small group of students who are mentored and taught by a single or multiple instructors. Some countries are considering large-scale tutoring to solve their education woes. They are recruiting student teachers and recent but unemployed college graduates for this purpose (Slavin, 2020).

Before COVID-19, private schools were closing at an historic rate, likely due to rising tuition costs (Sparks, 2020; Squire et al., 2019). However, with some public schools failing to reopen for face-to-face instruction this fall, many parents are taking a second look at private schools. Private schools frequently outperform traditional public schools on a variety of outcomes, and are particularly successful with marginalized students (Egalite & Wolf, 2016). It is likely that learning pods, as a version of a private school, can generate some of the academic benefits attributed to private schools at a fraction of the cost to families.

Finally, learning pods, with low student to teacher ratios could theoretically be high-dose learning environments with maximum capacity to differentiate, thus potentially providing the benefits associated with small class size and individualized learning (Chingos & Whitehurst, 2011; Schwartz, 2019). Similarly, the model allows for socialization, and mixed-age grouping, that could be an improvement to more isolated or siloed education models.

Parents with the resources and savvy to create learning pods are leading the way. Consequently, there is concern about those families left behind (Samuels & Prothero, 2020). We know that students with the least struggle most, and have the hardest time recovering what is lost. What can we do to ensure that learning pods are as strong and equitable as possible? Luckily, innovators are coming up with ideas to serve those most in need.

Established organizations like Big Brothers Big Sisters of America, the YMCA, and Boys and Girls Clubs of America are working to set up small pod "learning spaces" where students can access their virtual public-school curriculum in a safe environment under adult supervision (Kebede, 2020). Other community spaces such as museums, libraries, zoos, and national parks look to partner with funders to set up similar low-cost, high-impact learning hubs to foster more equitable access to the benefits of learning pods (Schimke & Aldrich, 2020).

Tutoring can be expanded to serve more children. Virtual tutoring networks, staffed by volunteers with moderate education and expertise, could also bring one-on-one instruction to more kids in need. For example, teens created a volunteer network serving hundreds of students in their area (Dorsey, 2020). Building tutoring networks with existing organizations could expedite the process and get thousands of tutors into the field quickly. Similarly, former Tennessee Governor Haslam came up with a plan, in partnership with Boys and Girls Clubs, to recruit college students to help tutor students across the state (Kraft & Goldstein, 2020; Wong, 2020). Plans like this one could be win-win propositions, by helping students and by investing in recent college graduates who face an uncertain job market due to COVID-19.

There are even funding options. The United Way, in partnership with other organizations, is offering "pod" funding for families in need. Similarly, Kentucky just approved a2,500 USD stipend to help in-home "centers" of up to 12 students get approved as legal childcare providers (Yetter, 2020).

Conclusions and policy recommendations

As schools across the country begin to open, policymakers must strive to adapt to evolving practices in real time. Clearly, many parents across the country are looking for options. While parents have a right to find, or create, schooling options that meet the needs of their families, every family wants the best option – in their judgment – for their child. States may want to craft explicit regulations to incentivize quality options and equitable access. Changes to regulations that would allow families to gather in small groups while still providing a safe learning atmosphere for students is a first step. For example, Massachusetts just moved to allow parents to form small learning groups that can be supervised by volunteer community organizations (Ebbert, 2020).

Funding is a crucial piece of the equity puzzle. Low-income parents need help setting up learning pods. Arizona allows the use of education savings account funds for micro-schools/learning pods, a policy that other states could copy (Duda, 2020).

Incentivizing the use of high-quality curricula, either through free access or stipends that incentivize use, is another strategy for ensuring at-home learning is rigorous.

Finally, helping parents find qualified teachers, for free, could help ensure higher quality instruction in learning pods. Creating apps or websites like Arkansas' ARTeachers.org, would connect certified teachers with teaching jobs. Currently, this website does not allow for private school job postings, but it could, thus providing more equitable access to qualified instructors. Hawaii, because it is a single district, and Alaska have similar unified job posting boards.

It is likely that learning pods are here to stay (Horn, 2020). Many parents will return to work in-person, and their students will return to face-to-face traditional schooling, but for some, this new education option will become permanent. Future research could easily include randomized control trials where student applicants are selected into learning pods, or are assigned by oversubscribed lotteries. These would be excellent tests of the impact of learning pods on academic as well as social emotional outcomes for students, their families, and their teachers. With standardized testing missing in action for Spring 2020, and in question for 2021 (Modan, 2020), implementing other stable interim assessments, such as NWEA's MAP testing, would help the research community with meaningful comparisons of academic growth.

Disclosure statement

No potential conflict of interest was reported by the author.

References

Ander, R., Guryan, J., & Ludwig, J. (2016). *Improving academic outcomes for disadvantaged students: Scaling up individualized tutorials.* The Hamilton Project. Retrieved from https://www.hamiltonproject.org/assets/files/improving_academic_outcomes_for_disadvantaged_students_pp.pdf?_ga=2.197003621.878040166.1599143585-180107006.1599143585

Bartholet, E. (2019). *Homeschooling: Parent rights absolutism vs. child rights to education and protection.* Retrieved from http://nrs.harvard.edu/urn-3:HUL.InstRepos:40108859

Beck, D., Watson, A., & Maranto, R. (2019). Do testing conditions explain cyber charter schools' failing grades. *American Journal of Distance Education, 33,* 46–58. doi:10.1080/08923647.2019.1554989

Blad, E. (2020). Private schools catch parents' eye as public school buildings stay shut. *Education Week,* Retrieved from https://www.edweek.org/ew/articles/2020/08/06/private-schools-catch-parents-eye-as-public.html

Burke, L. (2019). *Bringing achievement home: A review of the academic outcomes of home-schooling students in the united states.* Home School legal Defense Association. Retrieved from https://secureservercdn.net/45.40.149.34/n5e.cd2.myftpupload.com/wp-content/uploads/2020/04/Bringing-Achievment-Home.pdf

Chingos, M., & Whitehurst, G. (2011). *Class size: What research says and what it means for state policy.* Brookings. Retrieved from https://www.brookings.edu/research/class-size-what-research-says-and-what-it-means-for-state-policy/

Dorsey, D. (2020). *Coronavirus kindness: South Bay teens create tutor network for hundreds of students.* ABC. Retrieved from https://abc7news.com/coronavirus-impact-kindness-school/6053448/

Duda, J. (2020). *Microschools on the rise in Arizona, with COVID providing an added boost. AZ mirror.* Retrieved from https://www.azmirror.com/2020/07/28/microschools-on-the-rise-in-arizona-with-covid-providing-added-boost/

Dwyer, J., & Peters, S. (2019). *Homeschooling: The history and philosophy of a controversial practice.* Chicago: University of Chicago Press.

Ebbert, S. (2020). *State to allow remote learning pods, kids' programs outside schools. The boston globe.* Retrieved from https://www.bostonglobe.com/?p1=BGHeader_Logo

Egalite, A., & Wolf, P. (2016). A review of the empirical research on private school choice. *Peabody Journal of Education, 91*(4), 441–454.

Fox, M. (2020). *Desperate parents are turning to "learning pods" this fall. Here's what it can cost.* CNBC. Retrieved from https://www.cnbc.com/2020/08/10/parents-turn-to-learning-pods-this-fall-amid-covid-what-it-can-cost.html#:~:text=So%2Dcalled%20%E2%80%9Clearning%20pods%E2%80%9D,help%20being%20left%20left%20behind

Hollingsworth, H. (2020). Interest in homeschooling has 'exploded' amid COVID-19 pandemic. *Pittsburg post-gazette.* Retrieved from https://www.post-gazette.com/news/education/2020/08/12/Interest-in-homeschooling-has-exploded-amid-pandemic-COVID-19/stories/202008120094

Horn, M. (2015). The rise of altschool and other micro-schools: Combinations of private, blended, and at-home schooling meet needs of individual students. *Education Next, 15*(3), 77–79. Retrieved from https://www.educationnext.org/rise-micro-schools/

Horn, M. (2020). The rapid rise of pandemic pods: Will the parent response to COVID-19 lead to lasting change? *Education Next,* Retrieved from https://www.educationnext.org/rapid-rise-pandemic-pods-will-parent-response-covid-19-lead-to-lasting-changes/

Johnson, N. (2020). What is a homeschool co-op? *Parents.* Retrieved from https://www.parents.com/kids/education/what-is-a-homeschool-co-op/

Jones, D. (2020). Can parents hire a tutor this fall and call it homeschooling? Maybe. *The federalist*. Retrieved from https://thefederalist.com/2020/07/14/can-parents-hire-a-tutor-or-this-fall-and-call-it-homeschooling-maybe/

Kebede, L. (2020). Most Memphis students are starting the school year online. But from where? *Chalkbeat, tennessee*. Retrieved from https://tn.chalkbeat.org/2020/8/7/21359087/scs-students-are-starting-the-school-year-online-but-from-where

Kraft, M., & Goldstein, M. (2020). Getting tutoring right to reduce COVID-19 learning loss. *Brookings brown center chalkboard*. Retrieved from https://www.brookings.edu/blog/brown-center-chalkboard/2020/05/21/getting-tutoring-right-to-reduce-covid-19-learning-loss/

Maxouris, C. (2020). Covid-19 has parents frantically searching for school alternatives, even if they can't afford them. *CNN*. Retrieved from https://www.cnn.com/2020/07/19/us/parent-alternatives-school-fall/index.html

McDonald, K. (2020). The world's homeschooling moment. *Forbes*. Retrieved from https://www.forbes.com/sites/kerrymcdonald/2020/03/11/the-worlds-homeschooling-moment/#165b01fc550c

McQuiggan, M., Megra, M., & Grady, S. (2017). *Parent and family involvements in education: Results from the national household education surveys program of 2016, First Look,2017*. Retrieved from https://nces.ed.gov/pubs2017/2017102.pdf

Modan, N. (2020). States move toward waiving standardized tests for 2020–21. *Education dive*. Retrieved from https://www.educationdive.com/news/states-move-toward-waiving-standardized-tests-for-2020-21/580570/

Rheinheimer, D., Grace-Odeleye, B., Francois, G., & Kusorgbor, C. (2010). Tutoring: A support strategy for at-risk students. *Learning Assistance Review*, *15*, 23–34.

Samuels, C., & Prothero, A. (2020). Could 'pandemic pods' be a lifeline for parents or a threat to equity? *Education Week*, Retrieved from https://www.edweek.org/ew/articles/2020/07/29/could-the-pandemic-pod-be-a-lifeline.html

Sawchuk, S. (2020). High-dose tutoring is effective, but expensive. Ideas for making it work. *Education Week*, Retrieved from https://www.edweek.org/ew/articles/2020/08/20/high-dosage-tutoring-is-effective-but-expensive-ideas.html

Schimke, A., & Aldrich, M. (2020). Pods for all? Some districts and nonprofits are reimagining the remote learning trend. *Chalkbeat*. Retrieved from https://www.chalkbeat.org/2020/8/10/21362268/pods-for-all-some-districts-and-non-profits-are-reimagining-the-remote-learning-trend

Schwartz, S. (2019). One big barrier to personalized learning: Time. *Education Week*, Retrieved from https://www.edweek.org/ew/articles/2019/11/06/one-big-barrier-to-personalized-learning-time.html

Slavin, R. (2020). *Are the Dutch solving the covid slide with tutoring?* Retrieved from https://robertslavinsblog.wordpress.com/2020/06/18/are-the-dutch-solving-the-covid-slide-with-tutoring/

Slavin, R., & Steiner, D. (2020). Tutoring as an effective strategy in our troubled times. *Fordham institute, flypaper*. Retrieved from https://fordhaminstitute.org/national/commentary/tutoring-effective-strategy-our-troubled-times

Sparks, S. (2020). Catholic school closures rise amid COVID-19 recession. *Education Week*, Retrieved from https://www.edweek.org/ew/articles/2020/06/09/catholic-school-closures-rise-in-wake-of.html

Squire, J., King, M., & Trinidad, J. (2019). Working toward equitable access and affordability: How private schools and microschools seek to serve middle- and low-income students. *Bellwether education partners*. Retrieved from https://bellwethereducation.org/sites/default/files/Working%20Toward%20Equitable%20Access%20and%20Affordability_Bellwether.pdf

Vander Ark, T. (2017). What's the next big idea? Microschool networks. *Getting smart.* Retrieved from https://www.gettingsmart.com/2017/04/whats-the-next-big-idea-microschool-networks/

Wong, A. (2020). 'Time for innovation': How tutoring could be a key to lifting kids out of 'COVID slide'. *USA Today.* Retrieved from https://www.usatoday.com/story/news/education/2020/08/10/how-tutoring-could-key-lifting-kids-out-covid-slide/3319070001/

Woodworth, J., Raymond, M., Chirbas, K., Gonzalez, M., Negassi, Y., Snow, W., & Van Donge, C. (2015). *Online charter school study.* Retrieved from http://credo.stanford.edu/pdfs/Online%20Charter%20Study%20Final.pdf

Yetter, D. (2020). Kentucky announces revised rules for struggling child care centers to increase class size. *Courrier Journal.* Retrieved from https://www.courier-journal.com/story/news/education/2020/08/31/revised-rules-struggling-child-care-centers-allow-larger-classes/5656634002/

Reopening America's Schools: A Descriptive Look at How States and Large School Districts Navigated Fall 2020

David T. Marshall ⓘ and Martha Bradley-Dorsey ⓘ

ABSTRACT

The COVID-19 pandemic forced America's public schools to close in the latter half of the 2019–20 school year. Schools' reopening plans vary for 2020–21. We reviewed the reopening plans for all 50 states, as well as the largest 120 school districts in the United States with a particular focus on reopening modalities, mask-wearing guidance, the treatment of vulnerable students and staff, and fall sports. Several states recommend that schools reopen based on viral spread, while others recommend a particular modality (in-person, hybrid, or remote instruction). States varied most in their treatment of fall 2020 athletics. This descriptive work represents a first step in understanding how schools are reopening amidst the COVID-19 pandemic. We conclude with implications for school choice policy.

The COVID-19 viral pandemic disrupted the lives of people around the globe. Schooling has been no exception to this. In the United States, all but two states closed schools between March 12–23, with Nebraska and Maine holding out until April 1 and 2, respectively (Ballotpedia, 2020). Schools across the country remained closed for in-person instruction for the balance of the school year. Regardless of what a school district's transition to remote instruction looked like, the job of an educator looked radically different and became increasingly difficult. Marshall, Shannon, and Love (2020) surveyed teachers between mid-March and early April 2020 and found that more than 90% of respondents had never taught online before COVID-19 intervened. Teachers reported that all aspects of their job were more challenging during the transition to remote instruction. Teachers cited a range of challenges, including the inability to hold students accountable, a lack of adequate time to do the job well, and the inability to communicate with students in real time. Those responding to the survey also described challenges their student faced outside of school, including access to reliable internet and adequate resources. Teachers similarly cited their own challenges outside of school, including balancing the educational needs of their own children with those of their students.

This fall, states and school districts across the U.S. are making plans for how they are reopening their schools for the 2020–21 school year. COVID-19 has presented policymakers with a dilemma – keep schools open and risk the continued spread of the virus or close schools and realize the consequences of keeping children out of school. This dilemma extends beyond a pedagogical debate over learning modalities; there are a number of non-academic consequences related to school closures as well. These include sharp increases in child abuse (Sidpra, Abomeli, Hameed, Baker, & Mankad, 2020) and food insecurity (Wright & Merritt, 2020), as well as risks to mental health and wellbeing (Liu, Bao, Huang, Shi, & Lu, 2020; Van Lancker & Parolin, 2020). All of these issues are exacerbated for children living in poverty (Burgess & Sievertsen, 2020; Van Lancker & Parolin, 2020). Students with disabilities also lose access to school-based resources, and many struggle with remote instruction without in-person supports (Masonbrink & Hurley, 2020). Reopening schools for in-person instruction does involve the risk of the virus spreading. However, early evidence suggests that COVID-19 is far less common in younger children, and the vast majority of children who are infected with the virus have mild symptoms (Lee, Hu, Chen, Huang, & Hsueh, 2020).

The U.S. Department of Education has a webpage devoted to providing resources related to COVID-19 for schools, students, and families (2020). Among the resources is a link to the Center for Disease Control's (Centers for Disease Control and Prevention [CDC] 2020a) guidance on reopening schools, which notes that their guidelines and recommendations are not regulatory. Absent federal reopening requirements, each of the 50 states drafted their own guidance and recommendations. We present a snapshot of how state policymakers and, separately, how school district leaders were planning to reopen during this moment in time.

Method and data sources

Our work sought to answer the following research questions:

(1) What guidance are state-level education policymakers providing schools for reopening schools for the 2020–21 school year?
(2) How are the largest school districts in the United States opting to reopen their schools for the 2020–21 school year?
   (a) Do differences in reopening modalities exist in terms of total enrollment, race/ethnicity, and socioeconomic status?

To answer the first question, we examined the reopening guidance and plans for all 50 states between August 12–21, 2020. In the case of most states, a large document or two covered their guidance. Indeed, the Kansas State

Department of Education (2020) released the lengthiest such document at 1190 pages on August 17, 2020 that covers everything from kindergarten science instruction to health safety protocols. Other states, such as Missouri, opted to have a website with a plethora of links to smaller documents that offer much more limited and targeted guidance on reopening schools (Missouri Department of Elementary and Secondary Education, 2020b).

To answer the second research question, we examined the reopening modalities of the 120 largest school districts in the United States at two distinct time points: (1) August 5, 2020 and (2) August 21, 2020. As expected, some school districts amended their reopening plans between these two points in time. We acknowledge that August 21, 2020 is in some ways an arbitrary date; however, schools generally open in the United States anywhere between the first week in August and the day after Labor Day. August 21 represents a midway point between these two points in time and a point at which most reopening decisions were either beginning to be implemented or a couple of weeks away from being implemented. The purpose of this paper is to provide a snapshot of what reopening schools looked like amidst the COVID-19 pandemic.

State reopening plans and guidance

Our review of state reopening plans and guidance focused on a few key areas: (1) whether states had a recommended modality of learning; (2) the extent to which masks are going to be required; (3) how vulnerable populations will be treated; and (4) how sports will be handled for Fall 2020. See Appendix A to examine how all 50 states have handled these four issues.

Modalities of learning

There were several areas across state plans that were similar. Almost every state's plan allowed for decisions about reopening to be made at the local level and for decisions to vary across the state. Pennsylvania's plan is perhaps the most restrictive plan, as it is a phased reopening plan ordered by the governor (Pennsylvania Department of Education, 2020). By contrast, Mississippi's plan is the least restrictive; the Mississippi Department of Education (2020) is explicit in stating that it has no authority to direct schools' reopening plans. A number of states directly tie reopening modality to COVID-19 data. For example, Minnesota determines the learning model that is deployed based on the number of cases per 10,000 residents over the past two weeks (Minnesota Department of Education, 2020). If there are fewer than 10 cases per 10,000, then all students will learn in-person. A spike to 50 or more cases per 10,000 will force distance learning for everyone. Gradations in between call for a mix of in-person and hybrid instruction, prioritizing in-person instruction for elementary students.

States were also similar in their guidance for what to do when a case is reported. Louisiana is an example of a state that ties reopening to its governor's reopening phase. As of this writing, Louisiana is in Phase 2 and most systems will begin the school year with remote instruction. Maine, by contrast, has a Red/Yellow/Green guidance framework. A county is considered "Red" if there is high risk of the virus, and remote instruction is recommended. The "Yellow" distinction indicates that there is an elevated risk and hybrid instruction is recommended. A "Green" distinction indicates that there is low risk of the virus and schools should reopen in-person or hybrid. As of this writing, every county in Maine is listed as "Green." Almost every state involves local and state public health officials, recommends following CDC (2020b) guidance, and has a protocol for deep cleaning spaces that were used by an individual who has tested positive for the virus.

States that do not directly tie reopening to coronavirus cases handle their guidance in several ways. Some states, like Alabama, do not offer a recommendation and leave that decision to individual school districts (Alabama State Department of Education, 2020a, 2020b). Several states, including Arkansas, Florida, Illinois, and Massachusetts make explicit that the goal is to have in-person instruction. Florida's plan opens with several pages that discuss achievement gaps, and the danger that these gaps may widen with remote instruction (Florida Department of Education, 2020). The Massachusetts reopening begins similarly, stating that "there is a clear consensus from both education and medical groups: we must keep in mind not only the risks associated with COVID-19 for in-person school programs, but also the known challenges and consequences of keeping students out of school" (Massachusetts Department of Education, 2020, p. 3). Idaho's recommended modality is either in-person or hybrid, with their plan noting, "Despite incredible advances in digital learning, you can never replace the value and impact of in-person interaction with a professional, dedicated teacher" (Idaho Department of Education, 2020, p. 2); Rhode Island's guidance is similar. Alaska and Maryland's plans recommend their school districts consider in-person instruction for elementary students and remote instruction for older students. At least eight states recommend schools reopen with some type of hybrid instructional mode, with California, Illinois, Kentucky, and Maryland's plans all devoting space to articulating several types of hybrid modalities that might work.

Masks

Mask wearing is another area where state policies do not differ greatly. Almost every state either mandates mask wearing (either in their plan or via a governor's executive order) or strongly recommends individuals wear masks when at school. Several states, including Rhode Island and Wisconsin, invoke CDC (2020b) guidance in their discussions of mask wearing. Nebraska and West Virginia tie mask-wearing policy to transmission levels (Nebraska Department of Education, 2020; West Virginia Department of Education, 2020). Michigan and Colorado offer different recommendations for elementary and secondary schools, with both requiring middle and high school students to wear masks and only recommending masks for younger students (Colorado Department of Education, 2020; Governor Gretchen Whitmer, 2020). Ohio is the lone state that offers different guidance for instructional staff and students, and custodial and maintenance staff, recommending masks for the former and requiring their use for the latter (Ohio Department of Education, 2020). The reopening plans for Massachusetts and New Hampshire both recommend that students be given mask breaks throughout the day when they are able to be socially distanced from others, ideally either outdoors or indoors with open windows (Massachusetts Department of Elementary and Secondary Education, 2020; New Hampshire Department of Education, 2020). Overall, policies for mask wearing were similar across state contexts.

Vulnerable populations

Overall, states are similar in how they handle students who may be more vulnerable to contracting COVID-19 and developing serious symptoms. For the sake of this discussion, *vulnerable populations* refers to students, family members, and staff members who are at greater risk of experiencing adverse health outcomes due to COVID-19. Some of the reopening plans also describe academically at-risk students as a vulnerable population; however, this is not what we intend here. Most states allow families to decide whether to return to in-person instruction for those who are uncomfortable with returning to school, and 36 state plans explicitly suggest offering remote learning alternatives for these families. In terms of vulnerable staff who may have underlying conditions, eight states' plans simply recommend that a plan be created for those who may be at greater risk for the virus. Some states do not seem to address this at all, but those are in the minority. Several states including Alabama, Arkansas, Colorado, California, Nevada, Oklahoma, and Pennsylvania suggest that districts should find ways to encourage vulnerable staff to telework or provide alternate work duties that allow them to work from home. Connecticut and Alaska call for districts to consider reassigning vulnerable staff to remote teaching duties. At least three states' plans are explicit about developing flexible leave plans so that employees are not forced to deplete their earned leave for virus-related absences (whether they are due to exposure, a positive test, or for precautionary purposes). The recommendations from the Arkansas Department of Education (2020) suggest that school districts might consider placing vulnerable staff on administrative leave as one option to avoid them using all of their earned leave. Idaho ties how they deal with vulnerable staff to community transmission (Idaho Department of Education, 2020). If there is no community transmission in a county or municipality, staff are expected to come to work as usual. However, minimal community transmission triggers a reassignment process to allow them to work remotely. Hawaii and New Jersey's reopening plans recommend consulting with teachers' collective bargaining agreements when addressing the needs of vulnerable staff.

Fall sports

States vary widely in terms of how they intend to handle fall sports in 2020 (Stephens, 2020). Overall, states across the country are falling into one of four categories. A plurality of states are starting the fall with high school sports moving forward on schedule. A caveat to this is that there are districts within these states that are opting out of fall sports. For example, Pennsylvania has decided to move forward with fall sports; however, the School District of Philadelphia will not participate in football this fall (Anastasia, 2020). Several other states have decided to move forward with fall sports, albeit with a delayed start to the season and abridged schedules. A number of states have tabled all fall sports and have opted to move them to the spring semester. Finally, some states have moved football and volleyball to the spring, but are moving forward with low-risk sports like cross country, golf, and swimming. Perhaps the most interesting decision made around sports can be found in Vermont's guidance. Football as it is traditionally played will be replaced with seven-on-seven touch football. No decision has been made about whether to move traditional football to the spring. As of this writing, Maine has yet to decide about fall sports for the 2020–21 school year.

Summary

Overall, there are many similarities across state plans. Almost every state allows for alternative modalities of learning for vulnerable students, even if they attend school in a district that is reopening in-person. Almost all states allow local school districts to make decisions independent of the state bureaucracies, and almost all states either require or strongly recommend mask wearing during the pandemic. Perhaps most important, almost every state has made explicit overtures toward ensuring that instruction is equitable during this time of disruption. How that plays out across state lines might look very different between Florida and Pennsylvania, for example. However, ensuring equitable education is a stated value in almost every reopening plan. States differ the greatest in terms of their recommended modalities of learning and in terms of their decisions around fall sports.

District reopening modalities

Our review of district reopening plans focuses on two points in time – August 5, 2020 and August 21, 2020. A review of the 120 largest school districts in the United States by enrollment found that as of August 5, 71 planned to reopen schools with remote instruction (Lips, 2020). Of the remaining 49 school districts, 12 districts indicated that they planned to reopen schools with five days of in-person instruction each week. Thirty-six districts indicated that they would reopen with a hybrid plan intended to reduce the number of students in the building at any given time. We treated the state of Hawaii as a single school district since there are no districts in the state; all public schools report directly to the Hawaii Department of Education. As of August 5, Greenville County Schools (South Carolina) had not announced their decision regarding modality.

We explored the extent to which enrollment size, race/ethnicity, and economic disadvantage influenced the modality choices of districts. See Appendix B for a list of school districts included in this review and the modalities they selected in their reopening plans. We ran logistic regression analysis, operationalizing the dichotomous outcome variable as (1) offering some form of in-person instruction (including hybrid plans) and (2) only offering remote instruction as of August 5. None of three variables we included in our model were found to be statistically significant predictors. However, trends are seen in the data. Districts with larger nonwhite student populations and the poorest 25% of districts we examined were more likely to start the 2020–21 school year with remote instruction. See Table 1 for a comparison between districts offering in-person instruction and those offering remote instruction.

An examination of the largest school districts' reopening plans as of August 21 finds that several have shifted. Regardless of primary modality, every school district whose plan we examined was offering a remote learning option for families that wished to choose such an option. Eleven districts that initially announced they would reopen with a hybrid plan made the decision to open with remote instruction instead; Shelby County (TN), Dallas ISD (TX), and Boston Public Schools (MA) are examples of such districts. A Florida

Table 1. Comparing school district planned reopening modalities as of August 5, 2020.

	Race (% Nonwhite)		Poverty*		Enrollment**		
Modality	85±%	Less than 85%	High Poverty	Low Poverty	1–40	41–80	81–120
Offering in-person	2(6.5%)	10(11.4%)	1(3.3%)	11(12.2%)	5(12.5%)	4(10.3%)	3(7.5%)
Hybrid	6(19.4%)	31(35.2%)	6(20.0%)	31(34.4%)	11(27.5%)	13(33.3%)	13(32.5%)
All remote	23(74.2%)	55(62.5%)	23(76.7%)	47(52.2%)	24(60.0%)	22(56.4%)	24(60.0%)

Figures represent frequency counts with percentages in parentheses. Greenville Public Schools omitted from these figures. *High poverty operationalized as the poorest 25% of the largest 120 school districts. Low poverty operationalized as a district not being among the poorest 25%. **Districts are compared by enrollment. The largest 40 districts (1–40) are compared with the next largest 40 districts (41–80) and the 40 largest districts after that (81–120).

Department of Education Emergency Order mandates that schools in that state open fully[1] (Florida DOE Order No. 2020-EO-06, 2020). As such, nine Florida districts that initially announced they were opening with a hybrid option committed to opening school in-person by August 21. Miami-Dade, Broward, and Palm Beach counties sought waivers due to the high COVID-19 infection rates in South Florida. Most of the school districts that switched from a hybrid plan to in-person are located in Florida or Tennessee, with Detroit Public Schools (MI) being a notable exception. School districts offering hybrid instruction vary widely. For example, Greenville County Schools (SC) plans to reopen with one day of in-person instruction per week with the other four days of instruction being offered online. By contrast, Jordan School District in Utah will deliver in-person instruction Monday through Thursday; Friday is an optional day set aside for extension, remediation, and small group instruction that is delivered either in-person or online depending on teacher preference. Five districts whose plans were initially listed as hybrid are offering in-person instruction for elementary school five days a week, and are doing something different for middle and high school. Four of these five districts – Washoe County (NV), Cherry Creek (CO), Jefferson Parish (LA), and Capistrano Unified (CA) – are all offering secondary students hybrid instruction. Wichita Public Schools (KS) is opening school for elementary grades and starting the school year with secondary grades going remote.

An August 23, 2020 *Education Week* piece reported that "[a]s of August 21, 21 of the 25 largest school districts are choosing remote learning only as their back-to-school instructional model, affecting over 4.5 million students." Their reporting is indeed accurate if one only examines the largest 25 districts. Our examination of the largest 120 districts indicates that the largest 25 school districts are substantially doing what other large school districts are doing across the United States. Orange County (FL), Duval County (FL), and Cypress-Fairbanks ISD (TX) plan to reopen in-person, and New York City's public schools have announced a hybrid plan. However, some other district plans are more complicated. Hillsborough County Schools (FL) announced it would open remotely for the first week of school and give parents the option to have in-person instruction beginning in week 2. Hawaii is also difficult to categorize. Public schools in Hawaii on most islands are opening with in-person instruction; however, schools on the island of Oahu are reopening remotely. Oahu is where most Hawaiians live, and where the overwhelming majority of the state's COVID-19 cases have been reported (Hawaii Public Schools, 2020b). See Table 2 for a comparison of school districts by modality and by race, poverty, and enrollment for elementary grades as of August 21, 2020.

When we reran the same logistic regression model with an updated outcome variable reflecting district modality decisions made by August 21 for elementary-aged students, we found that race was a significant predictor. See

Table 2. Comparing school district planned reopening modalities for elementary as of August 21, 2020.

	Race (% Nonwhite)		Poverty*		Enrollment**		
Modality	85±%	Less than 85%	High Poverty	Low Poverty	1–40	41–80	81–120
Offering in-person	2(6.7%)	29(32.6%)	3(10.0%)	28(31.5%)	7(17.9%)	13(32.5%)	11(27.5%)
Hybrid	0(0.0%)	5(16.7%)	1(3.3%)	4(4.5%)	1(2.6%)	2(5.0%)	2(5.0%)
All remote	28(93.3%)	55(61.8%)	26(86.7%)	57(64.0%)	31(79.5%)	25(62.5%)	27(67.5%)

Figures represent frequency counts with percentages in parentheses. Hawaii's public schools are omitted from these figures. *High poverty operationalized as the poorest 25% of the largest 120 school districts. Low poverty operationalized as a district not being among the poorest 25%. **Districts are compared by enrollment. The largest 40 districts (1–40) are compared with the next largest 40 districts (41–80) and the 40 largest districts after that (81–120).

Table 3 for odds ratios and standard errors from this analysis. School districts serving student bodies that are 85% or more nonwhite were far more likely to reopen schools with remote learning than were districts with larger White student populations. Of the 30 districts with a student population that was greater than 85% nonwhite, only two are offering in-person instruction to start the 2020–21 school year.

Summary

Overall, more than two-thirds of the United States' largest school districts are reopening remotely for the 2020–21 school year. Enrollment size does not seem to be a factor in these decisions; the New York City Department of Education is the largest school district by far in America, serving almost a million students, and it is reopening with a hybrid plan. School districts that serve larger proportions of students who are nonwhite and living in higher degrees of poverty seem more likely to open remotely, even if these

Table 3. Logistic regression findings for August 21, 2020 school district elementary reopening plans.

Variable	OR(SE)
85%+ Nonwhite District	0.153*
	(0.126)
High Poverty District	0.597
	(0.394)
Large District	0.704
	(0.362)
Constant	0.705
	(0.180)
N	119
McFadden Pseudo R^2	.095

** $p <.01$; * $p <.05$; High poverty districts were operationalized as the 40 highest poverty districts among those included in these analyses. Large districts were operationalized as the 40 largest districts among those included in these analyses. The State of Hawaii was excluded from these analyses.

are not statistically significant in every instance. Unlike the initial plans that school districts release, a handful of districts are moving forward with in-person instruction for elementary students and either hybrid or remote instruction for older learners.

Discussion and limitations

The purpose of this paper was to describe what is happening in the 50 states and largest 120 school districts across the United States. Our examination revealed evidence of just how fluid these decisions are as schools grapple with a deadly pandemic while attempting to keep students' academic and athletic advancement on track. One of the biggest takeaways from this work is that despite the lack of a national blueprint for reopening, states made many similar decisions. For the most part, states offered school districts the latitude to make reopening modality decisions locally; offered similar guidance requiring or strongly recommending masks in schools; and recommend allowing families the ability to make the decision to begin the 2020–21 school year with remote instruction. There are areas in which they differ as well – including the recommendations whether to offer fall 2020 high school sports, as well as for how to approach protecting vulnerable adults working in schools. We begin here with an observation about school districts shifting from hybrid to in-person reopening plans, move to a discussion about younger learners, race and poverty, and sports, and conclude with implications for school choice and address limitations implicit in this work.

Districts changing from hybrid to in-person instruction

Between August 5 and August 21, 2020, several districts changed their stated modality from hybrid to in-person. Districts often explained that they selected hybrid instruction because it limits the number of students that are in school at any given time, making preventative measures like social distancing possible. Most of the districts we reviewed surveyed their parents and asked them about their reopening modality preferences. Although it was not explicitly stated in the plans that we reviewed, it is likely the case that several districts received a large enough response from those preferring remote learning that social distancing measures are possible with the remaining students whose families selected in-person instruction.

Prioritizing elementary students

Several states and school districts are explicit about the need to prioritize in-person instruction for younger learners. As previously mentioned, five school districts that initially opted for a hybrid model have moved toward a reopening that includes in-person instruction for elementary school and either hybrid or remote instruction for secondary grades. Several other districts like Douglas County School District in Colorado are opting to start the year with remote instruction, but have phased in reopening plans that have elementary grades returning to campus first. Several states similarly place a priority on younger students returning to school; Alaska, Maryland, and Minnesota are examples of such. Future research should follow students longitudinally and compare those who learn remotely in the coming year to those who receive in-person instruction.

Race, poverty, and reopening

Our early analyses presented here found that race and poverty seem to map onto district reopening plans. It is worth noting that we believed we would find the opposite when we began this project, particularly in terms of socioeconomic figures. We initially thought we would find that school districts serving larger portions of students living in poverty might be more likely to reopen than their counterparts, in part reflecting child-care and food needs of low income working families. While we fall short of making causal claims in this paper, our prediction was clearly incorrect. Only four of the 30 poorest districts are opening the school year with in-person instruction – Horry (SC), New York City, Detroit Public Schools, and Aldine ISD (TX). The same is true for race. Only two of the 31 districts that serve student bodies that are 85% or more nonwhite are opening their campuses this fall – Aldine ISD and Detroit.

There could be several explanations for this. Early evidence suggests that COVID-19 disproportionately impacts people of color (Hooper, Napoles, & Perez-Stable, 2020; Tai, Doubeni, Sia, & Wieland, 2020; Wright & Merritt, 2020). Compared to their White counterparts, people of color are more likely to die from the virus, are more likely to have underlying medical conditions that exacerbate the effects of COVID-19, are more likely to be frontline workers, and often have reduced access to health care services. Members of racial and ethnic minority groups place less trust in the government's response to the pandemic (Jaiswal, LoSchiavo, & Perlman, 2020), which might explain the decision to not have in-person instruction in districts that largely educate nonwhite students. It is also true that large cities tend to educate larger proportions of nonwhite students and students living in poverty, and be more densely populated, making the spread of a virus like COVID-19 easier. Large urban school districts are also more likely to have teachers organized in strong unions (Moe, 2011), and early analyses have found that school districts in areas with stronger unions are less likely to reopen with in-person instruction (DeAngeles & Makridis, 2020). In late July 2020, the American Federation of Teachers threatened to strike if their members were forced to return to schools they believed were unsafe (Will, 2020). Additional research should be conducted to better understand these trends.

Reopening and sports

The policy area where states varied the greatest in their reopening guidance is how fall 2020 sports are handled. Athletics, particularly high school football, play key roles in many U.S public schools. Sports teams unite school communities and facilitate information sharing, spreading social capital in part by helping connect students, parents, and taxpayers to local schools (Greene, 2013). On the other hand, athletics can detract from academics. Most male administrators are former athletic coaches, and may prioritize athletics over academics (Maranto, Carroll, Cheng, & Teodoro, 2018). In one of our states, it is widely believed that a key reason for reopening schools was the desire to have a fall football season, even though contact sports place students in closer proximity to one another than most classroom activities. Several states, including Texas and Iowa, are allowing students who are selecting remote instruction (presumably because they are at greater risk from the virus) to be eligible to play sports. Some entire districts, like Anchorage, AK, are fielding sports teams while their academic campuses are closed for in-person instruction. In some states, a tension exists between state guidance and local decisions. In states like Pennsylvania and Tennessee, fall sports are restarting on schedule with their largest school districts opting out of competition.

Our initial observations about which states were and were not moving forward with fall sports led us to wonder if politics played a role in these decisions. Accordingly, we collected data regarding whether states were having football season as usual, delaying it, or canceling it entirely (Stephens, 2020). The 19 states which are having high school football seasons proceed as usual in 2016 gave Donald Trump a mean of 54.73% of the vote, compared to 51.43% in the 14 states that are delaying football season for COVID-19, and just 40.93% for those that canceled fall football. States that are not playing football voted for Trump in fewer numbers than those that have announced plans to play high school football in 2020. Although this initial analysis yielded statistically significant results, it does not fully explain what is happening here. Indeed, Massachusetts – a state where less than one-third of the 2016 presidential vote went for President Trump – is moving forward with fall sports on schedule. Viral spread also does not seem to explain decisions about fall sports. According to the CDC (2020c), Vermont has a lower case rate (0.64 per 100,000 as of August 21, 2020) than all of the other 49 states, the District of Columbia, Puerto Rico, the Virgin Islands, and Guam. Yet, Vermont has canceled the fall 2020 football season, replacing tackle football with seven-on-seven touch football. Of the 18 states with case rates under 10 per 100,000, almost half (*n*= 8) have decided to forgo fall sports. Additional research should examine school reopening, sports, and factors that may explain the decisions that were made. It will be perhaps more important for medical researchers to help us understand the extent to which the virus spreads through contact sports and the impact that it has on high school athletes.

Implications for school choice

In many jurisdictions throughout the United States, few if any public school choice options exist for families. Their children attend schools based on their home address. Parents who are unsatisfied with their zoned school option and who have the means to do so can relocate to an address with more satisfactory schools or pay private school tuition (Marshall, 2017; Ryan, 2010; Sowell, 2020; Wells et al., 2009). Although some districts have magnet schools that parents can apply to (Wang & Herman, 2017), most traditional school systems offer parents few public choice options. The COVID-19 crisis has changed this. For school districts that are offering in-person instruction in some form, parents will have the choice to either enroll their child for in-person, or in some cases hybrid, instruction or to enroll their child in a remote learning option. Many of the plans we reviewed were explicit about families having the final decision regarding their child's education. We posit that the disruption caused by the pandemic represents a crossroads for public education in the United States. Will this be a watershed moment for school choice where parents seek increasingly diverse learning options for their children, including new options offered within traditional public school systems, a new wave of charter schools, or new approaches like micro schooling? Or, will this be a momentary disruption that finds most families returning to their traditional neighborhood schools and the status quo? Parents may emerge from this moment more empowered than ever before and ready to take greater responsibility over their children's education – or they may find themselves weary of the stress caused by the pandemic and ready for a return to what they were accustomed to prior to this disruption. It will be important to understand the decisions parents make in the wake of this moment in time and what the existence of new educational options (or lack thereof) means for student outcomes.

Limitations

This descriptive paper has several limitations. The reopening of America's schools in the fall of 2020 is a very fluid event. It is highly possible that districts that made one decision as of August 21, 2020 will choose differently before the school year begins, or that individual states' plans will have shifted since our review. Another limitation is that we only have policy decisions made at the state and school district level. Our analyses locate broad trends at the district level. It is also worth noting the nature of the 120 largest school districts. Fifty-seven of these districts, almost half, are located in either Florida, Texas, or California. Some states with large populations like New Jersey are not represented in our analysis of the school districts because their districts are small and have low enrollments relative to other states.

Every school district we reviewed is offering an online learning option this fall. This creates the possibility for one to compare the outcomes of students who engage in in-person instruction, those who receive remote instruction, and those who return to school with or opt for a hybrid modality. It will be interesting to make note of the types of students who select each modality where a choice is offered, and how they fare – not just academically, but in terms of social development as well. Finally, it is obvious that our analysis raises more questions than answers. We call for additional research in several areas, including how students fare academically under the various modalities employed, and whether these academic outcomes – or mental, physical, and social health outcomes – vary according to racial and demographic characteristics.

Note

1. As of this writing, this executive action is being challenged in court.

Disclosure statement

No potential conflict of interest was reported by the authors.

ORCID

David T. Marshall (iD) http://orcid.org/0000-0003-1467-7656
Martha Bradley-Dorsey (iD) http://orcid.org/0000-0002-9139-9402

References

Alabama State Department of Education. (2020a). *Roadmap to reopening schools.* Retrieved from https://www.alsde.edu/Documents/Roadmap%20for%20Reopening%20Schools%20June%2026%202020.pdf
Alabama State Department of Education. (2020b). *Dr. Mackey's update (July 29, 2020).* Retrieved from https://www.alsde.edu/COVID19%20Updates/Dr.%20Mackey%27s%20Update%20(July%2029,%202020).pdf
Alaska Department of Education & Early Development. (2020). *Alaska smart start 2020: Restart & reentry framework guidance for K-12 schools, 2020-2021 school year.* Retrieved from https://education.alaska.gov/news/COVID-19/Alaska%20Smart%20Start%202020%20Framework%20Guidance.pdf

Alaska School Activities Association. (2020). *COVID-19 updates*. Retrieved from https://asaa.org

Anastasia, P. (2020, August 21). PIAA gives the green light to fall high school sports in Pennsylvania. *Philadelphia Inquirer*. Retrieved from https://www.inquirer.com/high-school-sports/pennsylvania/piaa-fall-sports-high-school-football-coronavirus-20200821.htmlndemic.htm

Arizona Department of Education Office of Communications. (2020, July 21). *Superintendent Hoffman calls for reopening metrics, full funding for distance learning*. Retrieved from https://www.azed.gov/communications/2020/07/21/superintendent-hoffman-calls-for-reopening-metrics-full-funding-for-distance-learning/

Arkansas Division of Elementary & Secondary Education. (2020). *Arkansas ready to learn: Healthy school guide*. Retrieved from http://dese.ade.arkansas.gov/public/userfiles/Communications/Ready/Return_to_School_Guide_81220.pdf

Associated Press. (2020, August 13). *Wyoming announces COVID-19 testing program for teachers*. Retrieved from https://www.usnews.com/news/best-states/wyoming/articles/2020-08-13/wyoming-announces-covid-19-testing-program-for-teachers

Ballotpedia. (2020). *School closures in response to the coronavirus (COVID-19) pandemic, 2020*. Retrieved from https://ballotpedia.org/Debate_over_school_closures_during_the_coronavirus_(COVID-19)_pandemic,_2020#Background

Beckman, M., Executive Director, Montana High School Association. (2020, July 27). *Memorandum to MHSA school administrators re: Return to MHSA fall activities*. Retrieved from https://cdn3.sportngin.com/attachments/document/8b09-2216849/Tiers_-_Return_to_Fall_Activities_2020_Final_with_Ltr.pdf#_ga=2.99533270.91000749.1597257343-1775193290.1597257343

Bezjak, L. (2020, July 22). Decision affecting fate of SC high school sports season delayed. Here's what's next. *The State*, 4:50 p.m. Retrieved from https://www.thestate.com/sports/high-school/article244400927.html

Burgess, S., & Sievertsen, H. H. (2020). Schools, skills, and learning: The impact of COVID-19 on education. *VoxEu*. Retrieved from https://voxeu.org/article/impact-covid-19-education

California Department of Education. (2020, June). *Stronger together: A guidebook for the safe reopening of California's public schools*. Retrieved from https://www.cde.ca.gov/ls/he/hn/documents/strongertogether.pdf

Centers for Disease Control and Prevention. (2020a). *Schools and child care programs: Plan, prepare, and respond*. Retrieved from https://www.cdc.gov/coronavirus/2019-ncov/community/schools-childcare/index.html

Centers for Disease Control and Prevention. (2020b, updated August 11). *Guidance for K-12 school administrators on the use of cloth face coverings in schools*. Retrieved from https://www.cdc.gov/coronavirus/2019-ncov/community/schools-childcare/cloth-face-cover.html

Centers for Disease Control and Prevention. (2020c, updated August 23). *United States COVID-19 cases and deaths by state*. Retrieved from https://www.cdc.gov/covid-data-tracker/#cases

Colorado Department of Education. (2020, August 10). *Cases and outbreaks in schools - Template letters*. Retrieved from https://www.cde.state.co.us/communications/fall2020-cases-outbreaks

Colorado Department of Public Health & Environment. (2020). *Guidance for wearing masks*. Retrieved from https://covid19.colorado.gov/mask-guidance

Colorado Department of Public Health & Environment, Department of Education. (2020, July). *Reopening schools: Health guidance by COVID-19 phase*. Retrieved from https://www.cde.state.co.us/communications/20200720reopeningguidance

Connecticut State Department of Education. (2020a, August 3). *Adapt, advance, achieve: Connecticut's plan to learn and grow together.* Retrieved from https://portal.ct.gov/-/media/SDE/COVID-19/CTReopeningSchools.pdf

Connecticut State Department of Education. (2020b, June 25). *Plan for reimagining CT classrooms for continuous learning.* Retrieved from https://portal.ct.gov/-/media/SDE/COVID-19/ReimaginingCTClassrooms.pdf

DeAngeles, C. A., & Makridis, C. (2020, September 1). *Are school reopening decisions related to union influence?* SSRN. doi:10.2139/ssrn.3684867

Delaware Department of Education (2020). *Returning to school: Planning a safe, efficient, and equitable return to school for students and staff.* Retrieved from https://www.doe.k12.de.us/cms/lib/DE01922744/Centricity/Domain/599/ddoe_returningtoschool_guidance_final.pdf

Education Week. (2020, August 23). School districts' reopening plans: A snapshot. *Education Week.* Retrieved from https://www.edweek.org/ew/section/multimedia/school-districts-reopening-plans-a-snapshot.html.

Florida Department of Education. (2020). *Reopening Florida's schools and the CARES act.* Retrieved from http://www.fldoe.org/core/fileparse.php/19861/urlt/FLDOEReopeningCARESAct.pdf

Florida DOE Emergency Order No. 2020-EO-06. (2020). Retrieved from http://www.fldoe.org/core/fileparse.php/19861/urlt/DOE-2020-EO-06.pdf

Georgia Department of Education. (2020, July 30). *Georgia's path to recovery for K-12 schools.* Retrieved from https://www.georgiainsights.com/uploads/1/2/2/2/122221993/georgias_path_to_recovery_for_k-12_schools_-_v7-30-2020.pdf

Governor Gretchen Whitmer, COVID-19 Task Force on Education, Return to School Advisory Council. (2020, June 30). *MI safe schools: Michigan's 2020-21 return to school roadmap.* Retrieved from https://www.michigan.gov/documents/whitmer/MI_Safe_Schools_Roadmap_FINAL_695392_7.pdf

Governor Tim Walz, with Minnesota Departments of Education and Health. (2020, updated August 18). *Guidance for Minnesota public schools: Safe learning plan for 2020-21 - A localized, data-driven approach.* Retrieved from https://education.mn.gov/mdeprod/idcplg?IdcService=GET_FILE&dDocName=MDE033418&RevisionSelectionMethod=latestReleased&Rendition=primary

Governor's Economic Reopening Task Force. (2020, August 8). *Safer at home: Amateur & youth sports.* Retrieved from https://www.covidguidance.nh.gov/sites/g/files/ehbemt381/files/inline-documents/2020-05/guidance-amateur-youth-sports.pdf

Greene, J. P. (2013, February 6). Does athletic success come at the expense of academic success? *Education Next Blog.* Retrieved from https://www.educationnext.org/does-athletic-success-come-at-the-expense-of-academic-success/.

Groves, J. (2020, July 15). NMAA announces revised 2020-21 sports calendar. *Las Cruces Sun News.* Retrieved from https://www.lcsun-news.com/story/sports/high-school/football/2020/07/15/nmaa-announces-revised-2020-21-new-mexico-high-school-sports-calendar/5443107002/

Hawaii Department of Education. (2020a). *Return to learn: School reopening plan.* Retrieved from http://www.hawaiipublicschools.org/ConnectWithUs/MediaRoom/PressReleases/Pages/School-Reopening-Framework—Health-and-Safety.aspx

Hawaii Department of Education. (2020b). *HIDOE COVID-19 information and updates.* Retrieved from http://www.hawaiipublicschools.org/ConnectWithUs/MediaRoom/PressReleases/Pages/COVID-19-Information-Updates.aspx

Hooper, M. W., Napoles, A. M., & Perez-Stable, E. J. (2020). COVID-19 and racial/ethnic disparities. *Jama.* doi:10.1001/jama.2020.8598

Idaho Governor Brad Little, with Idaho State Board of Education, Idaho Department of Education, and Idaho Department of Health & Welfare. (2020, July 9). *Idaho back to school framework 2020*. Retrieved from https://www.sde.idaho.gov/re-opening/files/Idaho-Back-to-School-Framework-2020.pdf

Illinois State Board of Education. (2020a, updated regularly). *Coronavirus (COVID-19) updates and resources*. Retrieved from https://www.isbe.net/Pages/covid19.aspx

Illinois State Board of Education. (2020b, July 23). *Fall 2020 learning recommendations*. Retrieved from https://www.isbe.net/Documents/Fall-2020-Learning-Rec.pdf

Illinois State Board of Education, Illinois Department of Public Health. (2020, June 23). *Starting the 2020-21 school year: Part 3 - transition joint guidance*. Retrieved from https://www.isbe.net/Documents/Part-3-Transition-Planning-Phase-4.pdf

Indiana Department of Education. (2020a, March). *Indiana continuous learning guidance*. Retrieved from https://www.doe.in.gov/sites/default/files/news/indiana-continuous-learning-guidance-final.PDF

Indiana Department of Education. (2020b, updated and archived July 31). *Indiana's Considerations for Learning and Safe Schools (INCLASS)*. Retrieved from https://docs.google.com/document/d/1T1nQj3BrQRtT5QXVcVLGel14bOd5dSClWRggPuPE5dg/edit

Indiana Department of Education. (2020c, updated August 12). *COVID-19 resources for Indiana schools*. Retrieved from https://www.doe.in.gov/covid-19?utm_content=&utm_medium=email&utm_name=&utm_source=govdelivery&utm_term=

Institute for Health, Measurement, and Evaluation. (2020, updated September 3). *COVID-19 projections*. Retrieved from https://covid19.healthdata.org/united-states-of-america/arkansas?view=total-deaths&tab=trend

Iowa Department of Education. (2020). *Iowa return-to-learn support*. Retrieved from https://sites.google.com/iowa.gov/returntolearn

Iowa Department of Education, Iowa Department of Public Health. (2020, July 30). *Return to learn: Reopening Iowa's schools safely and responsibly*. Retrieved from https://educateiowa.gov/sites/files/ed/documents/2020-07-20ReopeningandPublicHealth.pdf

Jaiswal, J., LoSchiavo, C., & Perlman, D. C. (2020). Disinformation, misinformation and inequality-driven mistrust in the time of COVID-19: Lessons unlearned from AIDS denialism. *AIDS and Behavior, 24*(10), 2776–2780. doi:10.1007/s10461-020-02925-y

Kansas State Department of Education. (2020). *Navigating change: Kansas' guide to learning and school safety operations*. Retrieved from https://www.ksde.org/Teaching-Learning/Resources/Navigating-Change-Kansas-Guide-to-Learning-and-School-Safety-Operations.

Kentucky Department of Education. (2020a, May 15). *COVID-19 considerations for reopening schools: Initial guidance for schools and districts*. Retrieved from https://education.ky.gov/comm/Documents/Reopening%20Guidance%20%20051520kf_tkt%20421pm%20TM.pdf

Kentucky Department of Education. (2020b, August 18). *COVID-19 reopening resources*. Retrieved from https://education.ky.gov/comm/Pages/COVID-19-Reopening-Resources.aspx

Kolenich, J. (2020, July 27). VHSL votes 34-1 to postpone fall high school sports, pushing football to March. *Richmond Times-Dispatch*. Retrieved from https://richmond.com/sports/high-school/vhsl-votes-34-1-to-postpone-fall-high-school-sports-pushing-football-to-march/article_adc1e02e-b2a7-5c86-a314-9bde39c3c9bc.html

Lee, P., Hu, Y., Chen, P., Huang, Y., & Hsueh, P. (2020). Are children less susceptible to COVID-19? *Journal of Microbiology, Immunology, and Infection, 53*(3), 371–372. doi:10.1016/j.jmii.2020.02.011

Lips, D. (2020, August 5). A list of the 71 largest COVID-19 school closures. *Foundation for Research on Equal Opportunity*. Retrieved from https://freopp.org/70-of-the-nations-120-largest-school-districts-will-start-the-year-with-remote-instruction-and-no-b7c6b2d7a985

Liu, J. J., Bao, Y., Huang, X., Shi, J., & Lu, L. (2020). Mental health considerations for children quarantined because of COVID-19. *The Lancet Child & Adolescent Health, 4*(5), 347–349. doi:10.1016/S2352-4642.(20)30096-1

Louisiana Department of Education (2020a). *Coronavirus (COVID-19) (resource page).* Retrieved from https://www.louisianabelieves.com/resources/covid-19

Louisiana Department of Education. (2020b, updated July 28). *Strong start 2020: School reopening guidelines & resources.* Retrieved from https://www.louisianabelieves.com/docs/default-source/strong-start-2020/school-reopening-guidelines-and-resources.pdf?sfvrsn=c10e981f_28

Mackey, E. G.; Alabama State Superintendent of Education (2020, July 29). *Letter to district superintendents.* Retrieved from https://www.alsde.edu/COVID19%20Updates/Dr.%20Mackey%27s%20Update%20(July%2029,%202020).pdf

Maine Department of Education. (2020a). *Coronavirus update: Coronavirus (COVID-19) resources for schools.* Retrieved from https://www.maine.gov/doe/covid-19/

Maine Department of Education. (2020b, updated August 14). *Coronavirus update: Framework for reopening schools and returning to in-person instruction.* Retrieved from https://www.maine.gov/doe/framework

mainedoenews.net. (2020). *PK-12 and adult education public health guidance.* Retrieved from https://mainedoenews.net/wp-content/uploads/2020/08/School-Guidance-8-12-20-Final-8-am.pdf

Maranto, R., Carroll, K., Cheng, A., & Teodoro, M. P. (2018). Boys will be superintendents: School leadership as a gendered profession. *Phi Delta Kappan, 100*(2), 12–15. doi:10.1177/0031721718803563

Marshall, D. T. (2017). Equity and access in charter schools: Identifying issues and solutions. *Education Policy Analysis Archives, 25*(83), 1–18. doi:10.14507/epaa.25.2745

Marshall, D. T., Shannon, D. M., & Love, S. M. (2020). How teachers experienced the COVID-19 transition to remote instruction. *Kappan.* Retrieved from https://kappanonline.org/how-teachers-experienced-covid-19-transition-remote-instruction-marshall-shannon-love/

Maryland State Department of Education. (2020, June). *Maryland together: Maryland's recovery plan for education.* Retrieved from http://marylandpublicschools.org/newsroom/Documents/MSDERecoveryPlan.pdf

Masonbrink, A. R., & Hurley, E. (2020). Advocating for children during the COVID-19 school closures. *Pediatrics, 146*(3), e20201440. doi:10.1542/peds.2020-1440

Massachusetts Department of Elementary and Secondary Education. (2020, June 25). *Initial fall school reopening guidance.* Retrieved from http://www.doe.mass.edu/covid19/return-to-school/guidance.pdf

Minnesota Department of Health. (2020, August 12). *2020-2021 Planning guide for schools: Health considerations for navigating COVID-19.* Retrieved from https://www.health.state.mn.us/diseases/coronavirus/schools/k12planguide.pdf

Mississippi Department of Education. (2020). *Mississippi schools: Guidance for the 2020-21 school year.* Retrieved from https://www.mdek12.org/guidance2020-21

Missouri Department of Elementary and Secondary Education. (2020a). *Coronavirus (COVID-19) Information.* Retrieved from https://dese.mo.gov/communications/coronavirus-covid-19-information

Missouri Department of Elementary and Secondary Education. (2020b). *Show me strong recovery plan.* Retrieved from https://showmestrong.mo.gov/

Missouri School Boards Association's Center for Education Safety. (2020, August 4). *Pandemic recovery considerations: Re-entry and reopening of schools.* Retrieved from https://ams.embr.mobi/Documents/DocumentAttachment.aspx?C=ZfON&DID=GJGDM

Moe, T. M. (2011). Special interest: Teachers unions and America's public schools. Washington, DC: Brookings Institution Press

Montana Office of Public Instruction. (2020, updated July 27). *Reopening Montana schools guidance: Putting Montana students first.* Retrieved from http://opi.mt.gov/Portals/182/COVID-19/Reopening%20MT%20Schools%20Guidance-Final.pdf?ver=2020-07-02-114033-897

National Center for Education Statistics. (n.d.) *Enrollment, poverty, and federal funds for the 120 largest school districts, by enrollment size in 2016: 2015-16 adn fiscal year 2018.* Retrieved from https://nces.ed.gov/programs/digest/d18/tables/dt18_215.30.asp?current=yes

Nebraska Department of Education. (2020). *Launch Nebraska: Tools, actions, opportunities, and resources to support the complex planning and preparation needed by Nebraska school systems as they work to restart schools and support students as they transition back to school buildings.* Retrieved from https://www.launchne.com

New Hampshire Department of Education. (2020, July). *New hampshire grades K-12 back-to-school guidance.* Retrieved from https://www.covidguidance.nh.gov/sites/g/files/ehbemt381/files/inline-documents/sonh/k-12-back-to-school.pdf

New Jersey Department of Education. (2020a, updated periodically). *Restart & recovery plan: The road back.* Retrieved from https://nj.gov/education/reopening/

New Jersey Department of Education. (2020b, July 24). *Clarifying expectations regarding full-time remote learning options for families in 2020-2021 (Supplemental to restart & recovery plan: The road back).* Retrieved from https://nj.gov/education/reopening/updates/docs/7.24.20%20RtR%20Fulltime%20Remote%20Update.pdf

New Jersey State Interscholastic Athletic Association. (2020, May 26). *NJSIAA COVID-19 updates.* Retrieved from https://www.njsiaa.org/njsiaa-covid-19-updates

New Mexico Public Education Department. (2020, updated July 15). *New Mexico public education department reentry guidance.* Retrieved from https://webnew.ped.state.nm.us/wp-content/uploads/2020/07/20NMPED_ReentryGuide.pdf

New York State Department of Health. (2020, August 15). *Interim guidance for sports and recreation during the COVID-19 public health emergency.* Retrieved from https://www.governor.ny.gov/sites/governor.ny.gov/files/atoms/files/SportsAndRecreationMasterGuidance.pdf

New York State Education Department. (2020). *Recovering, rebuilding, and renewing: The spirit of New York's schools - Reopening guidance.* Retrieved from http://www.nysed.gov/common/nysed/files/programs/reopening-schools/nys-p12-school-reopening-guidance.pdf

North Dakota Department of Public Instruction. (2020). *ND K12 smart restart guidance 2020-2021.* Retrieved from https://www.nd.gov/dpi/familiescommunity/nddpi-updates-and-guidance-covid-19/nd-k12-smart-restart-guidance

Ohio Department of Education. (2020). *Reset and restart: Education planning for Ohio schools and districts.* Retrieved from http://education.ohio.gov/Topics/Reset-and-Restart

Ohio High School Athletic Association (2020, August 7). *OHSAA adjusts season if football is approved by governor.* Retrieved from https://ohsaa.org/news-media/articles/ohsaa-adjusts-season-if-football-is-approved-by-governor160

Oklahoma State Department of Education. (2020, updated August 5). *Return to learn Oklahoma: A framework for reopening schools.* Retrieved from https://sde.ok.gov/sites/default/files/Return%20to%20Learn%20Oklahoma.pdf

Oregon Department of Education. (2020, August 11). *Ready schools, safe learners: Guidance for school year 2020-21.* Retrieved from https://www.oregon.gov/ode/students-and-family/healthsafety/Pages/Planning-for-the-2020-21-School-Year.aspx

Pennsylvania Department of Education. (2020). *Guidance and resources for Pre-K to 12 schools during COVID-19.* Retrieved from https://www.education.pa.gov/Schools/safeschools/emer

gencyplanning/COVID-19/SchoolReopeningGuidance/ReopeningPreKto12/Pages/default.aspx

Public Schools of North Carolina (State Board of Education; Department of Public Instruction). (2020). *Lighting our way forward: North Carolina's guidebook for reopening public schools*. Retrieved from https://docs.google.com/document/d/1z5Mp2XzOOPkBYN4YvROz4YOyNIF2UoWq9EZfrjvN4x8/edit

Rhode Island Department of Education. (2020, updated 8/14). *Back to school RI: Reopening frequently asked questions, SY20-21*. Retrieved from https://www.ride.ri.gov/Portals/0/Uploads/Documents/COVID19/ReopeningFAQs.pdf?ver=2020-07-31-095926-290

Ryan, J. E. (2010). *Five miles away, a world apart: One city, two schools, and the story of educational opportunity in modern America*. Oxford: Oxford University Press.

Sidpra, J., Abomeli, D., Hameed, B., Baker, J., & Mankad, K. (2020). Rise in the incidence of abusive head trauma during the COVID-19 pandemic. *Archives of Disease in Childhood*, archdischild-2020-319872. doi:10.1136/archdischild-2020-319872

South Carolina Department of Education. (2020). *COVID-19 (Coronavirus) and South Carolina schools*. Retrieved from https://ed.sc.gov/newsroom/covid-19-coronavirus-and-south-carolina-schools/

South Dakota Department of Education. (2020). *Starting well 2020*. Retrieved from https://doe.sd.gov/coronavirus/startingwell.aspx

Sowell, T. (2020). *Charter schools and their enemies*. New York: Basic Books.

State of Nevada Executive Department, Governor Steve Sisolak. (2020, July 28). *Declaration of emergency: Directive 028*. Retrieved from http://www.doe.nv.gov/uploadedFiles/ndedoenvgov/content/News__Media/Press_Releases/2020_Documents/2020-07-28DeclarationofEmergencyDirective028.pdf

Stephens, M. (2020, August 18). Where the start of high school sports stands in all 50 states amid pandemic. *MaxPreps*. Retrieved from https://www.maxpreps.com/news/qiL5GOXkFkyfJ9jwZ8wb-g/where-the-start-of-high-school-sports-stands-in-all-50-states-amid-pandemic.htm

Tai, D. B. G., Doubeni, C. A., Sia, I. G., & Wieland, M. L. (2020). The disproportionate impact of COVID-19 on racial and ethnic minorities in the United States. *Clinical Infectious Diseases*. doi:10.1093/cid/ciaa815

Tennessee Department of Education. (2020). *Best for all central*. Retrieved from https://bestforall.tnedu.gov

Tennessee Department of Health (2020, updated August 7). *COVID-19 case response rubric*. Retrieved from https://www.tn.gov/content/dam/tn/education/health-&-safety/TDH%20COVID%20Case%20Response%20and%20School%20District%20Decision%20Making%20Protocol.pdf

Texas Education Agency. (2020). *Coronavirus (COVID-19) support and guidance*. Retrieved from https://tea.texas.gov/texas-schools/health-safety-discipline/covid/coronavirus-covid-19-support-and-guidance

Towne, S. (2020, August 5). Fall sports season delayed until mid-September for RI schools. *WPRI 12*. Retrieved from https://www.wpri.com/sports/high school/ri-interscholastic-league-fall-sports-update/

Utah State Board of Education. (2020). *Coronavirus information and resources*. Retrieved from https://www.schools.utah.gov/coronavirus

Van Lancker, W., & Parolin, Z. (2020). COVID-19, school closures, and child poverty: A social crisis in the making. *The Lancet Public Health*, 5(5), 243–244. doi:10.1016/S2468-2667(20)30084-0

Vermont Agency of Education. (2020a, revised August 11). *A strong and healthy start: Safety and health guidance for reopening schools, Fall 2020*. Retrieved from https://education.

vermont.gov/sites/aoe/files/documents/edu-vdh-guidance-strong-healthy-start-school-health-updated-8-11.pdf

Vermont Agency of Education. (2020b, August 19). *COVID-19 guidance for vermont schools*. Retrieved from https://education.vermont.gov/covid19#shs

Virginia Department of Education. (2020, updated July 6). *Recover, redesign, restart 2020*. Retrieved from http://www.doe.virginia.gov/support/health_medical/covid-19/recover-redesign-restart.shtml#

Wang, J., & Herman, J. (2017). Magnet schools: History, description, and effects. In R. A. Fox & N. K. Buchanan (Eds.), *The Wiley handbook of school choice* (pp. 180–193). West Sussex, UK: Wiley Blackwell.

Washington State Department of Health. (2020, updated August 5). *Decision tree for provision of in person learning among K-12 students at public and private schools during the COVID-19 pandemic*. Retrieved from https://www.doh.wa.gov/Portals/1/Documents/1600/corona virus/DecisionTree-K12schools.pdf

Wells, A. S., Baldridge, B., Duran, J., Lofton, R., Roda, A., Warner, M., & Grzesikowski, C. (2009). *Why boundaries matter: A study of five separate and unequal Long Island school districts*. New York: Teachers College Press.

West Virginia Department of Education (2020, updates provided). *School re-entry metrics & protocols*. Retrieved from https://wvde.us/school-reentry-metrics-protocols/

West Virginia Department of Education & West Virginia Department of Health & Human Resources. (2020, July 28). *West Virginia schools re-entry toolkit: COVID-19 guidance*. Retrieved from https://wvde.us/wp-content/uploads/2020/08/WV-School-Re-entry-Toolkit-072820-FORWEB-v5.pdf

Will, M. (2020, July 28). Strikes are an option to force schools to reopen safely, AFT president says. *Education Week*. Retrieved from https://blogs.edweek.org/teachers/teaching_now/2020/07/strikes_are_option_force_schools_to_reopen_safely_aft_president.html

Wisconsin Department of Public Instruction. (2020a). *Information on COVID-19*. Retrieved from https://dpi.wi.gov/sspw/2019-novel-coronavirus

Wisconsin Department of Public Instruction. (2020b). *Instructional models for flexibility*. Retrieved from https://dpi.wi.gov/education-forward/learning-landscape/instructional-models-for-flexibility

Wood, C. (2020, August 5). [Mississippi] Gov. Reeves issues new executive orders ahead of school reopenings. *WDAM7*, 10:08 AM. Retrieved from https://www.wdam.com/2020/08/05/gov-reeves-issues-new-executive-orders-ahead-school-reopenings/

Wright, J. E., & Merritt, C. C. (2020). Social equity and COVID-19: The case of African Americans. *Public Administration Review*. doi:10.1111/puar.13251

Wyoming Department of Education. (2020, July 1). *Smart start guidance*. Retrieved from https://1ddlxtt2jowkvs672myo6z14-wpengine.netdna-ssl.com/wp-content/uploads/2020/07/Smart-Start-Guidance.pdf

Appendix A

State reopening plans – recommended modalities, masks, vulnerable populations, and sports.

STATE	CASES/ 100 k	RECOMMENDED MODALITY	MASK POLICY	VULNERABLE POPULATIONS	FALL SPORTS	SOURCES
AL	23.77	Up to local districts	Required	Alt. work assignments for staff; remove learning options for students	On schedule	Alabama State Department of Education (2020a, 2020b); Mackey (2020)
AK	8.63	In-person for elementary; Remote for secondary	Recommended	Staff should support students through remote learning. Parents can opt for remote learning	Some districts delayed with abridged schedules	Alaska Department of Education (2020); Alaska School Activities (2020)
AZ	8.54	Up to local districts	Recommended	Telework and alt. work assignments for staff. Remote learning options for students	Delayed with abridged schedules	Arizona Department of Education (2020)
AR	29.01	In-person; based on health considerations	Recommended	Telework and alt. work assignments for staff	On schedule	Arkansas Department of Education (2020)
CA	16.64	In-person subject to local health clearance; Lists four examples of hybrid models	Required	Telework and flexible leave plans for staff that do not deplete earned leave. Remote learning options for students	No fall sports	California Department of Education (2020)
CO	6.09*	Up to local districts	Required for adults and students 11 and up; Recommended for students up to age 10	Provide alt. work duties that support working from home for staff; Remote learning options for students	No fall sports	Colorado Department of Public Health & Environment (2020); Colorado Department of Education (2020); Colorado Department of Public Health & Environment/ Department of Education (2020)
CT	2.36	In-person	Required	Allow at risk teachers to teach virtually & develop PD; Remote learning options for students	No fall sports	Connecticut State Department of Education (2020a, 2020b)

(Continued)

(Continued).

STATE	CASES/ 100 k	RECOMMENDED MODALITY	MASK POLICY	VULNERABLE POPULATIONS	FALL SPORTS	SOURCES
DE	5.33	Hybrid	Required for staff and students 4th grade and up; Recommended for students age 2–3rd grade	Allow at risk adults to maintain distance from others; allow for telework; Remote learning options for students	No fall sports	Delaware Department of Education (2020)
FL	22.12	In-person	Recommended	For at risk adults, take steps to reduce the no. of people they interact with; allow flexible leave options; Case-by-case accommodations for students	Delayed start	Florida Department of Education (2020)
GA	27.08	Up to local districts	Recommended	Offer special accommodations for staff including alt. teaching assignments; Remote learning options for students	All fall sports start on time except football. Delayed start for football with full season schedule	Georgia Department of Education (2020)
HI	15.33	In-person or hybrid, except for Oahu which starts with remote for four weeks, then hybrid	Required	Follow modified labor agreement; Students may opt for remote learning	On schedule	Hawaii Department of Education (2020a, 2020b)
ID	14.64	In-person or hybrid	Recommended	Normal operations if there is no community transmission; If there is minimal to moderate transmission, telework for adults and remote learning for students	On schedule	Idaho Department of Education (2020)
IL	16.93	In-person	Required for everyone over age 2	Recommends at-risk students consult with doctor	Golf, girls tennis, cross country, girls swimming and diving on schedule; Football moved to 2021	Illinois State Board of Education (2020a, 2020b); Illinois State Board of Education & Illinois Department of Public Health (2020)

(Continued)

(Continued).

STATE	CASES/ 100 k	RECOMMENDED MODALITY	MASK POLICY	VULNERABLE POPULATIONS	FALL SPORTS	SOURCES
IN	15.49	Hybrid with students attending either half days or alternate days	Recommended	Staff at risk encouraged to telework; Allow flexible sick leave policies; Remote learning options for students	On schedule	ndiana Department of Education (2020a, 2020b, 2020c)
IA	25.49	Guidance based on positive rate over 2 wk. period: 0–14% = In-person, hybrid as necessary; 15–20% = Hybrid, remote as necessary 21+% = Remote learning	Not recommended; Up to local districts	Remote learning options for students	On schedule with shortened seasons; Students attending via remote learning are eligible.	Iowa Department of Education (2020); Iowa Department of Health, Iowa Department of Education (2020)
KS	33.27	Up to local districts	Language suggests "should be recommended" but later in same section suggest "should be required" anytime social distancing or cohorting cannot be maintained	Put policies in place to protect privacy of individuals at higher risk for serious illness	All sports suspended	Kansas State Department of Education (2020)
KY	14.18	Suggests one of 4 models: scheduled rotations, synchronous opt-in, hybrid, fully online	Recommended for adults and students grades 1 and up.	Suggests districts should create policy regarding vulnerable staff and students	Delayed fall seasons	Kentucky Department of Education (2020a; 2020b)
LA	19.59	Guidance based on phase. As of this writing, state is in phase 2 so most systems will open remotely	Required for adults and students in grades 3 and up	Remote learning options for students	Delayed fall seasons	Louisiana Department of Education (2020a, 2020b)
ME	2.44	Guidance based on countywide viral spread with three categories: -Red (High risk, remote) -Yellow (Elevated risk, consider hybrid) - Green (Low risk, in-person or hybrid) As of this writing, all counties are listed as Green	Required for adults and students age 5 and up	Not discussed	No decisions made as of this writing	Maine Department of Education (2020a, 2020b); mainedocnews. com (2020)

(Continued)

(Continued).

STATE	CASES/ 100 k	RECOMMENDED MODALITY	MASK POLICY	VULNERABLE POPULATIONS	FALL SPORTS	SOURCES
MD	10.91	Offers range of options to consider: One-day rotation; two-day rotation; A/B weeks; elementary in-person with secondary remote	Recommended, up to local districts	Suggests identifying faculty with underlying conditions; Remote learning options for students	No fall sports	Maryland State Department of Education (2020)
MA	7.32	In-person	Required for adults and students grade 2 and up required	MDOE will work with districts to address staff at higher risk of severe illness; Remote learning options for students	On schedule	Massachusetts Department of Elementary and Secondary Education (2020)
MI	5.43*	Guidance depends on phase. Phases 4–6 allow for in-person learning; phases 1–3 require remote learning. As of this writing Northern MI is in Phase 5 and the rest of the state is in Phase 4	Required for staff and students in hallways, in common spaces, and during transit. Required in classrooms for grades 6–12. Strongly recommended in classrooms for grades K-5	Allow alt. work assignments for staff; Remote learning options for students	Football moved to spring 2021; rest of fall sports on schedule	Governor Gretchen Whitmer, COVID-19 Task Force on Education, Return to School Advisory Council (2020)
MN	14.82	Guidance depends on local bi-weekly case rates per 10,000 cases. 0–9 = in-person for all 10–19 = in-person for elementary, hybrid for secondary 20–29 = hybrid for all 30–49 = hybrid for elementary, remote for secondary 50+ = remote for all	Required age 2 and up	Have plan in place for alt. work assignments for staff. If adequate staffing is not possible, shift to an alt. learning model. Remote learning options for students.	Tennis, swimming/diving, and cross country on schedule. Football and girls volleyball allowed to practice, but competition moved to spring 2021	Gov. Tim Walz with Departments of Health and Education (2020); Minnesota Department of Health (2020)
MS	29.10	Prioritize in-person for younger students	Required	Remote learning options for students	On schedule	Mississippi Department of Education (2020); Wood (2020)

(Continued)

(Continued).

STATE	CASES/ 100 k	RECOMMENDED MODALITY	MASK POLICY	VULNERABLE POPULATIONS	FALL SPORTS	SOURCES
MO	20.34	Districts must submit alternative plans of instruction	Recommended	Eligible students can request enrollment in remote learning options	On schedule	Missouri Department of Elementary and Secondary Education (2020a, 2020b); Missouri School Board Association's Center for Education and Safety (2020)
MT	13.85	Up to local districts	Required	Follow CDC guidance	Dual events for golf, cross country; No fall football or volleyball	Montana Office of Public Instruction (2020); Beckman, M., Executive Director, Montana High School Association (2020)
NE	14.52	Guidance based on risk, 4 categories: Green = in-person, Yellow, enhanced mitigation; Orange = hybrid, Red = Remote learning	Not required when Green; Recommended when feasible for Yellow and above	Allow vulnerable teachers to teach remotely; Mandates outreach to families with at-risk students	On schedule	Nebraska Department of Education (2020)
NV	26.41	Hybrid	Required	Staff may be reassigned to work remotely; remote learning options for students	No fall sports	State of Nevada Executive Department, Governor Steve Sisolak (2020)
NH	1.55	Individuals choose between in-person, hybrid, and remote options	Recommended	Remote learning options for students	On schedule	New Hampshire Department of Education (2020); Governor's Economic Reopening Task Force (2020)
NJ	3.21	Up to local districts	Required for adults; Recommended for students	Consider unique needs of each staff member and consult with local bargaining units; Remote learning options for students	Delayed and abridged seasons	New Jersey Department of Education (2020a, 2020b); New Jersey State Interscholastic Athletic Association (2020)

(Continued)

(Continued).

STATE	CASES/ 100 k	RECOMMENDED MODALITY	MASK POLICY	VULNERABLE POPULATIONS	FALL SPORTS	SOURCES
NM	6.59	Hybrid	Required	Allow telework for staff; Remote options for students	No fall sports	New Mexico Public Education Department (2020); Groves (2020)
NY	3.57	Up to local districts	Follow NY State Dept. of Health Guidelines	District plans required to address this	Delayed seasons with no state championships	New York State Department of Health (2020); New York State Education Department (2020)
NC	18.96	Up to local districts	Required for symptomatic persons; Recommended for adults	Allow for alternative work arrangements for staff and learning arrangements for students including remote learning	Cross country, girls volleyball, and swimming and diving start in Nov. All other sports delayed until spring 2021	Public schools of North Carolina (2020)
ND	32.76	Guidance depends on health authorities' data with phased approach to in-person instruction	Not directly addressed	District level plans should address this	On schedule	North Dakota Department of Public Instruction (2020)
OH	9.01	In-person	Recommended for staff and students; Required for maintenance and custodial staff	Guidance references protecting health/safety of vulnerable staff/ students	On schedule	Ohio Department of Education (2020); Ohio High School Athletic Association (2020)
OK	27.29	Up to local districts	Recommended	Should discuss reentry with health care professionals	On schedule	Oklahoma State Department of Education (2020)
OR	6.35	Up to local districts	Required	High-risk staff may meet criteria for exclusion during pandemic; Districts directed to support high-risk personnel; Remote learning options for students	No fall sports	Oregon Department of Education (2020)

(Continued)

(Continued).

STATE	CASES/ 100 k	RECOMMENDED MODALITY	MASK POLICY	VULNERABLE POPULATIONS	FALL SPORTS	SOURCES
PA	5.58	Phased reopening plan per governor: Red = remote; Yellow = in-person with restrictions; Green = in-person with most restrictions eased As of this writing, all counties are Green; however, Allegheny and Philadelphia Counties have stricter guidance.	Required for everyone age 2 and up	Flexible attendance policies for staff, encourage telework; Remote learning options for students	On schedule, with Philadelphia public and Catholic leagues opting out	Pennsylvania Department of Education (2020); Anastasia (2020)
RI	14.46	Reopening based on community outbreak level; hybrid recommended for MS/HS if everyone cannot return in-person every day	Recommended	Remote learning options for students	Delayed start with abridged season	Rhode Island Department of Education (2020); Towne (2020)
SC	20.97	Up to local districts	Required	Plan discusses who might be at greater risk but offers no guidance	Delayed start with abridged season	South Carolina Department of Education (2020); Bezjak (2020)
SD	22.32	In-person	Up to local districts	Schools should make decisions about at-risk staff; Remote learning options for students	On schedule	South Dakota Department of Education (2020)
TN	24.81	Up to local districts	Required for everyone over age 2	Districts should develop plans to address at-risk staff; Remote learning options for students	On schedule with some districts like Shelby County (Memphis) opting out	Tennessee Department of Education (2020); Tennessee Department of Health (2020)
TX	20.20	Up to local districts, consider prioritizing in-person for elementary	Required	Allow staff to telework; remote learning options for students	Delayed seasons; Students enrolled in remote learning eligible	Texas Education Agency (2020)
UT	14.71	Up to local districts, recommends focus on individualized learning	Recommended	Identify high risk employees and mitigate risks; Alt. learning options for students	On schedule	Utah State Board of Education (2020)

(Continued)

(Continued).

STATE	CASES/ 100 k	RECOMMENDED MODALITY	MASK POLICY	VULNERABLE POPULATIONS	FALL SPORTS	SOURCES
VT	0.64	In-person	Required	Staff should consult with health care provider; Remote learning options for students	Football replaced with 7-on-7 touch football; girls volleyball moved outdoors; other fall sports on schedule	Vermont Agency of Education (2020a, 2020b)
VA	11.25	Based on phase. Phase 1 – mostly remote; Phase 2 – P-3 in-person, others remote; Phase 3 – all in-person with social distancing, might involve hybrid As of this writing, Va. is in Phase 3	Recommended for staff and students when social distancing cannot be maintained; Recommended in public spaces including hallways	Telework options for staff; Remote learning options for students	No fall sports	Virginia Department of Education (2020); Kolenich (2020)
WA	4.26*	Guidance based on cases per 100 k; Under 25 cases/100 k = in-person; 25–75/ 100 k = in-person for elementary, remote for secondary; Above 75/100 k = remote learning with limited in-person for students with highest needs	"Promote and ensure" for staff and students	Schools should have plans in place to protect staff and students at higher risk	No fall sports	Washington State Department of Health (2020)
WV	4.84	Guidance based on cases per 100 k; Green (3 or fewer/100 k); Yellow (3.1–9.9/ 100 k); Orange (10–24.9/100 k) = in-person; Red (25+/100 k) = remote learning	Based on guidance per 100 k; Green – grades 3 and up on buses; Yellow – Grades 3–5 on buses; 6–12 at all times; Orange – Required grades 3 and up	Schools should have plans in place to protect staff; Remote learning options for students	Delayed start	West Virginia Department of Education (2020); West Virginia Department of Health and Human Resources (2020)
WI	14.05	Up to districts; Guidance outlines a number of hybrid options	Recommended, follow CDC guidance	Develop flexibility for staff; plan to replace staff that are not returning for fall 2020; add positions for remote instruction; Remote learning options for students	Up to local districts; guidance allows for either delayed start with abridged fall seasons or moving fall sports to spring 2021	Wisconsin Department of Public Instruction (2020a, 2020b)

(Continued)

(Continued).

STATE	CASES/ 100 k	RECOMMENDED MODALITY	MASK POLICY	VULNERABLE POPULATIONS	FALL SPORTS	SOURCES
WY	10.98	Guidance based on viral spread; Tier I– in-person; Tier II – combination of in-person and intermittent closures; Tier III – remote learning As of this writing, WY is Tier I	Recommended	Remote and homebound learning options for students	On schedule	Wyoming Department of Education (2020); Associated Press (2020)

These data reflect our review of state plans between August 12–21, 2020. Case rates sourced from the Institute for Health, Measurement and Evaluation (2020) and reflect the data available for August 21, 2020. Three states denoted with (*) are missing data from August 21 and the data presented reflect their numbers as of August 20, 2020.

Appendix B

District enrollments and reopening modalities.

District	Enrollment	8/5/20 Modality	8/21/20 Modality
New York City, NY	984,462	Hybrid	Hybrid
Los Angeles Unified, CA	633,621	Remote	Remote
City of Chicago, IL	378,199	Remote	Remote
Miami-Dade, FL	357,249	Remote	Remote
Clark County, NV	326,953	Remote	Remote
Broward, FL	271,852	Remote	Remote
Houston ISD, TX	216,106	Remote	Remote
Hillsborough, FL	214,386	Hybrid	Remote*
Orange, FL	200,674	Hybrid	In-person
Palm Beach, FL	192,721	Hybrid	Remote
Fairfax County, VA	187,467	Remote	Remote
State of Hawaii	181,550	In-person	In-person/Remote**
Gwinnett County, GA	178,214	Remote	Remote
Wake County, NC	160,467	Remote	Remote
Montgomery County, MD	159,010	Remote	Remote
Dallas ISD, TX	157,886	Hybrid	Remote
Charlotte-Mecklenburg, NC	147,428	Remote	Remote
Philadelphia, PA	133,929	Remote	Remote
Prince George's CO, MD	130,814	Remote	Remote
Duval, FL	129,479	Hybrid	In-person
San Diego Unified, CA	128,040	Remote	Remote
Cypress-Fairbanks ISD, TX	114,868	In-person	In-person
Cobb County, GA	113,151	Remote	Remote
Baltimore County, MD	112,139	Remote	Remote
Shelby County, TN	111,403	Hybrid	Remote
Northside ISD, TX	106,145	In-person	Remote
Pinellas, FL	102,905	In-person	In-person
Polk, FL	102,295	In-person	In-person
DeKalb County, GA	101,284	Remote	Remote
Jefferson County, KY	99,813	Remote	Remote
Fulton County, GA	96,122	Remote	Remote
Lee, FL	92,686	Hybrid	In-person
Denver, CO	91,138	Remote	Remote
Albuquerque, NM	90,651	Hybrid	Remote
Prince William County, VA	89,345	Remote	Remote
Fort Worth ISD, TX	87,428	Remote	Remote
Jefferson County, CO	86,371	Hybrid	Remote
Davidson County, TN	85,163	Hybrid	Remote
Austin ISD, TX	83,067	Remote	Remote
Baltimore City, MD	82,354	Remote	Remote
Anne Arundel County, MD	81,379	Remote	Remote
Alpine, UT	8,957	In-person	In-person
Loudoun County, VA	78,348	Remote	Remote
Greenville, SC	76,918	TBD	Hybrid
Long Beach Unified, CA	76,428	Remote	Remote
Milwaukee, WI	76,206	Remote	Remote
Katy ISD, TX	75,428	Hybrid	In-person
Fort Bend ISD, TX	74,146	Remote	Remote

(Continued)

(Continued).

District	Enrollment	8/5/20 Modality	8/21/20 Modality
Brevard, FL	73,444	In-person	In-person
Fresno Unified, CA	73,356	Remote	Remote
Guilford County, NC	73,059	Remote	Remote
Davis, UT	72,987	Hybrid	Hybrid
Pasco, FL	72,493	Hybrid	In-person
Aldine ISD, TX	69,768	Hybrid	In-person
Granite, UT	69,580	Hybrid	In-person
Virginia Beach, VA	69,085	Remote	Remote
Seminole, FL	67,808	Hybrid	In-person
North East ISD, TX	67,531	Remote	Remote
Douglas County, CO	67,470	Hybrid	Remote
Washoe County, NV	66,671	In-person	In-person/Hybrid***
Mesa Unified, AZ	63,444	Remote	Remote
Elk Grove Unified, CA	63,061	Remote	Remote
Osceola, FL	63,031	Hybrid	In-person
Volusia, FL	63,028	Hybrid	In-person
Arlington ISD, TX	62,181	Remote	Remote
Knox County, TN	60,372	Hybrid	In-person
San Francisco Unified, CA	60,133	Remote	Remote
Chesterfield County, VA	60,060	Remote	Remote
Conroe ISD, TX	59,764	Remote	Remote
El Paso ISD, TX	59,424	Remote	Remote
Garland ISD, TX	57,133	Remote	Remote
Mobile County, AL	56,628	Remote	Remote
Pasadena ISD, TX	56,282	In-person	Remote
Frisco ISD, TX	55,923	Hybrid	In-person
Howard County, MD	55,626	Remote	Remote
Winston-Salem, NC	55,228	Hybrid	Remote
Cherry Creek, CO	54,852	Hybrid	In-person/Hybrid***
Santa Ana Unified, CA	54,505	Remote	Remote
Clayton County, GA	54,345	Remote	Remote
Seattle, WA	54,215	Remote	Remote
Plano ISD, TX	54,173	Remote	Remote
Boston, MA	53,640	Hybrid	Remote
Capistrano Unified, CA	53,613	Hybrid	In-person/Hybrid***
Jordan, UT	53,416	Hybrid	Hybrid
Lewisville ISD, TX	53,257	Remote	Remote
Corona-Norco Unified, CA	53,157	Remote	Remote
San Bernardino Unified, CA	53,152	Remote	Remote
San Antonio ISD, TX	52,514	Remote	Remote
Omaha, NE	52,344	In-person	Remote
Atlanta, GA	51,927	Remote	Remote
Klein ISD, TX	51,810	Remote	Remote
Henrico County, VA	51,425	Remote	Remote
Cumberland County, NC	51,194	Remote	Remote
Wichita, KS	50,600	Hybrid	In-person/Remote^
Columbus City, OH	50,331	Remote	Remote
Oakland Unified, CA	49,760	Remote	Remote
San Juan Unified, CA	49,255	Remote	Remote

(Continued)

(Continued).

District	Enrollment	8/5/20 Modality	8/21/20 Modality
Manatee, FL	48,884	Hybrid	In-person
Jefferson Parish, LA	48,668	Hybrid	In-person/Hybrid***
Charleston, SC	48,551	In-person	In-person
District of Columbia	48,462	Remote	Remote
Round Rock ISD, TX	48,321	Remote	Remote
Anchorage, AK	48,238	Remote	Remote
Portland, OR	48,173	Remote	Remote
Tucson, AZ	47,366	Remote	Remote
Brownsville ISD, TX	46,880	Remote	Remote
Sacramento City Unified, CA	46,815	Remote	Remote
Collier, FL	46,416	Hybrid	In-person
Alief ISD, TX	46,376	Remote	Remote
Forsyth County, GA	46,238	Hybrid	In-person
Detroit Public Schools, MI	45,455	Hybrid	In-person
Socorro ISD, TX	45,238	Hybrid	Remote
Hamilton County, TN	44,446	Hybrid	Hybrid
Chandler Unified, AZ	44,352	Remote	Remote
Garden Grove Unified, CA	44,223	Remote	Remote
Rutherford County, TN	44,149	Hybrid	In-person
Horry, SC	43,991	In-person	In-person
Killeen ISD, TX	43,782	Remote	Remote
United ISD, TX	43,660	Remote	Remote
Marion, FL	43,032	Hybrid	In-person

Enrollment figures from National Center for Education Statistics (n.d.). *Reopening modalities based on Lips (2020) and publicly available information found on each district's website.* * Hillsborough, FL reopening remote for one week, then offering in-person instruction; ** The island of Oahu is reopening remotely; the rest of Hawaii is reopening in-person; *** Elementary schools are reopening in-person; secondary schools reopening hybrid; ^ Elementary schools are reopening in-person; secondary schools are reopening remotely.

Are School Reopening Decisions Related to Funding? Evidence from over 12,000 Districts During the COVID-19 Pandemic

Corey A. DeAngelis and Christos A. Makridis

ABSTRACT

In theory, public school districts with more funding might be more likely to reopen in person if resources are a primary driver of their reopening decisions during the COVID-19 pandemic. However, it is also possible that these decisions are influenced by other factors including political partisanship, incentive structures, and special interests. Using data on over 12,000 school districts in the United States, we quantify the relationship between public school revenues and expenditures per student and their reopening decisions in Fall 2020. Across a range of statistical specifications, including comparisons of districts within the same county with one another, we find an economically and statistically significant positive association between remote instruction and revenue per student. Our models control for district-level demographic characteristics, together with county COVID-19 risk and partisanship variables. We also find that increases in the share of remote school districts in a state are associated with increases in the growth of counselors and social workers, relative to 2019, even after controlling for the overall employment decline in the state. Our results are consistent with models of rent seeking behavior by teachers unions with unintended consequences on children.

Introduction

The COVID-19 pandemic led to an overwhelming number of K-12 school closures, affecting at least 55 million public and private school students, covering nearly all of the K-12 student population.[1] While some schools successfully pivoted toward remote instruction, many students, especially younger students, experienced a substantial decline in learning outcomes and physical and mental health (Agostinelli, Doepke, Sorrenti, & Zilibotti, 2020; Christakis, Van Cleve, & Zimmerman, 2020; Green, 2021; Lee, 2020; McKinsey & Company, 2020; UNICEF, 2020; Varas, Menon, & Bellafiore,

2021). This has been further complicated by the impact of stay-at-home orders and regulations on child care that led to a decline in the demand for child care labor (Ali, Herbst, & Makridis, 2021a, 2021b).

While there is not yet causal evidence about the effects of school closures on learning outcomes, preliminary evidence is mounting. For example, a nationwide analysis by McKinsey & Company (2020) found that students lost about one to three months learning in terms of math and reading achievement from school closures. These learning losses have also generally been larger for students from disadvantaged groups, meaning school closures have exacerbated existing inequities in K-12 education (Agostinelli et al., 2020; McKinsey & Company, 2020).[2]

Many public school teachers' unions argued that they needed to remain closed for in-person instruction to curb the spread of the virus, but research suggests that reopening schools for in-person instruction was not associated with statistically or economically significant increases in local COVID-19 transmission or even hospitalizations (Billingsley et al., 2020; Christakis et al., 2020; DeAngelis & Makridis, 2021; Harris, Ziedan, & Hassig, 2021; Honein, Barrios, & Goldhaber et al., 2021; Ludvigsson, Engerström, Nordenhäll, & Larsson, 2021; Oster, 2020). That general pattern was not just present in the United States, but also across 191 countries (UNICEF, 2020). While Courtemanche, Le, Yelowitz, and Zimmer (2021) found a relationship between in-person school reopenings in fall 2020 in Texas and additional COVID-19 cases and deaths, recent evidence suggests such results could be a function of small samples (Chandra and Hoeg, 2022).

Research also found that school reopening decisions were strongly predicted by politics and union influence than measures of COVID-19 health risks (DeAngelis, 2020; DeAngelis & Makridis, 2021; Flanders, 2020; Harris et al., 2021; Hartney & Finger, 2021; Valant, 2020). Furthermore, to reopen schools for in-person instruction, many of these labor unions pushed for larger federal relief packages in The American Rescue Plan Act of 2021.

Moreover, Makridis and McNab (2020) found that the impact of COVID-19 on state budgets is between $79.9–125.2 billion, which is far below the stimulus bills that were proposed and that have been passed. The National Education Association additionally called for at least $175 billion in additional federal relief "to stabilize education funding."[3] Similarly, the President of the American Federation of Teachers, Randi Weingarten, wrote[4] that the $170 billion in education funding included in President Joe Biden's American Rescue Plan was "needed immediately to safely reopen schools for in-person teaching and learning [...]"

However, the Congressional Budget Office estimates that only about 5% of the funding allocated toward reopening K-12 public schools in person would have been spent in 2021; the rest would be paid out through 2028.[5] Furthermore, federal funding was on top of the $54 billion in federal funding for K-12 education in the Covid Relief Package[6] that was signed into law in December 2020 and the $13.2 billion for K-12 education in the CARES Act that was signed into law in March 2020, most of which remained unspent as of November 30th, 2020.[7]

The primary contribution of this study is to quantitatively explore whether there is a public policy rationale for intervening with additional funds to help school districts that taught remote in fall 2020. Using data on over 12,000 school districts, we provide robust evidence that school districts with greater funding were more likely to have learning fully remote as of Fall 2020, inconsistent with many of the claims by teachers unions that more funding was required for reopening. Our estimates are identified from variation across schools within the same county, controlling for enrollment and a wide array of demographic factors all at the district-level.

We also show that a percentage point increase in the share of school districts that opened remotely in fall 2020 was associated with a 0.35 percentage point increase in the growth rate of the number of job postings for counselors in a county between 2019 and 2020. This suggests remote instruction was also associated with a deterioration in mental health outcomes. Thus, we argue that union behavior over the pandemic was consistent with rent seeking models where unions lobby for additional resources that do not filter through to the public (i.e., K-12 learners).

The structure of the report is as follows. Section II provides a brief theoretical background about the debate between in-person and remote instruction as it relates to school funding. Section III presents the data and measurement strategy. Section IV provides the empirical specification. Section V discusses the main results. Section VI extends these results by exploring the effects of remote instruction on mental health outcomes using job posting data. Section VII concludes.

Theoretical framework

In theory, public school districts might be more likely to reopen for in-person instruction if they have more resources to cover the costs of reopening and if resources are indeed a major barrier to reopening schools in person. However, on average, private schools were more likely to reopen for in-person instruction in 2020 than public schools in the U.S., suggesting that incentives might have had something to do with reopening decisions (Henderson, Peterson, & West, 2021).

In the private sector, school leaders have a greater incentive to create value for learners since there is more competition: families can take their children's education dollars elsewhere if they are not sufficiently satisfied with the provided services (Chubb & Moe, 1988; DeAngelis & Holmes Erickson, 2018; Friedman, 1955). In the public sector, school districts receive children's

K-12 education funding despite the desires of individual families, and regardless of whether they open their doors for in-person instruction, in part because there are large transaction costs associated with switching out of residentially assigned schools – families would have to move residences to access a different public school, pay out of pocket for private school tuition and fees, or pay to cover the costs of home-based private education (Hanushek, Kain, Rivkin, & Branch, 2007). In fact, Hartney and Finger (2021) found evidence to suggest that competition from Catholic private schools was associated with a higher likelihood of nearby public school districts reopening for in-person instruction in 2020.

Some scholars have theorized that private schools have been more likely to reopen because they believe private schools are more well-funded than public schools, which would support the theory that reopening decisions are explained by resources.[8] However, there is no conclusive evidence that private schools are more well-funded than public schools on a per-student basis. On the contrary, Garet, Chan, and Sherman (1995) estimated that public K-12 schools spent an average of 43 to 52% more per student than private schools in the 1991–92 school year. A more recent analysis estimated that public K-12 school funding per student was about 80% higher than private school funding per student in the 2016–17 school year.[9] Another analysis similarly estimated that, on average, per-student funding was about 89% higher in public schools than private schools in 2018 (Van Kipnis, 2020). Moreover, K-12 private schools in the U.S. generally report tuition levels that are, on average, substantially lower than total public school revenues per student.[10]

Evidence suggests public school districts in areas with stronger teachers' unions were substantially less likely to reopen for in-person instruction in 2020 (DeAngelis & Makridis, 2021; Flanders, 2020; Harris et al., 2021; Hartney & Finger, 2021). It is possible that some public school teachers' unions pushed to remain closed for in-person instruction as a form of rent-seeking (Krueger, 1974; Tullock, 1967). In Oregon, for example, the teachers' union successfully lobbied to the government in March 2020 to make it illegal for families to move their children to virtual public charter schools.[11] That same month, the Pennsylvania Association of School Administrators similarly lobbied to make it illegal for families to switch to virtual public charter schools during the initial closures, and the president of the association admitted that their political action was an attempt to stop families seeking alternatives from leaving district-run schools so that they could keep taxpayer dollars in the traditional school system.[12]

In theory, more powerful public school teachers' unions could successfully leverage their influence to keep educational institutions closed for in-person instruction to bargain for additional funding, staffing, and supplies. Teachers' unions were in an especially favorable bargaining position in 2020 because taxpayers were already on the hook for funding the public school system regardless of whether in-person services were provided and because families usually did not have the option to take their children's taxpayer-funded K-12 education dollars elsewhere.

This convenient bargaining position was also theoretically amplified by the notion that special interest groups, in general, are advantaged by having members that are highly motivated by concentrated benefits whereas the costs are distributed across the rest of the population (Becker, 1983; Kahlenberg & Greene, 2012; Mitchell & Munger, 1991; Olson, 1965; Schattschneider, 1935). A relatively small special interest group can success-fully influence policy because they have a stronger incentive to take collective action and fight for concentrated benefits than the rest of the population because their costs are dispersed (Moe, 2005, 2006, 2011; Olson, 1965). This phenomenon is known as "rent seeking," which refers to the behavior by special interest groups to seek "rents" – or economic benefits – that are taken from another segment of the market. Here, for example, teacher's unions are thought of as extracting rents from taxpayers and students/parents.

If resources are a driver of schools reopening for in-person instruction in 2020, we might expect that, all else equal, public school funding per student would be positively associated with the decision to reopen in person. More resources might allow public school districts to cover the costs associated with providing an in-person learning environment if they have an incentive to cater to the needs of families. However, it is also possible that, all else equal, school districts with more funding might have been less likely to reopen in person if those districts experienced more influence from special interest groups includ-ing teachers' unions. Special interest groups have an incentive to lobby for additional benefits for their members while advocating for a reduction in costs associated with their jobs. In other words, we might expect to find a positive relationship between school district funding and the likelihood of reopening schools remotely because teachers' unions have pushed for both. In fact, a few studies have found that public school districts in areas with stronger teachers' unions were less likely to reopen in person in 2020 (e.g. DeAngelis & Makridis, 2021; Hartney & Finger, 2021). However, although billions of dollars have already been allocated in the name of reopening schools in person, no nation-wide analysis has actually examined whether the districts that switched to remote instruction are actually the districts that are also in greater need.

We contribute by providing the first analysis of the relationship between district-level funding per student and reopening decisions in the fall of 2020. We examine data from over 12,000 school districts in the U.S. and find that public school funding per student is either uncorrelated, or even negatively correlated, with reopening schools in person. In other words, across various analytic techniques and specifications, we do not find any evidence to suggest that district-level revenues or expenditures per student are positively associated with reopening schools in person.

Data and measurement

We use the latest and most comprehensive dataset on K-12 school reopening decisions from the fall of 2020 in the U.S. These school reopening decisions are publicly available at the MCH Strategic Data website and were updated through February 1st, 2021.[13] The dataset includes reopening plans reported by 13,448 K-12 public school districts enrolling around 47.9 million students, covering the vast majority of the estimated 50.7 million students in primary and secondary public schools in the U.S. in the 2020–21 school year.[14] For our empirical strategy, we omit districts that did not respond to the survey to avoid potential measurement error among non-respondents.

For our independent variable of interest, total revenues and expenditures per student, we use the latest publicly available district-level data at the National Center of Education Statistics Common Core of Data School District Finance Survey (F-33).[15] These district-level funding data are from the 2017–18 school year (fiscal year 2018). Although the latest available funding data are not from the 2020–21 school year, they should serve as valid proxies for current funding levels. One concern with the 2017–18 data as a proxy is that significant changes from one year to another could be correlated with unobserved determinants of reopening and/or local productivity. While only time will tell as more recent data becomes available, we test the credibility of our assumption that 2017 is a sufficient proxy by gathering annual data from 2006 to 2018 for each school. We subsequently estimate an autoregressive process with one lag. We obtain a coefficient of 0.99 on a one-year lag of logged total revenue and a coefficient of 0.95 on a one year lag of logged total revenue per member. This suggests that a good proxy for 2019–2020 is simply the value from the prior year, i.e. 2018–2019.

Our models include several control variables from various sources. First, we draw from the Stanford Education Data Archive (SEDA) to measure demographic characteristics at the district-level, including: the race distribution (the share who are Native American, Hispanic, Black, and White), and the share of males and females between age 25–64 in the labor force. These features are only available up until 2014, but since demographic characteristics tend to be fairly time-invariant, especially in more disaggregated geographical units, they are a useful proxy for 2020 values.[16] Second, we use a county-level control for the percent of Trump voters in the 2016 presidential election as reported by the MIT Election Data and Science Lab.[17] Finally, we use county-level controls for the number of COVID-19 cases and deaths as of July 30th 2020 from USA Facts.[18]

Figure 1 illustrates the percent of districts within each U.S. county in our dataset that are classified as "fully remote" by MCH Strategic Data. Notably, Florida, a state with public school funding per student that is about 29% lower than the national average according to the latest data from the U.S. Census Bureau, has most of its public schools open for in-person instruction.[19] In contrast, California – a state with about 38% higher per-student funding and stronger teachers' unions – mostly opted not to provide full-time in-person instruction.[20]

Next, we also summarize the means and standard deviations of our main variables of interest in Table 1 below. Roughly 24% of the school districts opened remotely in fall 2020. The average revenue per student is $16,563 in the pooled sample and statistically indistinguishable between those that are remote versus in-person. However, student enrollment is roughly twice as large in the remote districts. Not surprisingly, we also see a much higher vote share for Trump among districts that go in-person than those that go remote (59% versus 46%). There are no differences in terms of COVID-19 cases and deaths per capita between the two types of districts. The demographics are also fairly similar, although the districts that go in-person tend to have a higher concentration of Whites (84% versus 75%), but a lower share of college or more than college educated individuals. They also tend to have a $5,000 lower median household income than their remote counterparts.

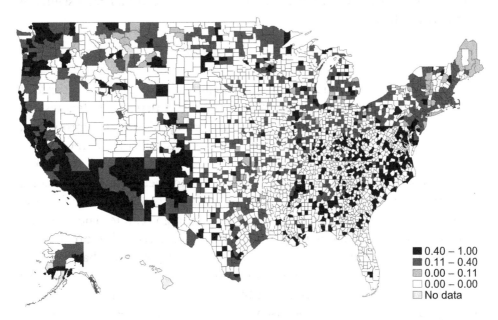

Figure 1. Percent of fully remote districts in fall 2020, across counties.

Table 1. Summary and descriptive statistics.

	Pooled		Remote		In-person	
	Mean	SD	Mean	SD	Mean	SD
Remote, %	0.24	0.43	1.00	0.00	0.00	0.00
Revenue/student, 2018	16,563	15,469	16,391	10,077	16,617	16,815
Student enrollment	3454	12,278	5736	18,912	2737	9144
Trump 2016 Vote, %	0.56	0.17	0.46	0.17	0.59	0.16
COVID-19 cases/capita	0.010	0.009	0.013	0.009	0.009	0.009
COVID-19 deaths/capita	0.000	0.000	0.000	0.000	0.000	0.000
Population	482,637	1,176,510	1,001,912	1,813,919	318,732	819,028
Male, %	0.50	0.02	0.49	0.02	0.50	0.02
Age under 18, %	0.22	0.03	0.23	0.03	0.22	0.03
Age 18–34, %	0.22	0.04	0.23	0.04	0.21	0.04
Age 35–64, %	0.39	0.03	0.38	0.03	0.39	0.03
Age over 64, %	0.17	0.04	0.16	0.04	0.18	0.04
White, %	0.82	0.14	0.75	0.16	0.84	0.13
Black, %	0.07	0.11	0.10	0.13	0.06	0.10
Married	0.50	0.06	0.48	0.06	0.51	0.06
Less than high school, %	0.12	0.06	0.13	0.06	0.12	0.05
Some college, %	0.31	0.05	0.30	0.05	0.31	0.05
College, %	0.16	0.06	0.18	0.06	0.16	0.06
More than college, %	0.10	0.05	0.11	0.06	0.09	0.05
Median household income	57,307	15,615	60,594	17,176	56,270	14,942
Observations	12,792		3069		9723	

Notes.–Sources: MCH Data, American Community Survey (2014–2018). The table reports the means and standard deviations for the main variables of interest in our statistical models. Remote, revenue per student, and enrollment are all measured at the school-district level. The remaining variables are all at the county-level.

Empirical specification

To understand the relationship between remote versus in-person learning and funding at the district-level, we estimate cross-sectional regressions of the following form

$$r_i = \gamma f_i + \phi e_i + g(D_i, \theta) + \xi_l + \varepsilon_i$$

where r_{il} denotes an indicator for whether district i has decided to conduct learning activities remotely (zero for hybrid and in-person), f denotes the logged district funding per student, e denotes logged student enrollment, $g(D, \theta)$ denotes a semi-parametric function of district-level demographic controls, and ξ denotes fixed effects on location (e.g., county or state). We cluster standard errors at the county-level and do not weight the observations.

The primary threat to identification is that districts with greater funding vary in ways that are correlated with the decision to go remote. The direction of the bias, however, is ambiguous. On one hand, districts with more funding may have access to better teachers and/or better infrastructure that cushions the effect of the pandemic on the community and students. If so, then our estimates will be upwards biased. On the other hand, if districts with more funding have more funding precisely because unions have the bargaining power to push for school closures, then our estimates will be downwards biased. The direction of the bias is, therefore, an empirical question.

We address the potential for omitted variables bias by including a wide array of district-level controls, including: the race distribution (the share who are Native American, Hispanic, Black, and White), and the share of males and females between age 25–64 in the labor force. By including the race distribution, we control for underlying correlates of minority student attendance and the especially adverse effects of the COVID-19 pandemic. Further, we control for the male and female labor force participation rates to control for differences in local labor market engagement. Beyond these district-level controls, we also include the share of Trump votes from 2016 to address concerns that we are simply detecting the effect of partisanship, which prior literature has found strongly predicts beliefs and behavior over the pandemic (Canes-Wrone et al., 2022).

Although these controls are helpful for removing cross-sectional heterogeneity that could otherwise bias our estimate of γ, we nonetheless introduce layers of geographic fixed effects. For example, state fixed effects remove time-invariant heterogeneity across states, which could reflect differences in state policymaking (e.g., more versus less lenient governors). Similarly, we introduce core business statistical area (CBSA) and county fixed effects, which add more granularity into our removal of potentially concerning unobserved heterogeneity. Even though there is no silver bullet to the presence of omitted variables, our wide array of controls and fixed effects help.

A final and remaining concern is that we are failing to control for unionization. While unionization is undoubtedly an important determinant of reopening decisions (DeAngelis, 2020; DeAngelis & Makridis, 2021; Flanders, 2020; Harris et al., 2021; Hartney & Finger, 2021; Valant, 2020), we do not want to "over control" for the mechanism. That is, if unionization is the driver of rent seeking behavior, then it will be highly correlated with both funding decisions and reopening. Nonetheless, as we will show, we control for county fixed effects, which isolates variation across school districts in the same county. Consistent with our interpretation of it as a mechanism, the magnitude of our coefficients declines, although remains significant.

Main results

Table 2 documents our main results. Columns 1–7 estimate our baseline equation using a linear probability model, whereas columns 8–9 use an ordered probit where a value of 3 denotes fully in person and a value of 1 denotes fully remote (and 2 denotes a hybrid model). Starting with column 1, the raw data shows little statistically or economically significant association between remote instruction and revenue per student: a 1% rise in revenue per member is linked with a 0.033 percentage point (pp) rise in the probability that a district switches to remote instruction, significant at

Table 2. The relationship between remote/in-person learning and funding.

Dep. var. =	Remote Instruction							In-person Index	
	(1)	(2)	(3)	(4)	(5)	(6)	(7)	(8)	(9)
log(Revenue/ Membership)	.033 *	.112***	.165***	.077***	.076***	.072***	.083***	−.084	−.105 *
	[.019]	[.021]	[.021]	[.016]	[.016]	[.016]	[.019]	[.053]	[.055]
log(Student Enrollment)		.064***	.066***	.035***	.035***	.030***	.041***	−.182***	−.176***
		[.005]	[.004]	[.004]	[.004]	[.004]	[.005]	[.013]	[.014]
Trump 2016 Vote, %				−.357***	−.367***	−.338***		1.468***	1.534***
				[.041]	[.042]	[.051]		[.125]	[.165]
COVID-19 cases/ capita					−1.063 *	−3.484***		1.470	7.136***
					[.553]	[.824]		[1.838]	[2.709]
COVID-19 deaths/ capita					3.430	31.440		5.124	−106.825
					[17.348]	[22.411]		[49.178]	[66.958]
R-squared	.00	.05	.18	.22	.22	.28	.36		
Sample Size	11,280	11,279	11,278	10,890	10,890	10,753	10,189	10,891	10,891
State FE	No	No	Yes	Yes	Yes	No	No	Yes	No
District Controls	No	No	No	Yes	Yes	Yes	Yes	Yes	Yes
CBSA FE	No	No	No	No	No	Yes	No	No	Yes
County FE	No	No	No	No	No	No	Yes	No	No

Notes.–Sources: MCH Data and the Stanford Education Data Archive (SEDA, 2014). The table reports the coefficients associated with regressions of an indicator for whether the school district has students in remote instruction in fall 2020 (columns 1–7) and an ordinal variable (1 = remote, 2 = hybrid, 3 = in-person) on logged revenue per membership, conditional on logged student enrollment in the school district, the county 2016 share of Trump voters, the county inverse hyperbolic sine of Covid-19 cases and deaths as of July 30th 2020, and a wide array of district-level demographic characteristics, including: the race distribution (the share who are Native American, Hispanic, Black, and White), and the share of males and females between age 25–64 in the labor force. Standard errors are clustered by county and observations are unweighted.

the 10% level. However, once we control for student enrollment in column 2, the coefficient grows in economic and statistical magnitude to 0.112. Next, we control for state fixed effects in column 3, differencing out variation in political governance structures that are correlated with reopening. We find an even stronger coefficient of 0.165, which is significant at the 1% level. We also continue to find a strong positive link between student enrollment and remote instruction.

So far, the coefficient on revenue per student has grown in significance, suggesting that these omitted variables were causing downwards bias. However, column 4 introduces the district-level controls, which reduces the estimate to 0.077 (albeit statistically significant at the 1% level). We have also included the 90–10, 90–50, and 50–10 income ratios as controls, but exclude them from the baseline because there are some districts with missing values. Not surprisingly, we also see that the 2016 Trump vote share is negatively correlated with remote instruction. Next, column 5 includes COVID-19 cases and deaths per capita, producing an identical coefficient on revenue per student. While infections per capita is negatively correlated with remote instruction, deaths per capita is positively correlated with it. Both are statistically noisy, however.

Next, column 6 introduces CBSA fixed effects, allowing us to compare districts in the same metropolitan area. Our estimate declines marginally, but remains statistically indistinguishable. Finally, column 7 introduces county fixed effects, comparing districts in the same county, but with the district-level covariates. Here, we find a robust and economically significant gradient of 0.072 on revenue per student. That is our strictest specification and the displayed county variables drop out. Finally, 8 and 9 present ordered probit results finding that public school district revenues per student are not statistically associated with reopening in person.

Across each of our specifications, we find a statistically significant and positive associations between student enrollment and remote instruction. Without any controls (column 2), a 10% rise in student enrollment is associated with a 0.64 percentage point increase in the probability the district goes remote. As we add controls and fixed effects, that declines to 0.35 percentage points. That is consistent with the view that larger schools might be more risk averse to remain in-person. We also find large and robust negative associations between the Trump vote share in 2016 and remote instruction. While we have also experimented with the number of union workers in a county as a control, the Trump share of votes is more direct and better measured. Finally, we see little association between COVID-19 cases and deaths with remote instruction: if anything, increases in COVID-19 cases are actually associated with declines in the probability of going remote within state.

We also present results as robustness using district-level revenues per student in 10,000s of dollars, rather than logged revenues per student, in Table 3. We present similar results as robustness using district-level logged expenditures per student, rather than revenues, in Table 4. When we use expenditures per student as our main right-hand-side variable, we find that the positive relationship between resources and the decision to go remote remains statistically significant up until county fixed effects are introduced. The relationship between expenditures per student and reopening status is statistically insignificant in the ordered probit models in columns 8 and 9 in Tables 3 and 4.

Another concern is that we might be overlooking variation in union power. While we do not have a comprehensive measure that is disaggregated at the district-level, or even fully at the county-level, we use data on union density at a state-level. However, including it as a control does not alter the results. Moreover, our results using county fixed effects implicitly control for differences in unionization under the assumption that union density is not changing at high frequencies within a county over time. We have also estimated specifications that contain fixed effects on zipcode, which produces similarly statistically insignificant estimates between school funding and the decision to go remote versus reopen.

Table 3. Robustness using level of school funding and remote/in-person learning.

Dep. var. =	Remote Instruction							In-person Index	
	(1)	(2)	(3)	(4)	(5)	(6)	(7)	(8)	(9)
Revenue/ Membership, '0000s	.009	.044***	.050***	.024***	.024***	.023***	.027***	−.028	−.038 *
	[.007]	[.008]	[.008]	[.006]	[.006]	[.006]	[.007]	[.021]	[.022]
log(Student Enrollment)		.063***	.063***	.033***	.033***	.028***	.040***	−.180***	−.174***
		[.005]	[.004]	[.004]	[.004]	[.004]	[.005]	[.012]	[.013]
Trump 2016 Vote, %				−.365***	−.375***	−.353***		1.477***	1.552***
				[.042]	[.042]	[.051]		[.125]	[.166]
COVID-19 cases/ capita					−1.156**	−3.644***		1.571	7.367***
					[.555]	[.833]		[1.840]	[2.721]
COVID-19 deaths/ capita					3.351	29.824		5.448	−105.281
					[17.518]	[22.524]		[49.250]	[66.819]
R-squared	.00	.05	.18	.22	.22	.28	.36		
Sample Size	11,280	11,279	11,278	10,890	10,890	10,753	10,189	10,891	10,891
State FE	No	No	Yes	Yes	Yes	No	No	Yes	No
District Controls	No	No	No	Yes	Yes	Yes	Yes	Yes	Yes
CBSA FE	No	No	No	No	No	Yes	No	No	Yes
County FE	No	No	No	No	No	No	Yes	No	No

Notes.–Sources: MCH Data and the Stanford Education Data Archive (SEDA, 2014). The table reports the coefficients associated with regressions of an indicator for whether the school district has students learning fully remotely in fall 2020 (columns 1–7) and an ordinal variable (1 = remote, 2 = hybrid, 3 = in-person) on revenue per membership (in tens of thousands), conditional on logged student enrollment in the school district, the county 2016 share of Trump voters, the county inverse hyperbolic sine of Covid-19 cases and deaths as of July 30th 2020, and a wide array of district-level demographic characteristics, including: the race distribution (the share who are Native American, Hispanic, Black, and White), and the share of males and females between age 25–64 in the labor force. Standard errors are clustered by county and observations are unweighted.

Although we are the first to provide a comprehensive analysis of the relationship between funding and reopening decisions, recent work by Roza (2021) has found similar results. In particular, she finds that that public school districts that are all or mostly remote in the 2020–21 school year generally demonstrated financial surpluses, suggesting that resources were not the primary reason that their schools did not reopen mostly in person.[21] For example, Los Angeles public schools, which opted to reopen remotely, had over a half a billion dollar – or about a $1,100 per student – funding surplus in the 2020–21 school year. Furthermore, Michigan school districts receiving more federal CARES Act funding were less likely to reopen (DeGrow & Rigterink, 2021).

Unintended consequences of remote instruction

The null, or even potentially positive, association between remote instruction and school funding casts doubt on the claim that giving school districts more money would make them more likely to be open for in-person instruction. Moreover, DeAngelis and Makridis (2021) show that union density, not coronavirus cases or deaths, is the strongest predictor of reopening decisions.

Table 4. Robustness using school expenditures and remote/in-person learning.

Dep. var. =	Remote Instruction							In-person Index	
	(1)	(2)	(3)	(4)	(5)	(6)	(7)	(8)	(9)
log(Expenditures)	.035**	.101***	.140***	.060***	.057***	.059***	.060***	−.071	−.099 *
	[.018]	[.018]	[.018]	[.015]	[.015]	[.015]	[.016]	[.049]	[.051]
log(Student Enrollment)		.063***	.063***	.033***	.033***	.028***	.039***	−.181***	−.176***
		[.005]	[.004]	[.004]	[.004]	[.004]	[.005]	[.012]	[.013]
Trump 2016 Vote, %				−.360***	−.334***	−.309***		1.433***	1.572***
				[.041]	[.043]	[.056]		[.127	[.175]
asinh(Covid-19 Cases)					−.040	−.316 *		.150	1.095 *
					[.086]	[.166]		[.334	[.574]
asinh(Covid-19 Deaths)					2.811	8.030**		−4.791	−20.055 *
					[2.238]	[3.126]		[7.814]	[10.767]
R-squared	.00	.05	.18	.22	.22	.28	.36		
Sample Size	11,280	11,279	11,278	10,890	10,890	10,753	10,189	10,891	10,891
State FE	No	No	Yes	Yes	Yes	No	No	Yes	No
District Controls	No	No	No	Yes	Yes	Yes	Yes	Yes	Yes
CBSA FE	No	No	No	No	No	Yes	No	No	Yes
County FE	No	No	No	No	No	No	Yes	No	No

Notes.–Sources: MCH Data and the Stanford Education Data Archive (SEDA, 2014). The table reports the coefficients associated with regressions of an indicator for whether the school district has students learning fully remotely in fall 2020 (columns 1–7) and an ordinal variable (1 = remote, 2 = hybrid, 3 = in-person) on logged school expenditures, conditional on logged student enrollment in the school district, the county 2016 share of Trump voters, the county inverse hyperbolic sine of Covid-19 cases and deaths as of July 30th 2020, and a wide array of district-level demographic characteristics, including: the race distribution (the share who are Native American, Hispanic, Black, and White), and the share of males and females between age 25–64 in the labor force. Standard errors are clustered by county and observations are unweighted.

These dual facts suggest that teacher unions have an incentive to leverage the pandemic to lobby for greater resources even if those resources are not used to drive greater value for students.

Already, there is emerging empirical evidence that remote instruction has had other unintended consequences, especially in lower academic achievement and learning outcomes for students (Agostinelli et al., 2020; Christakis et al., 2020; Hanushek & Woessmann, 2020; Kuhfeld, Tarasawa, Johnson, Ruzek, & Lewis, 2020; McKinsey & Company, 2020; Varas et al., 2021). Recent studies have also found that school closures disrupted the child care market (Ali, Herbst, & Makridis, 2021) and that women have disproportionately dropped out of the labor market to school their children (Boesch, Grunewald, Nunn, & Palmer, 2021; Lofton, Petrosky-Nadeau, & Seitelman, 2021).[22]

We now explore whether the rise in remote instruction might help explain the deterioration in mental health among children and their lack of access to in-person learning and socialization processes (Lee, 2020; Varas et al., 2021). There is growing descriptive evidence. For example, a national survey of parents with school-aged children conducted by Gallup in May 2020 found that 29% of respondents reported that their child was "already experiencing harm" to their emotional or mental health because of social distancing and school closures.[23] Zhang et al. (2020) compared reports of student mental health problems in China, before and after the pandemic started, finding that school closures were associated with an increase in depression, self-injury, and suicidal thoughts, plans, and attempts. Hawrilenko, Kroshus, Tandon, and Christakis (2021) found that "attending school remotely during the COVID-19 pandemic was associated with disproportionate mental health consequences for older and Black and Hispanic children as well as children from families with lower income." Makridis and Wu (2021) find that the counties that weathered the pandemic the best were the ones with the greatest social capital because shared norms and trust provided a glue during times of intense social isolation. Furthermore, Musaddiq, Stange, Bacher-Hicks, and Goodman (2021) find that private schooling over the pandemic expanded most in areas where most traditional public schooling went remote, consistent with substitution between public and private schooling among families.

To investigate this hypothesis more rigorously, we introduce new data from a labor market analytics company called Emsi, which scrapes the universe of online job postings. Their job postings data are advantageous because Emsi combines information from multiple platforms, such as Indeed and CareerBuilder.[24] We focus on job postings for each county by occupation, specifically education, counselors, and social workers (identified by standard occupational classification (SOC) codes). While we recognize that these job postings are imperfect measures of mental health in an area, we nonetheless view them as a useful proxy: greater mental health challenges will manifest in a greater demand for mental health professionals, i.e. a revealed preference proxy. Here, our sample is much smaller since we move from the district level to the county level. Some states have better coverage than others, so we also control for the number of districts per county.

We consider regressions of the 2019 to 2020 growth rate of job postings for separate occupations at a county-level on the share of districts that have gone remote, controlling for the growth rate of job postings in the county and our usual set of demographic features. While we may not be able to ascribe a fully causal interpretation to our estimates since we cannot control for all possible confounders, we nonetheless believe they are informative: in particular, our variation comes from comparisons of observationally equivalent counties in the same state that vary in their share of remote districts. Our set of controls is comprehensive: in addition to revenue per membership and student enrollment at the district-level, we control for country demographics and household income.

Table 5 documents these results. In columns 1–3, we focus on the growth rate of pre-school, kindergarten, elementary, middle school, and secondary school education jobs, which we broadly label as "education" jobs. While we do not find statistically significant effects, column 3 shows that a percentage point (pp) increase in the share of remote public school districts is associated with a 0.133 pp decline in education jobs with state fixed effects (significant at a 10% level), although it is not statistically significant when state fixed effects

Table 5. The effects of remote learning on mental health providers.

Dep. var. =	Education Jobs (Growth)			Counselor Jobs (Growth)			Social Work Jobs (Growth)		
	(1)	(2)	(3)	(4)	(5)	(6)	(7)	(8)	(9)
Remote Districts, %	−.063	−.083	−.133 *	.062	.098	.118	.122	.301	.369**
	[.051]	[.081]	[.080]	[.063]	[.115]	[.129]	[.098]	[.190]	[.178]
Total Job Postings 2019–20 Growth	.782***	.772***	.754***	1.238***	1.250***	1.127***	1.261***	1.266***	.929***
	[.075]	[.095]	[.091]	[.152]	[.140]	[.167]	[.294]	[.280]	[.310]
Log(Revenue/Membership)		.064	.300***		−.099	−.023		.200	.077
		[.099]	[.113]		[.075]	[.101]		[.139]	[.169]
Log(Student Enrollment)		.025	.014		−.029	−.032		−.007	.028
		[.018]	[.023]		[.031]	[.032]		[.038]	[.038]
Trump 2016 Vote, %		−.085	−.120		.161	−.193		.552	−.212
		[.246]	[.278]		[.278]	[.325]		[.541]	[.455]
R-squared	.21	.34	.49	.35	43	.52	.09	.23	.43
Sample Size	285	282	281	279	276	275	282	279	278
County Controls	No	Yes	Yes	No	Yes	Yes	No	Yes	Yes
State FE	No	No	Yes	No	No	Yes	No	No	Yes

Notes.–Sources: MCH Data and the American Community Survey (2014–2018). The table reports the coefficients associated with regressions of the 2019 to 2020 growth rate in a county for different categories of jobs – all of the education sector (SOC = 25), counselors (SOC = 211,010), and social workers (SOC = 211,020) – on the share of districts in a county that are remote as of Fall 2020, conditional on the logged number of districts in a county (to control for measurement error in the representativeness of districts in a county), logged revenue per member, logged student enrollment in the school district, the county 2016 share of Trump voters, the county inverse hyperbolic sine of Covid-19 cases and deaths as of July 30th 2020, and a wide array of county demographic characteristics, including: logged median household income, logged median housing values, logged population, the share that are male, the age distribution (the share under age 5, ages 5–9, ages 10–14, ages 15–17, ages 18–24, ages 25–34, ages 35–44, ages 45–54, ages 55–64, ages 65–74, ages 75–85, and ages 85+), the race distribution (the share white, the share black), the share that are married, and the education distribution (the share with less than a high school degree, some college, college, and more than college, normalized to those with a high school degree). We define education jobs as the sum of "Preschool Teachers, Except Special Education" (SOC 252011), "Kindergarten Teachers, Except Special Education" (SOC 252012), "Elementary School Teachers, Except Special Education" (SOC 252021), "Middle School Teachers, Except Special and Career/Technical Education" (SOC 252022), "Career/Technical Education Teachers, Middle School" (SCC 252023), "Secondary School Teachers, Except Special and Career/Technical Education" (SOC 252031), and "Career/Technical Education Teachers, Secondary School" (SOC 252032). Standard errors are clustered by county and observations are unweighted.

are omitted. This is not surprising: public schools that were remote-only likely had fewer students to serve, as some parents moved their students to private, charter, and home schools, or did not enroll their young children in schools at all (Flanders, 2021; Musaddiq et al., 2021; Scafidi, Tutterow, & Kavanagh, 2021). Remote instruction could also theoretically require fewer teachers and might depress schools' expectations for growth.

Turning to mental health related job postings, columns 4–6 show that increases in the share of remote districts are associated with increases in the growth of the number of job postings for counselors: under the preferred specification with state fixed effects, a 1 pp rise in the share of remote districts is associated with a 0.118 pp rise in the growth rate of counselors from 2019. While our estimates are fairly similar across specifications, we do not find statistically significant results, which may largely be driven by the small sample of counties available in our school district-level data. Nonetheless, when we focus on social workers, we do find a statistically and economically significant 0.369 pp increase in the growth rate of social work job postings. Moreover, the change in our marginal effects across specifications is consistent with a causal interpretation: failing to control for demographics and other dimensions of productivity (e.g., income) will cause downwards bias since areas with greater growth in counselors and social workers are negatively selected and less likely to go remote.[25] This suggests that the switch to remote instruction may have also been associated with family ruptures that manifested in an increased demand for social workers.

Admittedly, these results on the mental health effects are preliminary, but they point toward some of the unintended consequences of the shift to remote schooling. In particular, our use of job posting data, normalized to 2019 levels, is indicative of local expectations and demand for mental health services. Our assumption is that areas with higher demand for mental health services also have a greater need for them, thereby indicating that children locally might be struggling more. However, we suggest that future research validate these results using a larger sample of counties and actual data on mental health outcomes at a local level (e.g., number of suicides).

Conclusion

The COVID-19 pandemic has had a large effect on economic and social activity, particularly for youth. While many schools had reopened for in-person classes, many still had not by spring 2021. Given that teachers unions are requesting billions of extra dollars to reopen schools, it is worth knowing if schools with more resources were more likely to open for in-person instruction to start the fall 2020 semester. That is, is there evidence that more resources made it more likely that public school districts opened for in-person instruction to start the 2020–21 academic year? These decisions have been driven more by union preferences, rather than an actual scientific basis relating to rates of local COVID-19 infections or deaths (DeAngelis & Makridis, 2021).

This study provides the first and most comprehensive evaluation of the relationship between school funding and remote versus in-person learning strategies. Exploiting variation across school districts in the same county, controlling for demographic differences across districts, we find that there is a positive association between school funding and the decision to have students learning remotely as of Fall 2020. These results are highly robust across a wide array of specifications, ranging from the inclusion of different fixed effects to demographic controls to functional forms.

Both cases are inconsistent with the view that these remote districts needed more federal funding to reopen in person. In our specification with state fixed effects, the opposite is true. We also find that the increase in remote instruction in a county was associated with an economically and statistically significant increase in the number of job postings for counselors and social workers. Cumulatively, these results suggest that remote school districts had resources than their in-person learning districts, and that the surge in remote instruction may have led to other unintended consequences for mental health among the affected learners.

In sum, our results show that, even though teacher unions have advocated heavily for additional funding and for schools to continue remote instruction over in-person instruction, the school districts that have done teaching remotely already have greater resources. Furthermore, areas with more remote districts have more mental health problems and social disruption.

There are many reasons for interest groups, like teachers' unions, to advocate for policies that do not improve social welfare. Indeed, incentives exist for interest groups to promote their own objectives, which can sometimes be at the expense of social welfare. In this sense, our results are consistent with theories of rent seeking by interest groups such as teachers' unions (Krueger, 1974; Moe, 2011; Tullock, 1967). For example, Anzia and Moe (2015) find that unions increase the cost of government and that their returns to engaging in collective bargaining are especially large in high-stakes environments. As these political economy theories apply to teachers' unions, our results suggest that unions may have viewed the deliberations over the stimulus as an opportunity to secure large-scale funds under the guise of teacher health and safety.

Our research leaves several questions for future research. First, what is the effect of school funding on learning outcomes during a crisis, like the COVID-19 pandemic? Second, how have the funds from the 2020 CARES Act been used and what is their return on investment? One of the primary concerns associated with the stimulus has been that the request for funding has not been data-driven, but rather dictated by political partisanship, incentive structures, and special interests. Third, what are the factors behind the differential degrees of adaptation to the pandemic across schools? Our research takes a step forward in beginning to understand these types of questions.

Notes

1. Map: Coronavirus and School Closures in 2019–2020. EducationWeek. Retrieved from https://www.edweek.org/leadership/map-coronavirus-and-school-closures-in-2019-2020/2020/03.
2. Agostinelli et al. (2020), for example, found that "school closures have a large and persistent effect on educational outcomes that is highly unequal" and that "high school students from poor neighborhoods suffer a learning loss of 0.4 standard deviations, whereas children from rich neighborhoods remain unscathed." Christakis et al. (2020) found that missed instruction during 2020 could be associated with an estimated 13.8 million years of life lost associated with reductions in educational attainment based on U.S. studies.
3. Provide At Least $175 billion To Stabilize Education Funding & Reopen Schools Safely. National Education Association. Retrieved from https://educationvotes.nea.org/wp-content/uploads/2020/10/Funding-PPE-one-pager-0920.pdf.
4. Weingarten, R. (2021). A road map to safely reopen our schools. American Federation of Teachers. Retrieved from https://www.aft.org/column/road-map-safely-reopen-our-schools.
5. Reconciliation Recommendations of the House Committee on Education and Labor. Congressional Budget Office Cost Estimate. Retrieved from https://www.cbo.gov/system/files/2021-02/hEdandLaborreconciliationestimate.pdf.
6. Secretary DeVos Quickly Makes Available an Additional $54 Billion in COVID Relief Aid for K-12 Students, Teachers, and Schools. U.S. Department of Education. Retrieved from https://www.ed.gov/news/press-releases/secretary-devos-quickly-makes-available-additional-54-billion-covid-relief-aid-k-12-students-teachers-and-schools.
7. CARES Act: Education Stabilization Fund. U.S. Department of Education. Retrieved from https://covid-relief-data.ed.gov/.
8. Private schools pull students away from public schools. Axios. Retrieved from https://www.axios.com/private-schools-coronavirus-public-schools-d6aaf803-d458-4301-a3a7-71364b00a5b0.html.
9. Public School Funding Per Student Averages 80% More Than Private Schools. Just Facts. Retrieved from https://www.justfactsdaily.com/public-school-funding-per-student-averages-80-more-than-private-schools.
10. U.S. K-12 Education Spending Comparisons. Educational Freedom Institute. Retrieved from http://efinstitute.org/education-spending-comparisons/.
11. Oregon's Coronavirus Education Lockdown. The Wall Street Journal. Retrieved from https://www.wsj.com/articles/oregons-coronavirus-education-lockdown-11585697080.
12. Cyber charters in Pa. keep teaching amid confusion in coronavirus shutdown order. WHYY. Retrieved from https://whyy.org/articles/cyber-charters-in-pa-keep-teaching-amid-confusion-in-coronavirus-shutdown-order/.
13. COVID-19 IMPACT: School District Status. MCH Strategic Data. Retrieved from https://www.mchdata.com/covid19/schoolclosings.
14. Back to school statistics. Fast Facts. National Center for Education Statistics. Retrieved from https://nces.ed.gov/fastfacts/display.asp?id=372#PK12_enrollment.

15. Local Education Agency (School District) Finance Survey (F-33) Data, v.1a – Provisional. Common Core of Data. National Center for Education Statistics. Retrieved from https://nces.ed.gov/ccd/files.asp#Fiscal:1,LevelId:5,SchoolYearId:32, Page:1.
16. We thank an anonymous referee for the suggestion to use district-level data. We have also experimented with county-level controls from the American Community Survey (2014–2018) through the U.S. Census Bureau, including: age, race, population, education, and household income. The limitation with these is that they become collinear when we include the county fixed effects.
17. U.S. Presidential Elections. MIT Election Data and Science Lab (MEDSL). Retrieved from https://dataverse.harvard.edu/dataset.xhtml?persistentId=doi:10.7910/DVN/VOQCHQ.
18. USA Facts. US Coronavirus Cases and Deaths. Track COVID-19 Data Daily by State and County. Retrieved from https://usafacts.org/visualizations/coronavirus-COVID-19-spread-map.
19. Table 11. Summary Tables. 2018 Public Elementary-Secondary Education Finance Data. U.S. Census Bureau. Retrieved from https://www.census.gov/data/tables/2018/econ/school-finances/secondary-education-finance.html.
20. These data do not adjust for differences in cost of living.
21. Financial Turmoil: Open or Remote? What it Means for School District Budgets. Edunomics Lab at Georgetown University. Retrieved from https://edunomicslab.org/wp-content/uploads/2021/03/Financial-Turmoil-Webinar-Mar3.pdf.
22. How COVID-19 triggered America's first female recession in 50 years. The Economist. Retrieved from https://www.economist.com/graphic-detail/2021/03/08/how-COVID-19-triggered-americas-first-female-recession-in-50-years.
23. U.S. Parents Say COVID-19 Harming Child's Mental Health. Gallup. Retrieved from https://news.gallup.com/poll/312605/parents-say-covid-harming-child-mental-health.aspx; Social Factors Most Challenging in COVID-19 Distance Learning. Gallup. Retrieved from https://news.gallup.com/poll/312566/social-factors-challenging-covid-distance-learning.aspx.
24. These data have been used in several recent papers to study the effects of stay-at-home laws and other child care quality regulations, like child-to-staff ratios, on the demand for child care labor (Ali et al., 2021a, 2021b).
25. Specifically, unobserved heterogeneity in the capabilities of a county – that is, factors that might make a county under-resourced – will be positively correlated with increases in social workers and counselors since there might be more mental health challenges. However, those unobserved factors should be negatively correlated with the ability to go remote since, by construction, they have fewer resources and going remote might be tougher.

Acknowledgment

We would like to thank Emsi, specifically Kevin Kirchner, for providing us with the job posting data.

Disclosure statement

No potential conflict of interest was reported by the author(s).

ORCID

Corey A. DeAngelis (iD) http://orcid.org/0000-0003-4431-9489
Christos A. Makridis (iD) http://orcid.org/0000-0002-6547-5897

References

Agostinelli, F., Doepke, M., Sorrenti, G., & Zilibotti, F. (2020). *When the great equalizer shuts down: Schools, peers, and parents in pandemic times* (No. w28264). National Bureau of Economic Research.

Ali, U., Herbst, C., & Makridis, C. A. (2021a). The impact of COVID-19 on the U.S. Child care market: Evidence from stay-at-home orders. *Economics of Education Review, 82*, 102094. doi:10.1016/j.econedurev.2021.102094

Ali, U., Herbst, C., & Makridis, C. A. (2021b). Minimum quality regulations and the demand for child care labor. *Under Review.*

Anzia, S. F., & Moe, T. M. (2015). Public sector unions and the costs of government. *Journal of Politics, 77*(1), 114–127. doi:10.1086/678311

Becker, G. S. (1983). A theory of competition among pressure groups for political influence. *Quarterly Journal of Economics, 98*(3), 371–400. doi:10.2307/1886017

Billingsley, S., Brandén, M., Aradhya, S., Drefahl, S., Andersson, G., & Mussino, E. (2020). *Deaths in the frontline: Occupation-specific COVID-19 mortality risks in Sweden* (Stockholm Research Reports in Demography no. 2020:36). Stockholm University.

Boesch, T., Grunewald, R., Nunn, R., & Palmer, V. (2021). *Pandemic pushes mothers of young children out of the labor force.* Federal Reserve Bank of Minneapolis. Retrieved from https://www.minneapolisfed.org/article/2021/pandemic-pushes-mothers-of-young-children-out-of-the-labor-force

Brandice Canes-Wrone, J. T., & Christos, A. 2022 Makridis Title: Partisanship on an Emerging Issue: An Analysis of Mass and Elite Responses to COVID-19.

Christakis, D. A., Van Cleve, W., & Zimmerman, F. J. (2020). Estimation of US children's educational attainment and years of life lost associated with primary school closures during the coronavirus disease 2019 pandemic. *JAMA network open, 3*(11), e2028786–e2028786. doi:10.1001/jamanetworkopen.2020.28786

Chubb, J. E., & Moe, T. M. (1988). Politics, markets, and the organization of schools. *American Political Science Review, 82*(4), 1065–1087. doi:10.2307/1961750

Courtemanche, C. J., Le, A. H., Yelowitz, A., & Zimmer, R. (2021). *School reopenings, mobility, and COVID-19 spread: Evidence from Texas* (No. w28753). National Bureau of Economic Research.

DeAngelis, C. A., & Holmes Erickson, H. (2018). What leads to successful school choice programs? A review of the theories and evidence. *Cato Journal, 38*(1), 247–263.

DeAngelis, C. A. (2020). School reopenings linked to union influence and politics, not safety. *Reason Magazine.* Retrieved from https://reason.com/2020/08/19/school-reopenings-linked-to-union-influence-and-politics-not-safety/

DeAngelis, C. A., & Makridis, C. A. (2021). Are school reopening decisions related to union influence? *Forthcoming, Social Science Quarterly, 102*(5), 2266–2284. doi:10.1111/ssqu.12955

DeGrow, B., & Rigterink, A. (2021). *Money for nothing: Most federal COVID relief went to closed classrooms.* Mackinac Center for Public Policy. Retrieved from https://www.mackinac.org/money-for-nothing-most-federal-covid-relief-went-to-closed-classrooms

Flanders, W. (2020). *Politics in the pandemic: The role of unions in school reopening decisions.* Wisconsin Institute for Law & Liberty. Retrieved from https://www.will-law.org/wp-content/uploads/2020/12/reopening-brief.pdf

Flanders, W. (2021). Opting out: Enrollment trends in response to continued public school shutdowns. *Journal of School Choice, 15*(3), 331–343. doi:10.1080/15582159.2021.1917750

Friedman, M. (1955). The role of government in education. In R. A. Solo (Ed.), *Economics and the public interest* (pp. 123–144). New Brunswick, NJ: Rutgers University Press.

Garet, M., Chan, T. H., & Sherman, J. D. (1995). *Estimates of expenditures for private K-12 schools* (National Center for Education Statistics Working Paper Series). U.S. Department of Education.

Green, E. (2021). Surge of student suicides pushes Las Vegas schools to reopen. *New York Times.* Retrieved from https://www.nytimes.com/2021/01/24/us/politics/student-suicides-nevada-coronavirus.html

Hanushek, E. A., Kain, J. F., Rivkin, S. G., & Branch, G. F. (2007). Charter school quality and parental decision making with school choice. *Journal of Public Economics, 91*(5–6), 823–848. doi:10.1016/j.jpubeco.2006.09.014

Hanushek, E. A., & Woessmann, L. (2020). *The economic impacts of learning losses.* Organisation for Economic Co-operation and Development. Retrieved from https://www.oecd.org/education/The-economic-impacts-of-coronavirus-COVID-19-learning-losses.pdf

Harris, D., Ziedan, E., & Hassig, S. (2021). *The effects of school reopenings on COVID-19 hospitalizations.* National Center on Education Access and Choice. Retrieved from https://www.reachcentered.org/uploads/technicalreport/The-Effects-of-School-Reopenings-on-COVID-19-Hospitalizations-REACH-January-2021.pdf

Hartney, M., & Finger, L. (2021). Politics, markets, and pandemics: Public education's response to COVID-19. *Perspectives on Politics,* 1–17. doi:10.1017/S1537592721000955

Hawrilenko, M., Kroshus, E., Tandon, P., & Christakis, D. (2021). The association between school closures and child mental health during COVID-19. *JAMA Network Open, 4*(9), e2124092–e2124092. doi:10.1001/jamanetworkopen.2021.24092

Henderson, M. B., Peterson, P. E., & West, M. R. (2021). Pandemic parent survey finds perverse pattern: Students are more likely to be attending school in person where Covid is spreading more rapidly: Majority of students receiving fully remote instruction; private-school students more likely to be in person full time. *Education Next, 21*(2), 34–48.

Honein, M. A., Barrios, L. C., & Brooks, J. T. (2021). Data and policy to guide opening schools safely to limit the spread of SARS-CoV-2 infection. *JAMA, 325*(9), 823. doi:10.1001/jama.2021.0374

Honein, M.A., Barrios, L.C., & Brooks, J.T. (2021). Data and Policy to Guide Opening Schools Safely to Limit the Spread of SARS-CoV-2 Infection. *Jama, 325*(9), 823–824. doi:10.1001/jama.2021.0374

Kahlenberg, R. D., & Greene, J. P. (2012). Unions and the public interest: Is collective bargaining for teachers good for students? *Education Next, 12*(1), 60–69.

Krueger, A. O. (1974). The political economy of the rent-seeking society. *The American Economic Review, 64*(3), 291–303.

Kuhfeld, M., Tarasawa, B., Johnson, A., Ruzek, E., & Lewis, K. (2020). *Learning during COVID-19: Initial findings on students' reading and math achievement and growth.* NWEA. Retrieved from https://www.nwea.org/content/uploads/2020/11/Collaborative-brief-Learning-during-COVID-19.NOV2020.pdf

Lee, J. (2020). Mental health effects of school closures during COVID-19. *The Lancet Child & Adolescent Health, 4*(6), 421. doi:10.1016/S2352-4642(20)30109-7

Lofton, O., Petrosky-Nadeau, N., & Seitelman, L. (2021, February). *Parents in a pandemic labor market.* Federal Reserve Bank of San Francisco. Retrieved from https://www.frbsf.org/economic-research/files/wp2021-04.pdf

Ludvigsson, J. F., Engerström, L., Nordenhäll, C., & Larsson, E. (2021). Open schools, COVID-19, and child and teacher morbidity in Sweden. *New England Journal of Medicine, 384*(7), 669–671. doi:10.1056/NEJMc2026670

Makridis, C. A., & McNab, B. (2020). *The Fiscal cost of COVID-19: Evidence from the states* (SSRN working paper).

Makridis, C. A., & Rothwell, J. (2020). *The real cost of political polarization: Evidence from the COVID-19 pandemic* (SSRN Working Paper). https://journals.plos.org/plosone/article?id=10.1371/journal.pone.0245135.

Makridis, C. A., & Wu, C. (2021). How social capital helps communities weather the COVID-19 pandemic. *PLoS ONE, 16*(1).

McKinsey & Company. (2020). *COVID-19 and learning loss—disparities grow and students need help*. Retrieved from https://www.mckinsey.com/industries/public-and-social-sector/our-insights/COVID-19-and-learning-loss-disparities-grow-and-students-need-help

Mitchell, W. C., & Munger, M. C. (1991). Economic models of interest groups: An introductory survey. *American Journal of Political Science, 35*(2), 512–546. doi:10.2307/2111373

Moe, T. M. (2005). Teacher unions and school board elections. *Besieged: School Boards and the Euture of Education Politics*, 254–287. https://www.jstor.org/stable/10.7864/j.ctt127xjr.

Moe, T. M. (2006). Political control and the power of the agent. *The Journal of Law, Economics, and Organization, 22*(1), 1–29. doi:10.1093/jleo/ewj011

Moe, T. M. (2011). *Special interest: Teachers unions and America's public schools*. Washington DC, USA: Brookings Institution Press.

Musaddiq, T., Stange, K., Bacher-Hicks, A., & Goodman, J. (2021). *The pandemic's effect on demand for public schools, homeschooling, and private schools* (EdWorkingPaper No. 21-463). Annenberg Institute at Brown University.

Olson, M. (1965). *The logic of collective action*. Cambridge: Harvard University Press.

Oster, E. (2020). Schools are not spreading COVID-19. This new data makes the case. *Washington Post*. Retrieved from https://www.washingtonpost.com/opinions/2020/11/20/COVID-19-schools-data-reopening-safety/

Revisiting Pediatric COVID-19 Cases in Counties with and Without School Mask Requirements—United States, July July 20 2021 Ambarish Chandra and Tracy Beth Høeg https://papers.ssrn.com/sol3/papers.cfm?abstract_id=4118566

Roza, M. (2021). *Financial turmoil: Open or remote? What it means for school district budgets*. Washington DC, USA: Georgetown University, Edunomics Lab. Retrieved from https://edunomicslab.org/wp-content/uploads/2021/03/Financial-Turmoil-Webinar-Mar3.pdf

Scafidi, B., Tutterow, R., & Kavanagh, D. (2021). This time really is different: The effect of COVID-19 on independent K-12 school enrollments. *Journal of School Choice, 15*(3), 305–330. doi:10.1080/15582159.2021.1944722

Schattschneider, E. E. (1935). *Politics, pressures and the tariff*. New York City, NY, USA: Prentice-Hall, Inc. https://www.cambridge.org/core/journals/american-political-science-review/article/abs/politics-pressures-and-the-tariff-by-e-e-schattschneider-new-york-prentcehall-inc1935-pp-xi-301/D383F25CE172E7D824179315736A9C84.

Tullock, G. (1967). The welfare costs of tariffs, monopolies, and theft. *Western Economic Journal, 5*(3), 224–232.

Umair, A., Herbst, C., & Makridis, C. A. (2021). The Impact of Covid-19 on the U.S. Child Care Market: Evidence from Stay-at-Home Orders. *Economics of Education Review, 82.*

UNICEF. (2020). *Averting a lost COVID generation*. Retrieved from https://www.unicef.org/reports/averting-lost-generation-covid19-world-childrens-day-2020-brief

Valant, J. (2020). *School reopening plans linked to politics rather than public health*. Brookings Institution. Retrieved from https://www.brookings.edu/blog/brown-center-chalkboard/2020/07/29/school-reopening-plans-linked-to-politics-rather-than-public-health/

Van Kipnis, G. (2020). *Reform the K-12 government- school monopoly: Economics and facts.* American Institute for Economic Research. Retrieved from https://www.aier.org/article/ reform-the-k-12-government-school-monopoly-economics-and-facts/

Varas, J., Menon, V., & Bellafiore, R. (2021). *What's next for schools: Balancing the costs of school closures against COVID-19 health risks.* United States Congress Joint Economic Committee. Retrieved from https://www.jec.senate.gov/public/index.cfm/republicans/ 2021/2/what-s-next-for-schools-balancing-the-costs-of-school-closures-against-COVID -19-health-risks

Zhang, L., Zhang, D., Fang, J., Wan, Y., Tao, F., & Sun, Y. (2020). Assessment of mental health of Chinese primary school students before and after school closing and opening during the COVID-19 pandemic. *JAMA Network Open, 3*(9), e2021482–e2021482. doi:10.1001/ jamanetworkopen.2020.21482

The Longer Students Were Out of School, the Less They Learned

Harry Anthony Patrinos ⓘ

ABSTRACT

COVID-19 led to school closures and emergency remote learning. This paper analyzes school closures during the pandemic using a unique data base. The determinants of the duration of school closures estimates were used to instrument school closures – stringency of lockdown and vaccination – and causally estimate the impact of duration on learning. It is estimated that for every week that schools were closed, learning levels declined by almost 1% of a standard deviation. This means that a 20 week closure, for example, would reduce learning outcomes by 0.20 standard deviation, almost one year of schooling.

Introduction

COVID-19 school closures led to emergency remote-learning systems almost immediately. At its peak, nearly 1.6 billion learners in more than 190 countries, or 94% of the world's student population, were impacted by school closures (UNESCO, 2020). Students learned less when they were remote and attending high-poverty schools, which were hit hardest (Engzell, Frey, & Verhagen, 2021). Learning losses could cost this generation of students close to $15 trillion in lifetime earnings (Psacharopoulos, Collis, Patrinos, & Vegas, 2021). Worldwide, learning losses on average amount to 0.17 of a standard deviation (Patrinos, Vegas, & Carter-Rau, 2023), equivalent to roughly a one-half year's worth of learning[1].

I estimate the impact of the duration of school closures on learning. The longer the duration of the closures, then the greater the losses. For countries with robust learning loss data, average school closures were 21 weeks, leading to average losses of 0.23 standard deviation, almost a whole year's worth of learning. Each week of closures increases learning loss by 1% of a standard deviation. This will increase the education gaps between high and low socio-economic status students (Agostinelli, Doepke, Sorrenti, & Zilibotti, 2022), especially in lower-income countries (Kaffenberger, 2021). The main lesson learned is that if COVID continues as a low-intensity pandemic, or if a similar situation arises, keeping schools open should be a priority, as the evidence shows that the health benefits of school closures seemed to have been lower than the cost of learning losses (Allen, 2022; Davies et al., 2020, 2021; Gandini et al., 2021; Lee & Raszka, 2020; Ludvigsson, 2020; Raffetti & Di Baldassarre, 2022). The priority now should be to minimize the long-term impacts of school closures.

This paper contributes to several strands of the literature. First, it adds to the growing research on the impact of school closures on learning outcomes (Agostinelli, Doepke, Sorrenti, & Zilibotti, 2022; Belot & Webbink, 2010; Haelermans, Jacobs, van der Velden, van Vugt, & van Wetten, 2022), especially on the impact of duration on learning loss (Goldhaber et al., 2022; Jack, Halloran, Okun, & Oster, 2022). It also adds to the literature on the determinants of school closure duration (Kurmann & Lalé, 2021; Nitsche & Hudde, 2022). This paper uses unique data to estimate the precise impact per week of closures on learning loss across a variety of countries. From a human capital perspective, it makes sense that school closures would lead to learning loss since schooling is a productive endeavor (Becker, 1994); therefore, extending the time away from in-person instruction should lead to a reduction in learning outcomes. Programs to support learning loss mitigation have been explored.

Data

We supplement the robust data on learning losses compiled by Patrinos, Vegas, and Carter-Rau (2023) with a few more recent studies (see Annex 1 and https://microdata.worldbank.org/index.php/catalog/5367). Most refer to primary schooling. The number of weeks of school closure is compiled from the same studies. Not all surveys are nationally representative. In the United States, the learning loss surveys are representative, but school closure duration varied state to state, and our figure represents an average. In Nepal, the data come from a study that only includes adolescent girls from one disadvantaged district. Besides school closure and duration, other possible correlates of learning loss are included. One of those controls is the pandemic itself. We include the COVID-19 death rate per 100,000 population; the lockdown stringency index; and the vaccination rate.

We also control for national income. Since there are some reports that students in private schools lost less learning than others (Arenas & Gortázar, 2022; Jack, Halloran, Okun, & Oster, 2022; Wolf et al., 2021), we include the proportion of private schools as a control. To gauge to what extent connectivity helped, we include individuals using the internet (percent of the population). To measure preexisting school quality, we include the score from the World Bank's Harmonized Learning Outcomes (HLO). To measure the

Table 1. Means and Standard Deviations.

Variable	Mean	Std. Dev.	Source
Learning loss (SD)	0.23	0.16	see Annex 1 (Learning Loss COVID-19 2020–2022)
Weeks closed	20.78	18.21	see Annex 1
Death rate/100k	152.36	125.56	Johns Hopkins Coronavirus Resource Center
GDP p/c $US	21709	22717	World Bank
Private school (%)	14.84	14.10	World Bank
Internet (%)	69.44	25.12	International Telecommunication Union
School quality	462.08	89.97	Angrist et al. 2021
Vaccination rate	59.77	32.17	Oxford Coronavirus Government Response Tracker
Stringency index	56.29	8.90	Hale et al 2021
Union density	22.38	16.05	International Labour Organization
Democracy	7.02	4.76	Polity 5

strength of trade unions, we include the trade union density rate. We use the Polity5 dataset as the measure of democracy. See Table 1 for means, standard deviations, and sources.

School closures and learning losses

The literature suggests that school closures are an efficient strategy to reduce the overall duration of a pandemic (Bin Nafisah, Alamery, Al NafesaA, Aleid, & Brazanji, 2018). The decision to close down schools was primarily aimed at mitigating the spread of COVID-19 during the beginning of the pandemic (Raffetti & Di Baldassarre, 2022). Models from previous epidemics such as influenza suggested the role of schools as places that facilitate the spreading and the possible benefit from closure (Cauchemez, Valleron, Boëlle, Flahault, & Ferguson, 2008; Jackson, Mangtani, Hawker, Olowokure, & Vynnycky, 2014). It was estimated that since school holidays could lead to a 20–29% reduction in the rate at which influenza is transmitted to children, then this might work for COVID-19. School closures delay the epidemic peak if implemented earlier but do not eliminate it. Imperfect knowledge led to no guidance on how long the duration of closures should be. Democratic countries tended to implement closures more quickly from the start of the pandemic than those with a more authoritarian regime (Cronert, 2020).

Researchers using national data – for example, the United States national achievement test, NAEP – have shown that there is a significant correlation between the length of school closures and learning loss, confirming earlier research (Barnum, 2022; Goldhaber et al., 2022; Jack, Halloran, Okun, & Oster, 2022; Lehrer-Small, 2022; West, 2022). In the United States, public schools averaged less in-person teaching than private schools. These results are explained in large part by political preferences, vaccination rates, teacher unionization rates, and local labor conditions (Kurmann & Lalé, 2021). (Teacher) unionization

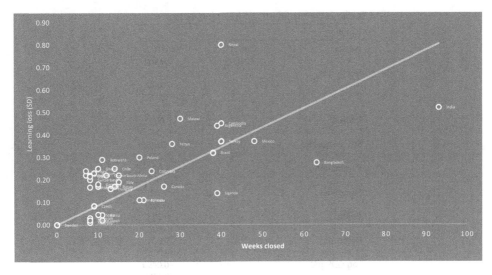

Figure 1. Learning Loss and Duration.

did not necessarily always favor school closures. For example, in Greece, teachers went on strike opposing the government's distance education plan (Lambropoulos, Vathi-Sarava, & Karatzia-Stavlioti, 2022). Nitsche and Hudde (2022) show that societal gender ideology has likely influenced school reopening policies – that is, countries with more supportive attitudes toward maternal employment reopened schools significantly sooner than those with less supportive attitudes toward maternal employment.

There is a clear link between weeks of school closures and learning loss (Figure 1). School closures were an exogenous event, brought about by the pandemic and the need to control the infection rates. Closures as part of national lockdowns were imposed. It turns out that an average learning loss of 0.23 standard deviation occurred on average with a school closure duration of 21 weeks in a sample of 41 countries (which represent 2/3 of the world's population).

We estimate learning loss, *LL*, in terms of standard deviations, as a result of weeks closed, *W*, and several control variables, X_n:

$$LL = \beta_1 W + \beta_n X_n + \varepsilon \tag{1}$$

In terms of learning loss, it makes little difference if the controls are included; all are insignificant, and they do not change the coefficient on school closures much (see Table 2). With or without controls, every week of school closures increases learning loss by almost 0.01 of a standard deviation; or 1% of a standard deviation. This means that a 20-week closure will reduce learning outcomes by the equivalent of almost ¾ of a year's worth of schooling. No other observed variable has an impact, so it is merely duration that counts.

Table 2. Determinants of Learning Loss.

Variable	1	2
Weeks	0.006***	0.007***
	(0.001)	(0.002)
Death rate		0.000
		(0.000)
Private		−0.0025
		(0.002)
Internet		0.0012
		(0.003)
School quality		−0.001
		(0.001)
Vaccination		0.001
		(0.001)
Stringency		0.000
		(0.003)
Union		0.002
		(0.002)
Democracy		0.005
		(0.006)
Log GDP p/c		−0.0499
		(0.048)
Constant	0.110*	0.568*
	(0.029)	(0.295)
Observations	41	41
R-squared	0.415	0.542

Note: Standard errors in parentheses.
*** $p<.01$, ** $p<.05$, * $p<.1$.

Given that there is little evidence that school closures reduced infection rates, then it is a high cost to pay, especially after it was deemed secure to open schools safely.

The determinants of duration of school closures

While closures were exogenous, the decision to remain closed longer was a conscious choice, especially after the American Academy of Pediatrics (2020) released, on June 24, 2020 , the first school guidance for safe in-person learning and the European Centre for Disease Prevention and Control (2020) released its recommendation on August 6, 2020 . By the time of the 2020–21 school year, it had become clear that it was possible to safely open schools (de Hoyos & Saavedra, 2021). By August 2020 evidence supported a marginal role of children as drivers of the first wave of infections (Munday et al., 2021). School reopening did not play a causal role in the increased number of new cases and hospitalizations in Italy during the period of September – October 2020 (Gandini et al., 2021), and it was not the main driver of the increased spreading of the COVID-19 UK variant in England at the beginning of 2021 (Davies et al., 2021). Moreover, school closures have no detectable effect on the contact patterns of adults (Cauchemez, Valleron, Boëlle, Flahault, & Ferguson, 2008). Other studies suggested that school closure during the 2009 H1N1 influenza epidemic in Pennsylvania would not have been worth the cost (Brown et al., 2011). Costs such as productivity losses of education professionals and parental wages outweigh the benefits in terms of decreased infection. Simulations showed that closing schools resulted in substantially higher net costs than not closing schools (Brown et al., 2011). Therefore, during the 2009 H1N1 epidemic, school closures could have resulted in substantial costs to society as the potential costs of lost productivity and childcare could have far outweighed the cost savings in preventing influenza cases. In other words, the likely beneficial impact of school closures is limited. At most, studies suggested that school closure can be a useful control measure during an influenza pandemic, particularly for reducing peak demand on health services, but they were not precise on the quantifiable benefits (Jackson, Mangtani, Hawker, Olowokure, & Vynnycky, 2014). It turned out that the actual benefits of school closure during the COVID-19 pandemic were less than expected (Raffetti & Di Baldassarre, 2022). Children have been less contagious than adults (Davies et al., 2020; Lee & Raszka, 2020; Ludvigsson, 2020). Allen (2022) calculates a number of cost/benefit ratios of lockdowns in terms of life-years saved in Canada. Using a mid-point estimate for costs and benefits of lives saved the reasonable estimate for Canada is a ratio of lost life due to lockdowns over lives saved of just 141 out of a population approaching 40 million.

We estimate the determinants of weeks closed using the same control variables. This is observational data used to estimate duration of closures by a set of independent variables. In our analysis, the only significant variables are GDP, private schooling, school quality, the stringency of lockdowns, and the vaccination rate (Table 3). Higher-income countries have a shorter duration of school closure. A low vaccination rate is associated with longer school closures. Similarly, more stringent lockdowns also increase the length of closures. Higher test scores before COVID-19 are correlated with longer school closures. This might suggest that when authorities believe their education system and therefore its distance education version is of high quality, then they tend to prolong school closures.[2] A higher proportion of private schools in a country leads to a longer duration of school closures. Interestingly, the death rate is not a factor, suggesting that school closures were not based on incidence of COVID-related fatalities.

While the unplanned closures were imposed on schools due to an external event, the duration of the closures was a choice, to some extent at least. To properly estimate the determinants of the duration and its impact on learning outcomes, then one needs to address potential endogeneity issues. Table 3 suggests that national income, private schooling, school quality, the stringency of lockdowns, and the vaccination rate are associated with the duration of school closures. Since stringency is related to closures, and quality and private schooling are related to learning outcomes, then we experiment with the vaccination rate as a possible

Table 3. Determinants of Duration of School Closures.

Variable	Coefficient
Death rate	−0.009
	(0.021)
Private	0.409**
	(0.166)
Internet	−0.0243
	(0.267)
School quality	0.139***
	(0.039)
Vaccination	−0.255**
	(0.098)
Stringency	0.486*
	(0.280)
Union	0.112
	(0.150)
Democracy	−0.355
	(0.552)
Log GDP p/c	−8.742*
	(4.566)
Constant	21.800
	(29.15)
Observations	41
R-squared	0.639

Note: Standard errors in parentheses.
*** $p<.01$, ** $p<.05$, * $p<.1$.

instrument. It could be argued that a high vaccination rate may lead to shorter school closures. A study shows that school closures can be minimized by regular testing and vaccination against COVID-19 (Colosi et al., 2022). The stringency index, a composite measure based on the strength of lockdown measures, can be used to measure how restrictive the measures were (Gros, Ounnas, & Yeung, 2021). Instrumental variables (IVs) are used to control for confounding and measurement error in observational studies. They allow for the possibility of making causal inferences with observational data. They adjust for both observed and unobserved confounding effects. We believe that the vaccination rate and the stringency index instrument for closures well and are unlikely to determine learning losses on their own. We instrument the duration of school closures using the vaccination rate and the stringency index using 2SLS. The first stage and IV results are presented in Table 4.

The vaccination rate and the stringency index turn out to be useful instruments. Since we do not have many degrees of freedom, we estimate a very parsimonious equation, explaining weeks closed with the vaccination rate. It turns out that a lower (higher) vaccination rate leads to a longer (shorter) duration of school closures, while a higher stringency index prolongs school closures. Therefore, we can tentatively conclude that the duration of school closures leads to a higher level of learning loss. In the IV estimates, a week of school closures leads to a 0.006 standard deviation increase in learning loss, just slightly higher than the OLS estimate.

Table 4. Determinants of Learning Loss.

Variable	First stage weeks closed	IV learning loss
Vaccination	−0.301**	
	(0.073)	
Stringency	1.021*	
	(0.262)	
Weeks		0.006***
		(0.002)
Constant	−18.723	0.111
	(14.567)	(0.034)
N	41	41
R-square	0.409	0.415
F-test	13.13	10.98
[p-value]	0.000	0.002
Sargan (overidentification) statistic		0.409
[p-value]		[0.5223]

Implications

In terms of learning loss, it makes little difference if the controls are included; all are insignificant. This suggests that school closures themselves were responsible for learning loss and the severity of that loss was primarily due to how long schools were kept closed. What matters is time spent in school. While pre-COVID learning levels varied considerably across countries, depending on many factors, learning happens if children go to school. Keeping schools open reduces learning losses, even in the poorest countries and in countries with low pre-COVID learning levels. This is especially important because research has found little evidence showing that school closures reduced infection rates.

Students learn less when they are not being taught in school buildings. Duration played a key role. The long-term impact may be increased education gaps, especially between students from high and low socioeconomic status.

The main lesson learned here is that if COVID continues as a low-intensity pandemic, or if a new, similar situation arises, keeping schools open should be a priority, as the evidence shows that the benefits of school closures seemed to have been lower than the cost of learning losses. However, the task at hand is to figure out how to accelerate learning and make up for the lost time. Fortunately, there are several things that work in terms of mitigating learning losses. These include online tutoring programs, which were shown to reduce learning loss significantly in several randomized controlled trials (see, for example, Carlana & La Ferrara, 2021; Gortazar, Hupkau, & Roldán, 2022; Kraft, List, Livingston, & Sadoff, 2022). A large-scale randomized trial testing low-technology interventions – SMS messages and phone calls – with parents to support their child in Botswana improved learning by 0.12 standard deviation (Angrist, Bergman, & Matsheng, 2022). Compensatory education works as well. In Tamil Nadu, India, two-thirds of the school closure learning deficit was made up within 6 months after school reopening, with a government-run after-school remediation program contributing one-quarter of the recovery (Singh, Romero, & Muralidharan, 2022). In Nigeria, a program designed to make up missed lessons during school closures led to a rebound within 2 months, and a recovery of all learning losses among students in low-cost schools (Adeniran, Okoye, Yedomiffi, & Wantchekon, 2022).

Conclusion

COVID-19 led to school closures and emergency remote-learning systems. The analysis investigated the impact of school closures using a unique data base. The determinants of the duration of school closures estimates were used to instrument school closures – stringency of lockdown and vaccination – and causally estimate the impact of duration on learning. It is concluded that for every week that schools were closed, learning levels declined by almost 1% of a standard deviation. This means that a 20 week closure, for example, would reduce learning outcomes by 0.20 standard deviation, almost one year of schooling.

The findings here could influence education policy decision-making. It would be wise for policy makers to be aware of the linkages between public health decisions – such as vaccinations – and the spillover effects on class time and learning. Such linkages have clear implications for the development of learning technologies (such as different applications for distance learning) and the resilience of learning outcomes.

Notes

1. This paper represents the opinions of the author and should not be attributed to the World Bank Group. Any errors are the fault of the author. I benefited from discussions at seminars at Wesleyan University, University of Mississippi, University of Maryland, Carleton University, University of Arkansas, GLO conference, ICFES, Global Schools Forum and FHi360. I received excellent comments from George Psacharopoulos, Robert Maranto, Xiaoxue Zhao, Chris Sakellariou, Vicente Garcia Moreno, Kevin Macdonald, Gustavo Arcia, David Marshall, Karthika Radhakrishnan-Nair, and Noah Yarrow.
2. Since we do not control for family size, then the relationship between higher test scores and longer duration school closures could be caused by smaller families. But since family size may be a proxy for development, it might be captured by GDP per capita.

Disclosure statement

No potential conflict of interest was reported by the author.

ORCID

Harry Anthony Patrinos (iD) http://orcid.org/0000-0002-4939-3568

References

Abufhele, A., Bravo, D., López Bóo, F., & Soto-Ramirez, P. 2022. Developmental losses in young children from pre-primary program closures during the COVID-19 pandemic. IZA Discussion Paper No. 15179.

Adeniran, A., Okoye, D., Yedomiffi, M. P., & Wantchekon, L. 2022. COVID-19 learning losses, parental investments, and recovery: evidence from low-cost private schools in Nigeria. RISE Working Paper Series 22/120.

Agostinelli, F., Doepke, M., Sorrenti, G., & Zilibotti, F. (2022). When the great equalizer shuts down: Schools, peers, and parents in pandemic times. *Journal of Public Economics, 206*, 104574. doi:10.1016/j.jpubeco.2021.104574

Allen, D. W. (2022). Covid-19 lockdown cost/benefits: A critical assessment of theliterature. *International Journal of the Economics of Business, 29*(1), 1–32. doi:10.1080/13571516.2021.1976051

Amelia, R., Kadarisma, G., Fitriani, N., & Ahmadi, Y. 2020. The effect of online mathematics learning on junior high school mathematic resilience during the COVID-19 pandemic. Journal of Physics: Conference Series, 5 August 2020, Cimahi, Indonesia, *1657*(1).

American Academy of Pediatrics. 2020. COVID-19 guidance for safe schools and promotion of in-person learning. https://www.aap.org

Angrist, N., Bergman, P., & Matsheng, M. (2022). Experimental evidence on learning using low-tech when school is out. *Nature Human Behavior, 6*(7), 941–950. doi:10.1038/s41562-022-01381-z

Angrist, N., Djankov, S., Goldberg, P. K., & Patrinos, H. A. (2021). Measuring human capital using global learning data. *Nature, 592*(7854), 403–408. doi:10.1038/s41586-021-03323-7

Ardington, C., Willis, G., & Kotze, J. (2021). COVID-19 learning losses: early grade reading in South Africa. *International Journal of Educational Development, 86*, 102480. doi:10.1016/j.ijedudev.2021.102480

Arenas, A., & Gortázar, L. 2022. Learning loss one year after school closures: evidence from the Basque Country. IEB Working Paper 2022/03.

Argentina, Ministerio de Educación de la Nación. 2022. Aprender 2021: Educación Primaria: informe nacional de resultados: análisis sobre los logros de aprendizaje y sus condiciones. https://www.argentina.gob.ar/sites/default/files/informe_aprender_2021_1.pdf

Asakawa, S., & Ohtake, F. 2021. Impact of temporary school closure due to COVID-19 on the academic achievement of elementary school students. Discussion Papers in Economics and Business 21-14, Osaka University, Graduate School of Economics.

Asim, S., Gera, R., & Singhal, A. (2022). *Learning Loss from Covid in Sub-Saharan Africa: Evidence from Malawi*. Washington DC: World Bank.

Barnum, M. (2022). Nation's report card: Massive drop in math scores, slide in reading linked to COVID disruption. *Chalkbeat*. https://www.chalkbeat.org/2022/10/24/23417139/naep-test-scores-pandemic-school-reopening

Becker, G. S. (1994). *Human capital revisited. In Human Capital: A Theoretical and Empirical Analysis with Special Reference to Education* (Third ed. pp. 15–28). Chicago: The University of Chicago Press.

Belot, M., & Webbink, D. (2010). Do Teacher Strikes Harm Educational Attainment of Students? *Labour, 24*(4), 391–406. doi:10.1111/j.1467-9914.2010.00494.x

Bielinski, J., Brown, R., & Wagner, K. (2021). *No Longer a Prediction: What New Data Tell Us About the Effects of 2020 Learning Disruptions*. Irvine, CA: Illuminate Education.

Bin Nafisah, S., Alamery, A. H., Al NafesaA, Aleid, B., & Brazanji, N. A. (2018). School closure during novel influenza: A systematic review. *Journal of Infection and Public Health, 11*(5), 657–661. doi:10.1016/j.jiph.2018.01.003

Birkelund, J. F., & Karlson, K. B. (2022). No Evidence of aMajor Learning Slide 14 Months into the COVID-19 Pandemic in Denmark. *European Societies*. Pre-publication.

Brown, S. T., Tai, J. H., Bailey, R. R., Cooley, P. C., Wheaton, W. D., Potter, M. A., & Lee, B. Y. (2011). Would school closure for the 2009 H1N1 influenza epidemic have been worth the cost? A computational simulation of Pennsylvania. *BioMed Central Public Health, 11*(1), 353. doi:10.1186/1471-2458-11-353

Carlana, M., & La Ferrara, E. (2021). Apart but connected: Online tutoring and student outcomes during the COVID-19 pandemic. *Social Science Research Network Electronic Journal*. doi:10.2139/ssrn.3785058

Cauchemez, S., Valleron, A. J., Boëlle, P. Y., Flahault, A., & Ferguson, N. M. (2008). Estimating the impact of school closure on influenza transmission from Sentinel data. *Nature, 452* (7188), 750–754. doi:10.1038/nature06732

Chaban, T. Y., Rameeva, R. S., Denisov, I. S., Kersha, Y. D., & Zvyagintsev, R. S. (2022). Rossiyskaya shkola v period pandemii COVID-19: Effekty pervykh dvukh voln i kachestvo obrazovaniya [Russian Schools during the COVID-19 Pandemic: Impact of the First Two Waves on the Quality of Education]. *Voprosy Obrazovaniya/Educational Studies Moscow, 1* (1), 160–188. doi:10.17323/1814-9545-2022-1-160-188

Clark, A. E., Nong, H., Zhu, H., & Zhu, R. (2021). Compensating for academic loss: Online learning and student performance during the COVID-19 pandemic. *China Economic Review, 68*, 68. doi:10.1016/j.chieco.2021.101629

Colosi, E., Bassignana, G., Contreras, D. A., Poirier, C., Boëlle, P. Y., Cauchemez, S. ... Colizza, V. (2022). Screening and vaccination against COVID-19 to minimise school closure: A modelling study. *The Lancet Infectious Diseases, 22*(7), 977–989. doi:10.1016/ S1473-3099(22)00138-4

Contini, D., Di Tommaso, M. L., Muratori, C., Piazzalunga, D., & Schiavon, L. (2022). Who lost the most? Mathematics achievement during the COVID-19 Pandemic. *The BE Journal of Economic Analysis & Policy, 22*(2), 399–408. doi:10.1515/bejeap-2021-0447

Coskun, K., & Kara, C. (2022). The impact of the COVID-19 pandemic on primary school students' mathematical reasoning skills: A mediation analysis. *London Review of Education, 20*(1), 1–15. doi:10.14324/LRE.20.1.19

Cronert, A. (2020). *Democracy, state capacity, and COVID-19 related school closures*. APSA Preprints. https://preprints.apsanet.org/engage/apsa/article-details/5ea8501b68bfcc00122e96ac

Davies, N. G., Abbott, S., Barnard, R. C., Jarvis, C. I., Kucharski, A. J., Munday, J. D. ... Washburne, A. D. (2021). Estimated transmissibility and impact of SARS-CoV-2 lineage B.1.1.7 in England. *Science, 372*(6538), 1–10. doi:10.1126/science.abg3055

Davies, N. G., Klepac, P., Liu, Y., Prem, K., Jit, M., Eggo, R. M., & Eggo, R. M. (2020). Age-dependent effects in the transmission and control of COVID-19 epidemics. *Nature Medicine, 26*(8), 1205–1211. doi:10.1038/s41591-020-0962-9

de Hoyos, R., & Saavedra, J. (2021). *It is time to return to learning*. World Bank. https://blogs. worldbank.org/education/it-time-return-learning

Domingue, B. W., Hough, H. J., Lang, D., & Yeatman, J. (2021). *Changing Patterns of Growth in Oral Reading Fluency During the COVID-19 Pandemic—Policy Brief*. Policy Analysis for California Education (PACE).

Education, W. (2021). Measuring impact of COVID-19 on learning in Rural Kenya. https:// www.whizzeducation.com/wp-content/uploads/Kenya-Covid-Impact-SCREEN.pdf

Education Policy Institute. (2021). *Understanding progress in the 2020/21 academic year: Interim findings.* London: Department for Education UK. Renaissance Learning.

Engzell, P., Frey, A., & Verhagen, M. 2021. Learning loss due to school closures during the COVID-19 pandemic. *Proceedings of the National Academy of Sciences. 118*(17): 1–7.

European Centre for Disease Prevention and Control. (2020). *COVID-19 in children and the role of school settings in COVID-19 transmission.* Stockholm: ECDC.

Gajderowicz, T. J., Jakubowski, M. J., Patrinos, H. A., & Wrona, S. M., 2022. Capturing the Educational and Economic Impacts of School Closures in Poland. World Bank Policy Research Working Paper No. 10253.

Gambi, L., & de Witte, K. 2021. The resiliency of school outcomes after the COVID-19 pandemic. Standardised test scores and inequality one year after long term school closures. FEB Research Report Department of Economics.

Gandini, S., Rainisio, M., Iannuzzo, M. L., Bellerba, F., Cecconi, F., & Scorrano, L. (2021). A cross-sectional and prospective cohort study of the role of schools in the SARS-CoV-2 second wave in Italy. *Lancet Regional Health-Europe, 5.* doi:10.1016/j.lanepe.2021.100092

Georgiou, G. (2021). Covid-19's impact on children's reading scores: Data trends and complementary interview. *The Reading League Journal, 2*(2), 3–33.

Goldhaber, D., Kane, T., McEachin, A., Morton, E., Patterson, T., & Staiger, D. 2022. The consequences of remote and hybrid instruction during the pandemic. NBER Working Paper No. w30010.

Gore, J., Fray, L., Miller, A., Harris, J., & Taggart, W. (2021). The impact of COVID-19 on student learning in New South Wales primary schools: An empirical study. *The Australian Educational Researcher, 48*(4), 605–637. doi:10.1007/s13384-021-00436-w

Gortazar, L., Hupkau, C., & Roldán, A. 2022. Online tutoring works: Experimental evidence from a program with vulnerable children. ESADE Center for Economic Policy and School of Public Policy, Spain, Working Paper (2).

Gros, D., Ounnas, A., & Yeung, T. Y. C. 2021. A new COVID policy stringency index for Europe. *COVID Economics, 66,* 115–137.

Haelermans, C., Jacobs, M., van der Velden, R., van Vugt, L., & van Wetten, S. 2022. Inequality in the effects of primary school closures due to the COVID-19 pandemic: Evidence from the Netherlands. *AEA Papers and Proceedings, 112:* 303–307.

Hale, T., Angrist, N., Goldszmidt, R., Kira, B., Petherick, A., Phillips, T. . . . Tatlow, H. (2021). A global panel database of pandemic policies (Oxford COVID-19 government response tracker). *Nature Human Behaviour, 5*(4), 529–538. doi:10.1038/s41562-021-01079-8

Hallin, A. E., Danielsson, H., Nordström, T., & Fälth, L. (2022). No learning loss in Sweden during the pandemic: Evidence from primary school reading assessments. *International Journal of Educational Research, 114,* 114. doi:10.1016/j.ijer.2022.102011

Hassan, H., Islam, A., Siddique, A., & Choon Wang, L. (2021). *Telementoring and home-schooling during school closures: A randomized experiment in rural Bangladesh* (No. 13). Munich: TUM School of Governance at the Technical University of Munich.

Hevia, F. J., Vergara-Lope Tristan, S., Velásquez-Durán, A., & Calderón Martín Del Campo, D. (2021). Estimation of the fundamental learning loss and learning poverty related to COVID-19 pandemic in Mexico. *International Journal of Educational Development, 88,* 102515. doi:10.1016/j.ijedudev.2021.102515

Jack, R., Halloran, C., Okun, J., & Oster, E. (2022). Pandemic schooling mode and student test scores: evidence from U.S. School Districts. *American Economic Review: Insights,* 1–28.

Jackson, C., Mangtani, P., Hawker, J., Olowokure, B., & Vynnycky, E. (2014). The effects of school closures on influenza outbreaks and pandemics: Systematic review of simulation studies. *PloS One, 9*(5), e97297. doi:10.1371/journal.pone.0097297

Kaffenberger, M. (2021). Modelling the long-run learning impact of the Covid-19 learning shock: Actions to (more than) mitigate loss. *International Journal of Educational Development, 81*, 102326. doi:10.1016/j.ijedudev.2020.102326

Kim, J., Rose, P., Tirunch, D. T., Sabates, R., & Woldehanna, T. (2021). Learning Inequalities Widen following COVID-19 school closures in Ethiopia. *Research on Improving Systems of Education (Rise).* https://riseprogramme.org/blog/learning-inequalities-widen-COVID-19-Ethiopia

Kogan, V., & Lavertu, S. (2021). *The COVID-19 pandemic and student achievement on Ohio's third-grade English language arts assessment.* Columbus: Ohio State University.

Korbel, V., & Prokop, D. (2021). *Czech students lost 3 months of learning after a year of the COVID-19 pandemic.* Prague: PAQ Research.

Kraft, M. A., List, J. A., Livingston, J. A., & Sadoff, S. 2022, . Online tutoring by college volunteers: Experimental evidence from a pilot program *AEA Papers and Proceedings, 112*: 614–618.

Kuhfeld, L. K., Ruzek, E., & McEachin, A. (2021). *Learning during COVID-19: Reading and math achievement in the 2020-21 school year.* Portland: NWEA.

Kurmann, A., & Lalé, E. 2021. School closures and effective in-person Learning during COVID-19: When, where, and for whom. School of Economics Working Paper Series 2021-18. LeBow College of Business Drexel University.

Lambropoulos, H., Vathi-Sarava, P., & Karatzia-Stavlioti, E. (2022). The impact of the COVID-19 Pandemic on Learning in Greece: Investigation of the University Entrance Exams. *European Journal of Education Studies, 9*(4), 67–89. doi:10.46827/ejes.v9i4.4230

Lee, B., & Raszka, W. V. (2020). COVID-19 Transmission and Children: The Child is Not to Blame. *Pediatrics, 146*, 1–3.

Lehrer-Small, A. 2022. Strong Link in Big City Districts' 4th-Grade Math Scores to School Closures. The 74. https://www.the74million.org/article/strong-link-in-big-city-districts-4th-grade-math-scores-to-school-closures/

Lerkkanen, M. K., Pakarinen, E., Salminen, J., & Torppa, M. (2022). Reading and math skills development among Finnish primary school children before and after COVID-19 school closure. *Reading and Writing, 36*, 263–288.

Lewis, K., Kuhfeld, M., Ruzek, E., & McEachin, A. (2021). *Learning during COVID-19: Reading and math achievement in the 2020-21 school year.* Portland: Center for School and Student Progress.

Lichand, G., Doria, C. A., & Leal-Neto, O. (2022). The impacts of remote learning in secondary education during the pandemic in Brazil. *Nature Human Behaviour, 6*, 1079–1086.

Locke, V. N., Patarapichayatham, C., & Lewis, S. (2021). *Learning Loss in Reading and Math in US Schools Due to the COVID-19 Pandemic.* Dallas, TX: Istation.

Ludewig, U., Kleinkorres, R., Schaufelberger, R., Schlitter, T., Lorenz, R., Koenig, C., and McElvany, N. (2022). COVID-19 Pandemic and Student Reading Achievement – Findings from a School Panel Study *Frontiers in Psychology, 13*, 1–15.

Ludvigsson, J. F. (2020). Children are unlikely to be the main drivers of the COVID-19 pandemic—A systematic review. *Acta paediatrica, 109*(8), 1525–1530.

Molnár, G., & Hermann, Z. (2023). Short- and long-term effects of COVID-related kindergarten and school closures on first- to eighth-grade students' school readiness skills and mathematics, reading and science learning. *Learning and Instruction, 83*, 1–13.

Munday, J. D., Sherratt, K., Meakin, S., Endo, A., Pearson, C. A. B., Hellewell, J. . . . Wallinga, J. (2021). Implications of the school-household network structure on SARS-CoV-2 transmission under school reopening strategies in England. *Nature Communications, 12*, 1942.

Nitsche, N., & Hudde, A. (2022). *Countries embracing maternal employment opened schools sooner after Covid-19 lockdowns* No. WP-2022-008. Rostock, Germany: Max Planck Institute for Demographic Research.

Patrinos, H., Vegas, E., & Carter-Rau, R. (2023). An Analysis of COVID-19 Student Learning Loss. In Jonathan Hamilton (Ed.), *The Oxford Research Encyclopedia of Economics and Finance*. Oxford: Oxford University Press.

Pier, L., Christian, M., Tymeson, H., & Meyer, R. H. (2021). COVID-19 Impacts on Student Learning: Evidence from Interim Assessments in California. In *Policy Analysis for California Education*. Stanford: PACE.

Psacharopoulos, G., Collis, V., Patrinos, H. A., & Vegas, E. (2021). The COVID-19 Cost of School Closures in Earnings and Income across the World. *Comparative Education Review, 65*(2), 271–287.

Raffetti, E., & Di Baldassarre, G. (2022). Do the Benefits of School Closure Outweigh Its Costs? *International Journal of Environmental Research and Public Health, 19*(5), 1–8.

Singh, A., Romero, M., & Muralidharan, K. 2022. COVID-19 Learning Loss and Recovery: Panel Data Evidence from India. RISE Working Paper Series. 22/112.

Skar, G. B. U., Graham, S., & Huebner, A. (2021). Learning Loss During the COVID-19 Pandemic and the Impact of Emergency Remote Instruction on First Grade Students' Writing: A Natural Experiment. *Journal of Educational Psychology, 114*(7), 1553–1566.

Tech, T. (2022). *Independent Evaluation of the Girls' Education Challenge Phase II (GEC II) – Evaluation Study 1: Effects of Covid-19 on Access and Learning in the GEC II Final Report* (PO 10019). Reading: Tetra Tech. https://girlseducationchallenge.org/media/as3lwuzx/gec-ii-evaluation-study-1-access-and-learning-final-report_february-2022.pdf

Thorn, W., & Vincent-Lancrin, S. (2021). *Schooling During a Pandemic: The Experience and Outcomes of Schoolchildren During the First Round of COVID-19 Lockdowns*. Paris: OECD.

Tomasik, M., Helbling, L., & Moser, U. (2020). Educational gains of in-person vs. distance learning in primary and secondary schools: A natural experiment during the COVID-19 pandemic 29 school closures in Switzerland. *International Journal of Psychology, 56*(4), 566–576.

UNESCO. (2020). UN Secretary-General warns of education catastrophe, pointing to UNESCO estimate of 24million learners at risk of dropping out. https://www.unesco.org/en/articles/un-secretary-general-warns-education-catastrophe-pointing-unesco-estimate-24-million-learners-risk-0

UNICEF. 2022. Learning Loss in the Covid-19 Pandemic Era: Evidence from the 2016-2021 Grade Six National Learning Assessment in Cambodia: Supplementary Technical Report for the 2021 Grade Six National Learning Assessment.

Uwezo, U. 2021. Are Our Children Learning? Illuminating the Covid-19 Learning Losses and Gains in Uganda. Uwezo National Learning Assessment Report, 2021. Kampala: Uwezo Uganda.

Vegas, E. (2022). *COVID-19's impact on learning losses and learning inequality in Colombia* (p. 599). Washington: Center for Universal Education at Brookings.

West, M. R. 2022. Nation's Report Card Shows Steep Declines in Student Learning. Education Next.

Wolf, S., Aurino, E., Suntheimer, N., Avornyo, E., Tsinigo, E., Jordan, J. . . . Behrman, J. R. 2021. Learning in the Time of a Pandemic and Implications for Returning to School: Effects of COVID-19 in Ghana. CPRE Working Papers.

Yarrow, N. B., Kim, H., Yoo, J., & Pfutze, T. (2022). *EdTech in COVID Korea: Learning with Inequality* (Innovation and Technology Note Series No. 7). Washington: World Bank.

Annex 1: Learning loss database

Country	Average learning losses (SD)	Weeks closed	Sources
Nepal	0.80	40	Tech (2022)
India	0.52	93	Singh, Romero, and Muralidharan (2022)
Malawi	0.47	30	Asim, Gera, and Singhal (2022)
Cambodia	0.45	40	UNICEF (2022)
Argentina	0.44	39	Argentina, Ministerio de Educación de la Nación (2022)
Mexico	0.37	48	Hevia, Vergara-Lope Tristan, Velásquez-Durán, and Calderón Martín Del Campo (2021)
Türkiye	0.37	40	Coskun and Kara (2022)
Kenya	0.36	28	Education (2021)
Brazil	0.32	38	Lichand, Doria, and Leal-Neto (2022)
Poland	0.30	20	Gajderowicz, Jakubowski, Patrinos, and Wrona (2022)
Botswana	0.29	11	Angrist, Bergman, and Matsheng (2022)
Bangladesh	0.28	63	Hassan, Islam, Siddique, and Choon Wang (2021)
Chile	0.25	14	Abufhele, Bravo, López Bóo, and Soto-Ramirez (2022)
Ghana	0.25	10	Wolf et al. (2021)
Colombia	0.24	23	Vegas (2022)
Norway	0.24	7	Skar, Graham, and Huebner (2021)
Belgium	0.23	9	Gambi and de Witte (2021)
China	0.22	7	Clark, Nong, Zhu, and Zhu (2021)
Finland	0.22	8	Lerkkanen, Pakarinen, Salminen, and Torppa (2022)
Greece	0.22	12	Lambropoulos, Vathi-Sarava, and Karatzia-Stavlioti (2022)
South Africa	0.22	15	Ardington, Willis, and Kotze (2021)
United States	0.22	8	Bielinski, Brown, and Wagner (2021); Domingue, Hough, Lang, and Yeatman (2021); Kogan and Lavertu (2021); Kuhfeld, Ruzek, and McEachin (2021); Lewis, Kuhfeld, Ruzek, and McEachin (2021); Locke, Patarapichayatham, and Lewis (2021); Pier, Christian, Tymeson, and Meyer (2021)
Switzerland	0.20	8	Tomasik, Helbling, and Moser (2020)
Italy	0.19	15	Contini, Di Tommaso, Muratori, Piazzalunga, and Schiavon (2022)
Germany	0.18	10	Ludewig et al. (2022)
Canada	0.17	26	Georgiou (2021)
England	0.17	10	Education Policy Institute (2021)
Netherlands	0.17	8	Haelermans, Jacobs, van der Velden, van Vugt, and van Wetten (2022)
Russian Federation	0.17	14	Chaban, Rameeva, Denisov, Kersha, and Zvyagintsev (2022)
Hungary	0.16	13	Molnár and Hermann (2023)
Uganda	0.14	39	Uwezo (2021)
Ethiopia	0.11	21	Kim, Rose, Tirunch, Sabates, and Woldehanna (2021)
Indonesia	0.11	20	Amelia, Kadarisma, Fitriani, and Ahmadi (2020)
Czechia	0.08	9	Korbel and Prokop (2021)
Spain	0.05	10	Arenas and Gortázar (2022)
Korea, Rep.	0.04	11	Yarrow, Kim, Yoo, and Pfutze (2022)
Denmark	0.03	8	Birkelund and Karlson (2022)
France	0.02	8	Thorn and Vincent-Lancrin (2021)
Japan	0.02	11	Asakawa and Ohtake (2021)
Australia	0.01	8	Gore, Fray, Miller, Harris, and Taggart (2021)
Sweden	0.00	0	Hallin, Danielsson, Nordström, and Fälth (2022)

Note: There could be considerable regional variability in the closure figures, especially in federal countries, such as the United States. Figures reported here consider full closures only.

COVID-19 and School Closures: A Narrative Review of Pediatric Mental Health Impacts

David T. Marshall (ID)

ABSTRACT

School closures were part of a larger COVID-19 mitigation effort. However, policymakers over-weighted concerns about the virus to the neglect of other aspects of pediatric health, including mental health. This narrative review summarizes findings from 40 studies. School closures appear to have been an ineffective mitigation strategy, yet children and adolescents experienced increased anxiety, depression, and loneliness, as well as an overall reduction of wellbeing. Suicidal ideation and incidence increased as well. Connecting with family and friends, even if virtually, improved these outcomes. Females and those living in poverty experienced worse mental health outcomes compared to their peers.

The SARS-CoV-2 (COVID-19) novel coronavirus pandemic that emerged in late 2019 affected all facets of life and schooling was no exception. Across the globe, schools were closed as part of a larger effort to curb the spread of COVID-19. Although some believed the disruption would be brief, schools remained closed in the United States for the duration of the 2019–2020 school year (Marshall & Bradley-Dorsey, 2022). Compared to countries in Europe and Asia, schools in the United States were much slower to return to in-person learning (Maranto, Queiroz, Melo, & Glenn, 2022; National Academies of Sciences, Engineering, and Medicine, 2020). The extent to which schools reopened for in-person learning for the 2020–2021 school year in the United States varied widely by context (Marshall & Bradley-Dorsey, 2020). Social psychologist Jonathan Haidt (2023) has argued that the teen mental health crisis began around 2012, fueled by smartphones and social media. Even if these trends predated the pandemic, they were exacerbated during the crisis by policy decisions that limited social interaction like lockdowns and school closures; adolescents were forced to live and learn in a manner that was further mediated by screens.

Compared to adults, children who contracted COVID-19 were much more likely to be asymptomatic or have mild symptoms and were far less likely to go to the hospital or die from the virus (Bhopal, Bhopal, & Bhopal, 2020;

European Centre for Disease Prevention and Control, 2020; Halleemunnissa, Didel, Swami, Singh, & Vyas, 2021; Lee, Hu, Chen, Huang, & Hsueh, 2020). A meta-analysis of 38 studies found that approximately half of all cases in children and adolescents resulted in mild symptoms or no symptoms at all, while only 1.2% of cases were critical (de Souza, Nada, Nogueira, Pereira, & Brandão, 2020). Children who were at the greatest risk had underlying conditions including Type 1 Diabetes, congenital cardiac or circulatory issues, and obesity (Kompaniyets et al., 2021). As of January 29, 2023, individuals under the age of 18 accounted for 1460 (0.13%) of the 1,101,953 deaths involving COVID-19 in the United States (National Center for Health Statistics [NCHS], 2023). Children are not at great risk from COVID-19, especially if they do not have underlying conditions. However, too often it seemed as if decisions about whether to close or reopen schools for in-person learning were made in a manner that focused solely on COVID-19-related impacts, neglecting other matters of pediatric health including mental health (Pfefferbaum, 2021).

Method

As of this writing, school closures are not being widely used as a tool to combat the virus; however, as new variants of COVID-19 and future pandemics emerge, it is important to understand the impact that closing schools had – both in terms of their effectiveness in COVID-19 mitigation, as well as the effect they had on the students whose education was disrupted. This narrative review summarizes findings from 40 academic studies related to pediatric mental health impacts, which were identified through searches of PubMed and the author's own files with the search terms "school closures," "COVID-19," and "coronavirus." All articles on the topic of pediatric or adolescent mental health were screened for inclusion. Only papers published in English were reviewed.

COVID-19 school closures

The logic of closing schools is rather straight-forward: schools are sites where hundreds of people gather, and they hold the potential to be epicenters of viral spread. Pivoting to remote learning allowed instruction to continue while teachers and students were physically apart, reducing the likelihood of COVID-19 spread. The decision to close schools privileged safety over learning. However, evidence suggests that schools were not vectors of transmission of the COVID-19 virus (Heavey, Casey, Kelly, Kelly, & McDarby, 2020; Xu et al., 2020). Auger et al. (2020) found that U.S. states that initially closed their schools earlier when rates of viral transmission were low saw the largest decrease in cases and associated deaths. However, studies conducted since the initial outbreak have found no association between a school's learning modality (e. g., in-person, hybrid, remote) and COVID-19 incidence or hospitalization rates (Espinito & Principi, 2020; Harris, Ziedan, & Hassig, 2021; Iwata, Doi, & Miyakoshi, 2020; Michelson & Samuels-Kalow, 2021; Varma et al., 2021). This can partly be explained by the fact that children do not exist in a vacuum where they are either in school or at home in isolation. When schools were closed, many children were in commercial care and still in contact with others, and especially for children of single parents or frontline workers, school closures made it more likely that they would be around grandparents or more vulnerable members of the population (Bourne, 2021). Overall, school closures have been an ineffective mitigation strategy for reducing adverse COVID-19 outcomes and it is worth considering the existing literature on other areas of pediatric health.

Pediatric mental health and school closures

Although COVID-19 is less harmful to children, the pandemic led to pediatric mental health that was much worse (Chu & Lake, 2021; Lui, Bao, Huang, Shi, & Lu, 2020; Naff, Williams, Furman-Darby, & Yeong, 2022; Stewart, Vasudeva, Van Dyke, & Poss, 2021; Van Lancker & Parolin, 2020). The lives of children and adolescents were disrupted severely during the pandemic. Structures and routines prior to the pandemic were disrupted, and people with whom children were accustomed to interacting were at least temporarily not as accessible. The loss of normalcy led to a sense of isolation and loneliness (Hawrilenko, Kroshus, Tandon, & Christakis, 2021; Isumi, Doi, Yamaoka, Takahashi, & Fujiwara, 2020; Magson et al., 2021; Salzano et al., 2021). At the same time mental health services were needed most among youth, the number of children and adolescents seeking help was reduced in some areas. Researchers compared Canadian child mental health assessments from 2018 and 2019 to those from 2020 and found that the number of assessments declined during the pandemic (Stewart, Vasudeva, Van Dyke, & Poss, 2021). The decrease was the greatest among patients from low-income households.

Students who attended school in person fared better in terms of their mental health than those who learned remotely during the pandemic. Hawrilenko, Kroshus, Tandon, and Christakis (2021) explored the mental health outcomes of U.S. students, comparing those who attended school remotely with those who attended in person during the 2020–2021 school year. They found that older students attending remotely struggled with their mental health more than students attending school in person. Black and Hispanic children, as well as those living in poverty also experienced more adverse mental health outcomes. Students living in higher concentrations of poverty were also less likely to have the requisite resources to engage in remote learning and more likely to have basic needs unmet (Hawrilenko, Kroshus, Tandon, & Christakis, 2021; Marshall et al., 2020).

Children and adolescents experienced greater anxiety, depression, and loneliness during school closures than they did prior to the pandemic (Bignardi et al., 2020; Duan et al., 2020; Kilincel, Kilincel, Muratdagi, Aydin, & Usta, 2021; Pisano et al., 2021; Tan, 2021). Duan et al. (2020) found that anxiety positively correlated with depression during the early months of the pandemic. Survey research conducted in China in March 2020 found that anxiety and depression were among the most prevalent symptoms found in children, with almost one-fourth of students reporting experiencing anxiety (Tang, Xiang, Cheung, & Xiang, 2020). A systematic review of the literature found that the duration of loneliness is correlated with mental health symptoms (Loades et al., 2020). Brooks et al. (2020) made a similar claim in their review of the evidence on the impact of quarantines on mental health. There was a sharp increase in teen suicide in the months following COVID-19 school closures and lockdowns (Hou, Mao, Dong, Cai, & Deng, 2020). This was especially true for adolescent females, for whom incidence of suicide increased as much as 50% from the year prior (Yard et al., 2021). Incidence of suicide spiked in May 2020, compared to March 2020. Interaction terms of month and school closure, however, were not found to be significant.

The influence of others

The ability to have positive interpersonal experiences reduced negative mental health impacts associated with the pandemic. In some cases, the lockdowns and school closures provided an opportunity for families to strengthen their relationships, and this was associated with positive mental health outcomes (Penner, Ortiz, & Sharp, 2021). Ellis, Dumas, and Forbes (2020) found a relationship between spending time with family and connecting with friends virtually during school closures and lower levels of depression. Similarly, Ng, Cosma, Svacina, Boniel-Nissim, and Badura (2021) found that 79% of adolescents in the Czech Republic reported positive interactions with family during school closures; however, girls reported reduced levels of mental well-being compared to boys. Student athletes who connected with their teammates during this time reported better mental health and well-being than those who did not (Grauspensperger, Benson, Kilmer, & Evans, 2020).

Studies exploring the impact of social media on pediatric mental health yielded mostly negative findings. A meta-analysis of 38 studies found a positive relationship between social media use and ill-being (Marciano, Ostroumova, Schulz, & Camerini, 2022), which is concerning given the elevated use of social media during the pandemic (Haidt, 2023). Ellis, Dumas, and Forbes (2020) found that social media use was related to increased loneliness and depression. Tan's (2021) systematic review of the literature echoed these findings. Survey research in the Gaza Strip found that social media use led to increased fear and panic among students, with female students psychologically affected more than males (Radwan, Radwan, & Radwan, 2020). However, Magis-Weinburg, Gys, Berger, Dornoff, and Dahl's (2021) longitudinal work with Peruvian adolescents suggests that social media can be either positive or negative, depending on how it is being used. Their findings suggest that students experienced more positive online experiences than negative. Negative online experiences were found to be positively related with loneliness whereas positive online experiences were found to be negatively related. Naff, Williams, Furman-Darby, and Yeong's (2022) systematic review of the literature found that while social media use was not a sufficient substitution for in person interactions, moderate use of social media was a positive coping strategy for youth during the pandemic. Given that almost all peer interactions moved from in person to digital during school closures, these more nuanced findings are important to recognize.

Student mental health and learning

Student mental health is important in and of itself. However, it is also foundational for learning. As Rossen and Cowan (2014) note, "Addressing student mental health is a prerequisite to learning and achievement, not an add-on or extracurricular luxury" (p. 8). Evidence suggests that students who learned remotely for longer periods of time suffered the greatest learning loss (Donnelly & Patrinos, 2022; Duckworth et al., 2021; Engzell, Frey, & Verhagen, 2021; Halloran, Jack, Okun, & Oster, 2021; Patrinos, 2023; Patrinos, Vegas, & Carter-Rau, 2022). Reckoning with the impact that the pandemic and associated lockdowns and school closures had on student mental health is an important part of addressing academic deficiencies. Although the overall trendlines are clear, it is worth noting that it is likely the case that certain groups of students with supportive home situations thrived during school closures and remote learning (e.g., introverts, students who were bullied in school). More research should be done to explore that possibility.

Conclusion

School closures were implemented at the start of the COVID-19 pandemic as part of a wider effort to slow the spread of the virus. Public policy always involves tradeoffs, and in the case of school closures, policymakers overweighted concerns about COVID-19 to the neglect of pediatric mental health. This especially became clear as evidence suggested that keeping schools closed was not an effective mitigation strategy against viral spread. During school closures, children and adolescents experienced increased anxiety, depression, and loneliness. Suicidal ideation and incidence increased as well. Connecting with family and friends, even if virtually, improved these outcomes, while social media use yielded mixed findings. Females and those living in poverty experienced worse mental health outcomes compared to their peers. It should be noted that impacts due to school closures cannot always be separated from those stemming from more general government lockdowns.

The central tradeoff in the policy decision to close schools was that it would help reduce COVID-19 spread, likely at the risk of reduced learning as well. However, the tradeoff failed. While students learned less and struggled with mental health while schools were closed, the anticipated benefit of reduced viral spread never transpired. Extended school closures as a policy response to COVID-19 were not particularly effective as a mitigation strategy, and they came with great costs in terms of the mental health of students. Policymakers should approach future pandemics and crises with more prudence and more fully consider the tradeoffs that exist when considering whether to close schools.

Acknowledgments

I am grateful to Harry Partrinos at the World Bank and Leanne Marshall at Auburn University for their feedback on this paper. This work is much improved because of their insights.

Disclosure statement

No potential conflict of interest was reported by the author.

ORCID

David T. Marshall ⓘ http://orcid.org/0000-0003-1467-7656

References

Auger, K. A., Shah, S. S., Richardson, T., Hartley, D., Hall, M., Warniment, A., & Timmons, K. (2020). Associations between statewide school closures and COVID-19 incidence and mortality in the US. *JAMA, 324*(9), 859–870. doi:10.1001/jama.2020.14348

Bhopal, S., Bhopal, J., & Bhopal, R. (2020). Children's mortality from COVID-19 compared with all-deaths and other relevant causes of death: Epidemiological information for decision-making by parents, teachers, clinicians and policymakers. *Public Health, 185*, 19–20. doi:10.1016/j.puhe.2020.05.047

Bignardi, G., Dalmaijer, E. S., Anwyl-Irvine, A. L., Smith, T. A., Siugdaite, R., Uh, S., & Astle, D. E. (2020). Longitudinal increases in childhood depression symptoms during the COVID-19 lockdown. *Archives of Disease in Childhood, 106*(8), 791–797. doi:10.1136/arch dischild-2020-320372

Bourne, R. A. (2021). *Economics in one virus: An introduction to economic reasoning through COVID-19*. Washington, DC: Cato Institute.

Brooks, S. K., Webster, R. K., Smith, L. E., Woodland, L., Wessely, S., Greenberg, N., & Rubin, G. J. (2020). The psychological impact of quarantine and how to reduce it: Rapid review of the evidence. *The Lancet, 395*(10227), 912–920. doi:10.1016/S0140-6736(20)30460-8

Chu, L., & Lake, R. (2021). *The kids are (really) not alright: A synthesis of COVID-19 student surveys.* Center for Reinventing Public Education. https://crpe.org/publications/kids-are-really-not-alright-synthesis-covid-19-student-surveys

de Souza, T. H., Nada, J. A., Nogueira, R. J. N., Pereira, R. M., & Brandão, M. B. (2020). Clinical manifestations of children with COVID-19: A systematic review. *Pediatric Pulmonology, 55* (8), 1892–1899. doi:10.1002/ppul.24885

Donnelly, R., & Patrinos, H. A. (2022). Learning loss during COVID-19: An early systematic review. *Prospects, 51*(4), 601–609. doi:10.1007/s11125-021-095582-6

Duan, L., Shao, X., Wang, Y., Huang, Y., Miao, J., Yang, X., & Zhu, G. (2020). An investigation of mental health status of children and adolescents in China during the outbreak of COVID-19. *Journal of Affective Disorders, 275,* 112–118. doi:10.1016/j.jad.2020.06.029

Duckworth, A. L., Kautz, T., Defnet, A., Satlof-Bedrick, E., Talamas, S., Lira, B., & Steinberg, L. (2021). Students attending school remotely suffer socially, emotionally, and academically. *Educational Researcher, 50*(7), 479–482. doi:10.3102/0013189X211031551

Ellis, W. E., Dumas, T. M., & Forbes, L. M. (2020). Physically isolated but socially connected: Psychological adjustment and stress among adolescents during the initial COVID-19 crisis. *Canadian Journal of Behaviroural Science, 52*(3), 177–187. doi:10.1037/cbs0000215

Engzell, P., Frey, A., & Verhagen, M. D. (2021). Learning loss due to school closures during the COVID-19 pandemic. *PNAS, 118*(17), e2022376118. doi:10.1073/pnas.2022376118

Espinito, S., & Principi, N. (2020). School closure during the coronavirus disease 2019 (COVID-19) pandemic. *JAMA Pediatrics, 174*(1), 921–922. doi:10.1001/jamapediatrics.2020.1892

European Centre for Disease Prevention and Control. (2020). Outbreak of novel coronavirus 2019 (COVID-19): Increased transmission globally – fifth update. Author. https://www.ecdc.europa.eu/sites/default/files/documents/RRA-outbreak-novel-coronavirus-disease-2019-increase-transmission-globally-COVID-19.pdf

Grauspensperger, S., Benson, A. J., Kilmer, J. R., & Evans, M. B. (2020). Social (un)distancing: Teammate interactions, athletic identify, and mental health of student athletes during the COVID-19 pandemic. *Journal of Adolescent Health, 67*(5), 662–670. doi:10.1016/j.jadohealth.2020.08.001

Haidt, J. (2023, February 8). The teen mental illness epidemic began around 2012. *Persuasion.* http://persuasion.community/p/haidt-the-teen-mental-illness-epidemic

Halleemunnissa, S., Didel, S., Swami, M. K., Singh, K., & Vyas, V. (2021). Children and COVID-19: Understanding impact on the growth trajectory of an evolving generation. *Children and Youth Services Review, 120,* 105754. doi:10.1016/j.child.youth.2020.105754

Halloran, C., Jack, R., Okun, J. C., & Oster, E. (2021). *Pandemic schooling mode and student test scores: Evidence from US states* (No. w29497). National Bureau of Economic Research. http://nber.org/papers/w29497

Harris, D. N., Ziedan, E., & Hassig, S. (2021). *The effects of school reopenings on COVID-19 hospitalizations.* National Center for Research on Education Access and Choice. https://www.reachcentered.org/publications/the-effects-of-school-reopenings-on-covid-19-hopsitalizations

Hawrilenko, M., Kroshus, E., Tandon, P., & Christakis, D. (2021). The association between school closures and child mental health during COVID-19. *The JAMA Network Open, 4*(9), e2124092. doi:10.1001/jamanetworkopen.2021.24092

Heavey, L., Casey, G., Kelly, C., Kelly, D., & McDarby, G. (2020). No evidence of secondary transmission of COVID-19 from children attending school in Ireland. *Eurosurveillance, 25* (21), 2000903. doi:10.2807/1560-7917.ES.2020.25.21.2000903

Hou, T., Mao, X., Dong, W., Cai, W., & Deng, G. (2020). Prevalence of and factors associated with mental health problems and suicidality among senior high school students in rural China during the COVID-19 outbreak. *Asian Journal of Psychiatry, 54*, 102305. doi:10.1016/j.ajp.2020.102305

Isumi, A., Doi, S., Yamaoka, Y., Takahashi, K., & Fujiwara, T. (2020). Do suicide rates in children and adolescents change during school closure in Japan? The acute effect of the first wave of COVID-19 pandemic on child and adolescent mental health. *Child Abuse & Neglect, 110*(2), 104680. doi:10.1016/j.chiabu.2020.104680

Iwata, K., Doi, A., & Miyakoshi, C. (2020). Was school closure effective in mitigating coronavirus disease 2019 (COVID-19)? Time series analysis using Bayesian inference. *International Journal of Infectious Diseases, 99*, 57–61. doi:10.1016/j.ijid.2020.07.052

Kilincel, S., Kilincel, O., Muratdagi, G., Aydin, A., & Usta, M. B. (2021). Factors affecting the anxiety levels of adolescents in home-quarantine during COVID-19 pandemic in Turkey. *Asia-Pacific Psychiatry, 13*(2), e26406. doi:10.1111/appy.12406

Kompaniyets, L., Agathis, N. T., Nelson, J. M., Preston, L. E., Ko, J. Y., Belay, B., Pennington, A. F., Danielson, M.L., DeSisto, C.L., Chevinsky, J.R., & Schieber, L.Z. (2021). Underlying medical conditions associated with severe COVID-19 illness among children. *The JAMA Network Open, 4*(6), e211182. doi:10.1001/jamanetworkopen.2021.11182

Lee, P., Hu, Y., Chen, P., Huang, Y., & Hsueh, P. (2020). Are children less susceptible to COVID-19? *Journal of Microbiology, Immunology, and Infection, 53*(3), 371–372. doi:10.1016/j.jmii.2020.02.011

Loades, M. E., Chatburn, E., Higson-Sweeney, N., Reynolds, S., Shafran, R., Brigden, A., & Crawley, E. (2020). Rapid systematic review: The impact of social isolation and loneliness on the mental health of children and adolescents in the context of COVID-19. *Journal of the American Academy of Child & Adolescent Psychiatry, 59*(11), 1218–1239. doi:10.1016/j.jaac.2020.05.009

Lui, J. J., Bao, Y., Huang, X., Shi, J., & Lu, L. (2020). Mental health considerations for children quarantined because of COVID-19. *Lancet Child & Adolescent Health, 4*(5), 347–349. doi:10.1016/S2352-4642(20)30096-1

Magis-Weinburg, L., Gys, C., Berger, E. L., Dornoff, S. E., & Dahl, R. E. (2021). Positive and negative online experiences and loneliness in Peruvian adolescents during the COVID-19 lockdown. *Journal of Research on Adolescence, 31*(3), 717–733. doi:10.1111/jora.12666

Magson, N. R., Freeman, J. Y., Rapee, R. M., Richardson, C. E., Oar, E. L., & Fardouly, J. (2021). Risk and protective factors for prospective changes in adolescent mental health during the COVID-19 pandemic. *Journal of Youth and Adolescence, 50*(1), 44–57. doi:10.1007/s10964-020-01332-9

Maranto, R., Queiroz, E., Melo, R., & Glenn, C. (2022). International differences in school responses to COVID-19. In D. T. Marshall (Ed.), *COVID-19 and the classroom: How schools navigated the great disruption* (pp. 165–181). Lanham, MD: Lexington Books.

Marciano, L., Ostroumova, M., Schulz, P. J., & Camerini, A. (2022). Digital media use and adolescents' mental health during the Covid-19 pandemic: A systematic review and meta-analysis. *Frontiers in Public Health, 9*, 793868. doi:10.3389/fpubh.2021.793868

Marshall, D. T., & Bradley-Dorsey, M. (2020). Reopening America's schools: A descriptive look at how states and large school districts are navigating fall 2020. *Journal of School Choice, 14*(4), 534–566. doi:10.1080/01626620.2020.17655897

Marshall, D. T., & Bradley-Dorsey, M. (2022). Reopening schools in the United States. In D. T. Marshall (Ed.), *COVID-19 and the classroom: How schools navigated the great disruption* (pp. 147–164). Lanham, MD: Lexington Books.

Marshall, D. T., Shannon, D. M., & Love, S. M. (2020). How teachers experienced the COVID-19 transition to remote instruction. *Phi Kappan Delta, 102*(3), 46–50. doi:10.1177/00311721720970702

Michelson, K. A., & Samuels-Kalow, M. E. (2021). Association of elementary school reopening status and county COVID-19 incidence. *Academic Pediatrics, 22*(4), 667–670. doi:10.1016/j.acap.2021.09.006

Naff, D., Williams, S., Furman-Darby, J., & Yeong, M. (2022). The mental health impacts of COVID-19 on PK-12 students: A systematic review of emerging literature. *AERA Open, 8* (1), 1–40. doi:10.1177/23328584221084722

National Academies of Sciences. (2020). *Engineering, and Medicine.* Washington, DC: National Academies Press.

National Center for Health Statistics. (2023). Weekly updates by selected demographic and geographic characteristics. Centers for Disease Control and Prevention. 2023 Jan 29. https://www.cdc.gov/nchs/nvss/vsrr/covid_weekly/index.htm#SexAndAge

Ng, K., Cosma, A., Svacina, K., Boniel-Nissim, M., & Badura, P. (2021). Czech adolescents' remote school and health experiences during the spring 2020 COVID-19 lockdown. *Preventative Medicine Reports, 22,* 101386. doi:10.1016/j.pmedr.2021.101386

Patrinos, H. A. (2023). *The longer students were out of school, the less they learned.* Washington, DC: World Bank.

Patrinos, H. A., Vegas, E., & Carter-Rau, R. (2022). *An analysis of COVID-19 student learning loss.* Policy Research Working Paper (No. 10033). World Bank: Washington, DC. https://openknowledge.worldbank.org/entities/publication/ce21738f-72d5-55ac-9876-23ac39efffea

Penner, P., Ortiz, J. H., & Sharp, C. (2021). Change in youth mental health during the COVID-19 pandemic in a majority Hispanic/Latinx US sample. *Journal of the American Academy of Child & Adolescent Psychiatry, 60*(4), 513–523. doi:10.1016/j.jaac.2020.12.027

Pfefferbaum, B. (2021). Challenges for child mental health raised by school closure and home confinement during the COVID-19 pandemic. *Current Psychiatry Reports, 23*(65). doi:10.1007/s11920-021-01279-z

Pisano, S., Cataone, G., Gritti, A., Almerico, L., Pezella, A., Santangelo, P. . . . Senese, V. P. (2021). Emotional symptoms and their related factors in adolescents during the acute phase of COVID-19 outbreak in South Italy. *Italian Journal of Pediatrics, 47*(86), 1–8. doi:10.1186/s13052-021-01036-1

Radwan, E., Radwan, A., & Radwan, W. (2020). The role of social media in spreading panic among primary and secondary school students during the COVID-19 pandemic: An online questionnaire study from the Gaza Strip, Palestine. *Heliyon, 6*(12), e05807. doi:10.1016/j.heliyon.2020.e05807

Rossen, E., & Cowan, K. C. (2014). Improving mental health in schools. *Phi Delta Kappan, 96* (4), 8–13. doi:10.1177/0031721714561438

Salzano, G., Passanisi, S., Pira, F., Sorrenti, L., LaMonica, G., Pajno, G. B. . . . Lombardo, F. (2021). Quarantine due to the COVID-19 pandemic from the perspective of adolescents: The crucial role of technology. *Italian Journal of Pediatrics, 47*(40), 1–5. doi:10.1186/s13052-021-00997-7

Stewart, S. L., Vasudeva, A. S., Van Dyke, J. N., & Poss, J. W. (2021). Child and youth mental health needs and service utilization during COVID-19. *Traumatology, 28*(3), 311–324. doi:10.1037/trm0000345

Tan, W. (2021). School closures were over-weighted against the mitigation of COVID-19 transmission: A literature review on the impact of school closures in the United States. *Medicine, 100*(3), e26709. doi:10.1097/MD.0000000000026709

Tang, S., Xiang, M., Cheung, T., & Xiang, T. (2020). Mental health and its correlates among children and adolescents during COVID-19 school closure: The importance of parent-child discussion. *Journal of Affective Disorders, 279,* 353–360. doi:10.1016/j.jad.2020.10.016

Van Lancker, W., & Parolin, Z. (2020). COVID-19, school closures, and child poverty: A social crisis in the making. *The Lancet Public Health, 5*(5), e243–244. doi:10.1016/S2468-2667(20)30084-0

Varma, J. K., Thamkittikasem, J., Whittemore, K., Alexander, M., Stephens, D. H., Arslanian, K., Bray, J., & Long, T.G. (2021). COVID-19 infections among students and staff in New York City public schools. *Pediatrics, 147*(5), e2021050605. doi:10.1542/peds.2021-050605

Xu, W., Li, X., Dozier, M., He, Y., Kirolos, A., Lang, Z. . . . Theodoratou, E. (2020). What is the evidence for transmission of COVID-19 by children in schools? *Journal of Global Health, 10* (2), 021104. doi:10.7189/jogh.10.021104

Yard, E., Radhakrishnan, L., Ballesteros, M., Sheppard, M., Gates, A., Stein, Z., & Stone, D. M. (2021). Emergency department visits for suspected suicide attempts among persons aged 12–25 years before and during the COVID-19 Pandemic — United States, January 2019–May 2021. *Morbidity and Mortality Weekly Report, 70*(24), 888–894. doi:10.15585/mmwr.mm7024e1

The Pre-Pandemic Growth in Online Public Education and the Factors that Predict It

Trevor Gratz, Dan Goldhaber ⓘ, and Nate Brown ⓘ

ABSTRACT

While spring of 2020 introduced virtual instruction to all public schools, virtual schooling had already been growing in most states. We focus on *pre*-COVID-19 changes to full-time virtual school enrollment in public schools, and provide evidence on the relationship between virtual school enrollment, internet speed, community demographics, and traditional K–12 school achievement levels. We find negative associations between online enrollment and test achievement in brick-and-mortar schools, and low internet speeds. There is some evidence that students are less likely to enroll in virtual schools as the share of students of their own demographic in brick-and-mortar schools increases.

Introduction

The spring of 2020 introduced virtual instruction to all public schools in the United States. However, virtual public schooling had been growing in most states well before it became ubiquitous in the wake of the COVID-19 pandemic. Indeed, there has been a significant expansion in publicly provided online options. Florida Virtual School, for instance, was started in 1997 (Florida Department of Education, 2021). Since then, full-time virtual schooling options have been introduced in 35 states and the District of Columbia.[1] While precise national estimates are hard to come by, there is evidence that the number of public school students enrolled full-time in online K–12 public education programs increased by nearly 50% from 2010 to 2020 (Wicks, 2010; National Center for Education Statistics National Center for Education Statistics, 2021b).[2]

Despite this rapid increase in virtual schooling, relatively little is known about the factors that predict the decisions of students/families to choose this option. This is an important gap in knowledge given that virtual schools are likely to continue, even after the pandemic, to play an important role in the schooling landscape. A number of large school systems, such as Fairfax County Public Schools (DeVoe, 2021), Fulton County Schools of Atlanta

(Singer, 2021), and Houston Independent School District (Carpenter, 2021), have announced plans to provide virtual school options in the fall of 2021.[3] Large districts are not alone. A recent RAND survey of school districts and charter management organizations finds that 20% of survey respondents "were considering, planning to adopt, or had already adopted a virtual school or fully online option" (Schwartz, Grant, Diliberti, Hunter, & Setodji, 2020, p. 11). And the recent passage of the 2021 Infrastructure and Jobs Act (H.R. 3684) included $63 billion to fund broadband development and access, reflecting needs identified given that many students have been online during the COVID-19 pandemic (McGill, 2021).

In this article, we focus on *pre*-COVID-19 changes to full-time virtual school enrollment in public schools and the factors that predict enrollment. Specifically, we use data from the Common Core of Data to track the growth in online public enrollment over four years and describe the demographics of students participating in virtual schools. We use unique data from Stride, an education management organization that provides online education. Stride is one of the largest providers of online education (based on student enrollment) in the U.S., representing approximately 25% of all fully virtual student enrollment. Stride data is combined with American Communities Survey, the Stanford Education Data Archive of student achievement, and Federal Communications Commission data to provide descriptive evidence on the relationship between virtual school enrollment, broadband access and quality, community demographics, and traditional (brick-and-mortar, a.k.a. neighborhood schools) K–12 school achievement levels.[4] We seek to answer the following:

(1) What were the pre-pandemic trends in full-time virtual school enrollment by different demographic groups?
(2) What factors predict virtual school enrollments? Specifically does the racial composition, standardized achievement of neighborhood school districts, and/or internet access and quality predict virtual school enrollments?

Ours study is one of only a handful of studies examining the predictors of online enrollment, the only study to use multi-state data, and one of the only to use panel data to determine how changes in these predictors lead to changes in enrollments.

We focus on *pre*-COVID-19 changes to full-time virtual school enrollment in public schools and the factors that predict enrollment. Relying on data from Stride, a large, virtual school education management organization, we provide descriptive evidence on the relationship between virtual school enrollment, broadband access and quality, community demographics, and traditional (brick-and-mortar) K–12 school achievement levels. We find negative associations between online enrollment and both income and test achievement in neighborhood brick-and-mortar schools. There is also evidence that enrollment rises nonlinearly with internet speed; in particular, internet speed appears to matter more for online enrollment at low speeds than for higher speeds. There is some evidence that virtual school enrollment depends on the demographics of neighborhood public schools, with students less likely to enroll in virtual schools as the share of students of their own demographic in neighborhood schools increases, but these results are not consistent across specifications.

Background

Despite the growth in virtual schooling over the past decade, tracking virtual schooling, its prevalence, and who is participating is spotty. Virtual K–12 schooling began in the early 1990s with a few schools (Gemin, Pape, Vashaw, & Watson, 2015), but estimates suggest that while 10 states allowed virtual K–12 schools in the 2001 school year (defined as Fall 2000 through Spring 2001) (Wicks, 2010), relatively few students utilized this option (Gulosino & Miron, 2017). Initially, virtual schooling started by providing online courses that were difficult to attain within students' neighborhood school districts. Some of the first courses offered online were Advanced Placement (AP) courses to students in rural or inner-city schools where no AP curriculum existed (Gemin et al., 2015).

The early 2000s witnessed ballooning of both state initiatives and law changes to permit virtual schooling (Molnar et al., 2013; Revenaugh, 2005), along with a significant increase in the number of students enrolled in virtual offerings (though not always entirely virtual according to the definition in footnote 1 above). For instance, between the 2000 and 2014 school years the best estimates[5] suggest full-time enrollment in virtual schools went from near zero to a quarter million students (Molnar et al., 2013).

Today virtual public schools can now, depending on the state, be operated by individual districts or schools (including charter schools), and not-for-profit as well as for-profit companies.[6] One of the largest providers of virtual and blended online learning is Stride, a for-profit education management organization. Launched in 2012, Stride has grown to cover roughly a quarter of the online enrollment in the U.S. Stride manages public, private, and charter schools, depending on the state, and are looking to continue their expansion of providing alternative learning options to traditional brick and mortar schools.[7]

Instruction in Stride schools, and virtual schools more generally, can be fully remote (i.e., replacing a student's entire K–12 education), supplemental (offering additional classes online with the student attending some in-person schooling), or blended (a single course has an in-person and online portion) (Wicks, 2010).

Prior to the 2013–2014 school year when the Common Core of Data (CCD) began tracking student enrollment in virtual schools, there was no standardized or centralized data collection informing national estimates of how many students were participating in virtual schools. Since 2013–14, the CCD asked whether or not a school identified as a virtual school, and offered the following definition:

> A public school that offers only instruction in which students and teachers are separated by time and/or location, and interaction occurs via computers and/or telecommunications technologies. A virtual school generally does not have a physical facility that allows students to attend classes on site

Beginning in the 2016–2017 school year, more nuanced data on the type of online schooling was collected (e.g., is instruction fully virtual, primarily virtual, or supplemental (Keaton, 2021)). Gulosino and Miron (2017) used the CCD to produce a national snapshot of student enrollment in virtual schools. They report 261,449 students enrolled in 454 virtual schools in the 2014–2015 school year, which represents about 0.5% of total K–12 public school enrollments in that year. They also find significant disparities by race/ethnicity in the likelihood of virtual schooling; for instance, White students represented about 50% of public school students, but nearly 70% of students enrolled in virtual schools. Ascertaining whether racial preferences are related to virtual schooling enrollment decisions is inherently speculative, but Gulosino and Miron suggest the "desire to evade racial integration" is partially responsible for the observed patterns.[8]

As we describe below, there is limited evidence about whether preferences for virtual schools are related to the demographics of neighborhood brick-and-mortar schools, but there is some evidence that demographics (and demographic change) influence schooling choices for private schools (Clotfelter, 1976, 2004; Sohoni & Saporito, 2009). For example, research dating back to the 1970s (Clotfelter, 1976) finds that after school desegregation, neighborhood schools with high minority shares saw larger attrition of White students from public schools to private schools.[9] It is not clear whether charter schools contribute to segregation. Charter schools could contribute to more integrated school systems by breaking the connection between residential segregation and school segregation (Swanson, 2017). On the other hand, families may exhibit preferences for same-race peers and in this light the ability to choose schools could contribute to segregation (Swanson, 2017). Importantly, brick-and-mortar charters, virtual charters, and public virtual schools may be less likely to influence school segregation than private schools because the wealth gap in the U.S. (Ashman & Neumuller, 2020) is more likely to influence private school enrollements than these publicly paid for schooling options.

To that end, research on whether or not charter schools increase or decrease segregation is mixed (Parker, 2012; Renzulli & Evans, 2005; Ritter, Jensen, Kisida, & Bowen, 2016).[10] Leveraging individual student-level moves between traditional schools and charter schools in Little Rock, Ritter et al. (2016) found that charter schools modestly decrease segregation because minority students are more likely to leave predominately minority schools. On the other hand, using a national sample of charter schools, Miron, Urschel, Mathis, and Tornquist (2010) found that on average charter schools were more segregated than traditional public schools. Still other studies find that charter schools can contribute to within-district desegregation and cross-district integration (Monarrez, Kisida, & Chingos, 2020). It appears that the extent to which charter schools influence segregation depends on a set of highly specific contextual factors. Given the impact of highly contextual factors on whether or not other non-traditional schools, such as charters, influence segregation it is possible our results will generalize poorly. Nevertheless, as we note below during the period of study Stride schools comprised a quarter of all fully virtual school enrollments, indicating that many of the contextual factors associated with the schools themselves should be similar for a large percentage of virtual students across the nation.

Prior studies disagree on the extent to which virtual school enrollment are related to the demographics of local brick-and-mortar public schools, or whether they lead to changes in school segregation (Gulosino & Miron, 2017; Mann, 2019). However, these studies use absolute measures of school segregation, that is, they document how isolated or exposed students of one racial group are to other racial groups. Importantly, they do not account for how segregated the broader school system is and/or residential segregation. And, both the measure of segregation and what constitutes "segregated," and the geographic level of comparison involve making arbitrary decisions that can influence conclusions about whether virtual schools lead to greater segregation of the school population. After reviewing the literature on charter school segregation, Ritter et al. (2016) argues that in order to say whether or not virtual schools (in Ritter et al.'s (2016) case charter schools) contribute to school segregation researchers need to show that students attending virtual schools would have been exposed to more diverse settings had they not attended virtual schools.[11] To fully understand this phenomenon, data linking the school students would have attended had they not gone to virtual schools is needed.

Using data from Pennsylvania between the 2009 and 2012 school years, Kotok, Frankenberg, Schafft, Mann, and Fuller (2017) examined the isolation index from neighborhood schools sending Black, White, and Hispanic students to virtual schools. They find that when Black and Latino students, and White students (depending on the geography of the school) leave neighborhood schools for virtual schools, the virtual schools are, on average, more racially isolated. One of the contributions of our work is to extend this type of analysis by examining over 25 states, 8 years later,[12] and to examine the decision to enroll in virtual schools across the distribution of neighborhood school district racial composition.

Another notable finding on virtual schooling is that there is considerable geographic variation in virtual school enrollment. Virtual schooling options exist within state-specific legal frameworks, leading to a diverse set of policies regulating virtual school. For instance, Oregon allows school districts to prohibit their students from enrolling in virtual schools if more than 3% of their students are enrolled (Oregon Department of Education, 2020), while Florida requires students to *take* one online course to earn a standard high school diploma (Hart, Jacob, & Loeb, 2020). Even within states, variation in utilization exists. Rural students are more likely to take online courses (Ahn & McEachin, 2017; Mann, Kotok, Frankenberg, Fuller, & Schafft, 2016), and one reason rural students are taking more online courses may be because specific courses are not offered at their in-person school (Hart et al., 2020).

To our knowledge, there is no large-scale multi-state evidence about participation in fully virtual schools by urbanicity. But variation in virtual schooling by urbanicity might be expected given differences in course offerings for small districts as well as broadband infrastructure. On one hand, small rural schools often lack the capacity or demand, to offer more advanced courses (Mann, Sponsler, Welch, & Wyatt, 2017), suggesting there may be greater rural demand for virtual options. On the other hand, the infrastructure needed to access and utilize virtual opportunities will be contingent on internet access and quality. As of 2015, roughly 39% of students were judged to lack internet or devices at home (National Center for Education Statistics, 2018). Concerns about the ability to engage with virtual schools due to technology constraints are framed around the availability and costs of high-speed internet in a student's neighborhood (Wheeler, 2020).

The Federal Communications Commission (FCC) estimates that 18 million people, primarily concentrated in rural areas, lack access to broadband (Federal Communications Commission(FCC), 2020). Because of the granularity of reporting for the FCC data (i.e., the census block rather than individual addresses), other research suggests this figure could be an undercount, representing only half of the true number of Americans without access to broadband (Busby & Tanberk, 2020). Moreover, access to broadband is not evenly distributed: disparities in access to the internet vary significantly by race, where in 2015, 93% of White students had some form of broadband in the home, compared to 81% and 73% for Black and American Indian/Alaskan Native students, respectively (National Center for Education Statistics, 2018). Additional disparities in access to the internet relate to geography as there are more students without access for students living in rural areas compared to suburban or urban areas (National Center for Education Statistics, 2018). These disparities may, in part, be explained by differences in socio-economic status, with 50% of households without broadband citing cost as one of the main reasons for not having it (Anderson, 2019).

Several qualitative studies suggest the reasons for choosing virtual schools are extremely varied; for example, students may have disabilities that prohibit them from attending brick-and-mortar schools or parents might desire a higher degree of customizability (Ahn, 2011; Marsh, Carr-Chellman, & Sockman, 2009). And there is a body of evidence exploring the influence of student achievement on enrollment decisions in the context of other schooling options. Murnane and Reardon (2018), for instance, find that 31% of parents report sending their child to private school because they believed private schools had better academics than their neighborhood school.[13] Similarly, parents report that a reason for electing to home school their child was a "dissatisfaction with academic instruction at other schools" (Kunzman & Gaither, 2013).

Experimental evidence of schools choice, as opposed to reported reasons for choices (in above studies), generally finds that the academic achievement of schools is a factor in parents' enrollment decisions,[14] but there is considerable heterogeneity in how much measures of school performance matters. Parents use proficiency rates on standardized tests to pick schools in a school choice model, but also exhibit preferences for schools with a higher percent of same-race students, and shorter distances from home (Glazerman & Dotter, 2017). Harris and Larsen (2015) find that non-academic preferences such as extra-curricular activities and distance from home are "at least as [important] as academic quality," and that low-income families have diminished preferences for academic outcomes.

An under-studied potential predictor of virtual school enrollment is the performance of neighborhood schools. To our knowledge there is one existing study on how traditional school performance, as measured by state standardized tests, might influence the choice to utilize virtual schools[15]. Mann and Baker (2019) found that the percent of students meeting proficiency on state standardized tests in a neighborhood school district is inversely related to the percent of students attending virtual schools in Pennsylvania. Importantly, the predictive power of standardized test has increased over time, which the authors speculate is due to parents' increasing knowledge about the poor academic performance of virtual schools. Given that Pennsylvania was an early adopter of online schooling, it is unclear if these finding will hold in other states and policy contexts (Mann & Baker, 2019).

As we describe below, the data we utilize allow us to characterize changes in virtual school enrollment by different demographic groups and by geographic region, and to assess the degree to which enrollment is associated with internet access and quality, or the performance or student demographics of neighborhood public schools. All of this represents novel contributions to our knowledge of virtual schooling.

Data

The data used in this study come from several sources. Information on public school enrollment come from the Common Core of Data (CCD) maintained by the National Center for Education Statistics (NCES). The CCD provides information on the physical location of every public school in the United States, key school characteristics such as the number of students on Free or Reduced Priced Lunch (FRPL), the racial makeup of students, and flags for the extent to which schools operate virtually. In our primary analysis, we categorize schools as being virtual if they are reported to be "Exclusively Virtual," but, below, we also show enrollment trends for more relaxed definitions of virtual schooling.[16]

The CCD began tracking virtual school status in the 2014 school year, but due to changes in how the data were reported starting in the 2017 school year, it is difficult to compare data across reporting periods. For this reason, and because data that we describe below were only available for the 2017 through 2020 school years, we focus our analysis on the 2017 through 2020 school years. The CCD school information are linked to district catchment zones that are maintained by the National Center for Education Statistics as part of the Education Demographics and Geographic Estimates database.

In Figure 1, we show how full-time virtual school enrollment as a percent of total K–12 enrollment varies across state and time. Over the past four years, both the number of states offering full-time virtual school and virtual school enrollment as a percent of total enrollment has grown. For example, in 2017, 31 states offered full-time virtual school, but by 2020, 35 states offered virtual school. Virtual school enrollment rose over this period in 87% of states offering virtual school in 2017, rising nationally from 212,311 to 293,689 students.

We use the CCD data to provide a national picture of changes over time in virtual school enrollments and assess how the CCD compares to a subset of virtual schools for which we have more nuanced data; we supplement the CCD data with information on students enrolled in Stride K12 virtual schools. Stride K12 (henceforth "Stride") is an education management organization that supports several virtual schools providing online programs and curriculum, and state-certified teachers for students wishing to enroll in online education.[17] While Stride supports online education for both public and

Panel A: 2020 Virtual School Enrollemnt as a Percent of Total Public School Enrollment

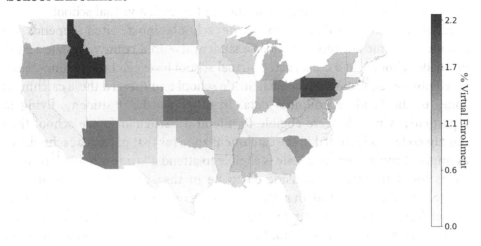

Panel B: Percent Change in Virtual School Enrollment Between 2017 and 2020

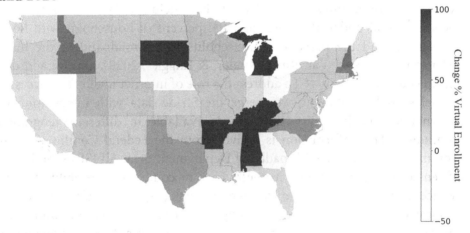

Figure 1. Growth in virtual school enrollment by state.

private schools, the data we use include only tuition-free public and public charter school enrollment. During the period of study, Stride made up 25% of all fully virtual school enrollments across the nation.[18]

The advantage of the Stride data is that it includes detailed information, not available in the school-level CCD data, on the attendance of students in virtual schools by their residential zip codes. Specifically, Stride provided us with an annual dataset for school years 2017 through 2020 containing the total enrollments at a specific Stride school (and race-specific enrollments) by student' residential zip code. Importantly, we have data on a student's residential zip code, so by using geolocation data students can be linked to the school district they would have likely attended had they not attended virtual school.

Eligibility for enrollment in Stride schools most often depends on a student's home address (i.e., does a student live in a county or state served by Stride schools). We constructed virtual school level catchment zones based on eligibility requirements for each Stride school and merged these catchment zones to the Stride enrollment data. In other words, if students living in a particular zip code were eligible to attend a particular Stride school then this zip code was included in the catchment zone for that particular school. For example, if any student in a state is eligible to attend a Stride school then all zip codes for that state are considered to be in the school's catchment zone (subject to the constraint that the zip code contained residential addresses and at least one child under 18 lived in the zip code).[19] Zip codes with no students enrolled in Stride schools, but within the catchment zone had their enrollment in Stride schools recorded as 0.[20]

We merge the Stride dataset to zip code-level information from the American Community Survey (ACS) that includes data on the median income,[21] total under 18 population, the percent of households with home computers, and the percent of households with broadband in the home (Manson, Schroeder, Van Riper, Kugler, & Ruggles, 2020), and we add data on zip codes' urbanicity.[22] To address the role of internet quality and access in virtual school enrollment, we merge the Stride data with information on Internet Service Provider (ISP) speeds available in different geographic locations.[23] This information is derived from the Federal Communications Commission (FCC) Fixed Broadband Deployment data. All ISPs submit a list of census blocks where they currently have or could have the ability to offer service to at least one location within each block (e.g., household or business), along with additional details pertaining to said service (e.g., minimum/maximum upload and download speeds).[24] The Fixed Broadband Deployment is collected every June and December of each year starting in June 2016 and continuing through June of 2020.[25] As of 2015, the FCC recommends a minimum download speed of 25 Megabits per second (Mbps) and a minimum upload speed of 5 Mbps (Federal Communications Commission (FCC), 2015). Different activities such as e-mail, streaming online radio and social media require the lowest download speed, while activities like streaming ultra HD video and telecommuting require higher download speeds.

Finally, using students' residential zip codes,[26] we link information about virtual school enrollments to achievement levels in local public schools derived from the Stanford Education Data Archive (SEDA) (Reardon et al., 2021).[27] SEDA data contain district by grade-level standardized assessment scores for math and reading. To get one measure of standardized achievement per subject, the average across grades within a district weighted by grade-level enrollment was taken for math and reading. In our main models described below, we take the average of these math and reading scores to get a composite measure of achievement.[28] SEDA data cover the 2009 through 2018 school years; however, the period of study for this paper is the 2017 through 2020 school years. To avoid including potentially endogenous measures of neighborhood district performance, the most recent available year of achievement data prior to the period of study was used for each school district.[29]

Table 1 provides summary statistics by school type and student demographics for the 2017 through 2020 school years. Statistics are provided for several different subgroups of schools: all public K–12 schools, all schools with some virtual component (both partially and fully virtual schools), fully virtual schools, and Stride schools. The sample characteristics for the dataset we use for much of the analytic work, the "Stride dataset," are in column (4) of Table 1. Schools with some virtual component comprised about eleven percent of school and year observations, and students attending schools with at least some virtual component made up about 9% of total enrollments, while fully virtual schools composed 0.5% of total enrollments. Fully virtual schools and Stride schools tend to enroll higher proportions of female students and White Students, and a lower proportion of Hispanic, Black, and Asian students. Stride schools often enroll students from anywhere in a state, whereas some fully virtual schools are district specific. Thus, it is not surprising that they tend to be much larger (approximately 3 times as large) compared to other fully virtual schools.[30] As we show in column (4), which is exclusive to the Stride data, there are only 73 schools representing 353,796 student-year observations (roughly 88,500 students per year) across 18,166 unique zip codes, but these 73 schools represent about a third of students enrolled in fully virtual schools.[31]

Table 1. Public school summary statistics.

	2017–2020			
	All (1)	Any Virtual Instruction (2)	Fully Virtual (3)	Stride (4)
School Average Enrollment	518	555	418	1361
	(454)	(579)	(1169)	(1743)
Percent				
Female	47.8%	47.8%	54.6%	53.0%
Native American	1.7%	2.0%	1.3%	1.7%
Asian	3.8%	3.2%	1.5%	2.4%
Black	14.9%	12.1%	8.8%	13.4%
Hispanic	23.9%	17.1%	16.6%	15.9%
Native Hawaiian/Pacific Islander	0.3%	0.3%	0.2%	0.5%
Multi-racial	4.0%	4.0%	4.9%	6.5%
White	51.3%	61.3%	66.6%	59.6%
Number of Schools	104,053	11,233	844	73
Students-Year Observations	201,375,072	18,551,735	1,074,436	353,796
Percent of Observations		9.2%	0.5%	0.2%

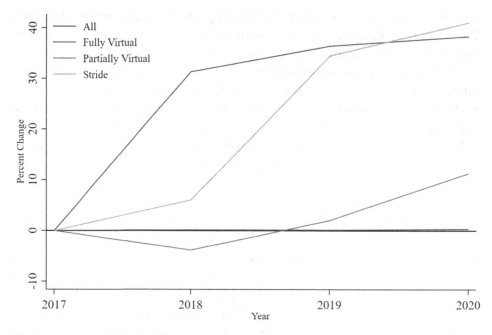

Figure 2. Percent changes in school enrollment: baseline 2017.

Both virtual and Stride schools saw considerable growth in enrollment over time: Using the 2017 school year as a baseline, Figure 2 depicts percent changes in enrollment by different types of virtual schools. Over the four years during the period of study, Stride school enrollment increased by just over 40%, roughly equal to the increase in other fully virtual schools, but a far higher increase than the roughly 10% increase in enrollment in partially virtual schools.

Table 2 provides summary statistics for students enrolled in Stride schools, and compares the demographics of Stride schools to the student demographics of neighborhood school districts students would likely have attended had they not attended Stride schools. (1) provides summary statistics for Stride students, column (2) for neighborhood school districts, and column (3) the differences between columns (1) and (2).[32]

On average, Stride students attend a school that is about 16% Black, 8% Hispanic, 65% White, and 11% other races. These demographics are quite different from the composition of average neighborhood school districts where the Stride students live, as the districts from which Stride schools draw are far more likely to enroll Hispanic students and relatively less likely to enroll White students.[33]

Table 2. Demographics of stride and neighborhood school districts for stride students' by race.

	Stride Schools	Neighborhood SDs	Difference
Percent Black	16.14	15.09	1.04
	(8.13)	(20.30)	
Percent Hispanic	8.24	24.10	−15.85 ***
	(7.48)	(23.03)	
Percent White	65.19	50.64	14.55 ***
	(13.21)	(28.56)	
Percent Other	10.43	10.17	0.26
	(10.53)	(9.28)	
N	353796		
Panel B: For Black Stride Students			
Percent Black	20.24	32.73	−12.49 ***
	(10.27)	(27.12)	
Percent Hispanic	7.73	24.52	−16.79 ***
	(7.68)	(22.17)	
Percent White	62.66	32.81	29.85 ***
	(13.59)	(24.37)	
Percent Other	9.38	9.94	−0.56
	(10.18)	(8.27)	
N	57097		
Panel C: For Hispanic Stride Students			
Percent Black	15.14	12.18	2.96 ***
	(7.02)	(15.12)	
Percent Hispanic	15.03	41.42	−26.40 ***
	(9.40)	(26.61)	
Percent White	59.89	36.93	22.96 ***
	(13.12)	(25.69)	
Percent Other	9.94	9.47	0.47
	(8.98)	(7.90)	
N	29159		
Panel D: For White Stride Students			
Percent Black	15.51	11.83	3.68 ***
	(7.56)	(17.20)	
Percent Hispanic	7.57	19.97	−12.40 ***
	(6.84)	(20.47)	
Percent White	67.87	58.73	9.14 ***
	(11.91)	(26.69)	
Percent Other	9.05	9.47	−0.42
	(9.04)	(8.40)	
N	230646		

Note: Mean and standard deviations of student demographics. To calculate p-values for the difference in characteristics, standard errors were clusterd at the Stride School – Neighborhood district pair.
*$p \leq 0.05$, **$p \leq 0.1$, ***$p \leq 0.001$.

Methods

The analytic dataset contains data on the total number of students living in a residential zip code for a given year linked to a specific Stride school, as well as a variety of demographic and geolocation-based covariates. We aim to assess the relationships between virtual school enrollment and potential predictors of enrollment, by estimating the following Poisson model[34]:

$$\ln(E_{STZ}) = \beta_1 AIS_{(T-1)Z} + \beta_2 Test_Z + \beta_3 X_{TZ} + \theta_T + U_Z + \delta_S + 1 * \log(Child_z)$$
$$+ \epsilon_{STZ}$$

$$(1)$$

In Equation (1), E_{STZ} is the total enrollment in virtual school S in year T, coming from residential zip code Z, and in Poisson regression is natural log transformed. $AIS_{(T-1)Z}$ is the average available internet download speed in the prior school year in zip code Z and is parameterized as a set of 0/1 indictors for the quintile of internet speeds,[35] $Test_Z$ is the most recent standardized average achievement of math and reading test scores prior to the 2017 school year (the start of the study period) for the neighborhood school district that is linked to zip code Z, and X_{TZ} is a vector of controls in year T in zip code Z. X_{TZ} contains the neighborhood districts' race/ethnicity composition, indicators for whether or not the neighborhood district ran their own fully or partially virtual schools, and the median income of the zip code. θ_T is a year fixed effect. U_Z is a factor variable for the urbanicity of the zip code with different categories: urban, micropolitan, town, and rural; the omitted category is urban.[36] δ_S is a Stride school fixed effect, and in some models is replaced by Stride school by neighborhood school district fixed effects.[37] Recall, that total enrollment in a Stride school is linked by year and residential zip code, so a positive and significant coefficient on, say, available internet speed would mean that zip codes with better available internet represent a larger share of students in a particular Stride school than zip codes with slower internet speeds linked to that particular Stride school. The inclusion of a Stride school fixed effect ensures coefficients are identified by enrollment changes in existing schools, and not by the opening or closing of schools tied to zip codes.

Fixed effects models are estimated as conditional Poisson models. To account for the fact that student enrollment in online education is constrained by the number of children under 18 in a given zip code, the exposure parameter, $1 * \log(Child_z)$, is included, where $Child_z$ is the number of children under age 18 living in zip code z. $\in_{STZ}$ is the error term and is clustered at the virtual school-zip code level.[38]

The coefficients from equation (1) describe the relationship between total enrollment and internet speeds, traditional brick-and-mortar neighborhood school district performance (judged by state assessments), and neighborhood school district racial composition. However, these coefficients may be biased by unobserved factors.[39] For example, areas with higher internet speeds may correlate with unobserved factors such as the ability of parents being able to stay in the home with children to facilitate online education.[40] Such a relationship would bias estimates of the coefficients for available internet speeds upwards. We address the potential for time-*invariant* unobserved heterogeneity by adding Stride school by zip code fixed effects to Equation (1) in place of $Test_Z$, the time-invariant components of X_{TZ} (e.g., median income), and urbanicity indicators. In this model, coefficients are identified by variation in total enrollment in Stride schools and zip code over-time.[41]

$$ln(E_{STZ}) = \beta_1 AIS_{(T-1)Z} + \beta_2 X_{TZ}^* + \theta_T + \pi_{SZ} + 1 * \log(Child_z) + \in_{STZ} \quad (2)$$

In Equation (2) E_{STZ} and $AIS_{(T-1)Z}$ are the same variables as in Equation (1), X_{TZ}^* includes only the time-variant variables of the original X_{TZ} vector (e.g., neighborhood district race compositions), and θ_T is a year fixed effect.[42] The virtual school by zip code fixed effects, π_{SZ}, remove time-invariant factors (but not dynamic) that might influencing the relationship between potential predictors and enrollment. As with available download speeds, we lag the neighborhood school district racial composition variables. The use of lags in equation (2) seeks to answer whether or not changes to the variables *precede* changes to total enrollment in the following year.

Results

Table 3 presents results from the Poisson models depicted by Equations (1) and (2) for all students enrolled in Stride schools, and Table 4 provides the results separately by student race/ethnicity (for the largest subcategories of students). The different specifications (across the columns) in the table include

Table 3. Factors predicting enrollment in virtual schools.

	(1)	(2)	(3)
Median Income (Per $1,000)	0.993 *	0.994 *	
	(0.000)	(0.000)	
Zip Code Urbanicity			
Micropolitan	1.003	1.004	
	(0.023)	(0.058)	
Town	0.970	0.983	
	(0.022)	(0.064)	
Rural	1.091 *	1.123	
	(0.044)	(0.076)	
Available Download Speeds Quintiles			
Quintile 2	1.073 *	1.017	1.047 *
	(0.020)	(0.015)	(0.015)
Quintile 3	1.100 *	1.086 *	1.148 *
	(0.022)	(0.020)	(0.019)
Quintile 4	1.096 *	1.056 *	1.145 *
	(0.025)	(0.022)	(0.022)
Quintile 5	1.088 *	1.051 *	1.173 *
	(0.027)	(0.025)	(0.025)
Neighborhood District Std. Achievement Score	0.831 *		
	(0.008)		
Neighborhood *SD* Percent			
Black	0.997 *	0.996	1.000
	(0.000)	(0.005)	(0.005)
Hispanic	0.988 *	1.006	1.010 *
	(0.001)	(0.005)	(0.005)
Other	0.993 *	1.001	1.002
	(0.001)	(0.004)	(0.003)
Fixed Effects			
Stride School	X		
Stride School by Neighborhood *SD*		X	
Stride School by Zip			X
Year	X	X	X
Observations	1,60,136	1,23,357	89,927

Note: *$p \leq 0.05$.
Total enrollment models are estimated with Poisson regression according to Equations (1) and (2) and include exposure parameters for the under 18 population in a given zip code. All errors are clustered at the school-zip code level.

Table 4. Differential associations between factors predicting enrollment in virtual schools by race and ethnicity.

	Black Enrollment			Hispanic Enrollment			White Enrollment		
	(1)	(2)	(3)	(4)	(5)	(6)	(7)	(8)	(9)
Median Income (Per $1,000)	1.000	1.002 *		1.001	1.004 *		0.990 *	0.987 *	
	(0.001)	(0.001)		(0.001)	(0.001)		(0.000)	(0.000)	
Zip Code Urbanicity									
Micropolitan	0.873 *	0.782		0.984	0.894		0.988	1.051	
	(0.039)	(0.112)		(0.048)	(0.193)		(0.023)	(0.063)	
Town	0.813 *	0.774		0.933	0.994		0.982	0.994	
	(0.052)	(0.162)		(0.063)	(0.344)		(0.023)	(0.070)	
Rural	0.876	0.588 *		1.049	1.127		1.054	1.122	
	(0.148)	(0.158)		(0.096)	(0.463)		(0.036)	(0.079)	
Available Download Speeds Quintiles									
Quintile 2	1.054	1.060	1.040	0.984	1.135 *	1.146 *	1.045 *	1.019	1.067 *
	(0.050)	(0.042)	(0.040)	(0.056)	(0.059)	(0.056)	(0.020)	(0.016)	(0.015)
Quintile 3	1.241 *	1.263 *	1.240 *	1.098	1.353 *	1.405 *	1.067 *	1.067 *	1.148 *
	(0.059)	(0.054)	(0.053)	(0.065)	(0.078)	(0.078)	(0.022)	(0.020)	(0.019)
Quintile 4	1.200 *	1.233 *	1.212 *	1.020	1.225 *	1.274 *	1.041	1.026	1.146 *
	(0.062)	(0.059)	(0.058)	(0.066)	(0.079)	(0.078)	(0.025)	(0.022)	(0.022)
Quintile 5	1.208 *	1.248 *	1.210 *	1.009	1.207 *	1.276 *	1.031	1.016	1.184 *
	(0.069)	(0.069)	(0.066)	(0.068)	(0.086)	(0.088)	(0.027)	(0.027)	(0.027)
Race-Specific Neighborhood District Std. Achievement Score	0.963			0.706 *			0.515 *		
	(0.060)			(0.050)			(0.014)		
Neighborhood *SD* Percent									
Black	0.997 *	1.008	1.010	1.001	1.088 *	1.105 *	1.002 *	0.997	1.001
	(0.001)	(0.009)	(0.009)	(0.001)	(0.021)	(0.019)	(0.000)	(0.006)	(0.006)
Hispanic	0.995 *	1.018	1.026 *	0.989 *	1.009	1.007	0.999	1.004	1.011 *
	(0.001)	(0.011)	(0.012)	(0.001)	(0.011)	(0.011)	(0.001)	(0.004)	(0.004)
Other	0.991 *	1.005	1.007	0.993 *	0.987	1.006	0.997 *	1.001	1.001
	(0.002)	(0.010)	(0.009)	(0.002)	(0.012)	(0.009)	(0.001)	(0.004)	(0.004)
Fixed Effects									
Stride School	X			X			X		
Stride School by Neighborhood *SD*		X			X			X	
Stride School by Zip			X			X			X
Year	X	X	X	X	X	X	X	X	X
Observations	1,16,298	55,942	30,817	1,44,003	56,217	27,277	1,59,918	1,17,558	80,579

Note: *$p \leq 0.05$.

Dependent variables are the number of Black, Hispanic, and White students enrolled in virtual schools, columns (1–3), (4–6), and (7–9) respectively. All models additionally control for the race-specific under 18 population at the zip code level through the exposure parameter. All errors are clustered at the school-zip code level.

different types of fixed effects. Column (1) includes Stride school fixed effects; in this specification, coefficients are identified by within Stride school variation across zip codes, and within the same zip code over time. In column (2) these fixed effects are replaced by Stride school by neighborhood school district fixed effects, so the coefficients are identified by cross zip code variation within a Stride school and neighborhood school district, and within zip code variation over time.[43] In essence, these are neighborhood school district catchment effects. Finally, in column (3), neighborhood school district fixed effects are replaced by Stride school by zip code fixed effects. In this specification the coefficients are identified by variation overtime within a Stride school and a single zip code.

All coefficients are reported as the incident rate ratio. Thus, for instance, if the coefficient on the top quintile of internet speed was 1.1, this would indicate that we would expect to see 1.1 times more students enrolling in online education from zip codes in the top quintile of internet speeds relative to the lowest quintile (the omitted category).

Factors predicting change in stride virtual school enrollments

Table 3 presents the Poisson regression coefficients from Equations (1) and (2), where the outcome is the total number of students from residential zip code Z enrolling in virtual school S. Prior to focusing on the coefficients of interest, it is worth noting that across the models, the median income of a zip code is negatively associated with online enrollment in all specifications. In particular, a $1,000 increase in median income is associated with a 0.6%–0.7% reduction in online enrollment. Rural zip codes enroll between 9% and 12% more students in online school than urban zip codes, after controlling for the under 18 population of the zip code. However, the inclusion of a Stride school by neighborhood school district fixed effect increases both the magnitude and standard error on the rural zip code indicators and is no longer statistically significant.[44] This is perhaps not surprising given that only 15% of neighborhood school districts contain at least 2 different urbanicity types. We note that these results hold even if a neighboring school district operates a virtual school (whether or not a neighborhood school district runs an online school is controlled for in all model). And, in an extension to these models, we run models controlling for the number of private schools located within a neighborhood school district's catchment zone, and find that their impact on our coefficients of interests is negligible.[45]

As hypothesized, internet speed is highly positive and predictive of online enrollment in all specifications. Focusing on columns (1) and (2), it is worth noting that the additional effect of moving from the bottom quintile to a higher internet speed quintile flattens out after the second or third quintile. Put another way, generally internet speed appears to matter more for online enrollment at low speeds than for higher speeds. As a specific example, based on the coefficient estimates in column (1), if all zip codes with internet speeds in quartile 1 and 2, instead had internet speeds at par with quartile 3, we would expect to see 925 more students per year enrolled in online education, which constitutes about a 1% increase in annual enrollment, and accounts for 9% of the annual increase to online enrollment. The findings on broadband speed that include Stride school by neighborhood school district fixed effects ((2)) and Stride school by zip code fixed effects (column (3)) are qualitatively similar.

There is also evidence that enrollment is dependent on the average test achievement of students' neighborhood schools. Students are less likely to enroll in Stride schools when neighborhood school test achievement rises: a 1 *SD* decrease in standardized test scores at neighborhood school districts is associated with a 17% increase in enrollment online.[46] This finding is consistent with Hanushek, Kain, Rivkin, and Branch (2007), who find that students are more likely to leave charter schools if their local schools perform well on state standardized tests.[47]

Finally, turning to the demographics of neighborhood schools, we find inconsistent evidence that the percent of students who are Black, Hispanic, or other races is associated with fewer students enrolling in online education. In particular, column (1) shows a negative relationship, whereas columns (2) and (3) show a mostly positive relationship. Because columns (2) and (3) include neighborhood school district fixed effects, the coefficients on neighborhood school district racial composition are identified solely by changes within the neighborhood school district overtime. Hence, these should be interpreted as, for example using column (2), a 1 percentage point increase to the Hispanic percent composition, results in a 0.6% increase in online enrollment. That being said, there is little variation in neighborhood district-wide racial composition over time. For instance, the average change between the percent of a district that is Black across two consecutive years is 0.05%. Because of this we choose to focus on the columns with Stride school fixed effects.

Do the results differ by race/ethnicity?

A Chow test confirms that the predictors of total enrollment vary by students race and ethnicity. Hence to ascertain the extent to which there are differential preferences for virtual schools by race and ethnicity, we estimate equation (1) and (2), but replaces E_{STZ} with E^*_{STZG} , the enrollment of racial group G in virtual school S in year T, coming from residential zip code Z. We also replace the overall neighborhood school district standardized test scores with race specific scores and replace the exposure parameter (the under 18 population) with the race specific under 18 population.[48] This analysis is focused on the three most populous racial sub-groups: Black, Hispanic, and White students. The results of this exercise are reported in Table 4.

Before turning to the regression models depicted in equations (1) and (2) we offer a descriptive picture of the racial composition of students leaving neighborhood school districts for virtual schools compared to the racial composition of the neighborhood school district they are leaving. The panels of Figure 3 separately plot the proportion of Black, Hispanic, and White students enrolled in virtual schools compared to the proportion of Black, Hispanic, and White students in neighborhood school districts.[49] The red line represents the marginal effects from a regression of the racial composition of Stride schools on a cubic of the racial composition of neighborhood school districts.[50] The green line represents a hypothetical case where the students leaving for virtual schools were perfectly representative of the neighborhood school district racial composition (i.e., the y = x line).

Starting in Panel A, when neighborhood school districts are between 0% and 20% Black, the virtual school enrollments from these districts are reflective of the neighborhood school district demographics, that is, the red line mirrors the green line. However, as the share of neighborhood school districts' enrollment of Black students increases, the share of Black students enrolled in virtual schools increases at a lower rate. In other words, the red line drops below the green. Panels B and C are an analogous figure for Hispanic and White students, respectively. Regardless of the demographic composition of the neighborhood school district, Hispanic students are underrepresented in virtual schools. White students tend to be overrepresented in virtual schools when the neighborhood school district is more nonwhite. While Figure 3 offers a descriptive picture of the differing racial compositions between virtual and neighborhood schools, it does not depict how changes in racial compositions are associated with changes in enrollment nor does it communicate the magnitude of these differences.

Table 4 presents the Poisson models depicted by equations (1) and (2) where the dependent variable, total enrollments in virtual schools, has been replaced by race specific enrollments. Median income is differentially predictive for Black, Hispanic, and White students; the relationship is positive and sometimes statistically significant for Black students, mixed for Hispanic students, and consistently negative and statistically significant for White students. More rural zip codes tend to have lower online Black enrollment (and sometimes statistically significant). Conversely, more rural zip codes have lower Hispanic and White enrollment in models without fixed effects, but higher (albeit not statistically significant) enrollment in models with fixed effects.

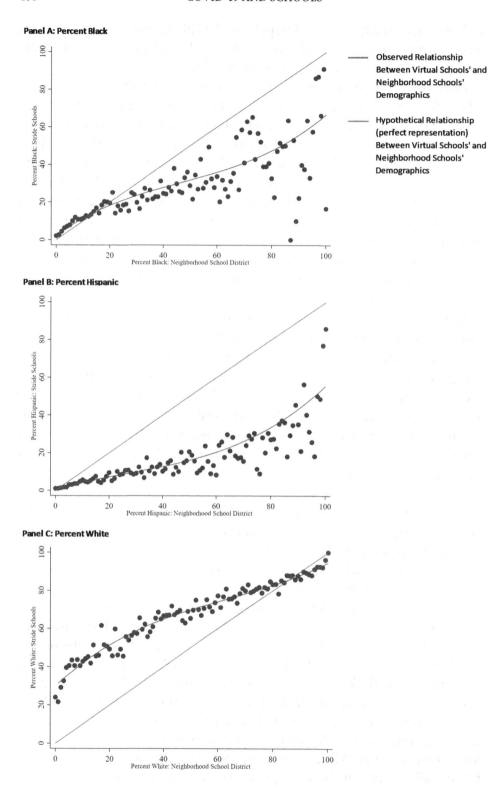

Figure 3. Neighborhood and virtual school racial compositions.

Internet speed is generally highly predictive of Black student enrollment in online school. For instance, in models with Stride school fixed effects, Black student enrollment in online education rises by 21% between zip codes with the slowest internet and those with the fastest. Similarly, internet speed is positive (in all models) and statistically significant (in models with Stride school by neighborhood school district fixed effects) in predicting Hispanic student enrollment in online school. Internet speed is positive, and sometimes statistically significant in predicting online enrollment for White students. Lastly, recall that coefficients in models with Stride school by zip code fixed effects are identified solely by variation within a zip code over time. Hence, the interpretation here for columns (3), (6), and (9) is that online enrollments increase *following* increases to internet speeds.

The findings on the relationship between neighborhood school district standardized achievement and Black student enrollment is negative, but insignificant, whereas Hispanic and White student enrollment is negatively associated with the standardized test scores of neighborhood school districts and statistically significant. While all coefficients on standardized achievement are negative, the magnitude of the coefficients differs substantially. For instance, in the models with Stride school fixed effects, if the neighborhood school district achievement decreases by 1 *SD* Black, Hispanic, and White student online enrollment increases by 4%, 29%, and 48%, respectively.

The findings on the racial composition of students' peers in their neighborhood school district are not terribly consistent across model specification. That said, we focus on the findings with the models with Stride school by neighborhood fixed effects and Stride school by zip code fixed effects as these models are identified by within neighborhood school district racial composition change.[51] These models suggest that there are small effects of neighborhood school demographics on the likelihood of online enrollment of various student subgroups, with the high-level finding that students of color are less likely to enroll in online education as the proportion of students of color rise in local districts, whereas White students are more likely to enroll in online education as the proportion of students of color increases.

Discussion and conclusion

Simple analyses of families' willingness to enroll in online education can mask the myriad factors that are related to and/or influence their decision-making process. Understanding the predictors of online enrollment will become increasingly important as enrollment in online settings surges as a consequence of families' experiences with online schooling during the COVID-19 pandemic.

After controlling for a rich suite of covariates, internet speed significantly predicts online enrollment, and higher speeds are associated with a 2%–10% increase in online enrollment. Moreover, the magnitude of the association flattens out by the second or third quintile of internet speed. This suggests that lower speeds act as a constraint on enrolling in online education, but that higher speeds do not tend to encourage enrollment once the speed constraint is passed. And, slow internet speeds may not only act as a constraint on the demand side for virtual schooling but also on the supply side. Patrick, Grissom, Woods, and Newsome (2021) found that during the pandemic, more rural districts with slower internet speeds provided fewer online education opportunities for their students. These findings suggest that the expressed desire of many districts to offer their own virtual school curriculum (Belsha, 2021; Singer, 2021) may be curtailed by poor internet infrastructure. And if districts do successfully start their own online curriculum they will still need to compete with well-established online schools (Mann, 2020).

Whether internet speeds act as a constraint on online education enrollment today may say little about whether they will act as a constraint in the future. Due to changes in behavior and technological advancements, over time the speeds required to maintain an acceptable connection have increased. For instance, up until 2010 the FCC considered download speeds of 4 Mbps to be broadband, whereas today the FCC considers speeds of 25 Mbps or more to be broadband (Federal Communications Commission (FCC), 2015). To maintain the same level of operability for online schooling, speeds will likely need to increase to match these technological changes.

When a neighborhood's internet infrastructure does improve, we find that online enrollment increases by 5%–17% the following year. During the period of study, available internet speed was rapidly expanding; the average available internet speed rose from 35 to 123 Mbps. However, since large jumps in the availability and quality of internet speed are potentially accompanied by other infrastructural changes, it is possible that these jumps in enrollment are picking up on other changes to infrastructure aside from changes to internet speed.

That being said, the $63 billion passed in the Infrastructure and Jobs Act (H. R. 3684) act to improve internet speeds and access has the potential to facilitate enrollment in online education (McGill, 2021). This is particularly relevant as nearly all students have now had some experience with online education due to the COVID-19 pandemic and are more familiar with online schooling.

The potential of more students enrolling in online education begs for an understanding of how these online schools perform. While we do not assess this here, we find that enrollment in online education is highly associated with the standardized achievement of neighborhood school districts. That is, lower academic performance in neighborhood school districts is associated with higher enrollment in online education. Parents and students may be leveraging information on districts' performance to make informed decision about enrolling in online education (Dougherty et al., 2009; Mann & Baker, 2019), though it is also possible that it reflects unobserved differences in preferences for different aspects of public schooling. For example, students' sense of safety at school has been shown to both be predictive of student achievement (Gronna & Chin-Chance, 1999; Mehta, Cornell, Fan, & Gregory, 2013), and predictive of enrollment in online education (Beck, Egalite, & Maranto, 2014). However, leveraging the Office of Civil Rights Harassment and Bullying data, we run an extension to our model with a control for the number of self-reported bullying incidents per student. While we find that the bullying rate is positively associated with enrollment in virtual schools, it has no impact on the relationship between achievement and enrollment.[52] However, future research is needed to fully disentangle the influence of school climate/safety on enrollment in virtual school.

What is clear is that the relationship between the achievement levels of brick-and-mortar schools and online school enrollment varies by student race/ethnicity, with a substantially stronger relationship between the two for White students than students of color. The reasons for this finding merit more investigation as the differential enrollment response portends greater school segregation by race as the online education sector grows. This issue also arises in terms of the finding of heterogeneous impacts on enrollment attributable to racial and ethnic composition of a student's local school district. Consistent with prior research (Gulosino & Miron, 2017), we find that online enrollment is positively associated with the White student population. For instance, if the percent of White students in a neighborhood school district increases by 10 percentage points, online enrollment increases by 6.5%.[53]

At first glance, this may appear inconsistent with prior research. Prior research has documented that as the share of minority students in local public schools rises, White student enrollment in alternative schooling environments, e.g., private schools, increases (Card, Mas, & Rothstein, 2008; Clotfelter, 1976). It is possible that White students' have an overall higher propensity for enrolling in online school, but when the brick-and-mortar school demographics start to change (i.e. the nonwhite percent share increases), enrollment in online schools for White students increases, and there is some evidence of this in the models that look at enrollment trends for different student subgroups.

Examining stated racial preferences, Hailey (2021) confirms this finding: White students prefer schools with more White students and fewer Black and/or Hispanic students. Hailey also finds that Black families prefer schools with more Black students and fewer White students, and Hispanic families prefer schools with more Hispanic students and fewer Black students. Using observed preferences (rather than expressed), our results broadly bear this out. Black students enroll in online school less if there are more Black and Hispanic students in the local school district relative to White students, Hispanic students enroll less often in online schools if there are more Hispanic students in the local school district, and White students are more likely to enroll in online education if there are more Black students in the local school district.

However, while these findings are statistically significant, the magnitudes could be considered modest. At most, we observe that if Black student enrollment in the neighborhood school district increases by 10 percentage points, then White student enrollment in online school increases by 2%. Given that the average school district is roughly 15% Black, a 10 percentage point increase in the Black student population in a neighborhood school district represents two-thirds of the average. To be clear, we are not arguing that White Flight does or does not exist, but rather that enrollment in online education does not appear to be a large and salient avenue of White Flight.

While many school systems have returned to in-person instruction (Burbio, 2021), there is evidence to suggest that online education will be an important policy issue in the future. Recent surveys suggest that a sizable share of parents, upward of 75%, support more online learning in the future (Laird, 2020). Indeed, due to parental demands, a number of school systems have decided to make online schools an option going forward. Our findings suggest that low internet speed is an important constraint on the likelihood that students utilize online options.

Notes

1. As described in Gemin et al. (2015), "Virtual schools are full-time online schools, sometimes referred to as cyber schools, which do not serve students at a physical facility. Teachers and students are geographically remote from one another, and all or most of the instruction is provided online. These may be virtual charter schools or non-charter virtual schools" (p. 6).
2. There is no census of full-time virtual public school students before the first year of tracking within the Common Core of Data, 2014. Wicks (2010) bases his best estimate of 2010 full-time virtual school enrollments off of survey data, and classifies it as "somewhat conservative". Such comparisons are challenging because definitions of full-time virtual school may be different. For instance, if "primarily virtual" schools are considered full-time virtual schools in the CCD then enrollment increased 120% since 2010. Regardless, the rise in virtual school enrollments is much higher than increases in overall enrollment (three percent) (National Center for Education Statistics, 2021a).
3. On the other hand, some states, such as New Jersey, will not allow school districts to offer virtual options in the 2021–2022 school year (Tully, 2021).
4. To be clear, we are not attempting to assess the quality of virtual K–12 education, rather whether achievement in brick-and-mortar schools predicts virtual school enrollment. For more on the limited evidence on the student achievement effects of online schooling, see Patrick and Powell (2009), Ahn and McEachin (2017), Molnar et al. (2019), and Sahni et al. (2021).

5. Estimates come from the annual National Education Policy Center on virtual schools. During this time no national data was collected in a standardized way. Instead, the authors estimate enrollment figures from reports on education management organizations and an annual report, *Keeping Pace*, paid for by the K–12 virtual schooling industry.

6. For a review of virtual charter enrollment by state see, Gill et al. (2015).

7. This is noteworthy as Stride is proactive in growing its enrollment via recruitment and advertising, and as such is expansion process may affect the makeup of online enrollments.

8. Mann (2019) uses the 2015–2016 CCD to examine racial segregation in online charter schools (not all of which are full-time virtual schools). He finds that 66% of students in virtual charter schools are White. Note that because of the difference in definitions between online schools and all online charter schools, it is impossible to tell if this four percent differential between Gulosino and Miron's study and Mann's reflects differences amongst virtual charter schools or differences in the definitions of virtual.

9. Clotfelter finds that there are tipping points, that is, White attrition to private schools becomes much more marked after the proportion of the nonwhite share reaches a certain threshold; in the case of Mississippi in the late 60s that threshold was approximately 57%. More recent work suggests that such tipping points exist in neighborhood composition (as opposed to school composition at much lower thresholds. Using a regression discontinuity design, Card et al. (2008) find that, depending on the city, White residents are more likely to leave a neighborhood when the minority share reaches 5–20%. School segregation tends to track housing segregation and this relationship has only gotten stronger over the past few decades (Frankenberg, 2013).

10. Recent research by Cordes and Laurito (2022) suggest that charter expasion has important consequences for school diversity and patterns are in flux.

11. For a full discussion on the complexity of measuring school segregation/integration, please see Ritter et al. (2016).

12. An important distinction considering the rate of change of information technology; for example, between the two periods of study, broadband access at home has climbed from 57% in 2008 to 70% in 2016 (Pew, 2021).

13. Murnane and Reardon argue that declines in private school enrollment between 1990 and 2010 are due in part to a narrowing gap in student achievement between public and private schools.

14. There is limited evidence on the academic effects of attending virtual schools, but the existing evidence suggests that student performance is lower in a virtual setting; Fitzpatrick, Berends, Ferrare, and Waddington (2020), for instance, find that on average students who switched from traditional schools to virtual charter schools in Indiana experienced negative effects on mathematics and ELA achievement.

15. There is limited evidence on the performance of students in virtual schools, but the available evidence shows that virtual schools had lower performance ratings and lower graduation rates than brick-and-mortar schools (Ahn & McEachin, 2017; Molnar et al., 2019); for instance, the graduation rate for virtual schools in 2019 was 50% compared to 84% for traditional public schools (Molnar et al., 2019).

16. Across the four years of this study the CCD records schools are coded as one of nine types: exclusively virtual, fully virtual, primarily virtual, supplemental virtual, virtual with face-to-face options, not virtual, no virtual instruction, missing, and not reported. Prior to the 2020 school year, "fully virtual" was used instead of "Exclusively Virtual", we code "fully virtual" schools in these earlier years as virtual schools. NCES collects data for a reference date of October 1st for a given school year, i.e., data reflect Fall enrollments. As such, all CCD utilized in this study predate potential COVID-19 induced enrollment pattern changes.

17. For more information on Stride K12 please visit https://www.k12.com/.

18. The CCD classifies some Stride schools in some years as partially virtual. For comparison, we calculate the above statistic only from CCD fully virtual CCD schools and fully virtual, per the CCD, Stride schools. While most Stride schools are fully virtual, because Stride schools can be partially virtual we refer to Stride schools as Stride schools from here on, as opposed to fully virtual schools.

19. Similarly, if students only from a single county are eligible to attend a Stride school, then all zip codes from that county constitute the catchment zone.

20. Students attending Stride schools were linked to Common Core District data by merging U.S. Census Bureau TIGER/Line shapefiles of zip codes to the National Center for Education Statistic's Education Demographic and Geographic Estimates for district boundaries. When a zip code intersected multiple districts, the zip code was assigned to the district with the most overlapping area.

21. Median Income as opposed to Free-or-Reduced-Price Lunch Eligibility was elected for two primary reasons. Median Income is available for all observations in our sample at the level our primary outcome is: enrollment in online education at the zip code level. Second, recent work recent by Fazlul, Koedel, and Parsons (2021) shows that FRPL is a crude proxy at the school-level for estimating school-level poverty, and measures of family income from the ACS are better at depicting poverty.

22. Data on a zip code's urbanicity come from the 2010 Rural-Urban Commuting Area Codes (RUCA) maintained by the U.S. Department of Agriculture. While not shown in the summary statistics, the breakdown of urbanicity in the analytic data is 56% Urban, 15% Micropolitan, 11% Town, and 18% Rural.

23. FCC data was linked to Stride K12 data (described below) through a zip code to census track crosswalk maintained by the Department of Housing and Urban Development (HUD): the USPS Zip crosswalk file. Because many census tracts can be matched to the same zip code, the HUD data also contains the percent of residential addresses that a particular census tract comprises of a zip code's total residential addresses. To get one observation per zip code, we took the mean of download speeds offered across intersecting census tracts and weighted by the share of residential addresses. Stride K12 and FCC data were merged by zip codes and year.

24. A note concerning these data from the FCC, "A provider that reports deployment of a particular technology and bandwidth in a census block may not necessarily offer that service everywhere in the block. Accordingly, a list of providers deployed in a census block does not necessarily reflect the number of choices available to any particular household or business location in that block, and the number of such providers in the census block does not purport to measure competition."

25. For more information on the granularity of the data see: https://broadbandmap.fcc.gov/#/

26. All analyses assume that students are not changing their residential zip codes so as to be able to enroll in online education. We believe that such changes are possible, but likely small because most online schools in this sample allow students from an entire state to enroll.

27. Specifically, the district cohort standardized datafile was used. The most recent available year was used for each school district. SEDA data was standardized within the sample and merged to residential zip codes in the Stride data by first merging SEDA data to district catchment boundaries maintained by NCES, and then spatially merging SEDA and zip code data.

28. The correlation between district level math and reading achievement was 0.89.

29. The code used to build and model the data is available at https://github.com/gratzt/Online_education.

30. This comports with prior research, who offer a descriptive snapshot of virtual schools in the 2014–15 school year (Gulosino & Miron, 2017).

31. We say "likely" because there are some zip codes that intersect multiple school districts. In these cases, we assume the neighborhood school district is the one most overlapping in area with the zip code. The median zip code has 89% of its area covered by one neighborhood school district. Zip codes with 0 children under the age of 18 (per the ACS data), zip codes with too few residents to warrant data collection in the ACS, and/or zip codes that were recorded as having zero residential addresses in the USPS zip code crosswalk dataset maintained by the U.S. Housing and Urban Development were dropped.

32. Statistical significance was calculated following equation 2.11 of Cameron, Gelbach, and Miller (2011) for testing the statistical significance of mean differences with clustered standard errors on more than one variable. For this analysis, observations were clustered at the Stride school and neighborhood school district level. All mean differences are weighted by the total enrollment of Stride schools or for particular student groups from the Stride schools.

33. Stride data provided information on enrollment by race/ethnicity and students residential zip codes. For this reason, it is difficult to compare variables other than these between Stride schools and neighborhood school districts.

34. We also estimate Equation (1) using ordinary least squares (OLS). Results are directionally consistent with those presented below, but we prefer the Poisson model given that OLS can produced biased estimates with low count data (Coxe, West, & Aiken, 2009); indeed we find the magnitudes of some key variables of interest to be significantly larger in OLS models than Poisson models. Lastly, we note that residual analysis suggests Poisson models fit the data substantially better than OLS. Results are available upon request.

35. We also estimated estimate Equation (1) with a cubic in available internet speeds. Results are qualitatively similar and available upon request.

36. Missing covariates were recorded as 0 and a missing dummy was added to the regression. Achievement data is missing for $1/16^{th}$ of the sample and income data is missing for $1/50^{th}$ of the sample. Models with listwise deletion are qualitatively similar and available upon request.

37. We also estimate models without Stride school fixed effects, but prefer the models with Stride effects given that Stride schools can focus on particular grades (and school levels) and/or different sub-populations of students. Models with state fixed effects are qualitatively similar to models with Stride school fixed effects and are available upon request.

38. Conditional Fixed Effect Poisson regression models cannot directly estimate clustered standard errors. To account for this, we follow Allison (2009) and bootstrap our models by sampling at the cluster level 1,000 times with replacement and run each model. Reported standard errors are the standard deviations of coefficients across the 1,000 models, and significance tests come from constructing the 95% confidence intervals using the 2.5 and 97.5 percentiles of coefficient estimates.

39. Unfortunately, school district panel student achievement data is not available for this period of study. Hence, no time series analyses were done using student achievement data.

40. This assumes that the relationship between wealthy areas and online enrollment is not fully accounted for by the median income of the zip code.

41. In some specifications, we replace school by zip code fixed effects with zip code fixed effects. We might expect differences between these models if new virtual schools open up or existing schools close. That is, school by zip code models capture changes in enrollment for existing schools, while zip code fixed effects capture changes in enrollment for existing schools and the entry or exit of schools. Results are qualitatively similar and available upon request.

42. Within this period of study, median income is time-invariant as it is only available at the zip code level through the American Community Survey's 5-year rolling average data.

43. There are an average of 2.7 zip codes per neighborhood school district.

44. Recall Poisson models control for the total number of students that could have enrolled in online school through the inclusion of the under 18 population as the exposure parameter. In raw differences, urban zip codes enroll more students in online education because the average number of children living in an urban zip code is higher than the number living in a rural zip code.
45. Relative to zero private schools being located in a neighborhood school district, five private schools or more is negatively associated with enrollment in virtual schools. These data come from Private School Universe Survey maintained by NCES. Results are available upon request.
46. Note that we elected not to estimate the model with Stride school by neighborhood school district fixed effects because the SEDA data only runs through the 2017–2018 school years, and are incomplete.
47. We also ran a model replacing average test achievement of students' neighborhood schools with the change in students' average test achievement between their most recent pre-study year and their second most recent pre-study year. The coefficient on the change in standardized test achievement is positive, but not statistically significant. Results are available upon request.
48. Note these under 18 population counts come from the American Communities Survey, which does not disaggregate data by race (and age). Instead, we use the zip codes overall racial composition to estimate the race specific under 18 population.
49. For visual clarity in the scatter plot, neighborhood school district compositions were averaged over 1% increments, however, the cubic regression is based off of the un-collapsed data.
50. The data was collapsed to the neighborhood school district level and all regressions include the same set of controls present in column (2) of Table (3).
51. While the number of students of a particular race enrolled in online schools is mechanically related to the percent of students from that race going to the neighborhood school districts, in practice Stride school enrollments are roughly 0.3% of the total neighborhood school district enrollments and likely do not strongly influence the coefficients on the racial composition of neighborhood school districts.
52. Results are available upon request.
53. Results are from a model similar to column (1) of Table 3, where the neighborhood school district percent Black, Hispanic, and Other have been replaced by percent White.

Disclosure statement

No potential conflict of interest was reported by the author(s).

Funding

This work was supported by the National Center for Analysis of Longitudinal Data in Education Research.

ORCID

Dan Goldhaber http://orcid.org/0000-0003-4260-4040
Nate Brown http://orcid.org/0000-0001-8146-6483

References

Ahn, J. (2011). Policy, technology, and practice in cyber charter schools: Framing the issues. *Teachers College Record: The Voice of Scholarship in Education, 113*(1), 1–26. doi:10.1177/016146811111300103

Ahn, J., & McEachin, A. (2017). Student enrollment patterns and achievement in Ohio's online charter schools. *Educational Researcher, 46*(1), 44–57. doi:10.3102/0013189X17692999

Allison, P. D. (2009). *Fixed effects models for count data: Fixed effects regression models* (pp. 49–69). Thousand Oaks, CA: SAGE.

Anderson, M. (2019, June 13). Mobile technology and home broadband 2019. Retrieved May 07, 2021, from https://www.pewresearch.org/internet/2019/06/13/mobile-technology-and-home-broadband-2019/

Ashman, H., & Neumuller, S. (2020). Can income differences explain the racial wealth gap? A quantitative analysis. *Review of Economic Dynamics, 35*, 220–239. doi:10.1016/j.red.2019.06.004

Beck, D., Egalite, A., & Maranto, R. (2014). Why they choose and how it goes: Comparing special education and general education cyber student perceptions. *Computers & Education, 76*, 70–79. doi:10.1016/j.compedu.2014.03.011

Belsha, K. (2021, May 26) Cheers and questions as some states and big school districts remove virtual learning option for fall. *Chalkbeat*. Retrieved from https://www.chalkbeat.org/2021/5/26/22455236/no-remote-learning-virtual-option-fall

Burbio. (2021). Burbio's K-12 school opening tracker. Retrieved May 6, 2021, from https://cai.burbio.com/school-opening-tracker/

Busby, J., & Tanberk, J. (2020). FCC reports broadband unavailable to 21.3 million Americans, broadbandNow study indicates 42 million do not have access. BroadbandNow Research.

Cameron, A. C., Gelbach, J. B., & Miller, D. L. (2011). Robust inference with multiway clustering. *Journal of Business and Economic Statistics, 29*(2), 238–249. doi:10.1198/jbes.2010.07136

Card, D., Mas, A., & Rothstein, J. (2008). Tipping and the Dynamics of Segregation. *The Quarterly Journal of Economics, 123*(1), 177–218. doi:10.1162/qjec.2008.123.1.177

Carpenter, J. (2021, March 25). *HISD hopes to offer online-only classes in 2021-22 - with one big change*. Houston Chronicle. https://www.houstonchronicle.com/news/houston-texas/education/article/HISD-hopes-to-offer-online-only-classes-in-16050391.php.

Clotfelter, C. T. (1976). School desegregation," tipping," and private school enrollment. *Journal of Human Resources, 11*(1), 28–50. doi:10.2307/145072

Clotfelter, C. T. (2004). Private schools, segregation, and the southern states. *Peabody Journal of Education, 79*(2), 74–97. doi:10.1207/s15327930pje7902_6

Cordes, S., & Laurito, A. (2022). Choice and change: The implications of charter school expansion for school and neighborhood diversity in NYC. (EdWorkingPaper: 22-556). Retrieved from Annenberg Institute at Brown University. 10.26300/d06m-2e33

Coxe, S., West, S. G., & Aiken, L. S. (2009). The analysis of count data: A gentle introduction to poisson regression and its alternatives. *Journal of Personality Assessment, 91*(2), 121–136. doi:10.1080/00223890802634175

DeVoe, J. (2021, May 6). *Fairfax county public schools to offer virtual option this fall with emphasis on in-person learning*. Reston Now. https://www.restonnow.com/2021/05/06/fairfax-county-public-schools-to-offer-virtual-option-this-fall-with-emphasis-on-in-person-learning/.

Dougherty, J., Harrelson, J., Maloney, L., Murphy, D., Smith, R., Snow, M., & Zannoni, D. (2009). School choice in suburbia: Test scores, race, and housing markets. *American Journal of Education, 115*(4), 523–548. doi:10.1086/599780

Fazlul, I., Koedel, C., & Parsons, E. (2021). Free and reduced-price meal eligibility does not measure student poverty: Evidence and policy significance. *EdWorkingPaper*, 21–415.

Federal Communications Commission (FCC). (2015). 2015 broadband progress report and notice of inquiry on immediate action to accelerate deployment. Washington, DC, USA, *Tech. Rep. FCC*, 15.

Federal Communications Commission(FCC). (2020). *2020 broadband deployment report* (Vol. FCC 20-50, Rep.). Washington, D.C.

Fitzpatrick, B. R., Berends, M., Ferrare, J. J., & Waddington, R. J. (2020). Virtual illusion: Comparing student achievement and teacher and classroom characteristics in online and brick-and-mortar charter schools. *Educational Researcher, 49*(3), 161–175. doi:10.3102/ 0013189X20909814

Florida Department of Education. (2021). Florida virtual school. Retrieved May 05, 2021, from http://www.fldoe.org/schools/school-choice/virtual-edu/florida-virtual-school/

Frankenberg, E. (2013). The role of residential segregation in contemporary school segregation. *Education and Urban Society, 45*(5), 548–570. doi:10.1177/0013124513486288

Gemin, B., Pape, L., Vashaw, L., & Watson, J. (2015). *Keeping pace with K-12 digital learning: An annual review of policy and practice.* Durango, Colorado: Evergreen Education Group.

Gill, B., Walsh, L., Wulsin, C. S., Matulewicz, H., Severn, V., Grau, E., & Kerwin, T. (2015). Inside online charter schools. A report of the national study of online charter schools. *Mathematica Policy Research, Inc.*

Glazerman, S., & Dotter, D. (2017). Market signals: Evidence on the determinants and consequences of school choice from a citywide lottery. *Educational Evaluation and Policy Analysis, 39*(4), 593–619. doi:10.3102/0162373717702964

Gronna, S. S., & Chin-Chance, S. A. (1999). Effects of school safety and school characteristics on grade 8 achievement: A multilevel analysis.

Gulosino, C., & Miron, G. (2017). Growth and performance of fully online and blended K-12 public schools. *Education Policy Analysis Archives, 25*, 124. doi:10.14507/epaa.25.2859

Hailey, C. A. (2021). Racial preferences for schools: Evidence from an experiment with White, Black, Latinx, and Asian parents and Students. *Sociology of Education, 95*(2), 110–132.

Hanushek, E. A., Kain, J. F., Rivkin, S. G., & Branch, G. F. (2007). Charter school quality and parental decision making with school choice. *Journal of Public Economics, 91*(5–6), 823–848. doi:10.1016/j.jpubeco.2006.09.014

Harris, D. N., & Larsen, M. (2015). What schools do families want (and why). In *Policy brief.* New Orleans, LA: Education Research Alliance for New Orleans, 1–67. Institutional Editor: Tulane University.

Hart, H., Jacob, B., & Loeb, S. (2020). Online course-taking and Expansion of curricular options in high school. In *EdWorkingPaper: 20-269.* Retrived from Annenberg Institute at Brown University. doi:10.26300/x3d2-7d79

Keaton, P. (2021, April 30). *Identifying Virtual Schools Using the Common Core of Data (CCD).* Retrieved May 06, 2021, from https://nces.ed.gov/blogs/nces/post/identifying-virtual-schools-using-the-common-core-of-data-ccd

Kotok, S., Frankenberg, E., Schafft, K. A., Mann, B. A., & Fuller, E. J. (2017). School choice, racial segregation, and poverty concentration: Evidence from Pennsylvania charter school transfers. *Educational Policy, 31*(4), 415–447. doi:10.1177/0895904815604112

Kunzman, R., & Gaither, M. (2013). Homeschooling: A comprehensive survey of the research. *Other Education, 2*(1), 4–59.

Laird, E. (2020, October 22). *Protecting students' privacy and advancing digital equity* (Rep.). Center for Democracy & Technology. HYPERLINK" https://cdt.org/insights/research-report-protecting-students-privacy-and-advancing-digital-equity/ " https://cdt.org/ insights/research-report-protecting-students-privacy-and-advancing-digital-equity/

Mann, B., Kotok, S., Frankenberg, E., Fuller, E., & Schafft, K. (2016). Choice, cyber charter schools, and the educational marketplace for rural school districts. *The Rural Educator, 37* (3), 17–29.

Mann, S., Sponsler, B., Welch, M., & Wyatt, J. (2017). Advanced placement access and success: How do rural schools stack up. *Education Commission of the States*, 1–12. https://www.Ecsorg/wpcontent/uploads/Advanced-Placement-Accessand-Success-How-do-rural-schools-stackup.pdf.

Mann, B., & Baker, D. P. (2019). Cyber charter schools and growing resource inequality among public districts: Geospatial patterns and consequences of a statewide choice policy in Pennsylvania, 2002–2014. *American Journal of Education, 125*(2), 147–171. doi:10.1086/701249

Mann, B. (2019). Whiteness and economic advantage in digital schooling: Diversity patterns and equity considerations for K-12 online charter schools. *Education Policy Analysis Archives, 27*(105), n105. doi:10.14507/epaa.27.4532

Mann, B. (2020). Compete, conform, or both? School district responses to statewide cyber charter schools. *Journal of School Choice, 14*(1), 49–74. doi:10.1080/15582159.2019.1566996

Manson, S., Schroeder, J., Van Riper, D., Kugler, T., & Ruggles, S. (2020). *IPUMS national historical geographic information system: Version 15.0* dataset. IPUMS: Minneapolis, MN. 2020 doi:10.18128/D050.V15.0

Marsh, R. M., Carr-Chellman, A. A., & Sockman, B. R. (2009). Why parents choose cyber charter schools. *TechTrends, 53*(4), 32–36.

McGill, M. H. (2021, November 8). *Infrastructure Bill includes billions for Broadband*. Axios. Retrieved November 9, 2021, from https://www.axios.com/infrastructure-bill-broadband-911dea37-b38d-4f33-901e-ec6eb73650c4.html.

Mehta, S. B., Cornell, D., Fan, X., & Gregory, A. (2013). Bullying climate and school engagement in ninth-grade students. *Journal of School Health, 83*(1), 45–52. doi:10.1111/j.1746-1561.2012.00746.x

Miron, G., Urschel, J., Mathis, W. J., & Tornquist, E. (2010). Schools without diversity: Education management organizations, Charter Schools and the Demographic Stratification of the American School System. Boulder and Tempe: Education and the Public Interest Center & Education Policy Research Unit. http://epicpolicy.org/publication/schools-without-diversity.

Molnar, A., Miron, G., Huerta, L., Cuban, L., Horvitz, B., Gulosino, C., ... Shafer, S. R. (2013). Virtual schools in the U.S. 2013: Politics, performance, policy, and research evidence. Boulder, CO: National Education Policy Center. Retrieved from http://nepc.colorado.edu/publication/virtualschools-annual-2013

Molnar, A., Miron, G., Elgeberi, N., Barbour, M. K., Huerta, L., Shafer, S. R., & Rice, J. K. (2019). *Virtual schools in the US 2019*. School of Education, University of Colorado Boulder. Boulder, CO: National Education Policy Center.

Monarrez, T., Kisida, B., & Chingos, M. M. (2020). The effect of charter schools on school segregation. *American Economic Journal. Economic Policy, 12*(1), 33–61. doi:10.1257/pol.20160555

Murnane, R. J., & Reardon, S. F. (2018). Long-term trends in private school enrollments by family income. *AERA Open, 4*(1), 2332858417751355. doi:10.1177/2332858417751355

National Center for Education Statistics. (2018). Student access to digital learning resources outside of the classroom (NCES 2017-098)

National Center for Education Statistics (2021a). *Digest of education statistics: 2019 table 105.20 enrollment in elementary, secondary, and degree-granting postsecondary institutions, by level and control of institution, enrollment level, and attendance status and sex of student: Selected years, fall 1990 through fall 2029.* Retrieved from https://nces.ed.gov/programs/digest/d19/tables/dt19_105.20.asp

National Center for Education Statistics (2021b). *State nonfiscal public elementary/secondary education survey data* (v 1.—Provisional) Dataset. Retrieved from https://nces.ed.gov/ccd/files.asp#Fiscal:2,LevelId:2,SchoolYearId:34,Page:1

Oregon Department of Education. (2020). Process to appeal a school district decision to deny student enrollment in a virtual charter school. Retrieved May 06, 2021, from https://www.oregon.gov/ode/learning-options/schooltypes/charter/Documents/ODEVirtualCSEnrollmentAppeal.pdf

Parker, W. (2012). From the failure of desegregation to the failure of choice. *Wash. UJL & Pol'y, 40,* 117.

Patrick, S., & Powell, A. (2009). A summary of research on the effectiveness of K-12 online learning. *International Association for K-12 Online Learning,* 1–11.

Patrick, S. K., Grissom, J. A., Woods, S. C., & Newsome, U. W. (2021). Broadband access, district policy, and student opportunities for remote learning during COVID-19 school closures. *AERA Open, 7,* 23328584211064298. doi:10.1177/23328584211064298

Reardon, S. F., Ho, A. D., Shear, B. R., Fahle, E. M., Kalogrides, D., Jang, H., & Chavez, B. (2021). Stanford education data archive (Version 4.0). Retrieved from http://purl.stanford.edu/db586ns4974.

Renzulli, L. A., & Evans, L. (2005). School choice, charter schools, and white flight. *Social Problems, 52*(3), 398–418. doi:10.1525/sp.2005.52.3.398

Research Center, P. 2019. Internet/broadband, Mobile, Social Media. Retrieved from: https://www.pewresearch.org/internet/fact-sheet/internet-broadband/

Revenaugh, M. (2005). K-8 virtual schools: A glimpse into the future. *Educational Leadership, 63*(4), 60.

Ritter, G. W., Jensen, N. C., Kisida, B., & Bowen, D. H. (2016). Urban school choice and integration: The effect of charter schools in Little Rock. *Education and Urban Society, 48*(6), 535–555. doi:10.1177/0013124514546219

Sahni, S. D., Polanin, J. R., Zhang, Q., Michaelson, L. E., Caverly, S., Polese, M. L., & Yang, J. (2021). A what works clearinghouse rapid evidence review of distance learning programs (WWC 2021-005REV). Washington, DC: U.S. Department of Education, Institute of Education Sciences, National Center for Education Evaluation and Regional Assistance, What Works Clearinghouse. Retrieved from https://ies.ed.gov/ncee/wwc/Docs/ReferenceResources/Distance_Learning_RER_508c.pdf

Schwartz, H. L., Grant, D., Diliberti, M., Hunter, G. P., & Setodji, C. M. (2020). *Remote learning is here to stay: Results from the first American school district panel survey.* RAND Corporation: Santa Monica, CA, Retrieved January, 11, 2021

Singer, N. (2021, April 11). *Online schools are here to stay, even after the pandemic.* The New York Times. https://www.nytimes.com/2021/04/11/technology/remote-learning-online-school.html.

Sohoni, D., & Saporito, S. (2009). Mapping school segregation: Using GIS to explore racial segregation between schools and their corresponding attendance areas. *American Journal of Education, 115*(4), 569–600. doi:10.1086/599782

Swanson, E. (2017). Can we have it all? A review of the impacts of school choice on racial integration. *Journal of School Choice, 11*(4), 507–526. doi:10.1080/15582159.2017.1395644

Tully, T. (2021, May 17). *New Jersey's governor removes the remote learning option for the next school year.* The New York Times. Retrieved January 4, 2022, from https://www.nytimes.com/2021/05/17/world/nj-schools-covid-virtual.html

Wheeler, T. (2020). *5 steps to get the internet to all Americans COVID-19 and the importance of universal broadband* (Rep.). The Brookings Institute.

Wicks, M. (2010). A national primer on K-12 online learning: Version 2. *International Association for K-12 Online Learning,* 1–50.

This Time Really Is Different: The Effect of COVID-19 on Independent K-12 School Enrollments

Benjamin Scafidi 🆔, Roger Tutterow, and Damian Kavanagh

ABSTRACT
The COVID-19 pandemic caused a severe economic recession in 2020. Historically, during economic recessions, there have been large declines in independent (private) school enrollments in the United States. Thus, it would be expected that the American independent school sector would have experienced significant enrollment declines between fall 2019 and fall 2020. But this time was different. In our sample, 70% of independent schools experienced increases in enrollment or level enrollments during the Pandemic Recession. In our multiple regression analyses, the main driver of this beneficial change in enrollments for independent schools was whether the public school districts that served their home county were open for only virtual instruction to start the 2020–21 academic year. We find suggestive evidence that a higher prevalence of county-level COVID-19, measured as deaths per capita, was associated with higher independent school enrollments as well. Economic conditions do not appear to have played a major role in changes in independent school enrollments.

Introduction

The onset of COVID-19 in early 2020 triggered a tragic health crisis in most of the world, including the United States. The health crisis led to an economic crisis as well. From February to April 2020, total non-farm payroll employment fell by 14.7% in the U.S. While employment experienced some recovery during subsequent months, it remained 7.5% below pre-recession levels in August 2020.[1] The unemployment rate surged from 3.5% pre-recession to 14.8% in April 2020 and had only improved to 8.4% by August 2020.[2]

By way of comparison, payroll employment fell by "only" 6.3% over a 26-month period during the "Great Recession" of 2008–09.[3] Thus, the negative employment shock during the Pandemic Recession came much faster and was much deeper relative to the negative employment shock during the Great Recession – where the latter had been the worst shock to American employment since the Great Depression.

Historically, when economic recessions hit the United States, enrollments in independent (private) K-12 schools have declined (National Center for Education Statistics, 2020). For example, during the Great Recession total independent school enrollments declined from 5.91 million in 2007 to 5.27 million in 2011 – a decline of almost 11% (National Center for Education Statistics, 2019a).

These declines in enrollment during economic downturns do not appear to be temporary – by 2017, total independent school enrollments were still about 190,000 students below their 2007 level.[4] In addition, public school enrollments increased by more than 1.4 million students between 2007 and 2017, so a decline in the school-aged population does not explain the decline in independent school enrollments during this time period (National Center for Education Statistics, 2019b).

Lower independent school enrollments due to economic recessions are of policy interest for two reasons. First, families are less likely to get their preferred array of educational and social aspects of schooling for their children if they prefer a given independent school to their public school alternative – but can no longer afford it. Second, student migration from the independent school sector to the public school sector increases costs to taxpayers, as state funding formulas tend to depend on student enrollment or attendance counts (Verstagen, 2018). Therefore, as more students migrate to public schools, state taxpayer costs will increase in order to fund larger state payments to public school districts.

A decline in independent school enrollments is to be expected during recessions, as households are more likely to experience unemployment and declines in income during these economic downturns. For the large majority of independent school students in the United States, their families must pay their cost of attendance, while public schools are universally available at a zero price, as their costs of capital and operation are paid by taxpayers.[5] While some families may prefer the educational and/or social offerings at independent schools for their children – and choose to pay for independent school attendance costs themselves – when parents and caregivers lose their jobs or experience significant declines in income, sending children to independent schools becomes less feasible financially. Based on experience from history, in April 2020, McCluskey (2020) warned that the K-12 independent school sector faced an "existential threat" in terms of the Pandemic Recession leading to severe enrollment declines.

Using data on 158 independent schools from fifteen states and the District of Columbia, in this paper we analyze the change in independent school enrollments between fall 2019 and fall 2020. Our main findings are that:

- 70% of independent schools experienced increases in enrollment or level enrollments during the Pandemic Recession. This is surprising given the severity of the Pandemic Recession.
- In our multiple regression analysis, the main driver of this beneficial change in enrollments for independent schools was whether the public school districts that served their home county were open for only virtual instruction to start the 2020–21 academic year.
  - In our sample, the learning modalities to start the 2020–21 academic year in the independent and public school sectors were mirror images of each other: while 75.5% of independent schools were open for full-time, face-to-face instruction, only 24.5% of public schools began the academic year with this learning modality.
- We find suggestive evidence that a higher prevalence of county-level COVID-19 – measured as deaths per capita – was associated with higher independent school enrollments as well.
- Economic conditions do not appear to have played a major role in changes in independent school enrollments.

The rest of this paper is organized as follows. First, we present some basic theory as to how families choose among school sectors. Next, we describe our data and empirical approach to analyzing changes in independent school enrollments between fall 2019 and fall 2020. Then, we report our findings and conclusions. To our knowledge, we are the first paper to analyze the anomalous enrollment patterns in K-12 independent schools in the United States during the recent and sharp economic recession. Given that independent school enrollments tended to remain the same or increase in the wake of the particularly acute Pandemic Recession, it appears that this time really was different, as compared to the effects of prior economic recessions on K-12 independent schools. The response of the public education sector to the health crisis appears to be a significant reason why independent school enrollments did well during the COVID-19 pandemic and recession – relative to previous economic recessions.

Theory

In this section, we present a simple theoretical model of how families choose school sectors, public or independent, to highlight the role of income changes on school enrollments across sectors.

Suppose each family can choose to educate their child in either the public (P) or independent (I) school sector. Let E^P and E^I denote vectors of the attributes of public and independent schools respectively. These attributes of each sector are both educational (including instructional modality) and non-educational (e.g., extracurricular activities, peers and religion). Let T^s denote the cost of attending school type s. All costs of operating the public school sector are covered by taxation while the costs of attending a school in the independent sector are borne by families themselves. Thus, $T^P = 0$ and $T^I > 0$.

Further, each family is endowed with a level of income where M_j denotes the income available to family j. This income can be used to purchase either education services or other consumption (X_j) which are purchased at price vector R. With this framework, each family faces the budget constraint $T^S + RX_j + \leq M_j$

Finally, let U_j (E^P, X_j) and U_j (E^I, X_j) represent the value to family j of enrolling their child in the public and independent sectors, respectively. This specification allows each family to have different preferences across the relative attributes of public and independent schools (including the instructional modality of each school). Thus, each family will solve the optimization problem of maximizing U_j (E^S, X_j) subject to $T^S + RX_j + \leq M_j$.

Obvious implications of the budget constraint are that as increases in M_j and reductions in T^S allow more options for selection of educational sector as well as more "other consumption."[6] Combining the preferences of the family and their budget constraint, we can write the value the family's optimal choice as a function of their income and the price of the educational sector they choose as V^S_j (T^S, M_j).[7]

The solution of the choice problem is trivial if the family prefers the public school even if the independent school were free. In this case, they will choose the public sector because they prefer the bundle E^P, and choosing the public sector allows them to devote all of their income to purchases of other goods.

However, the more interesting case is that in which the family prefers the attributes of the independent sector, but must consider the cost of attending the independent school. In this case, the optimal solution is to choose public school if V^P_j (0, M_j) > V^I_j (T^I, M_j) and to choose the independent school if V^P_j (0, M_j) < V^I_j (T^I, M_j). Given that in this case E^I is preferred to E^P, as M_j increases more families will opt for the independent school, perhaps with some families willing to sacrifice some consumption of other goods in order to consume the preferred E^I.[8]

While this model is a simplification of reality, its simplicity allows us to highlight two issues salient for the issues considered in this paper. First, a large body of empirical work suggests that choice of education sector is dependent on income as families incur a cost (T) of sending their children to the independent sector (see, for example, Lankford and Wyckoff (1992)).

Specifically, families with higher incomes will be more willing to send their children to the independent sector, all else equal, because T = 0 in the public sector and T > 0 in the independent sector. Since the Pandemic Recession caused many families to experience job losses and other economic hardships, it – like previous economic recessions – would be expected to result in a decline in enrollment in the independent school sector, due to the decrease in income.

Model Implication 1 – Decreases in family income caused by the Pandemic Recession will cause a decline in independent sector enrollments, all else equal.

A second implication of this simple model is that differential changes in E^I and E^P due to COVID-19 and each sector's response to the pandemic will impact the decisions of families regarding where to enroll their children in school. If the pandemic and its recession caused the value of E^I to increase relative to E^P, even if both values declined, then there would be an increase in independent sector enrollment, all else equal. Correspondingly, if the value of E^P increased relative to E^I, the model predicts that independent sector enrollments would decline, as families at the margin would switch their children to the public sector.

Model Implication 2 – Changes in the relative benefits from E^I and E^P due to COVID-19 and each sector's response to the pandemic will impact the school decisions of families such that the sector with the relative increase will experience an increase in enrollments, all else equal.

Given that we do not observe changes in tuition levels between fall 2019 and fall 2020 and that we do not observe most changes in the educational and other amenities offered by each sector, our simple model does not offer an unambiguous prediction as to whether independent school enrollments would ultimately increase or decrease due to COVID-19, the pandemic's economic effects, and each sector's response to the pandemic. That said, there are two observations that do shed light as to the direction of any COVID-19 effects. First, Lake, Gross, and Opalka (2020) report that a majority of public school districts did not require teachers to provide instruction to all students or grading of assignments for all or some students after schools shut down in March 2020. If families expected, on balance, that independent schools would provide relatively more E in the 2020–21 school year, then the model predicts that independent school enrollments would increase, all else equal.

Second, as shown in the next section, independent schools were much more likely to be open for full-time, face-to-face instruction than public schools in fall 2020. If parents valued face-to-face instruction more than they valued hybrid or virtual-only instruction, on balance, then the model predicts that independent school enrollments would increase, all else equal. To be clear, we do not observe relative changes in E between the public and independent sectors, so we cannot offer a definitive theoretical sign as to the effect of the pandemic on independent school enrollments. Even if the value of E^I increased relative to E^P, the observed decreases in income during the Pandemic Recession could offset some, all, or even overwhelm any beneficial changes in E for independent schools, which could still lead to a decline in enrollment in the independent sector. Thus, given the countervailing factors highlighted by this simple model, it remains an empirical question whether COVID-19 negatively or positively impacted independent school enrollments. We describe our data and empirical approach in the next two sections.

Data

To analyze the change in enrollments in independent schools between fall 2019 and fall 2020, the authors of this paper administered a very brief survey to independent school business officers to ask them questions about their enrollments in fall 2020 as compared to fall 2019; and to what extent their mode of school was fully in-person, a hybrid of in-person and virtual schooling, or fully virtual. These business officers were also asked to share their school's current tuition.

The survey was administered in November 2020 to business officers whose independent schools are a member of Mid-South Independent School Business Officers (MISBO). MISBO is a nonprofit association serving the business and operational needs of independent schools primarily located in the southeastern U.S. 158 school business officers from fifteen states and the District of Columbia responded to the survey out of 290 MISBO member schools invited to participate for a 54.5% response rate. There was no incentive for these business officers to complete the survey – the president of MISBO merely emailed MISBO members and asked them to complete the short survey. The exact survey questions and the states represented in our sample are listed in Appendix A. To maximize our survey response rate, we asked very few questions and did not ask questions that required much effort from respondents. The respondents are representative of the MISBO membership in the distribution of state, grade levels served, religious orientation, and size of school. However, as shown in Appendix A, the independent schools in our sample are not nationally representative. In particular, our schools are mostly from the southeastern United States, less likely to be Catholic or affiliated with another religion faith, and have larger enrollments as compared to the nation as a whole.

Since we observed the counties in which each of the independent schools in our sample are located, we merged county-level data on COVID-19 health and economic conditions into our survey data in order to analyze changes in independent school enrollments between fall 2019 and fall 2020.

We also merged in data as to whether the public school districts that served each county were fully in-person, a hybrid of in-person and virtual schooling, or fully virtual at the start of fall 2020. These data on public school district learning modalities were compiled by Education Week (2020). *Education Week* compiled information on learning modalities for 907 public school districts, including the 100 largest districts in the United States. For each county that houses the independent schools in our sample, the *Education*

Week database contained information for the learning modalities for the public school districts that served those counties.[9]

There was a stark difference in learning modalities between independent schools and the public school districts in their counties at the start of the fall 2020 semester. As shown in Figure 1 below, 75.5% of independent schools in our sample were open "full-time, face-to-face" to start the 2020–21 academic year. Of the public school districts that served their counties, only 24.5% were open for full-time, face-to-face learning to start the 2020–21 academic year.

The remaining 24.5% of independent schools were open for "hybrid, part time face-to-face" learning. Among the public school districts in their counties, 13.8% were open in a hybrid modality, while the remaining 61.6% were open in a fully virtual format, with children learning exclusively from home. No independent schools in our sample began the 2020–21 academic year in a fully virtual learning modality.

As a comparison, in the overall *Education Week* sample of 907 public school districts, 24% were fully open for face-to-face instruction and in our sample 24.5% of public school districts were fully face-to-face in fall 2020 – almost identical. However, the public school districts for the counties in our analysis were more likely to be open with virtual instruction only: 27% of the *Education Week* sample was open in a hybrid format, while only 13.8% of the public school districts in our analysis were open in a hybrid modality. Correspondingly, 49% of the districts in the full *Education Week* sample were in a virtual-only modality, while 61.6% of the public school districts that serve the counties in our sample were open only for virtual instruction.

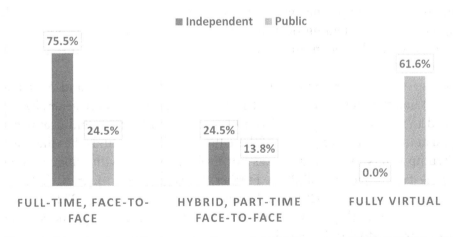

Figure 1. Educational modality by sector. Source: Fall 2020 Survey of MISBO members administered by the paper authors (N = 158) and matching public school districts from Education Week (2020).

However, the *Education Week* sample includes only the largest public school districts. A larger sample of public school districts shows that the independent schools in our sample were much more likely to be located in counties with public school districts that were fully virtual. MCH Strategic Data reports that for the 13,849 public school districts with complete data only 24.3% were open in a fully virtual format in fall 2020 (MCH Strategic Data, 2020). Thus, smaller public school districts were much less likely to be open in virtual-only formats to start the 2020–21 school year as compared to larger public school districts and the public school districts in the counties that house most of our independent school sample.

This stark difference in learning modalities across sectors is interesting because of the myriad school closings in spring 2020 and the ensuing debates about reopening. Starting in March 2020, the vast majority of American schools – both public and independent – closed for full-time face-to-face instruction (Kennedy, 2020). Over the ensuing summer, there were fierce debates about whether schools should reopen for face-to-face instruction to start the 2020–21 academic year. Advocates for full reopening pointed to studies that children in day-care centers were not getting COVID-19 at high rates; students were not learning much from home because traditional, in-person schools were not well-equipped to suddenly teach remotely; parents faced difficulties managing employment with the newfound daytime child care responsibilities; mental health concerns regarding students separated from their friends and teachers; and job furloughs among cafeteria, transportation, and other public school staff (North, 2020). Opponents of full reopening were concerned that full-time, face-to-face learning would lead to increased spread of COVID-19 among students and the community, especially among adult teachers and other school staff (Ibid). Considering both sectors as a whole, the public and independent schools in our sample navigated this tradeoff in very different ways with respect to their reopening decisions in fall 2020 with public schools much more likely to be open in a virtual-only format to start the 2020–21 school year.

Valant (2020), Hartney and Finger (2020), and DeAngelis and Makridis (2021a) find that public school modality opening decisions were generally not related to the incidence of COVID-19 (as measured by cases and deaths per capita at the county level). Each of these three studies also finds that the share of Trump voters in the county was positively associated with public schools opening face-to-face in fall 2020. Further, DeAngelis and Makridis (2021b), Hartney and Finger (2020) and Harris, Ziedan, and Hassig (2021) detect a positive relationship between teacher union strength and public schools opening in a virtual-only modality.

There also appear to have been two other relevant factors with respect to public school decisions. First, Hartney and Finger (2020) also find evidence that a larger presence of an exit option for families (more Catholic schools in the county) made it more likely that public schools returned to in-person learning. The revealed preference for in-person instruction is also shown by Flanders (2020) who found that Wisconsin public school districts that went fully remote in fall 2020 lost more students than their in-person counterparts. Second, DeAngelis and Makridis (2021a) build on their other work and find that having higher levels of per student funding were associated with districts opening with a virtual-only learning modality.

As shown above, the independent schools in our sample made very different decisions about fall 2020 learning modalities relative to the public school districts in their counties, and Valant (2020), Hartney and Finger (2020), DeAngelis and Makridis (2021a), and DeAngelis and Makridis (2021b) provide consistent evidence that political and other motivations, rather than health conditions, were a primary driver of public school decisions with respect to their choice of virtual-only, hybrid, or face-to-face instruction in fall 2020.

As shown in Figure 2, of the 158 independent schools in our analytic sample, 77 (48.7%) experienced an increase in enrollment between fall 2020 and fall 2019. 34 independent schools (21.5%) reported that their enrollments were "about the same" in fall 2020 relative to the prior fall. Of these 34 schools, 14 reported that they had excess demand for at least some grade levels – that is, these schools would have experienced an enrollment gain in fall 2020, if they had the capacity. The remaining 47 schools (29.8%) experienced an enrollment decline in fall 2020. Thus, just over 70% of independent schools in our sample experienced no enrollment decline during the severe COVID-19 economic recession.

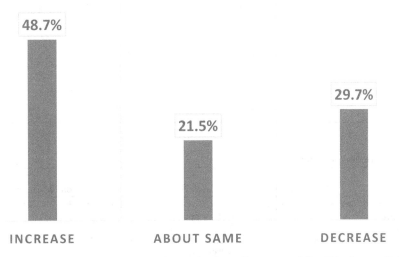

Figure 2. Enrollment trends at independent schools, Fall 2019 to Fall 2020. Source: Fall 2020 Survey of MISBO members administered by the paper authors (N = 158)

To explain changes in independent school enrollments between fall 2019 and fall 2020, we included variables in our multiple regression analyses measuring:

- The extent of COVID-19 in each school's county over the month of August 2020
- Economic conditions at the county level – as indicators of economic factors that impact the demand for independent schooling
- The learning modality (fully open, hybrid, or fully virtual) of the public school districts that serve the counties that house each independent school
- Independent school tuition levels, adjusted for differences in average wage levels across counties.

As shown in Table 1 below, we had two measures of the presence of COVID-19 in each county in August 2020 – when school learning modality decisions had to be made and when school enrollment decisions had to be made by families: the number of cases per 100,000 residents during the entire month of August 2020 (*cases_percapita*) and the number of deaths per 100,000 residents during the same month (*deaths_percapita*).[10] The mean number of cases per 100,000 residents was 611 and the mean number of deaths per 100,000 residents was 12.2, which were the number of cases and deaths during the

Table 1. Presence of COVID-19 in counties.

	Variable Name	Description	Mean	Standard Deviation	Minimum	Maximum
Cases Per	Capita	*cases_percapita*				
	Confirmed cases of COVID in the month of	August 2020 per 100,000 population of county	611.0	252.6	131.2	1535.7
Deaths Per	Capita	*deaths_percapita*	Death	from COVID in the month of		
		August 2020 per 100,000 population of county	12.2	8.5	0.0	49.4

Table 2. Economic variables.

	Variable Name	Description	Mean	Standard Deviation	Minimum	Maximum
Percent Change in Private Employment	*pct_change_employment*	% Change in private sector employment; 2Q2019 to 2Q2020	−0.090	0.036	−0.21	0.004
Real Tuition	*real_tuition*	Institutional tuition deflated by pre-pandemic and local wages	21.63	11.97	5.23	81.81

entire month per 100,000 county residents. However, there was substantial variation across the counties that house the independent schools in our sample – the low in cases per capita was 131.2, while the high was 1,535.7 per 100,000 residents. Two independent schools in our sample were in counties that experienced no COVID-19 deaths in August 2020, while the high was 49.4 deaths per 100,000 residents.

Several variables were considered as controls for economic factors that could affect independent school enrollments. As discussed below, the preferred model included *"pct_change_employment"* and *"real_tuition."*

The purpose of the economic variables was to control for pandemic-induced deterioration in the economic climate. Since previous recessions had induced a reduction in independent school parent employment, we expected economic factors to be relevant. Further, since the cost of tuition could be a factor considered in the decision between public and independent school, it was included as a control.

Several other local economic variables were considered including the percent annual change in average wages and in the number of establishments between the second quarter of 2019 and the second quarter of 2020.[11] It should be noted that average wage variables were complicated by the mix of industries that were impacted by the Pandemic Recession. Specifically, much of the job loss was in sectors with below average wages. As such, the average wage could be inflated by the disproportionate loss of lower paying jobs. Thus, percentage change in average wages may not be the best economic measure to capture decreases in the demand for independent schooling that would result from the Pandemic Recession. The average number of establishments increased by 3.9% between the second quarter of 2019 to the second quarter of 2020 – largely due to gains in the number of establishments in late 2019 and early 2020.

What we use in our preferred model in the next section is the percentage change in employment between the second quarter of 2019 and the second quarter of 2020. On average, county-level employment (the number of jobs) declined by 9% over this year in the counties in our sample. We also explored using shorter changes in each of these three economic variables – such as percent changes from the first quarter to the second quarter of 2020. As discussed in the next section, we explored myriad ways to measure these three economic variables and could not detect a relationship between changes in county-level economic conditions and changes in independent school enrollments – no matter which economic variables were used or what time period the percent change was calculated.

When we administered our brief survey to independent school business officers, we also asked them their tuition. We divided tuition by average weekly wages in the second quarter of 2020 to get a measure of "real" tuition levels – tuition levels that are related to families' ability to pay for independent schooling. There was substantial variation in these variables in our sample. This variable, *Real Tuition*, averaged 21.6 with a standard deviation of 12 (raw tuition levels ranged from a low of 4,500 USD to a high of 63,250 USD; and the average weekly wage in for sample was 1,130 USD).[12]

To check for robustness in our empirical models described in the next section, we coded schools that had level enrollments, but had excess demand, as (a) an enrollment increase and separately as (b) not an enrollment increase in various specifications.

Of the 159 responses to our survey, 158 had complete data necessary to estimate our empirical models that are described in the next section. For one independent school in our sample, data on the number of county-level COVID-19 cases and deaths was missing.

Empirical approach

In this section we present our empirical approach to analyze the factors associated with the anomalous changes in independent school enrollments in the United States between fall 2019 and fall 2020.

As shown above, 70% of independent schools in our sample experienced increases in enrollment or level enrollments in the middle of the Pandemic Recession. In this section, we estimate empirical models that seek to explain this anomaly. Specifically, we estimate the relationship between COVID-19 prevalence, economic conditions, and public and independent school learning modalities on independent school enrollment changes.

We estimated an empirical model using a multinomial logit (MNL) approach. In this specification, our dependent variable, a measure of independent school enrollment changes (*Enroll_status*), is a multinomial variable:

Enroll_status =3, if enrollment increased (between fall 2019 and fall 2020)

2, if enrollment stayed the same

1, if enrollment declined.

In a multinomial logit model, the dependent variable Y is a vector with indicators (equal to "0" for outcomes not realized and "1" for the outcome that was realized) for each of the possible discrete outcomes. One possible outcome is selected as the "baseline" case and then the relative probability of the occurrence of each of the other outcomes is modeled as a function of a set of explanatory variables. Specifically, if there are k possible outcomes of the dependent variable, and the baseline outcome is denoted by K, the relative probability of each of the other outcome is estimated with the model $ln \frac{Prob(Y_i=J)}{Prob(Y_i=K)} = \beta_J X_i$

Where β_J is a set of coefficients that are multiplied by the set of explanatory variables X_i. This model is estimated for each possible outcome of the dependent variable and then used to reveal the contribution of each explanatory variable on the likelihood of a dependent variable. Thus, for the k possible outcomes, there are k-1 sets of coefficients estimated (Maddala, 1986).

For the dependent variable, "decrease in enrollment" was chosen as our baseline case while "same" and "increase" were the other alternative outcomes.

We experimented coding the 14 schools that had no change in enrollments – but had excess demand – as "2" (enrollment stayed the same) and "3" (enrollment increased). Tables 3 and 4 (see also Figure 2) show that the percentage of schools that had an increase in enrollment goes from 48.4% if we code schools with excess demand as a "2" to 57.2% if we code these schools as a "3."

Essentially, the coding approach in Table 3 codes schools based on their actual enrollment patterns – while the approach in Table 4 codes schools based on the changes in demand that they experienced (considering that there were cases where capacity constraints prevented excess demand from being met). As discussed in the next section, the different coding choices do not impact our main results in significant ways.

Since our base outcome is $Enroll\_Status = 1$, enrollment declined between fall 2019 and fall 2020, we are estimating the probability that $Enroll\_Status = 2$ relative to this base case – controlling for the explanatory variables, and the probability that $Enroll\_Status = 3$ relative to the base case, also as a function of the explanatory variables. Thus, we will be estimating two sets of coefficients – one explaining the probability that $Enroll\_Status = 2$ and one set explaining the probability that $Enroll\_Status = 3$. The choice of which outcome is the base case is irrelevant to the implications taken from MNL estimation (Maddala, 1986). We present and discuss our MNL results in the next section.

Results

Our preferred specification from our multinomial logit (MNL) empirical approach includes schools with excess demand coded as increases in enrollment and with explanatory variables:

Table 3. Enrollment Change by Institution.

(Excess Demand Coded as Same Enroll)		
	Frequency	Percentage
Declined	48	30.2%
Stayed Same	34	21.4%
Increase	77	48.4%
Total	159	100.0%

Table 4. Enrollment change by institution.

(Excess Demand Coded as Increase Enroll)		
	Frequency	Percentage
Declined	48	30.2%
Stayed Same	20	12.6%
Increase	91	57.2%
Total	159	100.0%

176 COVID-19 AND SCHOOLS

- County level *deaths_percapita* to measure health conditions
- County level *pct_change_employment* to measure economic conditions
- *public_virtual* to measure the learning modality chosen by public school district that serves the county
- *real_tuition* to see if there is a relationship between tuition levels (adjusted by local average wage) and changes in enrollment.

This specification is preferred for the following reasons. First, we ran specifications including *cases_percapita* to measure health conditions, and the estimated coefficient on this variable was consistently near zero with z-scores close to zero as well. Thus, it appears, as shown in Table 5 below, that *deaths_percapita* was a more salient measure of health conditions to families deciding where to send their children to school.

Second, none of our economic variables – *pct_change_employment, pct_change_establishments, pct_change_wages* were ever close to statistical significance at conventional levels ($p < .31$ in Table 5 below was the closest it

Table 5. Coefficients for MNL model explaining change in independent school enrollment from fall 2019 to fall 2020.

Baseline: enroll_status = 1 ("decrease" in enrollment)
Dependent: enroll_status = 2 ("same" enrollment)

	Coefficient	Standard Error	Z-score	P-value
deaths_percapita	0.0535	0.0158	3.38	0.001
change_emp_annual	10.0445	9.8861	1.02	0.31
public_virtual	1.1028	0.5895	1.87	0.061
real_tuition	0.0091	0.0100	0.94	0.346
constant	−1.5764	0.7297	−2.16	0.031

Dependent variable: *enroll_status* =3 ("increase" in enrollment)

	Coefficient	Standard Error	Z-score	P-value
deaths_percapita	0.0042	0.0181	0.23	0.817
change_emp_annual	−1.4410	3.0339	−0.47	0.635
public_virtual	0.8108	0.3565	2.27	0.023
real_tuition	−0.0051	0.0138	−0.37	0.713
constant	0.1113	0.6582	0.17	0.866

Table 6. Marginal effects on the probability that Enroll_Status = 1, an enrollment decline.

	Estimated Marginal Effects	p-value
deaths_percapita	−0.027	0.254
change_emp_annual	−0.003	0.901
public_virtual	−0.173	0.009
real_tuition	0.010	0.747

Table 7. Marginal effects on the probability that Enroll_Status = 2, enrollment stayed about the same.

	Estimated Marginal Effects	p-value
deaths_percapita	0.021	0.019
change_emp_annual	0.007	0.643
public_virtual	0.060	0.257
real_tuition	−0.005	0.210

Table 8. Marginal effects on the probability that Enroll_Status = 3, an enrollment increase.

	Estimated Marginal Effects	p-value
deaths_percapita	0.005	0.529
change_emp_annual	−0.004	0.540
public_virtual	0.114	0.100
real_tuition	−0.005	0.536

came). Theoretically, it seems that pct_change_employment is the most salient variable, given the nature of the Pandemic Recession (average wages increased because many low wage industries were closed due to health conditions, etc.). That said, as shown in Appendix B, using the other measures of economic conditions changes none of the main inferences reported in this section.

Third, *public_hybrid* (=1 if the public school district started fall 2020 with a hybrid learning modality) was never close to statistical significance and had very small point estimates in all specifications we ran.

Appendix B contains the results of several other specifications, and the takeaway from Appendix B is that the main inferences from the MNL results reported in Table 5 below are robust across specifications. As an example, the choice of coding for the dependent variable also did not impact the implications of the results.

We clustered by state to generate the standard errors in Table 5 and in all specifications in Appendix B.

As shown in Table 5 above, health conditions measured by *deaths_percapita* had a positive and statistically significant effect ($p < .002$) on the probability that an independent school experienced no enrollment change – relative to the base case of an enrollment decline. There was essentially no impact of *deaths_percapita* on the likelihood of enrollment experiencing an increase, as the estimated coefficient was small (we discuss marginal effects below) and the z-score equaled 0.23.

Employment and economic conditions as measured by *pct_change_employment* and *real_tuition* did not have statistically significant impacts on the likelihood that schools experienced no change or an increase in enrollment. However, when the public school districts in their county opened in a virtual-only learning modality for fall 2020 (*public_virtual* = 1) there was a positive impact on both experiencing no enrollment decline (*enroll_status* = 2) and an enrollment increase (*enroll_status* = 3), $p < .07$ and $p < .03$, respectively.

Marginal effects

Since they are part of non-linear functions, it is difficult to visualize the effect sizes of MNL coefficient estimates. In this subsection, we discuss the marginal effects of the coefficient estimates listed above in Table 5. The marginal effects of *public_virtual* are the effects of changing from *public_virtual* = 0 to *public_virtual* = 1. The marginal effects of all the other variables are the effect of a one standard deviation increase in these continuous variables, where the standard deviations are listed in Tables 1 and 2 above. Marginal effects across all three outcomes sum to "1," because the MNL model produces estimates of the probabilities of each of the three outcomes occurring, and the probabilities sum to "1" by construction.

We report in Tables 6, 7, and 8, respectively, the marginal effect of each variable on the likelihood that independent schools would experience (a) a decline in enrollment (*enroll_status* = 1); (b) enrollment that would stay about the same (*enroll_status* = 2); and (c) an enrollment increase (*enroll_status* = 3).

In our sample, 29.8% of independent schools experienced an enrollment decline between fall 2019 and fall 2020. To ascertain the practical significance of each variable, readers should compare the marginal effects of each variable on the probability of an enrollment decline to this 29.8% figure. As shown above, a one standard deviation increase in *deaths_percapita* over the month of August 2020 (8.54 per 100,000 county residents) decreased the likelihood that an independent school experienced an enrollment decline by 2.7 percentage points – an almost 10% decrease in the likelihood of experiencing an enrollment decline. This estimated marginal effect is not statistically significant at conventional levels ($p < .26$). The *deaths_percapita* marginal effect on the probability that enrollment stayed the same (*enroll_status* = 2) is statistically significant ($p < .02$) and increased this probability by 2.1 percentage points. The marginal effect of this variable on the likelihood of enrollment increases was very small and statistically insignificant.

The marginal effect of *pct_change_employment* on the likelihood that enrollment declined, stayed the same, or increased was less one percentage point in each case with very large *p*-values. Thus, we detect no impact of economic conditions on independent school enrollments in the wake of the Pandemic Recession – a sharp break with the history of independent school enrollments during recessions.

There is a massive effect of public school districts choosing to have a virtual-only learning modality (*public_virtual* =1) at the start of fall 2020. Specifically, when the public school district that served the county opened the school year in a virtual-only format, that decreased the likelihood that an independent school would experience an enrollment decline by 17.3 percentage points ($p < .01$) – a 58% decrease in the likelihood of losing enrollment. The effect of *public_virtual* on the likelihood of enrollment staying about the same was a positive 6 percentage points ($p < .26$). The effect of *public_virtual* on enrollment increases for independent schools was 11.4 percentage points ($p < .11$).

We could detect no effect of *real_tuition* on the likelihood of independent schools losing enrollment, as the estimated marginal effect of a one standard deviation increase in *real_tuition* was only one percentage point and not close to statistical significance ($p < .75$).

The main limitations of our analysis and results are the sample size (N = 158) and that our data come from only fifteen states and the District of Columbia. However, given the stark contrast in learning modalities chosen at the start of fall 2020 between public school districts and independent schools and the very large and statistically significant marginal effects of the virtual-only learning modality in public schools on independent school enrollments, we are confident that "this time was different" because of the different choices made by public school districts and independent schools.

Concluding remarks

Historically, when economic recessions hit the United States, enrollments in independent (private) K-12 schools have declined. Given that 70% of the independent schools in our sample experienced enrollment increases or had enrollments remain the same during the particularly acute Pandemic Recession, it appears that this time really was different, as compared to the effects of prior economic recessions on K-12 independent schools. To our knowledge, we are the first paper to analyze this anomalous enrollment pattern in K-12 independent schools in the United States during the recent and sharp economic recession caused by the COVID-19 pandemic.

Internet searches yield myriad examples of anecdotal evidence that parents switched their children from public to private schools because the former opened in only a fully virtual modality. For example, Dickler (2020) describes the condition of a parent whose public school decided to be virtual, causing a "slight nervous breakdown" and a frantic search for an appropriate independent school. In the same article, Dickler notes that an educational consultant in New York, while helping families find independent schools, reported "my phone is ringing off the hook with New York City public school families applying to private middle and high schools."

The response of the public education sector to the health crisis appears to have been a significant reason why independent school enrollments did relatively well during the COVID-19 pandemic and recession. Specifically, independent school enrollments tended to increase when the public school districts that serve their counties were open in only a fully virtual learning modality for fall 2020. Valant (2020), Hartney and Finger (2020), and DeAngelis and Makridis (2021a; 2021b) find that public school modality opening decisions were generally not related to the incidence of COVID-19; that the share of Trump voters in the county was positively associated with public schools opening face-to-face in fall 2020; and DeAngelis and Makridis (2021b) and Hartney and Finger (2020) detect a positive relationship between teacher union strength and public schools opening in a virtual-only modality.

Hartney and Finger (2020) added that partisan politics drove the "tone and direction of school districts' reopening plans" more than markets or health conditions (p. 18).

In our data, the differences in learning modalities in fall 2020 were stark across sectors:

- 75.5% of independent schools in our sample were open for full-time, face-to-face learning.
- Of the public school districts that served the counties in our sample, only 24.5% were open for full-time, face-to-face learning.

Hartney and Finger (2020) also find evidence that a larger presence of Catholic schools in the county made it more likely that public schools returned to in-person learning. As our results indicate, it was rational for public school districts to be concerned that students would migrate from the public to the independent education sector when the former was open for virtual instruction only.

While political decisions made by public school districts appear to have been important, surprisingly, economic variables do not seem to be associated with enrollment changes in independent schools between fall 2019 and fall 2020 – again, this is a sharp break with history.

Finally, we cannot detect any evidence that the following variables had any impact on independent school enrollments during the COVID-19 pandemic: tuition levels, tuition levels adjusted for differences in average wages across counties, COVID cases per capita, or whether public schools began the 2020–21 academic year in a hybrid learning modality. That is, we estimated very small effect sizes for each of these variables and the z-scores were very close to zero in our regression models. As a caveat to each of these null results – our sample size is small. Perhaps a much larger sample would have been able to detect effects of some of these covariates on independent school enrollments.

While over two-thirds of independent schools in our sample experienced level enrollments or enrollment increases between fall 2019 and fall 2020, 29.7% of independent schools in our sample did experience enrollment declines. Thus, the fact that enrollments held up relatively well as compared to prior economic recessions in the independent school sector as a whole does not mean that all independent schools thrived during the Pandemic Recession. To highlight this issue, McCluskey (2021) documents that 132 independent schools – or about four-tenths of one percent of all independent schools nationwide – were closed or merged with other schools due to COVID-19 and/or its associated recession.

Homeschooling also increased significantly in fall 2020. According to the U.S. Bureau of the Census Household Pulse Survey, the number of students being homeschooled rose from 3.2 million just prior to the pandemic to 5.0 million in the August 2020, a rise from 4.8 to 8.7% of all school-aged children (Duvall, 2021). Nevertheless, Duvall also notes, "the homeschool population declined the following month, perhaps suggesting that some parents decided to reenroll their children in traditional schools after attempting to homeschool for a brief time." Future work should examine whether this rise in homeschooling was related to public school modality decisions and other factors.

In addition, future work should also analyze the extent to which independent school enrollments and homeschooling remain level or elevated in fall 2021 and beyond – as the acute health and economic effects of COVID-19 subside. Perhaps the elevated levels of independent school enrollments and homeschooling will persist into the future, or perhaps many students will return to public schools if health conditions are markedly improved and public schools are open for face-to-face instruction in fall 2021.

Notes

1. These employment figures were tabulated from the Bureau of Labor Statistics Current Employment Statistics, which is housed in the U.S. Department of Labor (Bureau of Labor Statistics, 2021).
2. Ibid.
3. Ibid.
4. As another example, independent school enrollments also declined significantly between 2001 and 2003, while public school enrollments increased. While not the focus of this paper, some independent school families may switch to homeschooling during economic downturns as well.
5. There is a significant and growing proportion of independent school students who have at least some of their cost of attendance paid by taxpayers through education choice programs. According to EdChoice, as of 2020, there were 1.28 million students who received an average of $2,805 in taxpayer support to defray the cost of their independent school education – which translates to 11.6% of independent school students and 1% of all school-aged children (EdChoice, 2020).
6. The variation in income may be idiosyncratic to a specific family or broad-based across the community as would be likely in a recession.
7. In the language of microeconomic theory, $U(.)$ and $V(.)$ are direct and indirect utility functions. See for example, Varian (1992). The superscript on $V(.)$ does not denote a different value function, but rather reports if the optimal choice included a public or independent school. To simplify our analysis, we assume prices of other consumption (R) is fixed so its presence in $V(.)$ is implicit.
8. Technically, the independent school could reduce their effective price (increased "discounting") in response to a recession to provide some partial offset to the effect of failing income. However, the offset would not be complete unless one assumes that the demand for independent education is perfectly elastic or the supply is perfectly inelastic – neither of which is likely the case.
9. For almost all of our sample, one public school district served each county. For states that had more than one public school district serving the county, we used the data for the

largest public school district in our analysis. Using other reasonable approaches to coding learning modalities for nearby public schools did not change our point estimates or statistical significance of key variables in any important way – that is, effect sizes and significance levels were essentially unchanged.

10. The source of these data on COVID-19 cases and deaths per county for August 2020 were retrieved from USA FACTS (www.usafacts.org). USA FACTS was created by former Microsoft CEO Steve Ballmer to provide more transparency about the American population and governments at the federal, state, and local levels. USA FACTS partners with Penn Wharton Budget Model at the University of Pennsylvania and the Institute for Economic Policy Research at Stanford University to provide the data available on their website.

11. Establishments are single physical locations where individuals are employed. Therefore, a given business firm may encompass more than one establishment. For example, if a given grocery store chain has two stores at separate locations within a given county, that would be counted as two establishments. Each of these three economic variables were pulled from: Employment private employers, Private establishments, Average weekly wage private employers, Quarterly Census of Employment and Wages, Bureau of Labor Statistics, U.S. Department of Labor, https://www.bls.gov/cew

12. To maximize our survey response rate, we did not ask respondents their exact enrollments for fall 2019. The maximum tuition level in the sample of $63,250 is a boarding school whose tuition fee is inclusive of room and board.

ORCID

Benjamin Scafidi ⓘD http://orcid.org/0000-0001-9431-4200

References

Bureau of Labor Statistics. (2021a). Current employment statistics (CES) - National, Bureau of Labor Statistics, U.S. Department of Labor, https://www.bls.gov/ces/

DeAngelis, C., & Makridis, C. (2021a). Are school reopening decisions related to funding? Evidence from over 12,000 districts during the Covid-19 pandemic. Retrieved from https://papers.ssrn.com/sol3/papers.cfm?abstract_id=3799694

DeAngelis, C., & Makridis, C. (2021b). Are school reopening decisions related to union influence? *Social Science Quarterly*. doi:10.1111/ssqu.12955

Dickler, J. (2020, November 8). Families jump to private schools as coronavirus drags on. CNBC. https://www.cnbc.com/2020/11/08/coronavirus-why-families-are-jumping-to-private-schools.html

Duvall, S. (2021). A research note: Number of homeschool students growing rapidly. Forthcoming. *Journal of School Choice*, 1–10. doi:10.1080/15582159.2021.1912563

EdChoice (2020). *School choice in America dashboard*. Retrieved January 30, 2021, from https://www.edchoice.org/school-choice/school-choice-in-america/

Education Week. (2020, December 15). School districts' reopening plans: A snapshot. Retrieved from https://www.edweek.org/leadership/school-districts-reopening-plans-a-snapshot/2020/07

Flanders, W. (2020). Opting out: Enrollment trends in response to continued public school shutdowns. Policy brief. Wisconsin Institute for Law & Liberty. Retrieved from https://www.

will-law.org/wp-content/uploads/2020/12/2020-12-10-reopening-and-enrollment-trends1. pdf

Harris, D. N., Ziedan, E., & Hassig, S. (2021) The effects of school reopening on Covid-19 hospitalizations. National Center for Research on Education Access and Choice. Retrieved from https://www.reachcentered.org/publications/the-effects-of-school-reopenings-on-covid-19-hospitalizations

Hartney, M. T., & Finger, L. K. (2020). Politics, markets, and pandemics: Public education's response to COVID-19. (EdWorkingPaper: 20-304). doi:10.26300/8ff8-3945

Kennedy, M. (2020). 45 states have closed all schools because of the coronavirus. American School and University. Retrieved from https://www.asumag.com/safety-security/crisis-disaster-planning-management/article/21126638/friday-morning-update-45-states-have-closed-all-schools-because-of-the-coronavirus

Lake, R., Gross, B., & Opalka, A. (2020, June 16).Analysis: just 1 in three districts required teachers to deliver instruction this Spring. They mustn't be left on their own again. The74million. https://www.the74million.org/article/analysis-just-1-in-3-districts-required-teachers-to-deliver-instruction-this-spring-they-mustnt-be-left-on-their-own-again-in-the-fall/

Lankford, H., & Wyckoff, J. (1992). Primary and secondary school choice among public and religious alternatives. *Economics of Education Review*, *11*(4), 317–337. doi:10.1016/0272-7757(92)90040-A

Maddala, G. S. (1986). *Limited-dependent and qualitative variables in econometrics*. Cambridge, England: Cambridge University Press.

McCluskey, N. (2020, April 13). Private schools face an existential threat. Cato Institute Blog. Retrieved from https://www.cato.org/blog/private-schools-face-existential-threat

McCluskey, N. (2021, April 13). Private schooling after a year of COVID-19: How the private sector fared and how to keep it healthy. Policy Analysis No. 914. Cato Institute. Retrieved from https://www.cato.org/policy-analysis/private-schooling-after-year-covid-19-how-private-sector-has-fared-how-keep-it

National Center for Education Statistics. (2017-18). Private school universe survey 2017-18. Table 4. Retrieved from https://nces.ed.gov/surveys/pss/tables/TABLE04fl1718.asp

National Center for Education Statistics. (2019a). Digest of education statistics. Table 205.20. Retrieved from https://nces.ed.gov/programs/digest/d19/tables/dt19_205.20.asp?current=yes

National Center for Education Statistics (2019b). Digest of education statistics. Table 203.10. Retrieved from https://nces.ed.gov/programs/digest/d19/tables/dt19_203.10.asp?current=yes.

National Center for Education Statistics. (2020, May).The condition of education: Private school enrollment. Retrieved from https://nces.ed.gov/programs/coe/indicator_cgc.asp

North, A. (2020, July 10). The debate over reopening America's K-12 schools, explained. Vox. Retrieved from https://www.vox.com/2020/7/10/21310099/schools-reopen-open-reopening-trump-public-covid

Strategic Data, M. C. H.. (2020). "Fall 2020 School District Covid Operating Plans (History)." https://www.mchdata.com/Subscription.

USA FACTS. *Data on COVID-19 cases and deaths*. www.usafacts.org

Valant, J. (2020, July 29). School reopening plans linked to politics rather than public health. Brookings Institution. Retrieved from https://www.brookings.edu/blog/brown-centerchalkboard/2020/07/29/school-reopening-plans-linked-to-politics-rather-than-public-health/

Varian, H. (1992). *Microeconomic Analysis* (Third ed.). New York: W.W. Norton & Company.

Verstagen, D. (2018). A 50-state survey of school finance policies and programs. https://schoolfinancesdav.wordpress.com/

Appendix A. Survey Questions and the Distribution of Responses by State

Below are the questions we asked to the business officers whose schools are members of Mid-South Independent School Business Officers (MISBO). The survey was deployed in November 2020 through e-mail with two reminder e-mails to those who had not completed the survey. The MISBO membership includes 340 schools located primarily in the southeastern United States. Of these 340, 290 business officers were invited to participate in the survey; for the remaining schools, contact information did not include the business officer.

The survey was as follows:

(1) What county (COUNTY not country) is your school in?
(2) What state is your school in?
(3) Roughly, what is your tuition (an average within about $500)?
(4) What is your enrollment?
(5) For the current school year (and with a margin of 5 students or more), relative to last year, did your enrollment:
    (a) INCREASE
    (b) DECREASE
    (c) STAY ABOUT THE SAME
(6) If your enrollment this year is "about the same" as last year, is it the case that you had excess demand but were unable to add more students because you were at capacity?
    (a) Yes
    (b) No
    (c) doesn't apply
(7) Currently, is your school:
    (a) FULL TIME, FACE-TO-FACE
    (b) HYBRID, PART TIME FACE-TO-FACE
    (c) FULLY VIRTUAL

Below are the fifteen states and the District of Columbia represented in our sample of independent schools.

State	Number of Schools Responding	Percent of Respondents	Cumulative Percent	Other demographic descriptions of responding schools	
AL	8	5.06%	5.06%	Catholic schools	3.75%
AR	1	0.63%	5.70%	Other Christian denomination	30.00%
CA	1	0.63%	6.33%	Other religion	3.75%
CO	2	1.27%	7.59%	150 to 299 students	14.48%
DC	3	1.90%	9.49%	300 to 499 students	21.25%
FL	24	15.19%	24.68%	Over 500 students	57.50%
GA	49	31.01%	55.70%	Special education emphasis	7.50%
IL	1	0.63%	56.33%	K-8 only	20.75%
KY	1	0.63%	56.96%	High school only	9.43%
MD	3	1.90%	58.86%	K-12	69.81%
MO	2	1.27%	60.13%		
NC	19	12.03%	72.15%		
SC	9	5.70%	77.85%		
TN	18	11.39%	89.24%		
TX	2	1.27%	90.51%		
VA	15	9.49%	100.00%		

Comparing the characteristics of the independent schools in our sample, as shown in the table above, with the 2017–18 Private School Universe Survey (PSS) shows some differences between our sample and the PSS, where the latter endeavors to be a national census of independent schools. All national data in the rest of this appendix come from the PSS. First, only 3.75% of schools in our sample are Catholic, while the corresponding national figure from the PSS is 21.7%. This difference is due to the lower rate of Catholic schooling in the southeastern United States. The independent schools in our sample are also more likely to be secular. Specifically, 44.7% of independent schools in the PSS are nonsectarian, as compared to 62.5% in our sample (National Center for Education Statistics, 2017–18).

The independent schools in our sample also tend to be larger than the national average, 57.5% of schools in our sample have over 500 students as compared to only 6.2% in the PSS. This difference is size may be due to the fact that in our sample 69.81% have grades K-12, while only 29.3% of independent schools in the PSS have all grades K-12. Other schools in both our sample and the PSS have only elementary or secondary grades, but not both. Finally, 6.1% of PSS schools have a special education focus, while 7.5% of our sample schools have this focus (National Center for Education Statistics, 2017–18). Given these differences, we do not claim that our sample is nationally representative.

While we do not claim that our sample is nationally representative, it is a good representation of the overall MISBO membership. Non-Catholic Christian schools comprise 34.02% of the MISBO membership and 30% of the sample. Nearly half of the MISBO member schools, 48.35%, have student bodies larger than 500 and the corresponding figure in the sample is 57.5%. Finally, 65.17% of schools in MISBO serve grades K-12 and in the sample, 69.81% serve grades K-12.

Appendix B. Other Empirical Model Specifications to Analyze Changes in Independent School Enrollments

In this appendix we report the results of seven different empirical specifications to show that the main results in the body of the paper are robust across specifications—and to show that certain variables like county-level COVID-19 (*cases_percapita*) and the economic variables do not seem to be associated with changes in private school enrollments between fall 2019 and fall 2020.

In Tables A1 and A2 below, we show the marginal effects from our preferred MNL specification that was reported in the body of the paper—with one change. In Table A1, we replaced *change_emp_annual* (the annual change in county-level employment) with *change_wages_annual* (the percent annual change in average wages from Q2 2019 to Q2 2020). In Table A2, the economic variable we used in place of *change_emp_annual* was *change_estab_annual* (the percent annual change in the number of establishments for this same time period).

Please recall that in our sample, 29.8% of independent schools experienced an enrollment decline between fall 2019 and fall 2020. To ascertain the practical significance of each variable,

Table A1. Marginal effects on the probability that Enroll_Status = 1, an enrollment decline. *change_wages_annual* is the economic variable.

	Estimated Marginal Effects	p-value
deaths_percapita	−0.030	0.306
change_wages_annual	−0.006	0.940
public_virtual	−0.164	0.025
real_tuition	0.0006	0.816

Table A2. Marginal effects on the probability that Enroll_Status = 1, an enrollment decline. *change_estab_annual* is the economic variable.

	Estimated Marginal Effects	p-value
deaths_percapita	−0.020	0.365
change_estab_annual	−0.014	0.635
public_virtual	−0.158	0.022
real_tuition	−0.00005	0.983

readers should compare the marginal effects of each variable on the probability of an enrollment decline to this 29.8% figure. Also recall that the marginal effects for *public_virtual* are the difference between *public_virtual* = 0 and *public_virtual* = 1. Each of the other covariates are continuous variables, so the marginal effects are the effect of a one standard deviation increase.

In both of the above specifications, the estimated coefficients on the economic variables and *real_tuition* have very small marginal effects and are not close to statistical significance. The effect sizes of public_virtual are almost identical to what is in our preferred specification and this variable is statistically significant ($p < .03$) in both of these specifications (Tables A1 and A2). *Deaths_percapita* is not statistically significant, as was the case in our preferred results, and the effect sizes are almost identical to our preferred specification. The statistical significance of the marginal effect of *deaths_percapita* on enroll_status = 2 (no change in enrollment) is about the same as our preferred results ($p < .002$) in this specification (not shown).

In Table A3 we display the marginal effects from estimates with one change to our preferred MNL specification—we used county-level *cases_percapita* from August 2020 as our measure of the health conditions present in the county, instead of *deaths_percapita*. As shown below, it appears that *cases_percapita* was not as salient to families when they were making decisions on where to send their children to school—not as salient as *deaths_percapita*. The marginal effect of *cases_percapita* is approximately zero with a very large p-value. This result was the case for every other specification we tried for *cases_percapita*. While we find some evidence that *deaths_percapita* were associated with keeping enrollments level, we can detect no evidence that *cases_percapita* had any effect on independent school enrollments.

Table A4 shows the marginal effects from estimates with one change to our preferred MNL specification—the dependent variable codes schools with excess demand as having no change in enrollment (*enroll_status* = 2). Thus, independent schools who reported that they had no enrollment changes between fall 2019 and fall 2020, yet had excess demand, were coded as having no enrollment change. As seen below, this coding change does not impact the main conclusions in the body of the paper.

For the empirical specification in Table A5 below, we changed the dependent variable to be dichotomous, Y = 1 if the independent school experienced no enrollment decrease between fall 2019 and fall 2020, and Y = 0 if the school did experience an enrollment decrease. This specification increases our degrees of freedom, as it requires only one set of coefficients to be

Table A3. Marginal effects on the probability that *Enroll_Status* = 1, an enrollment decline. *cases_percapita* is the health variable.

	Estimated Marginal Effects	p-value
cases_percapita	−0.00002	0.885
change_emp_annual	−0.002	0.851
public_virtual	−0.162	0.034
real_tuition	0.0008	0.804

Table A4. Marginal effects on the probability that Enroll_Status = 1, an enrollment decline. Independent schools with excess demand were coded as experiencing no enrollment change.

	Estimated Marginal Effects	p-value
deaths_percapita	−0.030	0.223
change_emp_annual	−0.008	0.938
public_virtual	−0.173	0.023
real_tuition	0.0008	0.796

Table A5. OLS estimates of the preferred model independent variables with a dichotomous dependent variable.

R-squared = 0.0353						
dep var =0 if enroll decrease **equals 1 if no enroll decrease**						
	Coefficient	**Std. Err**	**t**	**P>|t|**	**[95% Conf. Interval**	
deaths_percapita	0.0034	0.0025	1.34	0.2	−0.0020	0.0088
change_emp_annual	0.0916	0.7006	0.13	0.898	−1.4017	1.5848
public_virtual	0.1815	0.0752	2.41	0.029	0.0212	0.3418
Treal	−0.0006	0.0027	−0.22	0.832	−0.0063	0.0052
constant	0.5693	0.1278	4.46	0	0.2970	0.8416

Table A6. Marginal effects on the probability that *enroll_status* = , an enrollment decline. *Estimated model as an ordered logit.*

	Estimated Marginal Effects	p-value
deaths_percapita	−0.002	0.819
change_emp_annual	−0.002	0.708
public_virtual	−0.142	0.009
real_tuition	0.0007	0.323

estimated. We display the ordinary least squares (OLS) results below. The virtue of OLS is that it is easy to interpret effect sizes from the coefficient estimates. For example, when public schools in the county were open only for virtual instruction (public_virtual = 1), the likelihood of private schools experiencing a decline in enrollment fell by 18.15 percentage points—very close to our preferred results from the MNL specification in the body of the paper. The other implications from the preferred MNL specification are highly similar to this OLS specification as well.

In Table A6 below we report the results of estimating our model as an ordered logit, instead of multinomial logit (MNL). The results are almost identical to the MNL results reported in the body of the paper.

In Table A7 we report the results of estimating our MNL model with squared terms for all three continuous variables. The implications of these are almost identical to the MNL results reported in the body of the paper.

Finally, we estimated a few dozen other specifications (employed an ordered probit approach, shorter changes in economic variables, public schools opening in a hybrid modality as a covariate; independent school learning modality as a covariate, etc.), and none of them yielded results that would have changed the main conclusions in this paper. The latter variable, independent school learning modality, is theoretically endogenous, as independent schools concerned about losing enrollment during the pandemic may have been more likely to open for face-to-face instruction. Given this endogeneity issue, we do not report an empirical specification with independent school learning modality as a covariate.

Table A7. Marginal effects on the probability that *enroll_status* = 1, an enrollment decline. *Multinomial logit results with squared terms for all continuous variables.*

	Estimated Marginal Effects	p-value
deaths_percapita	0.001	0.894
change_emp_annual	0.084	0.816
public_virtual	−0.184	0.010
real_tuition	0.003	0.633
deaths_percapita_squared	−0.0001	0.671
change_emp_annual	−0.0002	0.881
real_tuition	−0.00002	0.760

Opting Out: Enrollment Trends in Response to Continued Public School Shutdowns

Will Flanders ⓘ

ABSTRACT
Research has found that fall 2020 school district reopening decisions appear to be driven more by politics and teachers unions than by the local presence of COVID-19. But what are the implications of those decisions for enrollment trends? Using recently released enrollment data from the state of Wisconsin, this study goes further to show whether school district decisions to go virtual, as opposed to in-person, led families to make other educational choices including enrollment in virtual schools, or delaying enrollment in school. We find that school districts that chose virtual learning to start the 2020 school year saw the largest enrollment declines, while families gravitated toward private schools and school districts with existing virtual schools.

Introduction

The COVID-19 pandemic severely affected almost every aspect of American life – from the workplace to grocery shopping. But perhaps few impacts will be more consequential than the impact on students in K-12 education. In the spring 2020 semester, when little was known about the virus, schools throughout the country shut down in-person instruction. Over time, the growing consensus among healthcare experts has been that reopenings can occur safely. Indeed, Director of the National Institute for Allergies and Infectious Disease Anthony Fauci remarked that we ought to "close the bars and open the schools," highlighting the relative safety of reopening schools relative to other public activities (Fowler, 2020). Even more compelling, a meta-analysis of more than 130 studies found consistent evidence that reopening schools can be done safely (Bailey, 2021). Yet even as health experts have increasingly gone on record in support of opening schools (Insights for Education, 2020; Kampe, Lehfeld, Buda, Buchholz, & Haas, 2020), many districts made the decision to remain shut down for the fall semester Figure 1.

Research has found that these decisions were driven less by real fears about COVID-19 than by pressure from teachers unions (DeAngelis & Makridis, 2020; Flanders, 2020; Hartney & Finger, 2020) and local politics (Flanders,

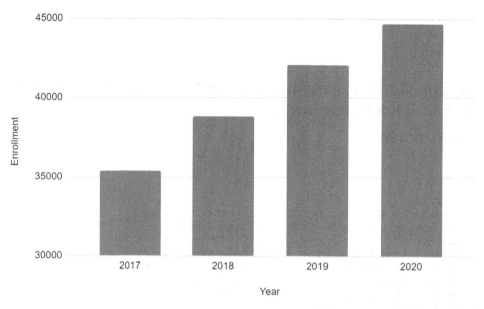

Figure 1. School Choice Program Enrollment, 2017-2020 School Years Wisconsin

2020; Hartney & Finger, 2020). But what has been the reaction of families to these decisions?

Using data from Wisconsin on school district enrollment combined with data on school district reopening decisions, we seek to answer that question. Like in many other situations, we find that parents behave in a rational manner when it comes to reopenings: opting out of schools that aren't meeting the needs of their families for schools better equipped to educate their children or delaying enrolling in school entirely.

Literature review

There are many reasons that families may find continued virtual education does not meet the educational needs of their children. A study from Germany examined the amount of time that children were spending on school-related activities since the pandemic began (Woessmann et al., 2020). The research found that students were only spending about half the time they were prior to the pandemic on learning, while spending more time on television and video games. The resulting loss of learning may be more profound in math than in reading (Kuhfeld, Tarasawa, Johnson, Ruzek, & Lewis, 2020). Researchers at the Center for Reinventing Public Education analyzed the performance of a nationally-representative sample of school districts. They found that just one third of school districts had an expectation that teachers would regularly deliver in instruction (Lake, Gross, & Opalka, 2020). In Wisconsin, parents were surveyed during the early stages of the pandemic. More than 80% report that their children were spending less than 20 hours per week on school work. The largest percentage at the high school level were spending 10 hours or less (Flanders, 2020a).

This reduced focus on learning could have long-term economic consequences. A recent study by Hanushek and Woessman (2020) estimated that students who miss just one third of a year of schooling would reduce their lifelong earnings potential by 3%. This would, in turn, result in a loss of GDP in present value of a staggering 14.2 USD billion to the U.S. If learning loss continues through the fall, that cost would essentially double to 27.9 USD billion. Given that families have an intrinsic desire for their children to do well in life, they are likely to do all they can to avoid the realization of these economic costs to their own children. These losses have only grown since this work was released.

What's worse, these losses are not evenly spread across the population. The fact that virtual education relies on technology means that many lower-income families and those in rural areas without ready access to high-speed internet may be most likely to suffer. According to polling from the Pew Research Center, low-income parents are far more concerned about their children falling behind than parents from other income groups (Horowitz, 2020). Dorn, Hancock, Sarakatsannis, and Viruleg (2020) estimate that achievement gaps between low-income and wealthier students could grow by as much as 15–20% after the pandemic. The implications of these losses may reach beyond academic achievement. A recent study used the relationship between educational achievement and life expectancy to estimate an aggregate 13.8 million years of life lost among those of school age during school closure (Christakis, Van Cleve, & Zimmerman, 2020).

These reopening decisions often appear to be driven by factors beyond the pandemic. Valant (2020) was among the first to note that reopening decisions were more highly correlated with local politics as measured by Trump support than with coronavirus cases. DeAngelis and Makridis (2021a) examined data on more than 800 school districts around the country, and determined that those in areas with a stronger teacher's union presence were more likely to close than those in areas with weaker unions independent of COVID-19 rates. Hartney and Finger (2020) utilize a national database that tracks school reopening decisions to reach similar conclusions. Closer to the Wisconsin dataset used here, Flanders (2020) used a comprehensive database of union presence in districts throughout the state of Wisconsin to conclude that unions and local politics drove reopening decisions while COVID-19 rates were insignificantly related to that outcome. Such decisions do not appear to be related to funding either. A study by DeAngelis and Makridis (2021b) found that better funded districts were equally or more likely to go virtual.

If reopening decisions are not being driven primarily by the local threat of the virus, it is likely that dissatisfaction may be increasing among families who are being forced into homeschooling. Existing research suggests that families behave rationally when the traditional public-school environment isn't meeting their children's needs. For example, in New York's public school system, families are more likely to enroll in schools with better academic outcomes when provided simple information about these schools (Corcoran, Jennings, Cohodes, & Sattin-Bajaj, 2016). In Milwaukee, academics and student safety drive enrollment in the city's school voucher program (DeAngelis and Flanders 2018). If parents find the virtual school environment dissatisfying, we would expect them to make alternative choices. The broad availability of public school choice in Wisconsin makes this an ideal venue to examine this proposition.

Public school choice and virtual charters

Wisconsin has a relatively permissive open enrollment program that allows families to open enroll out of their home district into other surrounding districts that may better fit their needs. Each year, school districts decide on the number of seats they will open. School districts are not required to open any seats, however most districts in the state participate broadly, as the program offers financial benefit to the receiving district (Kava, 2019). Families are allowed to apply to up to three districts per year, and may specify the school within the district they wish to attend. The window for traditional open enrollment opens in February and closes in the first week of April. However, there is an alternative application process that is open year-round that many virtual schools made a push to make known during the summer as districts were deciding how to handle the Fall semester (RightWisconsin, 2020).

The open enrollment program is the largest school choice program in the state of Wisconsin, with over 62,000 students participating according to the most recent data. The program is growing: 7.3% of Wisconsin students were enrolled in the program during the 2018–19 school year compared to 1.10% in 2001–02 (RightWisconsin, 2020).

Wisconsin also has a number of virtual schools that may be better equipped to meet the needs of students forced into at-home education. In Wisconsin, all virtual public schools are considered to be charter schools. Virtual charter schools are organized, like other public schools, under the umbrella of a school district. Currently, the state has 52 virtual charter schools operating with 44 school districts. Many of these schools have been in operation for several years, and are likely to have effective processes in place for online education. Families apply to the virtual charter schools through the same open enrollment process that is used to apply to other public schools in the state.

Theory

As we have seen in the previous section, families in Wisconsin have the ability to "vote with their feet" when it comes to where they send their children to school. Based on the evidence of dissatisfaction around school reopening decisions, I expect that enrollment will decline in districts that made the decision to go fully virtual. The decision to change schools is likely based around two key desires: the desire among some families for their children to be in school full time, and the desire among other families for their child to be enrolled in a virtual school program that has a proven track record of success. Consequently, I expect that districts that made the decision to go virtual since the outbreak of the pandemic will see enrollment decline, while districts with virtual schools that existed prior to the pandemic will also experience growth.

Methods

The dependent variable in this analysis is the percent change in enrollment between the 2019–20 school year and the 2020–21 school year. To account for the possibility that some districts may simply be shrinking faster than others for reasons beyond the decision to go virtual, we include a number of control variables in the analysis. These variables include the percentage change in enrollment during the previous two years, the percentage of students in the district who are African American, and the share of low-income students in the district. These variables are included to account for the possibility that the popularly documented differential effect of the pandemic on disadvantaged groups (e.g. King & Guadiano, 2020) has made them more likely to look for alternative enrollment options. These variables are all also measured during the 2020–21 school year. Finally, the population of the area in which the school district is located is included in the model.

Our key independent variable is *Move to Virtual*. This variable takes on a value of "1" if a district went to virtual education to start the 2020–21 school year and a "0" if other methods were utilized. For simplicity, only districts that went fully virtual are coded as "1" here. Districts that utilized hybrid models of educating students in-person for a few days per week, or those that educated students in different grades using different means, are not considered.[1] Consequently, our model can be considered a cautious estimate of the impact on enrollment of moving to virtual education.

Formally, for each district:

$$\Delta\text{Enrollment} = \alpha + \beta_1(\textit{Move to Virtual}) + \beta_2(\text{Lagged } \Delta \text{ Enrollment}) + \beta_3(\text{Controls}) + e \tag{1}$$

We are also interested in whether districts that have previously established virtual schools are attractive to parents. Theoretically, such schools may have worked out many of the "kinks" surrounding virtual education that traditional school districts are only beginning to consider. To address this possibility, we run a second model with *Existing Virtual* as the variable of interest, and all previously mentioned variables still included. This variable is coded as "1" if the district had a virtual school in place prior to the 2020–21 school year, and a "0" otherwise.[2]

Thus the second model[3]:

$$\Delta \text{Enrollment} = \alpha + \beta_1 (\textit{Move to Virtual}) + \beta_2 (\text{Lagged } \Delta \text{ Enrollment}) \\ + \beta_3 (\text{Controls}) + \beta_4 (\text{Existing Vitrual School}) + e^4 \qquad (2)$$

Results

Table 1 displays the summary statistics for our key variables. At this level, one can see that enrollment declines increased substantially relative to the previous year, 18 to 19. This year, enrollment declined by 2.67% statewide whereas enrollment declined by 0.3% in the previous year. This 790% increase in enrollment declines suggests an important impact of the pandemic on Wisconsin schools. Other things to note among our key variables: about 10% of districts throughout the state have an established virtual charter school. While we cannot tell how spread out such charters are throughout the state from this data, it does suggest that a substantial share of the state's population may have access to such schools.

Finally, we note that approximately 8% of districts throughout the state went fully virtual. Again, recall that this number does not include schools that utilized a hybrid model or went virtual later in the year.

Table 2 displays the results from the analysis in Equation (1). Of note first is that many of the control variables behave in the manner that we might expect. For example, a strong predictor of 2019–20 enrollment change is the 2018–19 enrollment change. It appears that the pandemic did not shift overall trends of which districts in the state are growing, and which are shrinking.[4]

Area population was insignificantly related to enrollment changes, though the coefficient on the variable is negative. This may be consistent with trends that have been observed of people moving out of close, crowded urban areas during the pandemic on the margins. On our variable of interest, it appears that the decision to go fully virtual did have a negative effect on student enrollment. Districts that went virtual saw an approximately 3 percentage point larger decline in enrollment than other districts throughout the state ($p < .05$).[5]

Table 3 below adds the *established virtual charter school* variable to the model. Recall that this is a binary variable taking on a value of "1" in districts that already had a virtual school in place prior to the pandemic. Our previous

COVID-19 AND SCHOOLS

Table 1. Summary statistics for key variables.

Variable	Mean(SD)	N
Enrollment Change 2020–21	−0.0267(0.0589)	415
Decision to go Virtual	0.0819(0.2746)	415
Established Virtual School	0.1060(0.3082)	415
Enrollment Change 2019–20	−0.0034(0.0337)	415
Share African American	0.0215(0.0526)	415
Share Economically Disadvantaged	0.3760(0.1625)	415
Population (100,000s)	1.432(2.1092)	415

Table 2. Enrollment change & decision to go virtual.

VARIABLES	Enrollment Change 2020–21
Enrollment Change 2019–20	0.3570***
	(0.0829)
Decision to go Virtual	−0.0289**
	(0.0121)
African American Share	0.3060***
	(0.0665)
Economically Disadvantaged Share	−0.0322
	(0.0197)
Population (100,000s)	−0.0023
	(0.00182)
Constant	−0.0144*
	(0.00869)
Observations	415
R-squared	0.101

Standard errors in parentheses.
*** $p < 0.01$, ** $p < 0.05$, * $p < 0.1$.

Table 3. Enrollment change & established virtual schools.

VARIABLES	Enrollment Change 2020–21
Enrollment Change 2019–20	0.3160***
	(0.0806)
Decision to go Virtual	−0.0304***
	(0.0117)
Established Virtual School	0.0469***
	(0.00883)
African American Share	0.2780***
	(0.0646)
Economically Disadvantaged Share	−0.0399**
	(0.0191)
Population (100,000s)	−0.0019
	(0.00176)
Constant	−0.0165*
	(0.00843)
Observations	415
R squared	0.159

Standard errors in parentheses.
*** $p < 0.01$, ** $p < 0.05$, * $p < 0.1$.

key variables function much the same way with the addition of this variable. In this model, the decision to go virtual is related to an approximate 3 percentage point decline in enrollment ($p < .01$). Because we are now accounting for movement to existing virtual schools, it arguably represents the decline in enrollment from parents who were dissatisfied with virtual education in general as opposed to that offered by a particular public school district.[6]

That said, having an established virtual charter school appears to have an independent, positive effect on enrollment. Such districts saw an enrollment increase of about 4.6 percentage point holding all other variables constant.

Discussion

The next logical question is, of course, where else are families moving? While virtual charters have seen substantial growth, they cannot entirely account for the downward enrollment trend in 2020. Other research has found that the largest enrollment declines statewide occurred in the Kindergarten and pre-Kindergarten cohorts, while drops at other grade levels were far closer to what is seen in a regular school year (Flanders, 2020a).

It also appears that families continued to be interested in the state's private school choice programs. The programs continue to grow by about 2–3,000 students per year, and this year was no exception. About 2,700 additional students took advantage of private school choice this year, suggesting such schools continue to offer a viable alternative for many families even during the pandemic. Greater enrollment growth occurred in the out-state programs than the Milwaukee Parental Choice Program (MPCP). Enrollment in the MPCP went up by 63 students, while the statewide program grew by 2,379, and the Racine program grew by 186. The school choice program focused on special needs students grew by 380 students.

There is a growing literature that suggests that many parents throughout the country have been dissatisfied with the decision of school districts to only provide virtual education contrary to the preponderance of scientific evidence that it is generally safe to keep schools open with reasonable protocols in place (DeAngelis & Makridis, 2020). However, the literature has yet to establish that this decision-making was inconsistent with the needs of families. This paper lends support to that hypothesis. It appears that some parents were willing to "vote with their feet" and seek out other educational options when districts decided to go fully virtual. Families enrolled out of such districts into districts that were offering in-person instruction, or had established virtual school protocols that were likely more well organized than what could be created during this chaotic time.

This study provides even further evidence that families are willing and able to use school choice options when made available to them. It also shows that traditional, district-based educational models have a tenuous hold on families, and that making inter-district movement viable can have broad implications during periods of change. While it remains to be seen whether the enrollment shifts observed during the pandemic become permanent, there is the possibility that we are at the front-end of radical shift in the mode of delivery for education.

Notes

1. Other districts have gone virtual subsequent to the school year starting. These districts are not considered either as we are interested in the enrollment decisions that parents made prior to the school year.
2. A full list of virtual charter schools in Wisconsin is included as an Appendix to this document as shown in Appendix Table A2.
3. To account for the potential of non-linearity in the data, an alternative model with squared terms included for each control variable is found in Appendix Table A3. No meaningful change in the key results occurred from this analysis.
4. Looking at longer term trends, the 18–19 decline is far more consistent with average declines seen over the years.
5. As a falsification test, we utilize 18–19 enrollment change as an alternative dependent variable. Theoretically, if other trends in the district explain the relationship to the decision to go virtual, this variable would also be significantly related to the decision to go virtual. Appendix Table A1 shows the results and an insignificant relationship.
6. In order to fully bolster this claim, it would be important to account for enrollment at nearby private schools that went virtual and offered in-person instruction. However, this information is not currently available. Future research may attempt to resolve this question.

Disclosure statement

No potential conflict of interest was reported by the author(s).

ORCID

Will Flanders ⓘ http://orcid.org/0000-0001-8284-4853

References

Bailey, J. (2021). Is it safe to reopen schools? *Center for Reinventing Public Education Policy Report*. Retrieved from https://www.crpe.org/sites/default/files/3-12_is_it_safe_to_reopen_schools_an_extensive_review_of_the_research_1.pdf

Christakis, D., Van Cleve, W., & Zimmerman, F. J. (2020). Estimation of US children's educational attainment and years of life lost associated with primary school closures during the coronavirus disease. *JAMA Network Open*, *3*(11), e2028786. doi:10.1001/jamanetworkopen.2020.28786

Corcoran, S., Jennings, J. L., Cohodes, S. R., & Sattin-Bajaj, C. (2016). *Leveling the playing field for high school choice: Results from a field experiment of informational interventions*

(Working Paper). National Bureau of Labor Statistics. Retrieved from https://www.nber.org/papers/w24471

DeAngelis, C., & Flanders, W. (2018). The education marketplace: The predictors of school growth and closure in Milwaukee. *Journal of School Choice, 13*(3), 355–379. doi:10.1080/15582159.2019.1595949

DeAngelis, C. A., & Makridis, C. A. (2021a). Are school reopening decisions related to union influence? *Social Science Quarterly.* doi:10.1111/ssqu.12955

DeAngelis, C. A., & Makridis, C. A. (2021b). *Are school reopening decisions related to funding? Evidence from over 12,000 districts during the COVID-19 pandemic* (SSRN Working Paper). Retrieved from https://papers.ssrn.com/sol3/papers.cfm?abstract_id=3799694

Dorn, E., Hancock, B., Sarakatsannis, J., & Viruleg, E. (2020). COVID-19 and student learning in the United States: The hurt could last a lifetime. *McKinsey.* Retrieved from https://www.mckinsey.com/industries/public-and-social-sector/our-insights/covid-19-and-student-learning-in-the-united-states-the-hurt-could-last-a-lifetime

Flanders, W. (2020). *Politics in the pandemic: The role of unions in school reopening decisions* (Working Paper). Retrieved from https://will-law.org/wp-content/uploads/2020/12/reopening-brief.pdf

Flanders, W. (2020a). Poll: Messaging reopening in Wisconsin. *Wisconsin Institute for Law & Liberty Policy Memo.* Retrieved from https://will-law.org/wp-content/uploads/2020/12/reopen-wisconsin-poll_final_2.pdf

Fowler, H. (2020). Close bars and keep schools open, Fauci says. Has that worked in other countries? *Miami Herald.* Retrieved from https://www.miamiherald.com/news/coronavirus/article247504030.html

Haines, S. (2020). Teachers union puts tombstones in Madison to push for virtual classes. *WTMJ Milwaukee.* Retrieved from https://www.tmj4.com/news/local-news/teachers-put-up-tombstone-signs-in-madison-to-push-for-virtual-classes

Hamel, L., Kearney, A., Lopes, L., Munana, C., & Brody, M. (2020). KFFTracking poll-July 2020. *Kaiser Family Foundation.* Retrieved from https://www.kff.org/coronavirus-covid-19/report/kff-health-tracking-poll-july-2020/

Hanushek, E., & Woessman, L. (2020). The economic impacts of learning loss. *OECD.* Retrieved from http://www.oecd.org/education/The-economic-impacts-of-coronavirus-covid-19-learning-losses.pdf

Hartney, M., & Finger, L. (2020). *Politics, markets, and pandemics: Public education's response to COVID-19. EdWorking Paper.*

Horowitz, J. (2020). Lower-income parents most concerned about their children falling behind amid COVID-19 school closures. *Pew Research Center FactTank.* Retrieved from https://www.pewresearch.org/fact-tank/2020/04/15/lower-income-parents-most-concerned-about-their-children-falling-behind-amid-covid-19-school-closures/

Insights for Education. (2020). *COVID-19 and schools: What we can learn from six months of closures and reopening.* Retrieved from https://education.org/facts-and-insights#f09a6e46-8c5f-4d01-8297-d2a3f6c8f873

Kampe, E., Lehfeld, A.-S., Buda, S., Buchholz, U., & Haas, W. (2020). Surveillance of COVID-19 school outbreaks, Germany, March to August 2020. *Eurosurveillance, 25*, 1–6.

Kava, R. (2019). *Open enrollment program* (Wisconsin Legislative Fiscal Bureau Informational Paper 26). Retrieved from https://docs.legis.wisconsin.gov/misc/lfb/informational_papers/january_2019/0026_open_enrollment_program_informational_paper_26.pdf

Kim, J., Choe, Y. J., Lee, J., Park, Y. J., Park, O., Han, M. S., ... Cho, E. H. (2020). Role of children in household transmission of COVID-19. *Archives of Disease in Childhood*, archdischild-2020-319910. Published Online. doi:10.1136/archdischild-2020-319910

King, M., & Guadiano, N. (2020). The pandemic could widen the achievement gap. A generation of students is at risk. *Politico*. Retrieved from https://www.politico.com/news/2020/09/23/how-the-coronavirus-is-making-school-segregation-worse–420839

Kuhfeld, M., Tarasawa, B., Johnson, A., Ruzek, E., & Lewis, K. (2020). Learning during COVID-19: Initial findings on students' reading and math achievement and growth *NWEA Research*. Retrieved from https://www.nwea.org/content/uploads/2020/11/Collaborative-brief-Learning-during-COVID-19.NOV2020.pdf

Lake, R., Gross, B., & Opalka, A. (2020). Analysis: Just 1 in 3 districts required teachers to deliver instruction this spring. They mustn't be left on their own again in the fall *Center for Reinventing Public Education Policy Brief*. Retrieved from https://www.crpe.org/sites/default/files/final_national_sample_brief_2020.pdf

Oster, E. (2020). Schools aren't superspreaders. *The Atlantic*. Retrieved from https://www.theatlantic.com/ideas/archive/2020/10/schools-arent-superspreaders/616669/

RightWisconsin. (2020). *Not happy with your district's back to school plans? You can still transfer into online public charter schools in Wisconsin*. Retrieved from https://rightwisconsin.com/2020/08/14/not-happy-with-your-districts-back-to-school-plans-you-can-still-transfer-into-online-public-charter-schools-in-wisconsin

Valant, J. (2020). School reopening decisions linked to politics rather than public health. *Brookings Institute Brown Center Chalk Board*. Retrieved from https://www.brookings.edu/blog/brown-center-chalkboard/2020/07/29/school-reopening-plans-linked-to-politics-rather-than-public-health/

Woessmann, L., Freundl, V., Grewenig, E., Lergetporer, P., Werner, K., & Zierow, L. (2020). Education in the corona crisis: How did the schoolchildren spend the time the schools were closed and which educational measures do the Germans advocate? *Ifo Schnelldienst, 7*, 3.

Appendix A.

Table A1. Falsification test with previous year's enrollment change.

VARIABLES	(1) Enrollment Change 2019–20
Enrollment Change 18–19	0.0774*
	(0.0445)
Decision to go Virtual	−0.0051
	(0.00719)
African American Share	0.0360
	(0.0406)
Economically Disadvantaged Share	−0.0272**
	(0.0117)
Population (100,000s)	−0.0003
	(0.00109)
Constant	0.0072
	(0.00515)
Observations	415
R-squared	0.026

Standard errors in parentheses.
*** $p < 0.01$, ** $p < 0.05$, * $p < 0.1$.

Table A2. Additional control for previous enrollment change.

VARIABLES	(1) Enrollment Change 2020–21
Enrollment Change 2019–20	0.329***
	(0.0817)
Enrollment Change 2018–17	0.2920***
	(0.0734)
Decision to go Virtual	−0.026**
	(0.0119)
Share African American	0.245***
	(0.0671)
Share Economically Disadvantaged	−0.0282
	(0.0194)
Population (100,000s)	−0.00145
	(0.00180)
Constant	−0.0149*
	(0.00854)
Observations	415
R-squared	0.134

Standard errors in parentheses.
*** $p < 0.01$, ** $p < 0.05$, * $p < 0.1$.

Table A3. Results with squared terms included.

VARIABLES	(1) Enrollment Change 2020–21
Enrollment Change 2019–20	0.3190***
	(0.0831)
Decision to go Virtual	−0.0249**
	(0.0118)
Established Virtual School	0.0483***
	(0.00883)
Share African American	−0.2230
	(0.167)
Share Economically Disadvantaged	−0.0003
	(0.0691)
Population (100,000s)	0.0095*
	(0.00524)
African American^2	1.140***
	(0.348)
Economically Disadvantaged^2	−0.0244
	(0.0815)
Population (100,000s)^2	−0.0011**
	(0.000532)
Enrollment Change 2019–20^2	1.4820
	(1.067)
Constant	−0.0319**
	(0.0161)
Observations	415
R-squared	0.193

Standard errors in parentheses.
*** $p < 0.01$, ** $p < 0.05$, * $p < 0.1$.

COVID-19 Safety Concerns, School Governance Models, and Instructional Modes: An Exploration of School Quality Perspectives during the Pandemic

Jason Jabbari [ID], Takeshi Terada, Ethan Greenstein, and Evan Rhinesmith

ABSTRACT

This paper explores how parents' COVID-19 safety concerns relate to school governance models (SGMs), instructional modes (i.e. in-person, hybrid, online), and perceptions of school quality during the pandemic. Leveraging two waves of household survey data across 47 states and the District of Columbia, we first conduct a series of multinomial regression analyses to explore the extent that parents' safety concerns relate to SGMs, as well as the extant that SGMs relate to instructional modes. We then explore the extent that parents' safety concerns, SGMs, and instructional modes relate to perceptions of school quality. We also examine whether the relationship between SGMs and perceptions of school quality vary across instructional modes. We find that parents' safety concerns varied widely across SGMs and that when considering these variations, SGMs appeared to be able to match parents' safety concerns with appropriate instructional modes. Although charter and private schools were consistently associated with better perceptions of school quality, we did not observe frequent associations between instructional modes (e.g. virtual instruction) and perceptions of school quality. However, we did find that the relationship between SGMs and perceptions of school quality significantly varied across instructional modes, such that hybrid instruction tended to increase the likelihood of perceiving poor school quality at charter schools but decrease these perceptions in private schools. We conclude with implications for policy and practice.

Introduction

Following the outbreak of the COVID-19 pandemic in the Spring of 2020, nearly all k-12 students in the U.S. experienced a disruption in in-person instruction, and many schools continued remote instruction during the 2020–2021 school year. Research has demonstrated that remote instruction can have deleterious effects on student learning (Goldhaber et al., 2022). Moreover, the quality of remote instruction can differ between schools (Dawson, 2022), and its prevalence can vary across neighborhood and school contexts (see, for example, Camp & Zamarro, 2022). Therefore, the pandemic can be seen as further stratifying learning opportunities and in some cases exacerbating some of the preexisting inequalities across student demographic characteristics and social contexts (Goldberg, 2021).

However, given that families can differ in their pandemic safety concerns, including the tradeoffs between the risks and benefits associated with in-person learning, different instructional offerings can – in some cases – be seen meeting the preferences of certain parents (Barnum, 2021). These preferences can be met by parental choice of schools or instructional modes or, conversely, by schools' responses to parental concerns. Pertaining to parental choice, preferences can be met (a) through previous actions – by parents having chosen a school that aligns with their safety concerns and related preferences or (b) through current actions – by parents choosing an instructional mode within a current school or by choosing a new school altogether that aligns with their safety concerns and related preferences. At the same time, schools can be seen as responding to parents' concerns and preferences through the type of instruction offered to students during the pandemic (see, for example, Houston & Steinberg, 2022).

School governance models (i.e. traditional public, charter, and private) are an important facet of parental choice in their child's education and have been related to both instructional mode and parent perceptions of school quality during the pandemic (Henderson, Peterson, & West, 2021). Nevertheless, despite the importance of understanding how parents' safety concerns relate to school governance models (SGMs), instructional modes (i.e. in-person, hybrid, and online), and perceptions of school quality during the pandemic, research has yet to explore these relationships simultaneously, nor the ways in which instructional modes may moderate the relationships among SGMs and school quality. To fill the gap in the research, we ask the following questions:

(1) How do parental safety concerns, as well as the tradeoffs between in-person learning risks and benefits, relate to school governance models (SGMs), instructional modes, and perceptions of school quality during the COVID-19 pandemic?
(2) How do SGMs relate to instructional modes and perceptions of school quality during the COVID-19 pandemic?
(3) How do school instructional modes relate to perceptions of school quality during the COVID-19 pandemic?
(4) Does the relationship between SGMs and perceptions of school quality during the pandemic vary across instructional mode?

To answer these questions, we use two waves of household survey data across 47 states and the District of Columbia to conduct series of multinomial regression analyses among COVID-19 safety concerns, SGMs, instructional modes, and perceptions of school quality. We then interact SGMs and instructional modes in our model examining perceptions of school quality. We find that parents' safety concerns varied across SGMs, that instructional modes appear to match the safety concerns associated with SGMs for most respondents, and that the relationship between SGMs and perceptions of school quality significantly varies across instructional modes.

Literature review

In an effort to mitigate the spread of COVID-19 during the early stages of the pandemic, all 50 states opted to cease in-person learning in K-12 schools (Auger et al., 2020). In the preliminary stages of the pandemic, states that closed schools earlier – when COVID-19 cases were lowest – saw the largest relative reduction in cases and deaths relative to states that closed later on (Auger et al., 2020).[1] Similarly, each additional day delaying state-mandated school closures following the first reported COVID-19 case was associated with 1.5 to 2.4% more COVID-19 deaths per capita (Rauscher & Burns, 2021). Taken together, these studies show an association between closing schools when COVID-19 cases were still low and keeping COVID-19 incidences and mortalities low.

As the pandemic continued into the 2020–21 academic year, schools across the country planned for a return to distance learning with some estimates showing that nearly 60% of students began the school year virtually (Dorn, Hancock, Sarakatsannis, & Viruleg, 2020). However, several states opted to return to in-person learning as the school year progressed. According to a survey of nearly 600 public school district leaders in 46 states, while only 41% of public school districts offered in-person instruction in the fall, this increased to 54% by the winter of 2021 (Hodgman, Rickles, Carminucci, & Garret, 2021). In many states, while executive orders led to the initial school closures, return decisions were often made by local districts (Grossman et al., 2021). As these decisions did not always reflect trends in COVID-19 cases (DeAngelis & Makridis, 2021), it is important to consider both the factors that influence instructional modalities, such as parental safety concerns, as well as influence of instructional modalities on school quality perceptions. Moreover, as many parents were not provided with the option to choose their instructional mode, it is also important to consider the role of school governance models (SGMs) in these relationships. We proceed by reviewing the related research on parental safety concerns, SGMs, and instructional modalities during the pandemic.

Parental safety concerns

Parental safety concerns and school governance models

The relationship between parents' safety concerns and school governance models may be explained by a school's level of social closure and trust. Here, social closure in education refers to the sociological phenomenon where a tight-knit community of families enrolling in a particular school (e.g. a Catholic school) are able to enforce norms that result in desirable outcomes (Fasang, Mangino, & Brückner, 2014). As the pandemic spread, boundaries – an essential aspect of social closure – became an important element in families' daily lives, as it allowed families to partially control their vulnerability to the virus. In addition to drawing boundaries of exposure, families also needed to trust individuals within their boundaries to limit their own exposure to the virus. While social closure and greater levels of trust within schools can be particularly advantageous during the COVID-19 pandemic, these attributes are not randomly distributed across school contexts. Rather, both social closure and greater levels of trust have often been associated with private schools. For example, Coleman and Hoffer (1987) found greater levels of social closure in Catholic schools; Bryk and Schneider (2002) found greater levels of trust in Catholic schools as well. While research has yet to explore how levels of social closure and trust vary across SGMs during the pandemic, research has pointed to the important role of trust in schools as parents navigated health risks associated with school re-opening in the preliminary stages of the pandemic (Fersch, Schneider-Kamp, & Breidahl, 2022).

In addition to trusting the health safety of schools and other parents, concerns of safety also involve weighing the risks and benefits of in-person learning. Despite increase spread of COVID-19 in areas that offered more in-person instruction, private school parents – who are more likely to have a child learning in-person – were more likely to be satisfied with their child's school and less likely to report a negative effect of mitigation measures on learning (Henderson et al., 2021). Here, private school parents might perceive the benefits of in-person learning to outweigh the risks of potentially having their child exposed to COVID-19.

Parental safety concerns and instructional mode

Perceived COVID-19 risks are associated with protective health behaviors (de Bruin & Bennett, 2020), and evaluations of risks and benefits are both strongly correlated, as well as related to an individual's affective evaluation of an activity (Alhakami & Slovic, 1994). Thus, it is unsurprising that parents perceived the risks and benefits of in-person learning differently and therefore made different decisions on learning modality. While much of the research has focused on choices *between*, rather than *within*, schools (Musaddiq, Stange, Bacher-Hicks, & Goodman, 2022), some schools did offer parents choices between in-person and remote instruction – especially during and after the 2021–2022 school year (Belsha & Barnum, 2022).

While little research has explored these choices, it is important to consider parents' safety concerns. A survey of parents conducted in the summer and fall of 2020 found that the majority of parents reported that student health was their top concern, followed by academic development, personal health, and student mental health (Anderson, Hughes, & Trivedi, 2021). Considering fall 2020 plans, a nationally representative survey administered in June of 2020 found that, 31% of parents would probably or definitely keep their child home in the coming fall, while 49% of parents would probably or definitely send their child to school (Kroshus, Hawrilenko, Tandon, & Christakis, 2020). The factors associated with planning to keep children home in the fall included lower incomes, higher rates of unemployment, greater job flexibilities, greater fears of illness, and less confidence in schools (2020). Furthermore, a qualitative study of Latinx families in Houston, Texas discovered that many parents sacrificed in-person learning to protect the health of their children and family networks, and when in-person learning was necessary (e.g. for working mothers), school safety protocols became incredibly important for parents (Szabo, 2021). However, parents' values and subsequent plans may be due – in part – to limited knowledge of school safety and COVID-19 risks. For example, recent research by (Polikoff, 2021) found that informational text messages that addressed student well-being and safety concerns increased the willingness of parents (who were initially unsure) to send their child back for in person learning. Recent research by Lessler and his colleagues (2021) demonstrated that schools implementing safety and mitigation strategies are effective at limiting the COVID-19 risks associated with in-person learning, such that the risks mirror those in the surrounding community.

Additionally, as in-person learning was more prevalent in areas with more rapid spreading of COVID-19 (Henderson et al., 2021), it is likely that some parents placed greater value on the benefits associated with in-person learning rather than the risks of their children potentially getting sick. Finally, it is important to note that during the 2020–2021 school year most parents were getting the type of instruction that they wanted for their children. In a survey conducted in January of 2021, 89% of parents who preferred remote learning (42% of all parents) were receiving remote instruction, while 74% of parents who preferred in-person learning (36% of all parents) were receiving in-person instruction (Barnum, 2021).

Parental safety concerns and school quality

School physical safety is one of the most important factors in parents' satisfaction with their child's school (Friedman, Bobrowski, & Geraci, 2006). However, satisfaction with schools and perceived school quality are not the same. Rather, much of the literature on parents' perceptions of school quality focuses on student achievement (Gibbons & Silva, 2011). Nevertheless, given that the relationship between school physical safety and student achievement (Kutsyuruba, Klinger & Hussain, 2015), there is reason to believe that perceptions of health safety will be strongly related to perceptions of school quality. As the literature on perceptions of health safety and school quality has yet to take COVID-19 into consideration – a situation in which safety may actually be antithetical to student achievement – it is important to consider the risks and rewards of student achievement during the pandemic. In this regard, fall 2020 survey data found that parents whose children were learning in-person were less likely to state that they perceived COVID-19 mitigation measures in schools as having a negative effect on protection from COVID-19, academic achievement, emotional wellbeing, social relationships, and physical fitness – despite more rapid transmissions in these areas (Henderson et al., 2021). When considering that parents of children attending schools in-person are more likely to be satisfied with instruction, less likely to report learning less, and more likely to state that they were aware of at least one positive COVID-19 case being reported in their child's school (Henderson et al., 2021), we can infer that these parents are either perceiving the environment to be safe for learning or are placing greater value on in-person instruction.

School governance models

School governance models and instructional modes

As described by Hartney and Finger (2022), one way in which school governance models may be related to instructional modes during COVID-19 is through responsiveness to institutional environments (Chubb & Moe, 1990). While constituencies within these institutional environments are numerous, teacher unions have historically been better organized and more politically active than other constituencies (Moe, 2011), which was likely the case during COVID-19 (Hartney & Finger, 2022). Thus, traditional public schools, in which teacher unions are often strongest, may be more responsive to their desires (Hartney & Finger, 2022). Despite some parents wanting more in-person instruction (Barnum, 2021), teacher unions often expressed safety concerns – especially in the early part of the pandemic (Hartney & Finger, 2022). However, while evidence from fall 2020 polling suggests that private school students (60%) were more likely to receive in-person instruction than traditional public school students (24%), charter schools students (18%) were *not* more likely to receive in-person instruction than traditional public school students (Henderson et al., 2021).

In addition to the potential for constituency groups to influence decisions concerning school instructional modes, schools may have also felt pressure from "alternatives" in a given school market. For example, Hartney and Finger (2022) use the MCH Strategic Dataset, containing fall reopening data for over

70% of the nation's public schools, to better understand the influence of market pressures on instructional modes. The authors find that public schools were more likely to open in-person if there was a larger share of private – specifically Catholic – schools nearby opening in-person, demonstrating the sensitivity of these decisions to the local "market" (Hartney & Finger, 2022). Furthermore, research from Musaddiq and her colleagues (2022) use longitudinal administrative data from Michigan and the Census Household Pulse Survey, finding that private school enrollments increased in areas where local schools opted for remote instruction. Similarly, research by Scadafi, Tutterow, and Kavanagh (2021) demonstrate that 70% of independent schools increased their enrollment in the 2020–2021 school year, which was largely due to virtual instruction offered by surrounding public schools. Flanders (2021) confirms these trends with data from Wisconsin, finding that school districts who started the 2020–2021 school year virtually experienced significant declines in enrollment.

School governance models and school quality

Beyond the relationship between school instructional mode and school quality, which will be explained in the following section, there is another way in which school governance models may be related to school quality: innovation. As charter schools did not appear to offer more in-person instruction during the pandemic, innovation may provide an explanation for a potential increase in school quality at these schools. The relationships between SGMs and innovation are based on market theories of governance, which suggest that schools with less bureaucratic structures, such as charter and private schools, will be more likely to innovate their practices in order to better meet to the preferences of "customers" (Chubb & Moe, 1990). Although much of the evidence on such innovation is lacking (Lubienski, 2003), parental involvement does appear to predict innovation in charter schools (Preston, Goldring, Berends, & Cannata, 2012).

Given the importance of parental involvement in virtual instruction, it is possible that charter schools were able to offer higher quality virtual instruction or more attractive hybrid options. Based on summer 2020 parent survey results, Carpenter and Dunn (2020) found that charter schools offered more video and software instruction, as opposed to pen and paper instruction, than both traditional public and private schools during the early stages of the pandemic. Carpenter and Dunn (2020) also found that both charter and private schools offered more highly structured and interactive learning experiences than traditional public schools, while also holding higher expectations of students and engaging in more frequent communication with parents.

According to data from the National Center for Education Statistics (2021), total public school enrollment between 2019–20 and 2020–21 fell by 3%. Additionally, in a nationally representative survey of parents of school-aged children, the reported share of parents enrolling their children in district schools dropped by 9 points (from 81% to 72%) between the spring 2020 shutdown and the fall 2020 return (Henderson et al., 2021). As traditional district enrollments declined, choice-based school sectors (public charter schools, private schools, and homeschooling options) increased over the same period. Over this period, charter school enrollments increased from 5% to 8%, private school enrollment increased from 8% to 11%, and instances of homeschooling increased from 6% to 8% (Henderson et al., 2021).

Instructional modes and school quality

The relationship between instructional modes and school quality has been examined in studies that focus on the ability for schools to provide support (Haller & Novita, 2021), learning resources (Jabbari et al., 2022), and instructional practices across different learning modalities during the pandemic. Survey data from Spring 2020 demonstrate that lack of attendance collections, check-ins, grading, and progress-monitoring led to low expectations for learning (Gross & Opalka, 2020). Even when schools were able to plan for instruction in the 2020–2021 school year, significant barriers existed across homes and neighborhoods, such as lack of supervision, internet enabled devices, and access to high-speed internet (Domina, Renzulli, Murray, Garza, & Perez, 2021).

Unsurprisingly, research confirms the difficulties associated with virtual instruction. In a longitudinal cohort analysis comparing MAP Growth assessments of nearly 5 million 3rd-8th grade students from Fall 2019 and Fall 2020, Kuhfeld et al., 2020) found that math scores were 5–10 percentage points lower on average in Fall 2020 than previous years. Additionally, leveraging testing data across 12 states, Halloran, Jack, Okun, and Oster (2021) found that the declines in pass rates were largest in districts with less in-person instruction. Finally, using data from over 2.1 million students across 10,000 schools in 49 states, Goldhaber et al. (2022) found that remote instruction widened achievement gaps across race and school poverty.

Data, methods, and results

Data and sample

Data for our empirical analysis comes from the Socioeconomic Impacts of COVID-19 Survey (SEICS) administered by the Social Policy Institute at Washington University in St. Louis (Roll et al., 2021).[2] SEICS is a 5-wave, online survey for adults collected at quarterly intervals between April 2020 and June 2021. The samples for these surveys are drawn from a large, online panel provider and are constructed using a quota sampling technique to ensure the samples are representative of the U.S. population in terms of age, race/ethnicity, income, and gender. Each wave of the survey has approximately 5,000 respondents from all 50 U.S. states and the District of Columbia, and respondents can participate in multiple waves of the survey, allowing us to track their outcomes and experiences during COVID-19 over time. Respondents from wave 1 were prioritized for-follow-up waves. While follow-up rates varied in waves 2–5, it is important to note that each subsequent wave employed the same quota sampling technique to ensure sample representativeness. The survey responses collected through this study undergo several quality checks to ensure the reliability of the data. These quality checks involve assessing the speed of responses during the survey, post-hoc checks of the consistency of responses both within and across surveys, and a within-survey commitment exercise to elicit reliable responses.

For the present study, we focus on survey participants who are parents. For parents with two children or more, we randomly assigned one of the children and asked parents to respond to questions for the assigned child. While research has demonstrated that online, non-probability samples using Qualtrics panels tend to generate samples that closely approximate those of the General Social Survey (Zack et al., 2019), we focus on a subset of survey takers who have school-aged children, which does not ensure national representativeness.[3] Nevertheless, our sample does collect a robust set of information for households across 47 states and the District of Columbia.

Our study leverages the second and third waves of the SEICS, which was administered from August to September 2020 (Wave 2) and from November to December 2020 (Wave 3), as these waves capture school enrollment factors and perceptions of learning in the first school semester of the 2020–2021 school year. In particular, this semester occurred *after* the initial outbreak (when almost all schools operated virtually) and *before* the wide distribution of the vaccines (when many schools operated in-person), which allows for an optimal amount of variation in experiences. For the purposes of this study, respondents who did not provide a response to the items used in the analysis were excluded using listwise deletion. Most notably, parents with children below pre-school and past high school were removed from the sample, as well as families who were currently home-schooling their children. After removing these respondents, we had a sample of 1,832 observations. After removing additional respondents with missing variables on other study measures (roughly 7%), the final analytical sample included 1,699 observations from 1,413 parents across the two survey waves (286 parents responded in both waves; 1127 parents responded in only one of the waves). Finally, as SEICS is a household survey, parents of the same children could only respond during the same wave if they resided in separate households, which would be extremely rare for a survey of this type.

Measures

For parental beliefs about school safety, we used Likert scale items (1 = strongly/somewhat disagree; 2 = neither agree nor disagree; 3 = somewhat/strongly) to measure parents' reaction to the following statements:

Other parents are safe: other parents do their best to keep their children safe during the pandemic.

School is safe: your child's school provides a safe learning environment during the pandemic.

In-person benefits outweigh the risks: the benefits of in-person class outweigh the risks during the pandemic.

For school governance model, we asked parents to select the type of school that their child currently attends (1 = public school; 2 = charter school; 3 = private or parochial school); similarly, for instructional mode, we asked parents to select the type of instruction that their child is currently receiving (1 = in-person only; 2 = online only; 3 = a mix of in-person and online or "hybrid"). For school quality, we measured respondents' perceptions of school quality both *before* (retrospectively) and *during* the pandemic (1 = very poor/poor; 2 = average; 3 = very good/excellent).

In addition to our main study variables, we also include a variety of characteristics relating to politics, the pandemic, children, and parents. Starting with politics, we account for *political party identification* (1 = Independent/Other; 2 = Republican; 3 = Democrat). Moving on to the pandemic, we account for *survey wave, county COVID-19 cases* (number of COVID per county cases/1000), *urbanicity* (1 = metro area; 2 non-metro area), and *state of residence*. These measures account for differences in local COVID-19 contexts and state policies, which had large influences on schools' instructional modes (see Marshall & Bradley-Dorsey, 2020). In terms of child characteristics, we include: *grade level* (1 = pre-school; 2 = kindergarten through; 3 = 1st through 2nd grades; 4 = 3rd through 5th grades; 5 = 6th through 8th grades; 6 = 9th through 12th grades), and *diagnosed learning disability status* (1 = no; 2 = yes).

Finally we include a variety of demographic and parent characteristics, including: *age, gender* (1 = male; 2 = female); *race/ethnicity* (1 = White; 2 = Black; 3 = Asian; 4 = Hispanic; 5 = other); *primary language spoken at home* (1 = not English; 2 = English); *educational attainment* (1 = less than Bachelor's degree; 2 = Bachelor's degree or higher); *number of children* (1 = one kid; 2 = two kids; 3 = three or more kids); *area median income* (AMI) level (1 = less than 50% of the AMI [low]; 2 = between 50% and 80% of the AMI [moderate]; 3 = between 80% and 120% [middle]; and 4 = above 120% [high]); *respondent employment status* (1 = working full-time; 2 = working part-time; 3 = not working); *partner/spouse's employment status* (1 = working full-time; 2 = working part-time; 3 = not working; 4 = does not have a partner/ spouse); and *whether or not a household member lost a job or income due to COVID 19* (1 = no; 2 = yes).

Analytic strategy

As our three main variables of interest – school governance models, instructional modes, and school quality – all had three categories, we used multinomial logistic regression. Specifically, we first construct a series of multinomial logistic models predicting SGMs, instructional modes, and perceptions of school quality. We then interact SGMs and instructional modes in our model predicting perceptions of school quality. In our SGM model, we account for safety concerns, politics, pandemic characteristics, child characteristics, and parent characteristics/other demographic characteristics. In our instructional mode model, we also include SGMs. In our school quality model, we also include instructional mode, as well as a measure of pre-pandemic school quality. Sets of characteristics are included one at a time in order to demonstrate potential confounding or mediating effects. Additionally, as some respondents participated in both waves, we clustered standard errors at the individual level.[4] Finally, as our data is treated as cross-sectional and we do not model temporal choices of schools governance models nor instructional modes, it is important to note that our regression models do not imply directional relationships (e.g. X causes Y). This is particularly true for our models predicting school governance models and instructional modes. Rather, we present associations with school governance models and instructional modes to provide a general understanding of the characteristics related to these educational contexts and modalities. For all analyses, we used Stata version 16.1.

Equation 1. School Governance Model

$$\ln\left(\frac{\Pr(Y_i = Charter)}{\Pr(Y_i = Public)}\right) = \beta_0 + \beta_1 X^{\text{Concerns}} + \beta_2 X^{\text{Politics}} + \beta_3 X^{\text{COVID-19}} + \beta_4 X^{\text{Student}} + \beta_5 X^{\text{Parent}}$$

$$\ln\left(\frac{\Pr(Y_i = Private)}{\Pr(Y_i = Public)}\right) = \beta_0 + \beta_1 X^{\text{Concerns}} + \beta_2 X^{\text{Politics}} + \beta_3 X^{\text{COVID-19}} + \beta_4 X^{\text{Student}} + \beta_5 X^{\text{Parent}}$$

Equation 2. Instructional Mode

$$\ln\left(\frac{\Pr(Y_i = Online)}{\Pr(Y_i = In\ Person)}\right) = \beta_0 + \beta_1 X^{\text{Concerns}} + \beta_2 X^{\text{Politics}}$$
$$+ \beta_3 X^{\text{SGM}} \beta_4 X^{\text{COVID}-19} + \beta_5 X^{\text{Student}} + \beta_6 X^{\text{Parent}}$$

$$\ln\left(\frac{\Pr(Y_i = Hyrbrid)}{\Pr(Y_i = In\ Person)}\right) = \beta_0 + \beta_1 X^{\text{Concerns}} + \beta_2 X^{\text{Politics}}$$
$$+ \beta_3 X^{\text{SGM}} \beta_4 X^{\text{COVID}-19} + \beta_5 X^{\text{Student}} + \beta_6 X^{\text{Parent}}$$

Equation 3. School Quality

$$\ln\left(\frac{\Pr(Y_i = Good)}{\Pr(Y_i = Average)}\right) = \beta_0 + \beta_1 X^{\text{Concerns}} + \beta_2 X^{\text{Politics}} + \beta_3 X^{\text{SGM}}$$
$$+ \beta_3 X^{\text{Mode}} + \beta_5 X^{\text{SGM}} * X^{\text{Mode}} + \ldots$$

$$\ln\left(\frac{\Pr(Y_i = Poor)}{\Pr(Y_i = Average)}\right) = \beta_0 + \beta_1 X^{\text{Concerns}} + \beta_2 X^{\text{Politics}} + \beta_3 X^{\text{SGM}}$$
$$+ \beta_3 X^{\text{Mode}} + \beta_5 X^{\text{SGM}} * X^{\text{Mode}} + \ldots$$

Results

Sample description

Tables 1 and 2 contain descriptive statistics for the sample. Starting with our dependent variables, 72.2% of the sample had children enrolled in traditional public schools, while 10.0% of children were enrolled in public charter schools and 17.8% of children were enrolled in private or parochial schools. In terms of school governance model (SGM), 50.5% of the respondents had children that were engaged in online instruction, while 22.1% were engaged in in-person instruction, and 27.4% were engaged in hybrid instruction. For school quality, 44.0% of the respondents felt that the quality of the school instruction was good during the pandemic, 39.5% felt that the quality was neither good nor poor, and 16.5% felt that the quality was poor; prior to the pandemic, while 64.8% felt that the quality was good, 26.4% felt that the quality was neither good nor poor, and 8.8% felt that the quality was poor.

When considering parental concerns and politics, 60.9% of the respondents agreed that their children's school provided a safe learning environment during the pandemic, while 12.5% disagreed, and 26.6% neither agreed nor disagreed. In addition, 58.6% of the respondents agreed that other parents would do their best to keep their children safe during the pandemic, while 13.4% disagreed, and 28% neither agreed nor disagreed. Concerning the risks and rewards for in-person instruction, 48.2% of the respondents agreed that

Table 1. Descriptive statistics for categorical variables.

Variable	Percentage
School governance model	
Public	72.16
Charter	10.01
Private/parochial	17.83
Instruction mode	
In-person	22.07
Online	50.5
Hybrid	27.43
School quality during the pandemic	
Poor	16.54
Neutral	39.49
Good	43.97
Pre-pandemic school quality	
Poor	8.77
Neutral	26.43
Good	64.8
Health safety: school is safe	
Disagree	12.54
Neither agree/Disagree	26.55
Agree	60.92
Health safety: other parents are safe	
Disagree	13.36
Neither agree/Disagree	28.02
Agree	58.62
Health safety: in-person benefits outweigh risks	
Disagree	24.43
Neither agree/Disagree	27.43
Agree	48.15
Political party	
Republican	30.02
Democrat	40.02
Independent/Other	29.96
Wave	
2	48.15
3	51.85
Urbanicity	
Metro area	87.52
Non-metro area	12.48
Grade level	
Pre-school	8.71
Kindergarten through	7.53
1st through 2nd grade	10.89
3rd through 5th grade	19.42
6th through 8th grade	19.42
9th through 12th grade	34.02
Learning disability	
No	81.46
Yes	18.54
Gender	
Male	48.2
Female	51.8
Race/Ethnicity	
White	58.74
Black	12.3
Asian	5.59
Hispanic	21.07
Other	2.3
Primary language	
Non-English	4.47
English	95.53

(*Continued*)

Table 1. (Continued).

Variable	Percentage
Bachelor's degree	
Less than Bachelor degree	26.55
Bachelor degree or higher	73.45
Number of kids	
One	47.32
Two	39.55
Three or more	13.13
Area median income (AMI)	
Low: (0–50%] AMI	27.31
Moderate: (50–80%] AMI	17.3
Middle: (80–120%] AMI	21.13
High: 120% + AMI	34.26
Employment status	
Working full-time	68.51
Working part-time	10.18
Not working	21.31
Spouse's employment status	
Working full-time	57.74
Working part-time	8.83
Not working	15.48
Single	17.95
Job/income loss due to the pandemic	
No	63.15
Yes	36.85

Table 2. Descriptive statistics for numeric variables.

Variable	Mean	SD	Min	Max
COVID cases per county/1,000	39.37	73.75	0	466.46
Age	39.38	10.65	18	89

the benefits of in-person learning outweigh the risks during the pandemic, while 24.4% disagreed, and 27.4% neither agreed nor disagreed. For political party identification, 40% of the respondents consider themselves Democrats, 30% consider themselves Republican, and the rest (30%) consider themselves to be Independent or from another party.

Concerning child, parent, and other demographic characteristics, 34% of the respondents' children were 9th through 12th graders, 19.4% were the 6th through 8th graders, 19.4% were 3rd through 5th graders, 10.9% were 1st through 2nd graders, and 16.2% were preschoolers or kindergartners. The majority of respondents identified as White (58.7%) and female (51.8%), spoke English as their primary language (95.5%), had a bachelor's degree or higher (73.5%), and lived in a metro area (87.5%). Considering family size, 47.3% of respondents had one child, 39.6 had two children, and 13.1% had three or more children. Regarding income, 27.3% of the respondents had low incomes, 17.3% had moderate incomes, 21.1% had middle incomes, and 34.3% had high incomes. In terms of employment characteristics, the majority of the respondents worked full-time (68.5%) and had spouses or partners that worked full-time (57.7%). Additionally, over a third of the respondents (36.9%) lost their job or income due to the pandemic. Finally, the average age of respondents in our sample was 39.4, and the average COVID cases per county (divided by 1,000) was also 39.4.

Analytic results

In our analytic models, we present our results in relative risk ratios (RRRs) and describe these coefficients as a percent increase or decrease in the risk (or chance) of an event occurring. A RRR is equivalent, but not identical, to an odds ratio in a binary regression model (e.g., logistic regression). Whereas odds ratios compare the odds of an event occurring in one group compared with another, RRRs compare the risk of an event in one group versus the risk in the reference group. Similar to an odds ratio, the range of a RRR extends from zero to positive infinity, and an association is positive if its ratio is significantly greater than 1 and an association is negative if the ratio is significantly less than 1.

Associations with School Governance Models (SGMs)

In Table 3, we describe how parents' perceptions of health safety and their political party identification relate to school governance models. In these models, traditional public schools are set as the reference category. First, we explore school health safety concerns (Model 1), finding that when compared to neutral perceptions of school health safety, disagreeing that one's school was safe was significantly associated with a 92% increase in the chance of attending a charter school compared to a traditional public school (RRR: 1.923; $p < .05$). On the other hand, disagreeing that the benefits of in-person learning outweigh the risks was significantly associated with a 46% decrease in the chance of attending a charter school (RRR: 0.537; $p < .05$). Second, we added political party to Model 1, finding that when compared to identifying as an independent (or from another party), identifying as Republican was significantly associated with increased chances of attending both a charter (RRR: 1.688; $p < .05$) and a private school (RRR: 1.978; $p < .001$), while identifying as a Democrat was significantly associated with increased chances of attending a charter school (RRR: 1.681; $p < .05$) and marginally associated with increased chances of attending a private school (OR: 1.367; $p < .10$) (Model 2).

When accounting for COVID-19-related characteristics (Model 3), characteristics of respondents' children (Model 4), and parent/other demographic characteristics (Model 5), some of these associations slightly altered. For example, when accounting for COVID-19-related characteristics in Model 3, agreeing that a child's school was safe was now marginally associated with increased chances of attending a private school (RRR: 1.395; $p < .10$). Furthermore, when accounting for child and parent characteristics in Model

Table 3. Perceptions of safety and school governance models: multinomial logistic results (reference category: traditional public schools).

	MODEL 1		MODEL 2		MODEL 3		MODEL 4		MODEL 5	
	Charter	Private	Charter	Private	Charter	Private	Charter	Private	Charter	Private
Child school is safe (*reference = Neither agree nor disagree*)										
Disagree	1.923*	1.112	1.941*	1.15	2.151**	1.258	1.753[+]	1.069	1.843*	0.993
	(0.554)	(0.292)	(0.556)	(0.3)	(0.638)	(0.347)	(0.544)	(0.3)	(0.573)	(0.286)
Agree	1.171	1.26	1.163	1.27	1.281	1.395[+]	1.298	1.327	1.457	1.282
	(0.285)	(0.233)	(0.282)	(0.235)	(0.319)	(0.267)	(0.33)	(0.256)	(0.375)	(0.267)
Other parents are safe (*reference = Neither agree nor disagree*)										
Disagree	1.281	0.942	1.294	0.932	1.415	0.965	1.395	1.019	1.221	1.136
	(0.376)	(0.24)	(0.377)	(0.237)	(0.432)	(0.261)	(0.433)	(0.278)	(0.392)	(0.317)
Agree	0.95	1.243	0.921	1.185	0.888	1.173	0.888	1.195	0.813	1.188
	(0.228)	(0.221)	(0.218)	(0.21)	(0.219)	(0.215)	(0.222)	(0.224)	(0.208)	(0.238)
In-person benefits outweigh safety risks (*reference = Neither agree nor disagree*)										
Disagree	0.537*	0.722	0.536*	0.745	0.514**	0.719	0.552*	0.701	0.617[+]	0.791
	(0.133)	(0.153)	(0.133)	(0.159)	(0.131)	(0.158)	(0.147)	(0.156)	(0.164)	(0.185)
Agree	0.764	1.268	0.767	1.239	0.77	1.227	0.665[+]	1.129	0.638[+]	0.933
	(0.155)	(0.218)	(0.158)	(0.215)	(0.171)	(0.221)	(0.152)	(0.208)	(0.149)	(0.186)
Political party (*reference = Independent*)										
Republican			1.688*	1.978***	1.797*	2.026***	1.557[+]	1.937***	1.608[+]	1.534*
			(0.389)	(0.372)	(0.442)	(0.394)	(0.393)	(0.378)	(0.43)	(0.324)
Democrat			1.681*	1.367[+]	1.787**	1.307	1.600*	1.274	1.520[+]	1.145
			(0.352)	(0.254)	(0.39)	(0.253)	(0.363)	(0.251)	(0.368)	(0.245)
Number of COVID cases per County/1000					1.003**	1.004***	1.003*	1.004***	1.002	1.004***
					(0.00129)	(0.00116)	(0.00135)	(0.00117)	(0.00149)	(0.00127)
Wave (*reference = Wave 2*)										
wave = 3					0.568***	1.047	0.581**	1.027	0.611**	0.984
					(0.0952)	(0.128)	(0.102)	(0.129)	(0.111)	(0.135)
Rural-urban continuum (*reference = Metro area*)										
Non-metro area					0.596	0.852	0.613	0.833	0.589	1.025
					(0.214)	(0.227)	(0.225)	(0.224)	(0.234)	(0.298)
Grade level (*reference = Pre-school*)										
Kindergarten through							1.187	0.339**	1.384	0.324**
							(0.429)	(0.124)	(0.543)	(0.127)
1st through 2nd Grade							0.564	0.284***	0.723	0.315**

(*Continued*)

Table 3. (Continued).

	MODEL 1		MODEL 2		MODEL 3		MODEL 4		MODEL 5	
	Charter	Private	Charter	Private	Charter	Private	Charter	Private	Charter	Private
3rd through 5th Grade							0.524+ (0.176) [(0.203)]	0.513* (0.141) [(0.0933)]	0.741 (0.273) [(0.28)]	0.504* (0.154) [(0.112)]
6th through 8th Grade							0.346** (0.121)	0.418** (0.115)	0.485+ (0.185)	0.442** (0.135)
9th through 12th Grade							0.343** (0.112)	0.289*** (0.0782)	0.553 (0.204)	0.387** (0.119)
Learning disability (*reference = No*)										
Yes							3.090*** (0.624)	1.287 (0.229)	2.352*** (0.528)	1.325 (0.257)
Age									0.986 (0.0119)	0.977* (0.0111)
Gender (*reference = Male*)										
Female									0.783 (0.162)	0.645* (0.117)
Ethnicity (*reference = White*)										
Black									2.161** (0.642)	0.665 (0.211)
Asian									0.733 (0.431)	0.249* (0.138)
Hispanic									1.018 (0.287)	0.524** (0.115)
Other									1.028 (0.763)	1.121 (0.687)
Primary language (*reference = Non-English*)										
English									1.064 (0.554)	0.425* (0.166)
Bachelor's degree (*reference = Less than Bachelor degree*)										
Bachelor Degree or Higher									1.059 (0.243)	2.967*** (0.735)
Number of kids (*reference = One*)										
Two									1.255 (0.282)	1.145 (0.201)
Three or more									0.674	0.624+

(Continued)

Table 3. (Continued).

	MODEL 1		MODEL 2		MODEL 3		MODEL 4		MODEL 5	
	Charter	Private	Charter	Private	Charter	Private	Charter	Private	Charter	Private
									(0.216)	(0.174)
Area median income (*reference = Low: (0–30%] AMI*)										
Moderate: (50–80%] AMI									0.657	1.402
									(0.197)	(0.376)
Middle: (80–120%] AMI									0.712	1.601[+]
									(0.225)	(0.418)
High: 120% + AMI									0.828	1.361
									(0.224)	(0.345)
Employment status (*reference = Working full-time*)										
Working part-time									1.47	0.839
									(0.433)	(0.258)
Not working									0.541*	0.578[+]
									(0.159)	(0.163)
Spouse's employment status (*reference = Working full-time*)										
Working part-time									1.414	1.543[+]
									(0.398)	(0.394)
Not working									0.772	0.843
									(0.245)	(0.206)
Single									0.460*	0.410**
									(0.17)	(0.124)
Job or income loss due to the pandemic (*reference = No*)										
Yes									1.877**	1.155
									(0.396)	(0.191)
Constant	0.149***	0.175***	0.104***	0.127***	0.228*	0.121**	0.418	0.341	0.491	1.288
	(0.0281)	(0.0321)	(0.0249)	(0.0282)	(0.162)	(0.0846)	(0.342)	(0.263)	(0.601)	(1.223)
Observations	1699		1699		1699		1699		1699	
Pseudo R^2	0.015		0.024		0.079		0.114		0.184	

Exponentiated coefficients are represented as relative risk ratios (RRR).
Standard errors in parentheses and clustered at the individual level.
Starting in Model 3, state fixed effects are controlled for.
[+]$p < 0.10$, * $p < 0.05$, ** $p < 0.01$, *** $p < 0.001$.

4 (RRR: 0.655; $p < .10$) and Model 5 (RRR: 0.638; $p < .10$), agreeing that the in-person benefits of learning outweigh the risks was now marginally associated with decreased chances of attending a charter school. Moreover, when accounting for COVID-19-related characteristics (Model 3), the relationship between identifying as a Democrat and attending a private school were no longer significant.

Associations with instruction modes

In Table 4, we describe how parents' perceptions of health safety, their political party identification, and school governance models (SGMs) relate to instruction modes. In these models, in-person instruction was set as the reference category. First, we explore school health safety concerns (Model 6), finding that that when compared to neutral perceptions of school health safety, disagreeing that one's school was safe was significantly associated with a 44% decrease in the chance of receiving virtual instruction (RRR: 0.563; $p < .05$) and marginally associated with a 43% decrease in the chance of receiving hybrid instruction (RRR: 0.571; $p < .05$) compared to in-person instruction. Alternatively, agreeing that one's school was safe was significantly associated with a 41% decrease in the chance of receiving virtual instruction (RRR: 0.586; $p < .01$). When compared to neutral perceptions, disagreeing that the benefits of in-person learning outweigh the risks was significantly associated with a 128% increase in the chance of receiving virtual instruction (RRR: 2.277; $p < .001$), while agreeing that the benefits of in-person learning outweigh the risks was significantly associated with decreased chances of virtual (RRR: 0.529; $p < .001$) and hybrid instruction (RRR: 0.489; $p < .001$). Additionally, when political party identification was added in Model 7, we find that when compared to identifying as an independent, identifying as a Republican was significantly associated with decreased chances of virtual (RRR: 0.612; $p < .01$) and hybrid instruction (RRR: 0.568; $p < .01$). Finally, when SGMs were added in Model 8 we find that when compared to traditional public schools, being enrolled in a charter school was significantly associated with a 121% increase in the chance of receiving virtual instruction (RRR: 2.207; $p < .01$), while being enrolled in a private school was significantly associated with a 44% decrease in the chance of receiving virtual instruction (RRR: 0.561; $p < .001$).

Similar to the previous set of results, some of these associations slightly altered in subsequent models. Specifically, disagreeing that one's school was safe was no longer associated with hybrid instruction when child character-istics were added in Model 10. Additionally, when COVID-19-related char-acteristics were added in Model 9, attending a private school was no longer associated with hybrid instruction.

Table 4. Perceptions of safety, school governance models, and instruction mode: multinomial logistic results (reference category: in-person instruction).

	MODEL 6		MODEL 7		MODEL 8		MODEL 9		MODEL 10		MODEL 11	
	Online	Hybrid	Online	Hybrid	Online	Hybrid	Online	Hybrid	Online	Hybrid	Online	Hybrid
Child's school is safe (reference = Neither agree nor disagree)												
Disagree	0.563*	0.571[+]	0.540*	0.556*	0.515*	0.561[+]	0.507*	0.558[+]	0.542*	0.616	0.550[+]	0.594
	(0.144)	(0.171)	(0.138)	(0.166)	(0.136)	(0.17)	(0.149)	(0.182)	(0.161)	(0.205)	(0.168)	(0.2)
Agree	0.586**	0.863	0.576**	0.864	0.574**	0.869	0.485***	0.822	0.489***	0.817	0.504***	0.809
	(0.108)	(0.177)	(0.106)	(0.176)	(0.108)	(0.179)	(0.0961)	(0.179)	(0.0992)	(0.182)	(0.104)	(0.181)
Other parents are safe (reference = Neither agree nor disagree)												
Disagree	1.409	1.081	1.45	1.091	1.41	1.094	1.473	0.962	1.381	0.872	1.476	0.947
	(0.348)	(0.294)	(0.355)	(0.295)	(0.352)	(0.3)	(0.402)	(0.276)	(0.381)	(0.254)	(0.416)	(0.282)
Agree	1.14	1.198	1.191	1.253	1.222	1.269	1.293	1.193	1.273	1.182	1.317	1.249
	(0.19)	(0.223)	(0.199)	(0.233)	(0.209)	(0.239)	(0.24)	(0.242)	(0.243)	(0.245)	(0.257)	(0.262)
In-person benefits outweigh safety risks (reference = Neither agree nor disagree)												
Disagree	2.277***	1.048	2.191***	1.019	2.280***	1.006	2.529***	1.036	2.549***	1.032	2.736***	1.089
	(0.494)	(0.254)	(0.476)	(0.248)	(0.501)	(0.247)	(0.596)	(0.267)	(0.609)	(0.27)	(0.691)	(0.296)
Agree	0.529***	0.489***	0.547***	0.497***	0.570***	0.501***	0.576***	0.480***	0.600**	0.531**	0.604*	0.522**
	(0.0886)	(0.0886)	(0.0924)	(0.0902)	(0.0972)	(0.0917)	(0.109)	(0.0936)	(0.116)	(0.106)	(0.122)	(0.107)
Political party (reference = Independent)												
Republican			0.612**	0.568**	0.629*	0.591**	0.695[+]	0.583*	0.706[+]	0.591*	0.774	0.600*
			(0.111)	(0.111)	(0.115)	(0.117)	(0.136)	(0.122)	(0.138)	(0.125)	(0.158)	(0.129)
Democrat			1.133	0.811	1.126	0.823	1.138	0.775	1.164	0.809	1.182	0.801
			(0.202)	(0.156)	(0.201)	(0.158)	(0.214)	(0.157)	(0.219)	(0.164)	(0.229)	(0.167)
School governance model (reference = Public)												
Charter					2.207**	0.826	2.134**	0.819	2.373**	1.052	2.287**	1.109
					(0.571)	(0.259)	(0.616)	(0.263)	(0.722)	(0.353)	(0.714)	(0.38)
Private/parochial					0.561***	0.739[+]	0.500***	0.734	0.533**	0.82	0.544**	0.776
					(0.0969)	(0.134)	(0.0968)	(0.148)	(0.103)	(0.166)	(0.111)	(0.168)
Number of COVID cases per County/1000							1	1	1	1	1	1
							(0.00138)	(0.00167)	(0.00137)	(0.0017)	(0.0014)	(0.00171)
Wave (reference = Wave 2)												
wave = 3							0.81	0.679**	0.82	0.686*	0.882	0.694*
							(0.108)	(0.0976)	(0.111)	(0.101)	(0.124)	(0.105)

(Continued)

Table 4. (Continued).

	MODEL 6		MODEL 7		MODEL 8		MODEL 9		MODEL 10		MODEL 11	
	Online	Hybrid	Online	Hybrid	Online	Hybrid	Online	Hybrid	Online	Hybrid	Online	Hybrid
Rural-urban continuum (reference = Metro area)												
Non-metro area							0.507**	0.664+	0.518**	0.684	0.559*	0.717
							(0.119)	(0.158)	(0.122)	(0.163)	(0.136)	(0.174)
Grade level (reference = Pre-school)												
Kindergarten through									2.683**	3.267**	2.930**	3.544**
									(0.972)	(1.361)	(1.08)	(1.512)
1st through 2nd grade									1.694+	1.567	1.719+	1.625
									(0.515)	(0.57)	(0.546)	(0.613)
3rd through 5th grade									2.601**	3.236***	2.759**	3.231***
									(0.78)	(1.094)	(0.875)	(1.142)
6th through 8th grade									2.245**	4.000***	2.331**	4.171***
									(0.654)	(1.288)	(0.733)	(1.435)
9th through 12th grade									2.391**	3.794***	2.609**	4.012***
									(0.651)	(1.177)	(0.789)	(1.365)
Learning disability (reference = No)												
Yes									0.935	0.664+	0.996	0.779
									(0.186)	(0.144)	(0.207)	(0.176)
Age											0.997	0.988
											(0.00866)	(0.00877)
Gender (reference = Male)												
Female											0.814	0.938
											(0.147)	(0.183)
Ethnicity (reference = White)												
Black											1.492	0.944
											(0.42)	(0.283)
Asian											3.816**	1.174
											(1.704)	(0.661)
Hispanic											1.194	1.142
											(0.282)	(0.297)
Other											1.271	0.998
											(0.679)	(0.592)
Primary language (reference = Non-English)												
English											0.78	0.62
											(0.311)	(0.271)

(Continued)

Table 4. (Continued).

	MODEL 6		MODEL 7		MODEL 8		MODEL 9		MODEL 10		MODEL 11	
	Online	Hybrid	Online	Hybrid	Online	Hybrid	Online	Hybrid	Online	Hybrid	Online	Hybrid
Bachelor's degree (reference = Less than Bachelor degree)												
Bachelor degree or Higher											1.128	1.213
											(0.237)	(0.266)
Number of kids (reference = One)												
Two											0.952	0.826
											(0.164)	(0.151)
Three or more											1.156	0.997
											(0.292)	(0.262)
Area median income (reference = Low: (0–30%] AMI)												
Moderate: (50–80%] AMI											1.161	1.432
											(0.285)	(0.358)
Middle: (80–120%] AMI											0.768	0.972
											(0.186)	(0.249)
High: 120% + AMI											0.941	1.251
											(0.232)	(0.316)
Employment status (reference = Working full-time)												
Working part-time											1.32	1
											(0.363)	(0.309)
Not working											0.878	0.913
											(0.181)	(0.202)
Spouse's employment status (reference = Working full-time)												
Working part-time											1.383	1.153
											(0.411)	(0.372)
Not working											1.698*	1.532[+]
											(0.409)	(0.38)
Single											0.936	0.957
											(0.231)	(0.251)
Job or income loss due to the pandemic (reference = No)												
Yes											1.02	0.680*
											(0.168)	(0.123)
Constant	3.572***	1.937***	3.900***	2.461***	3.865***	2.572***	0.789	2.197	0.343	0.663	0.294	1.313
	(0.631)	(0.371)	(0.785)	(0.541)	(0.789)	(0.569)	(0.563)	(1.07)	(0.269)	(0.398)	(0.292)	(1.122)
Observations	1699		1699		1699		1699		1699		1699	
Pseudo R^2	0.039		0.045		0.058		0.148		0.161		0.178	

Exponentiated coefficients are represented as relative risk ratios (RRR).
Standard errors in parentheses and clustered at the individual level.
Starting in Model 9, state fixed effects are controlled for.
[+]$p < 0.10$, * $p < 0.05$, ** $p < 0.01$, *** $p < 0.001$.

Associations with perceptions of school quality

7In Table 5, we describe how parents' perceptions of health safety, their political party identification, SGMs, and instruction modes relate to perceptions of school quality, when controlling for pre-pandemic perceptions of school quality. In these models, neutral perceptions of school quality was set as the reference category. First, we explore pre-pandemic perceptions of school quality (Model 12), finding that when compared to neutral perceptions of pre-pandemic school quality, poor pre-pandemic perceptions of school quality was significantly associated with increased chances of both poor (RRR: 3.415; $p < .001$) and good perceptions of school quality during the pandemic (RRR: 2.918; $p < .001$), while good pre-pandemic perceptions of school quality was significantly associated with a 480% increase in the chances of good perceptions of school quality during the pandemic (RRR: 5.796; $p < .001$). When compared to neutral perceptions of school health safety, disagreeing that one's school was safe was marginally associated with a 50% increase in the chance of perceiving good school quality during the pandemic (RRR: 1.506; $p < .10$), while agreeing that one's school was safe was significantly associated with a 97% increase in the chances of perceiving good school quality during the pandemic (RRR: 1.967; $p < .001$). When compared to neutral perceptions of other parents' health safety, agreeing that other parents were safe was significantly associated with a 39% increase in the chances of perceiving good school quality during the pandemic (RRR: 1.387; $p < .05$). In addition, when compared to neutral perceptions of in-person benefits, disagreeing that the benefits of in-person learning outweigh the risks was significantly associated with a 72% increase in the chances of perceiving poor school quality during the pandemic (RRR: 1.724; $p < .01$), while agreeing that the benefits of in-person learning outweigh the risks was significantly associated increased chances of perceiving both poor (RRR: 1.509; $p < .01$) and good (RRR: 1.430; $p < .01$) school quality during the pandemic.

When political party identification was added in Model 13, we find that when compared to identifying as an Independent, identifying as a Republican was significantly associated with a 94% increase in the chances of perceiving good school quality during the pandemic (RRR: 1.937; $p < .001$), while identifying as a Democrat was marginally associated with 30% decrease in the chances of perceiving good school quality during the pandemic (RRR: 0.700; $p < .10$). Additionally, when SGMs were added in Model 14, we find that when compared to public schools, being enrolled in a charter school was significantly associated with a 119% increase in the chances of perceiving good school quality during the pandemic (RRR: 2.190; $p < .001$), while being enrolled in private or parochial school was marginally associated with a 38% decrease in the chances of perceiving poor school quality during the pandemic (RRR: 0.621; $p < .10$) and significantly associated with a 156% increase in the chances of perceiving good school quality during the pandemic (RRR: 2.558; $p < .001$). Finally, when instructional modes were added in Model 16, we find

Table 5. Perceptions of safety, school governance models, instruction mode, and school quality: multinomial logistic results (reference category: neutral school quality).

	MODEL 12		MODEL 13		MODEL 14		MODEL 15		MODEL 16		MODEL 17		MODEL 18		MODEL 19		MODEL 20	
	Poor	Good	Poor	Good	Poor	Good	Poor	Good	Poor	Good	Poor	Good	Poor	Good	Poor	Good	Poor	Good
Pre-pandemic school quality																		
(reference = Neutral)																		
Poor	3.415***	2.918***	3.408***	2.757***	3.597***	2.443**	3.385***	2.668***	3.587***	2.406**	3.799***	2.562**	3.756***	2.374**	4.144***	2.440**	4.442***	2.403**
	(0.816)	(0.774)	(0.824)	(0.737)	(0.874)	(0.673)	(0.818)	(0.717)	(0.873)	(0.664)	(0.982)	(0.736)	(0.979)	(0.688)	(1.112)	(0.715)	(1.196)	(0.707)
Good	1.063	5.796***	1.063	5.923***	1.041	6.164***	1.059	5.930***	1.04	6.176***	0.948	7.272***	0.928	7.317***	0.922	7.920***	0.918	7.920***
	(0.187)	(0.918)	(0.187)	(0.945)	(0.184)	(0.975)	(0.187)	(0.947)	(0.183)	(0.979)	(0.179)	(1.219)	(0.177)	(1.233)	(0.179)	(1.395)	(0.181)	(1.408)
Child's school is safe																		
(reference = Neither agree nor disagree)																		
Disagree	1.506+	1.129	1.553+	1.175	1.585+	1.132	1.544+	1.158	1.575+	1.124	1.509	1.118	1.466	1.043	1.332	1.031	1.358	1.035
	(0.355)	(0.288)	(0.369)	(0.3)	(0.378)	(0.292)	(0.367)	(0.297)	(0.376)	(0.292)	(0.386)	(0.294)	(0.382)	(0.275)	(0.356)	(0.279)	(0.365)	(0.279)
Agree	1.013	1.967***	1.035	1.991***	1.037	1.958***	1.031	2.012***	1.034	1.987***	1.01	1.998***	0.995	1.966***	0.957	2.055***	0.911	2.080***
	(0.205)	(0.323)	(0.212)	(0.325)	(0.214)	(0.318)	(0.212)	(0.329)	(0.214)	(0.323)	(0.225)	(0.344)	(0.222)	(0.338)	(0.215)	(0.362)	(0.206)	(0.369)
Other parents are safe																		
(reference = Neither agree nor disagree)																		
Disagree	1.259	1.39	1.226	1.391	1.224	1.385	1.239	1.402	1.233	1.39	1.327	1.305	1.357	1.351	1.334	1.296	1.289	1.328
	(0.285)	(0.328)	(0.278)	(0.329)	(0.279)	(0.329)	(0.281)	(0.332)	(0.281)	(0.331)	(0.316)	(0.33)	(0.324)	(0.341)	(0.324)	(0.338)	(0.316)	(0.346)
Agree	0.855	1.387+	0.843	1.338+	0.847	1.330+	0.843	1.354+	0.849	1.342+	0.841	1.328+	0.85	1.338+	0.794	1.306	0.777	1.319
	(0.16)	(0.222)	(0.159)	(0.215)	(0.161)	(0.214)	(0.159)	(0.218)	(0.161)	(0.216)	(0.169)	(0.223)	(0.173)	(0.225)	(0.164)	(0.223)	(0.162)	(0.226)
In-person benefits outweigh safety risks																		
(reference = Neither agree nor disagree))																		
Disagree	1.724**	1.206	1.771**	1.239	1.715**	1.309	1.795**	1.2	1.745**	1.262	1.772**	1.251	1.754*	1.268	1.653*	1.301	1.679*	1.269
	(0.349)	(0.217)	(0.36)	(0.222)	(0.348)	(0.237)	(0.369)	(0.219)	(0.359)	(0.232)	(0.389)	(0.235)	(0.385)	(0.239)	(0.376)	(0.248)	(0.386)	(0.244)
Agree	1.509*	1.430*	1.483*	1.391*	1.462+	1.381*	1.464+	1.338+	1.448+	1.340+	1.475+	1.326+	1.471+	1.294	1.362	1.292	1.377	1.279
	(0.295)	(0.219)	(0.29)	(0.215)	(0.285)	(0.215)	(0.287)	(0.208)	(0.284)	(0.21)	(0.305)	(0.222)	(0.308)	(0.218)	(0.295)	(0.223)	(0.299)	(0.221)
Political party																		
(reference = Independent)																		
Republican			1.049	1.937***	1.069	1.745***	1.039	1.894***	1.06	1.713**	1.066	1.774***	1.07	1.749**	1.02	1.802***	1.034	1.777**
			(0.204)	(0.317)	(0.211)	(0.29)	(0.203)	(0.31)	(0.21)	(0.286)	(0.227)	(0.304)	(0.229)	(0.302)	(0.221)	(0.32)	(0.226)	(0.316)
Democrat			0.700*	1.265	0.712*	1.196	0.702*	1.25	0.714+	1.18	0.744	1.171	0.74	1.165	0.682+	1.132	0.692+	1.115
			(0.126)	(0.188)	(0.128)	(0.18)	(0.126)	(0.187)	(0.129)	(0.179)	(0.138)	(0.186)	(0.138)	(0.186)	(0.134)	(0.19)	(0.138)	(0.189)
School governance model																		
(reference = Public)																		
Charter					0.688	2.190***			0.7	2.128***	0.603+	2.281***	0.616+	2.151***	0.566+	2.048**	0.115*	3.064*
					(0.184)	(0.478			(0.188)	(0.465)	(0.175)	(0.523)	(0.18)	(0.499)	(0.173)	(0.485)	(0.123)	(1.639)
Private/parochial					0.621+	2.558***			0.613+	2.558***	0.532*	2.460***	0.513*	2.357***	0.465*	2.308***	1.07	2.085*
					(0.158)	(0.424			(0.156)	(0.427)	(0.142)	(0.427)	(0.138)	(0.41)	(0.131)	(0.432)	(0.466)	(0.694)

(Continued)

Table 5. (Continued).

	MODEL 12		MODEL 13		MODEL 14		MODEL 15		MODEL 16		MODEL 17		MODEL 18		MODEL 19		MODEL 20	
	Poor	Good	Poor	Good	Poor	Good	Poor	Good	Poor	Good	Poor	Good	Poor	Good	Poor	Good	Poor	Good
Instruction mode																		
(reference = In-person only)																		
Online							0.866	0.88	0.877	0.938	0.789	1.031	0.803	1.064	0.802	1.101	0.904	1.118
							(0.176)	(0.136)	(0.18)	(0.151)	(0.178)	(0.177)	(0.182)	(0.183)	(0.188)	(0.192)	(0.244)	(0.23)
Hybrid							0.937	0.667*	0.954	0.709*	0.904	0.725[+]	0.921	0.758	0.936	0.77	1.067	0.717
							(0.208)	(0.113)	(0.214)	(0.123)	(0.219)	(0.135)	(0.223)	(0.142)	(0.234)	(0.146)	(0.305)	(0.162)
Number of COVID cases per County/1000											1	1	0.999	1	0.999	1	0.999	1
											(0.00158)	(0.00105)	(0.00161)	(0.00107)	(0.00159)	(0.00112)	(0.00159)	(0.00112)
Wave																		
(reference = Wave 2)																		
wave = 3											0.700*	1.290*	0.692*	1.288*	0.677*	1.264[+]	0.673*	1.255[+]
											(0.108)	(0.158)	(0.108)	(0.158)	(0.109)	(0.16)	(0.11)	(0.159)
Rural-urban continuum																		
(reference = Metro area)																		
Non-metro area											0.905	0.949	0.908	0.955	0.862	0.939	0.869	0.95
											(0.221)	(0.207)	(0.224)	(0.209)	(0.221)	(0.209)	(0.221)	(0.212)
Grade level																		
(reference = Pre-school)																		
Kindergarten through													0.478[+]	0.579[+]	0.405*	0.558[+]	0.424[+]	0.530[+]
													(0.211)	(0.185)	(0.186)	(0.181)	(0.196)	(0.174)
1st through 2nd Grade													0.753	0.570[+]	0.67	0.608	0.687	0.579[+]
													(0.274)	(0.175)	(0.253)	(0.191)	(0.261)	(0.185)
3rd through 5th Grade													0.796	0.622[+]	0.645	0.654	0.68	0.619[+]
													(0.272)	(0.171)	(0.225)	(0.188)	(0.24)	(0.18)
6th through 8th Grade													0.745	0.724	0.599	0.789	0.619	0.756
													(0.256)	(0.199)	(0.212)	(0.229)	(0.221)	(0.222)
9th through 12th Grade													0.652	0.638[+]	0.533[+]	0.75	0.552[+]	0.721
													(0.208)	(0.163)	(0.184)	(0.206)	(0.191)	(0.2)
Learning disability																		
(reference = No)																		
Yes													0.89	1.359[+]	0.862	1.322	0.9	1.307
													(0.199)	(0.231)	(0.203)	(0.241)	(0.212)	(0.239)

(Continued)

Table 5. (Continued).

	MODEL 12		MODEL 13		MODEL 14		MODEL 15		MODEL 16		MODEL 17		MODEL 18		MODEL 19		MODEL 20	
	Poor	Good	Poor	Good	Poor	Good	Poor	Good	Poor	Good	Poor	Good	Poor	Good	Poor	Good	Poor	Good
Age															1.014	0.989	1.013	0.989
															(0.00877)	(0.00727)	(0.00881)	(0.00731)
Gender *(reference = Male)*																		
Female															1.213	0.660**	1.26	0.657**
															(0.229)	(0.101)	(0.24)	(0.101)
Ethnicity *(reference = White)*																		
Black															1.098	1.554*	1.12	1.564*
															(0.303)	(0.328)	(0.311)	(0.331)
Asian															0.520+	0.756	0.514+	0.753
															(0.197)	(0.231)	(0.196)	(0.231)
Hispanic															0.573*	0.99	0.565*	0.982
															(0.136)	(0.198)	(0.136)	(0.197)
Other															0.565	1.25	0.599	1.245
															(0.34)	(0.547)	(0.366)	(0.544)
Primary language *(reference = Non-English)*																		
English															1.454	1.069	1.468	1.06
															(0.747)	(0.311)	(0.76)	(0.308)
Bachelor's degree *(reference = Less than Bachelor degree)*																		
Bachelor Degree or Higher															0.922	0.928	0.958	0.917
															(0.196)	(0.169)	(0.205)	(0.167)
Number of kids *(reference = One)*																		
Two															1.271	1.181	1.27	1.176
															(0.229)	(0.171)	(0.233)	(0.172)
Three or more															1.265	1.096	1.243	1.097
															(0.339)	(0.233)	(0.336)	(0.234)
Area median income *(reference = Low: (0–30%) AMI)*																		
Moderate: (50–80%) AMI															1.451	0.813	1.521	0.807
															(0.371)	(0.173)	(0.392)	(0.172)
Middle: (80–120%) AMI															1.459	0.9	1.477	0.904
															(0.394)	(0.184)	(0.4)	(0.186)
High: 120% + AMI															1.604+	0.699+	1.656*	0.704+
															(0.405)	(0.143)	(0.421)	(0.145)
Employment status *(reference = Working full-time)*																		
Working part-time															1.327	0.932	1.289	0.944
															(0.371)	(0.239)	(0.365)	(0.241)

(Continued)

Table 5. (Continued).

	MODEL 12		MODEL 13		MODEL 14		MODEL 15		MODEL 16		MODEL 17		MODEL 18		MODEL 19		MODEL 20	
	Poor	Good	Poor	Good	Poor	Good	Poor	Good	Poor	Good	Poor	Good	Poor	Good	Poor	Good	Poor	Good
Not working															0.811	1.082	0.826	1.068
															(0.173)	(0.199)	(0.178)	(0.196)
Spouse's employment status (reference = Working full-\time)																		
Working part-time															0.661	0.941	0.663	0.938
															(0.213)	(0.233)	(0.216)	(0.234)
Not working															1.17	0.689+	1.206	0.676*
															(0.289)	(0.134)	(0.301)	(0.132)
Single															1.189	0.876	1.223	0.876
															(0.292)	(0.188)	(0.303)	(0.188)
Job or income loss due to the pandemic (reference = No)																		
Yes															1.709**	0.851	1.713**	0.85
															(0.298)	(0.129)	(0.301)	(0.129)
SGM * Mode																		
Charter * Online																	4.775	0.559
																	(5.358)	(0.343)
Charter * Hybrid																	10.22+	0.948
																	(12.7)	(0.732)
Private/parochial * Online																	0.309+	1.138
																	(0.216)	(0.494)
Private/parochial * Hybrid																	0.227*	1.284
																	(0.153)	(0.59)
Constant	0.237***	0.121***	0.267***	0.0907***	0.290***	0.0737***	0.295***	0.111***	0.315***	0.0857***	0.801	0.0621***	1.175	0.0936***	0.366	0.202*	0.319	0.216*
	(0.0419)	(0.0214)	(0.0533)	(0.0188)	(0.0586)	(0.0157)	(0.076)	(0.0262)	(0.0815)	(0.0213)	(0.457)	(0.0365)	(0.76)	(0.0593)	(0.328)	(0.156)	(0.291)	(0.168)
Observations	1699		1699		1699		1699		1699		1699		1699		1699		1699	
Pseudo R^2	0.118		0.126		0.146		0.128		0.147		0.192		0.196		0.214		0.218	

Exponentiated coefficients are represented as relative risk ratios (RRR).
Standard errors in parentheses and clustered at the individual level.
Starting in Model 17, state fixed effects are controlled for.
$^+ p < 0.10$, $* p < 0.05$, $** p < 0.01$, $*** p < 0.001$.

that when compared to in-person instruction, hybrid instruction was significantly associated with a 29% decrease in the chances of perceiving good school quality during the pandemic (RRR: 0.709; $p < .05$).[5]

Similar to the previous sets of results, some of these associations slightly altered in subsequent models. Specifically, disagreeing that one's school was safe was no longer associated with poor perceptions of school quality when COVID-19-related characteristics were added in Model 17, while agreeing that other parents were safe was no longer associated with good perceptions of school quality when parent characteristics are added in Model 19. Furthermore, agreeing that the in-person benefits outweigh the risks were no longer associated with good perceptions of school quality when child characteristics were added in Model 18 and no longer associated with poor perceptions of school quality when parent characteristics were added in Model 19. Moreover, identifying as a Democratic was no longer associated with poor perceptions of school quality when COVID-19-related characteristics were added in Model 17 or when child characteristics were added in Model 18. Additionally, when COVID-19-related characteristics were added in Model 17, attending a charter school became marginally associated with a decrease in the chances of perceiving poor school quality (RRR: 0.603; $p < .10$). Finally, when child characteristics were added in Model 18, hybrid instruction is no longer associated with good perceptions of school quality.

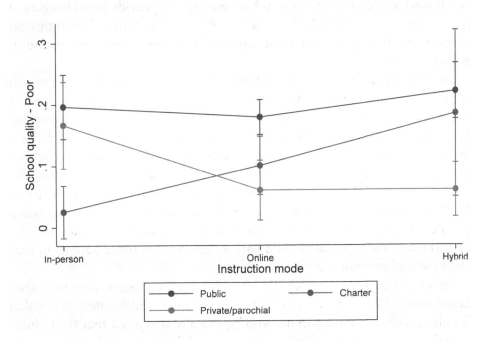

Figure 1. Marginal plot for interactions between school governance models and instruction modes when predicting poor school quality.

Lastly, interactions between school governance models and instructional modes were included in Model 20. For ease of interpretation, we provide a marginal probability plot for poor perceptions of school quality (Figure 1). Here, we see that attending a charter school is associated with increased probabilities of perceiving poor school quality when students are engaged in hybrid instruction, while attending a private school is associated lowered probabilities of perceiving poor school quality when students are engaged in online and hybrid instruction.

Discussion

The COVID-19 pandemic altered the mode of instruction for millions of students, which had implications for the quality of instruction received during the 2020–2021 school year. Recent research has explored the relationship between instructional mode and school quality, finding that instructional mode, and by extension, school quality has varied widely across students; this variation can be seen as further stratifying learning opportunities – and in some cases – exacerbating preexisting inequalities (Jabbari et al., 2022). However, research has yet to explore the factors associated with instructional mode – especially when considering parents perceptions of health safety and school governance models (SGMs). By exploring how parents' health safety concerns are associated with school governance models, as well as instructional modes and perceptions of school quality, we provide novel insights on how schools can respond to the concerns of parents in times of crisis through instructional strategies and if these responses can lead to better perceptions of school quality.

First, we explored the relationships between health safety concerns and school governance models. We find that charter school parents (i.e. parents associated with attending a charter school) are more likely to disagree that their school was safe, yet less likely to disagree that the in-person benefits of learning outweigh the risks – perhaps because they have chosen these schools for their children. Moreover, despite previous research demonstrating that private schools tend to have higher levels of social closure (Coleman & Hoffer, 1987) and trust (Bryk & Schneider, 2002), we only find one instance where private school parents feel that their school is (marginally) more safe and find no instances where private school parents believe that other parents in their child's school are more safe.

Second, we explore how COVID-19 health safety concerns relate to instructional mode. We find heterogeneity across school health safety and online learning, such that both parents who agreed and disagreed that their child's school was safe were less likely to have their child receive online instruction, which may signal the lack of choices that parents had in their instructional mode. At the same time, those that agreed that in-person benefits outweighed the risk were less likely to receive both online and hybrid instruction, demonstrating a potential match between health safety concerns and instructional mode. Republicans were also less likely to have their children engage in both online and hybrid instruction, which held even after we account for COVID-19-related, child, and parent characteristics, suggesting political sorting associated with the pandemic (Grossmann et al., 2021). Despite charter school parents believing that the benefits of in-person learning outweigh the risks, charter schools were more likely to receive online instruction, even after accounting for all other characteristics. Given that parents did not view these schools as safe, it is possible that these schools may not have been able to offer in-person instruction safely. As such, this finding offers mixed implications for charter schools' purported responsiveness to parental desires during the pandemic: while parents may have been more willing to endure some of risks associated with in-person instruction, there may have been a point at which this could not occur safely. Finally, private schools parents were both less likely to have their children engage in both online and hybrid schools, which may reflect school health safety, political attitudes (Republicans were more likely to attend private schools), or a lack of school resources to offer other learning options.

Third, we explore the relationships among parental concerns, SGMs, instructional modes, and school quality perceptions. Starting with parental concerns, feelings of health safety were often associated with good perceptions of school quality, supporting previous research on the importance of health safety and school quality. Additionally, when accounting for all other characteristics – including instructional mode, disagreeing that the benefits of in-person learning outweigh the risks was associated with poor perceptions of school quality. This notion of caution may point to unobserved school-related factors beyond instruction that children may not have been able to take part in, which may negatively affect how parents perceive the quality of their child's education. Despite offering different instructional modes, both charter and private schools were associated with improved school quality, suggesting that it was not merely the mode of instruction offered, but also the type of school that was offering it. While much of the research thus far has demonstrated the ineffectiveness of online instruction (Goldhaber et al., 2022), given the health safety concerns of parents and the differences in instructional offerings across SGMs, we were surprised to not find a significant association between online learning and perceptions of school quality. While hybrid instructional mode was associated with poor school quality, the significance of this relationship dissipated after we accounted for child characteristics. Here, we can infer that schools had a difficult time simultaneously offering multiple modes of instruction, but that this difficulty may reflect certain child characteristics, such as grade level.

Finally, we found marginally and statistically significant moderation across SGMs and instructional modes. Hybrid instruction tended to increase the likelihood of perceiving poor school quality at charter schools, but decrease these perceptions in private schools. Online learning also tended to decrease the likelihood of perceiving poor school quality at private schools. Given that private schools are often smaller, they may have been able to provide more tailored instruction in virtual or semi-virtual spaces. Furthermore, as private schools tended to offer in-person instruction, the ones that did offer virtual or hybrid instruction may have had additional resources that allowed them to do so, which could have increased the quality of learning and subsequent perceptions of school quality. Of course, these resources could also extend from the families that send their children to private schools. In our sample, private school families were more likely to have a bachelor's degree and higher incomes.

Through these analyses, we demonstrate that perceptions of high-quality education during the pandemic was not based on a "one-size-fits-all" model. Rather, schools appear to respond – in part – to the health safety concerns of parents through their instructional offerings. Moreover, alternative school governance models – even though they tended to offer different modes of instruction – had similar associations with better perceptions school quality, suggesting that school quality during the pandemic may have been less about the instructional mode offered and more about the *schools* offering these modes of instruction. This is also supported by the fact that those with positive pre-pandemic perceptions of school quality were also more likely to have positive perceptions of school quality during the pandemic.

Implications

This study has multiple implications for policy and practice. First, as both charter and private schools appear to be better able to match parents' COVID-19 health safety concerns with instructional modes *and* more likely to provide higher levels of perceived school quality, traditional public schools should consider ways in which they too can better meet the concerns of parents and adapt instructional modes accordingly. Particularly evident in our moderation model, there does not appear to be a one-size-fits-all method to instructional modes during the pandemic. Thus, schools should rely on the mode that works best for their staff and students, while also meeting the concerns of parents. Moreover, as hybrid instruction was related to worse school quality perceptions in charter schools, these schools may want to consider providing one instructional mode to the best of their ability, rather than multiple instructional modes at once (as is often the case with hybrid instruction).

Additionally, when considering the relationships among parents' health safety concerns and perceptions of school quality, schools leaders should consider ways both to improve the health safety of their schools, as well as measures that can help ensure the health and safety of the families they server. Recent research by Kearney and Childs (2021) demonstrates how multi-tiered systems of support can help schools remain open – both safely and effectively. As the pandemic continues to wax and wane and new variants continue to emerge, future research should also consider the role of communal pledges, testing, and vaccine policies on perceptions of health safety. Finally, while parents must ultimately decide how they weigh the benefits and risks for their children, schools can provide families with accurate information that can help them make informed decisions.

Limitations

Despite the novel contributions of this paper to the research field, this study is not without its limitations. First, while multiple waves of data were used in this analyses with repeated observations for some of the participants, our sample did not allow us to utilize a longitudinal design. Second, while we were able to account for a comprehensive array of COVID-19-related characteristics, as well as a robust set of child and parent demographic characteristics in our models, we were not able fully account for parents' decisions to enroll in various SGMs, nor schools' decisions to adopt various instructional modes. Therefore, we are not able to make causal claims. Finally, while we account for both SGM enrollment and instructional mode received, due to our survey design and sample, we cannot delineate among parents who changed SGMs during the pandemic or parents who had the option of choosing their child's instructional modes in our analysis. We are also unable to account for parents who made decisions to exit formal schooling entirely (e.g. through home-schooling or learning pods[6]). Future research can build on this study by leveraging longitudinal administrative data that contains student- and school-level information and a variety of family and neighborhood characteristics, while also considering alternative modes of education, such as homeschooling and pandemic "pods."[7]

Notes

1. Specifically, closing schools when cumulative COVID-19 incidences were in the lowest quartile compared to the highest quartile was associated with fewer COVID-19 cases and deaths per 100,000 (Auger et al., 2020)
2. This study was approved by Washington University in St. Louis's Institutional Review Board, and all participants consented to participate in the survey.
3. For example, our sample population tends to have higher rates of bachelor degree attainment than the U.S. adult population.

4. While multiple responses from a given parent can strengthen our analysis from a time-point perspective, there may be some unobserved bias in who chooses to respond to subsequent waves.
5. These results were not substantially different when estimated without the presence of SGMs (Model 15), suggesting that SGMs do not appear to explain the relationship between instructional mode and perceptions of school quality.
6. These decisions may also be strongly related to parents safety concerns (Watson, 2020).
7. For example, recent research has found that per-pupil expenditures were also related to instructional mode (DeAngelis & Makridis, 2022). Moreover, Marshall (2022) has recently explored how pandemic pods influenced private education.

Disclosure statement

No potential conflict of interest was reported by the authors.

Funding

This work was supported by the JP Morgan Chase Foundation, the Mastercard Center for Inclusive Growth, and the Annie E. Casey Foundation, but the views expressed herein are solely those of the authors.

ORCID

Jason Jabbari (iD) http://orcid.org/0000-0002-0196-4966

References

Alhakami, A. S., & Slovic, P. (1994). A psychological study of the inverse relationship between perceived risk and perceived benefit. *Risk Analysis, 14*(6), 1085–1096. doi:10.1111/j.1539-6924.1994.tb00080.x

Anderson, J. R., Hughes, J. L., & Trivedi, M. H. (2021). School personnel and parents' concerns related to COVID-19 pandemic's impact related to schools. *School Psychology Review, 50*(4), 519–529. doi:10.1080/2372966X.2020.1862626

Auger, K. A., Shah, S. S., Richardson, T., Hartley, D., Hall, M., Warniment, A., . . . Thomson, J. E. (2020). Association between statewide school closure and COVID-19 incidence and mortality in the US. *Jama, 324*(9), 859–870. doi:10.1001/jama.2020.14348

Barnum, M. (2021). Polls show most–though not all–parents are getting the type of instruction they want for their kids.

Belsha, K., & Barnum, M. (2022, June 6). Sticking around: Most big districts will offer virtual learning this fall, a sign of pandemic's effect. Chalkbeat. Retrieved from https://www.chalkbeat.org

Bryk, A., & Schneider, B. (2002). *Trust in schools: A core resource for improvement.* New York, NY: Russell Sage Foundation.

Camp, A. M., & Zamarro, G. (2022). Determinants of ethnic differences in school modality choices during the COVID-19 crisis. *Educational Researcher, 51*(1), 6–16. doi:10.3102/0013189X211057562

Carpenter, D., & Dunn, J. (2020). We're all teachers now: Remote learning during COVID-19. *Journal of School Choice, 14*(4), 567–594. doi:10.1080/15582159.2020.1822727

Chubb, J. E., & Moe, T. M. (1990). America's public schools: Choice is a panacea. *The Brookings Review, 8*(3), 4–12. doi:10.2307/20080159

Coleman, J. S., & Hoffer, T. (1987). Public and private schools: The impact of communities.

Dawson, M. (2022). Student Growth during COVID-19: Grade-level readiness matters.

DeAngelis, C. A., & Makridis, C. (2021). Are school reopening decisions related to union influence? *Social Science Quarterly, 102*(5), 2266–2284. doi:10.1111/ssqu.12955

DeAngelis, C. A., & Makridis, C. A. (2022). Are school reopening decisions related to funding? Evidence from over 12,000 districts during the COVID-19 pandemic. *Journal of School Choice, 16*(3), 454–476.

de Bruin, W. B., & Bennett, D. (2020). Relationships between initial COVID-19 risk perceptions and protective health behaviors: A national survey. *American Journal of Preventive Medicine, 59*(2), 157–167. doi:10.1016/j.amepre.2020.05.001

Domina, T., Renzulli, L., Murray, B., Garza, A. N., & Perez, L. (2021). Remote or removed: Predicting successful engagement with online learning during COVID-19. *Socius, 7*, 2378023120988200. doi:10.1177/2378023120988200

Dorn, E., Hancock, B., Sarakatsannis, J., & Viruleg, E. (2020, December 8). *COVID-19 and learning loss—disparities grow and students need help.* McKinsey & Company.

Fasang, A. E., Mangino, W., & Brückner, H. (2014, March). Social closure and educational attainment. *Sociological Forum, 29*(1), 137–164. doi:10.1111/socf.12073

Fersch, B., Schneider-Kamp, A., & Breidahl, K. N. (2022). Anxiety and trust in times of health crisis: How parents navigated health risks during the early phases of the COVID-19 pandemic in Denmark. *Health, Risk & Society, 24*(1–2), 36–53. doi:10.1080/13698575.2022.2028743

Flanders, W. (2021). Opting out: Enrollment trends in response to continued public school shutdowns. *Journal of School Choice, 15*(3), 331–343. doi:10.1080/15582159.2021.1917750

Friedman, B. A., Bobrowski, P. E., & Geraci, J. (2006). Parents' school satisfaction: Ethnic similarities and differences. *Journal of Educational Administration, 44*(5), 471–486. doi:10.1108/09578230610683769

Gibbons S and Silva O. (2011). School quality, child wellbeing and parents' satisfaction. Economics of Education Review, 30(2), 312–331. 10.1016/j.econedurev.2010.11.001

Goldberg, S. B. (2021). *Education in a pandemic: The disparate impacts of COVID-19 on America's students.* USA: Department of Education.

Goldhaber, D., Kane, T. J., McEachin, A., Morton, E., Patterson, T., & Staiger, D. O. (2022). *The consequences of remote and hybrid instruction during the pandemic (No. w30010).* National Bureau of Economic Research.

Grossmann, M., Reckhow, S., Strunk, K. O., & Turner, M. (2021). All states close but red districts reopen: The politics of in-person schooling during the COVID-19 pandemic. *Educational Researcher, 50*(9), 637–648. doi:10.3102/0013189X211048840

Gross, B., & Opalka, A. (2020). *Too many schools leave learning to chance during the pandemic.* Center on reinventing public education.

Haller, T., & Novita, S. (2021). In *Frontiers in Education, 6*, 700441. doi:10.3389/feduc.2021.700441

Halloran, C., Jack, R., Okun, J. C., & Oster, E. (2021). *Pandemic schooling mode and studenttest scores: Evidence from US states (No. w29497).* National Bureau of Economic Research.

Hartney, M. T., & Finger, L. K. (2022). Politics, markets, and pandemics: Public education's response to COVID-19. *Perspectives on Politics, 20*(2), 457–473. doi:10.1017/S1537592721000955

Henderson, M. B., Peterson, P. E., & West, M. R. (2021). Pandemic parent survey finds perverse pattern: Students are more likely to be attending school in person where covid is spreading more rapidly. *Education Next, 21*(2), 34–49.

Hodgman, S., Rickles, J., Carminucci, J., & Garret, M. (2021, June). National Survey of Public Education's response to COVID-19. Retrieved from https://www.air.org/sites/default/files/2021-07/research-brief-covid-survey-differences-instructional-modes-june-2021_0.pdf

Houston, D. M., & Steinberg, M. P. (2022). Public support for educators and in-person instruction during the Covid-19 pandemic. *(EdWorkingPaper: 22-575)*. Annenberg Institute at Brown University. doi:10.26300/ek3z-x247

Jabbari, J., Chun, Y., Johnson Jr, O., Grinstein-Weiss, M., & McDermott, L. (2022). Perceptions of School Quality and Student Learning During the Pandemic: Exploring the Role of Students, Families, Schools, and Neighborhoods. Socius, 8, 23780231221142955.

Kearney, C. A., & Childs, J. (2021). A multi-tiered systems of support blueprint for re-opening schools following COVID-19 shutdown. *Children and Youth Services Review, 122*, 105919. doi:10.1016/j.childyouth.2020.105919

Kroshus, E., Hawrilenko, M., Tandon, P. S., & Christakis, D. A. (2020). Plans of US parents regarding school attendance for their children in the fall of 2020: A national survey. *JAMA Pediatrics, 174*(11), 1093–1101. doi:10.1001/jamapediatrics.2020.3864

Kuhfeld, M., Soland, J., Tarasawa, B., Johnson, A., Ruzek, E., & Lewis, K. (2020). Learning during COVID-19: Initial findings on students' reading and math achievement and growth. *Collaborative for Student Growth.* NWEA Research. Retrieved from https://www.nwea.org/content/uploads/2020/11/Collaborative-brief-Learning-during-COVID-19.NOV2020.pdf

Kutsyuruba, B., Klinger, D. A., & Hussain, A. (2015). Relationships among school climate, school safety, and student achievement and well☐being: a review of the literature. Review of Education, 3(2), 103–135.

Lessler, J., Grabowski, M. K., Grantz, K. H., Badillo-Goicoechea, E., Metcalf, C. J. E., Lupton-Smith, C., ... Stuart, E. A. (2021). Household COVID-19 risk and in-person schooling. *Science, 372*(6546), 1092–1097. doi:10.1126/science.abh2939

Lubienski, C. (2003). Innovation in education markets: Theory and evidence on the impact of competition and choice in charter schools. *American Educational Research Journal, 40*(2), 395–443. doi:10.3102/00028312040002395

Marshall, D. T. (2022). COVID-19 and the classroom: How schools navigated the great disruption.

Marshall, D. T., & Bradley-Dorsey, M. (2020). Reopening America's schools: A descriptive look at how states and large school districts are navigating fall 2020. *Journal of School Choice, 14* (4), 534–566. doi:10.1080/15582159.2020.1822731

Moe, T. M. (2011). Special interest: Teachers unions and America's public schools. Washington, DC: Brookings Institution Press.

Musaddiq, T., Stange, K. M., Bacher-Hicks, A., & Goodman, J. (2022). The Pandemic's effect on demand for public schools, homeschooling, and private schools. *Journal of Public Economics.* 212, 104710.

National Center for Education Statistics. (2021, June 28). *Nation's public school enrollment dropped 3 percent in 2020-21.* Retrieved from https://bit.ly/3waonSb

Polikoff, M. S., Silver, D., Garland, M., Saavedra, A. R., Rapaport, A., Fienberg, M., ... Yoo, P. (2021). The impact of a messaging intervention on parents' school hesitancy during COVID-19. *Educational Researcher, 51*(3), 231–234. 0013189X211070813. doi:10.3102/0013189x211061732

Preston, C., Goldring, E., Berends, M., & Cannata, M. (2012). School innovation in district context: Comparing traditional public schools and charter schools. *Economics of Education Review, 31*(2), 318–330. doi:10.1016/j.econedurev.2011.07.016

Rauscher, E., & Burns, A. (2021). Unequal opportunity spreaders: Higher COVID-19 deaths with later school closure in the United States. *Sociological Perspectives, 64*(5), 831–856. doi:10.1177/07311214211005486

Roll, S., Bufe, S., Chun, Y., & Grinstein-Weiss, M. (2021). The Socioeconomic Impacts of COVID-19 Study: Survey Methodology Report. Retrieved from: https://openscholarship.wustl.edu/cgi/viewcontent.cgi?article=1053&context=spi_research

Scafidi, B., Tutterow, R., & Kavanagh, D. (2021). This time really is different: The effect of COVID-19 on independent K-12 school enrollments. *Journal of School Choice, 15*(3), 305–330. doi:10.1080/15582159.2021.1944722

Szabo, J. (2021). Online or in-person instruction? Factors influencing COVID-19 schooling decisions among latinx families in Houston, Texas. *Aera Open, 7.*

Watson, A. R. (2020). Parent-created "Schools" in the US. *Journal of School Choice, 14*(4), 595–603. doi:10.1080/15582159.2020.1836801

Zack, E. S., Kennedy, J., & Long, J. S. (2019). Can nonprobability samples be used for social science research? A cautionary tale. Survey Research Methods, 13(2), 215–227

Teacher Morale, Job Satisfaction, and Burnout in Schools of Choice Following the COVID-19 Pandemic

David T. Marshall ⓘD, Natalie M. Neugebauer ⓘD, Tim Pressley ⓘD, and Katrina Brown-Aliffi ⓘD

ABSTRACT
Student enrollment patterns have been studied during the COVID-19 pandemic, with many families seeking alternatives to traditional public schools. Less is known about teacher experiences in these alternatives. We explored predictors of teacher job satisfaction, burnout, and morale. Of particular interest was whether these presented differently across school types. We surveyed teachers nationwide ($n = 798$) in May 2022. Three linear regression models were tested. Results suggested that teacher autonomy and administrative support were significant predictors in each model. Private school teachers experienced greater job satisfaction and morale than traditional public school teachers; charter school teachers had greater levels of morale.

The SARS-CoV-2 (COVID-19) pandemic disrupted most facets of life in the United States, and schooling was no exception. In the spring of 2020, schools closed for in-person learning as part of a wider effort to curb the spread of the virus (Bourne, 2021; Marshall, 2022). In the past two years, several challenges and changes to traditional teaching approaches have been associated with increased teacher attrition rates (Marshall et al., 2022a; Marshall et al., 2022b; Zamarro, Camp, Fuchsman, & McGee, 2022). Research conducted early in the pandemic found that teachers had higher burnout, anxiety, and workloads (Chan, Sharkey, Lawrie, Arch, & Nylund-Gibson, 2021; Pressley et al., 2021). Teacher burnout and attrition have been persistent issues within the profession (Menter, 2022); however, these issues have been exacerbated in the wake of the pandemic.

In the fall of 2020, schools reopened offering a wide range of instructional plans, which included fully in-person, hybrid, or fully virtual instruction, often depending on the number of local cases of COVID-19 (Marshall & Bradley-Dorsey, 2020). While state-level guidance and plans were based on COVID-19 case rates (e.g., Minnesota), actual decisions that were made at the district level often reflected local politics more than science (DeAngelis & Makridis, 2021; Grossmann, Reckhow, Strunk, & Turner, 2021; Hartney & Finger, 2021). During the 2020–2021 school year, schools in states like Florida offered in-person instruction for most of the year, while schools in states like California were remote for most or all of the school year (Marshall & Bradley-Dorsey, 2022). Within state contexts, school districts varied in their approaches to schooling during the 2020–2021 school year (DeAngelis & Makridis, 2022; Grossmann, Reckhow, Strunk, & Turner, 2021; Marshall & Bradley-Dorsey, 2020). While society worked to maintain a sense of normalcy, many teachers struggled with balancing their teaching responsibilities and their families' safety and needs, leading to higher anxiety levels among teachers (Allen, Jerrim, & Sims, 2020; Jones & Kessler, 2020). Studies also showed that increased teacher burnout rates were associated with COVID-related health concerns, administrative support, changes in instructional approaches, and parent communication (Hutchison et al., 2022; Marshall et al., 2022c; Marshall et al., in press; Zamarro, Camp, Fuchsman, & McGee, 2022). This was especially true for teachers at schools with high levels of poverty, where several teachers reported needing more support compared to teachers at more affluent schools (Kraft, Simon, & Lyon, 2021; Slavin & Storey, 2020). Higher levels of stress and burnout became more pervasive as teachers (1) were asked to follow new instructional requirements and approaches; (2) failed to receive adequate support for the continual changes; and (3) saw their workloads increase (Chan, Sharkey, Lawrie, Arch, & Nylund-Gibson, 2021; Love & Marshall, 2022; Ma et al., 2022; Marshall et al., in press; McCarthy, Blaydes, Weppner, & Lambert, 2022; Sokal, Trudel, & Babb, 2021).

Schools of choice during COVID-19

An emerging body of work has explored student enrollment patterns amidst the pandemic across school sectors. Public schools' responses to the pandemic left many families seeking alternatives for their children's education. Some families wanted in-person learning for their children and lived in areas where public schools were not offering this. As such, private and charter schools that offered in-person learning options became more attractive. Scafidi, Tutterow, and Kavanagh (2021) found that independent school enrollments increased by 70% during the 2020–2021 school year. A report from the National Alliance for Public Charter Schools found that charter school enrollment also grew during this time, increasing by seven percent during the 2020–2021 school year (Veney & Jacobs, 2021). Of the 42 states they analyzed, 39 states experienced enrollment increases in their charter sector. Some families left public schools altogether, opting to homeschool their children (Musaddiq, Stange, Bacher-Hicks, & Goodman, 2022) or create what became known as "pandemic pods" – or learning pods – that involved the schooling of children from a small number of families together (Watson, 2022). While much focus has been placed on families "voting with their feet" and increasingly opting for alternatives to traditional public schools (TPS), much less focus has been placed on the experiences of teachers in these alternatives during the pandemic.

Entering the 2021–2022 school year, schools tasked teachers with catching up students who were behind academically due to COVID-19 (e.g., Halloran, Jack, Okun, & Oster, 2021), while providing regular instruction and implementing COVID-19 safety protocols. In most contexts, schools had resumed normal operation, perhaps apart from mask-wearing requirements. The purpose of this study was to explore teachers' morale, job satisfaction, and burnout levels at the conclusion of the 2021–2022 school year and learn if these constructs presented differently for teachers who taught in different sectors. Specifically, we asked the following questions:

(1) Do relationships between teaching in a school of choice, teacher morale, job satisfaction, and teacher burnout exist following the COVID-19 pandemic?
(2) Do teachers who teach in charter and private schools experience different levels of autonomy than teachers in traditional public schools (TPS)?
(3) Do teachers who teach in charter and private schools experience different levels of administrative support than teachers in TPS?

Teacher job satisfaction and retention

Ample literature has established a link between teacher job satisfaction and the intention (or lack thereof) to leave the teaching profession (e.g., Skaalvik & Skaalvik, 2011). In schools of choice – particularly in charter schools – a tension exists whereby teachers tend to enjoy at least some aspects of their job, but also have greater attrition rates on average than teachers in TPS. The findings around job satisfaction and charter schools are mixed. Malloy and Wohlstetter (2003) examined 40 case studies with teachers in the charter sector and found that teachers generally enjoyed their teaching environments and working with their colleagues. Other studies have found that TPS teachers reported slightly higher job satisfaction levels than charter school teachers (Erichsen & Reynolds, 2020; Roch & Sai, 2016). Teachers in standalone charter schools were found to have greater levels of satisfaction than teachers in schools run by education management organizations (EMOs) or charter management organizations (CMOs) (Roch & Sai, 2016). Ndoye, Imig, and Parker (2010) conducted survey research in North Carolina and found that charter school teachers were more likely to report an intention to leave their jobs than their TPS counterparts. However, the literature suggests that supportive and effective school leadership is a predictor of teachers remaining in their jobs (Ndoye, Imig, & Parker, 2010; Torres, 2016). In the private school sector, Lopes and Oliveira (2020) conducted a multilevel analysis of teacher and school determinants of job satisfaction and found that teaching in a private school was the strongest predictor.

Teacher burnout

Teaching has always been a difficult job and attrition was an issue prior to the COVID-19 pandemic, with over half of teachers leaving the profession within their first five years (Ingersoll et al., 2014; Ryan et al., 2017) and between 8–16% of teachers leaving annually (National Center for Education Statistics, 2016; Steiner & Woo, 2021). During the 2020–2021 school year, studies found that between 25% and 55% of teachers considered leaving their job (Jotkoff, 2022; Marshall et al., 2022a; Steiner & Woo, 2021). However, the general trend from several national reports on teacher attrition did not find an increase in teachers leaving teaching, but only an increase of teacher burnout and lower job satisfaction (Rosenberg & Anderson, 2021; Zamarro, Camp, Fuchsman, & McGee, 2022). This could be partly explained by research conducted by Nguyen et al. (2022) which suggests that teachers who express an intention to leave the profession do not always do so. It is important to note that specific subgroups of teachers, such as teachers at high-poverty schools and early career teachers, did have an increase in attrition during the spring of 2021 (Rosenberg & Anderson, 2021). At the state level, several reports have found slight increases in teacher attrition in Arkansas (Camp, Zamarro, & McGee, 2022), North Carolina (Bastian & Fuller, 2022), California, (Carver-Thomas, Leung, & Burns, 2021), and Washington (Goldhaber & Theobald, 2022). In a follow-up to their 2022 study, Camp, Zamarro, and McGee (2023) found teacher attrition trends continued to grow in Arkansas, with 5% of teachers leaving teaching before the 2021–2022 school year.

By the conclusion of the 2021–2022 school year, about three-fourths of teachers reported considering leaving the profession (Agyapong, Obuobi-Donkor, Burback, & Wei, 2022; Marshall et al., 2022b). This is important because of the negative relationship between teacher burnout and self-efficacy (Billett, Turner, & Li, 2022; Savas, Bozgeyik, & Eser, 2014; Skaalvik & Skaalvik, 2010). Teachers who do not feel they can succeed in their jobs become demoralized. Teachers in charter schools, especially those associated with larger CMOs, have historically had high attrition levels and often work more hours per week than their TPS counterparts (Oberfield, 2017; Pondiscio, 2019). Fusco (2017) has termed large CMOs like KIPP, Uncommon Schools, Achievement First, and Success Academies as "burnout factories" – a nod to their long hours and high attrition rates. By contrast, Waychunas (2022) found that teachers in "no excuses" charter schools "created professional subcultures where novice teachers feel simultaneously challenged and supported" (p. 56).

During the pandemic, factors contributing to burnout included anxiety about the virus itself, managing multiple instructional modalities, and a lack of administrative support (Agyapong, Obuobi-Donkor, Burback, & Wei, 2022; Hutchison et al., 2022; Pressley, 2021). At the conclusion of the 2020–2021 school year, approximately 9 in 10 teachers reported feeling burned out (Marshall et al., 2022d). Similarly, Kotowski, Davis, Barratt, Davis, and Kotowski (2022) found that more than a year into the pandemic, 72% of teachers they surveyed reported feeling very or extremely stressed out, 57% reported feeling very or extremely burned out, and more than half struggled to find a satisfactory work-life balance. Teachers also reported high levels of stress, burnout, and job dissatisfaction due to the challenges they faced with providing online instruction (Minihan et al., 2022; Walter & Fox, 2021), changes in teaching approaches (Robinson et al., 2022), and increased workloads during COVID-19 (Chan, Sharkey, Lawrie, Arch, & Nylund-Gibson, 2021; Sokal, Trudel, & Babb, 2021). There continues to be a need to investigate teacher burnout, especially in charter schools, as the pandemic has likely exacerbated many trends prior to 2020.

Teacher morale

Teacher morale has been defined as the degree to which a person's needs are satisfied and their perception of how the job situation brought that state of satisfaction to fruition (Remple & Bentley, 1970). Teacher morale has been positively associated with student achievement (e.g., Houchard, 2005), motivation, effort, and job satisfaction (Huysman, 2008). Furthermore, morale has been negatively associated with job performance and attachment to students (Lumsden, Huitinga, Lumsden, & Dijkstra, 1998). A study of teachers in Pakistan found that teacher morale was similar between private and public school teachers (Miraj, Reba, & Din, 2018). Malik's (2021) research at an elementary charter school in Texas found that participants who felt empowered and had a sense of belonging to the school community also had high morale and work performance levels. In Merseth's (2009) book exploring five successful urban charter schools, she noted that a commonality they shared was that they each had teacher retention committees in place to keep track of teacher morale and listen to teacher concerns.

During the pandemic, survey research found that 29% of teachers reported low morale at the conclusion of the 2020–2021 school year, a figure that almost doubled to 56% by the conclusion of the 2021–2022 school year (Marshall et al., 2022b). These findings contradict what one might have initially thought – that things would improve upon a return to normalcy. As such, exploring job satisfaction, burnout, and morale in K-12 schools remains important.

Method

Several studies have explored teacher job satisfaction, burnout, morale, and well-being at the beginning of the pandemic (e.g., Kush, Badillo-Goicoechea, Musci, & Stuart, 2021; Rogowska & Meres, 2022) and during the first full year of teaching during COVID-19 (e.g., Hutchison et al., 2022; Zamarro, Camp, Fuchsman, & McGee, 2022). As COVID-19 and its effects waned in 2022, teachers still faced increased expectations for supporting students, incorporating technology used during the pandemic, and being flexible with students and teachers for COVID-related absences (e.g., virtual learning and covering of other classes). This exploratory study focused on understanding teacher experiences at the end of the 2021–2022 school year. Specifically, we were interested in learning what predicted teacher job satisfaction, burnout, and morale, with a particular interest in learning whether this presented differently in schools of choice.

Procedures and sampling

To collect information on teachers' perspectives, researchers used convenience and snowball sampling from May 4–18, 2022. This time period was selected because most teachers were in the last few weeks of the school year, which allowed an opportunity for them to reflect on their experience including ever-changing COVID-19 policies throughout the academic year. Study participants had to be currently employed PK-12 teachers in the United States at the time of the survey administration in order to be eligible to participate. IRB approval was received prior to initiating research activities.[1] Researchers provided an anonymized survey link to personal networks in addition to posting it on social media sites including Facebook, Twitter, and Reddit. We posted a link to the survey in teacher and teaching-related Facebook groups and subreddit pages, and used teaching-related, trending hashtags to post the link on Twitter. Using social media platforms allowed for an extensive sample of teachers from across the United States to participate in the current study. The survey was also emailed to recent graduates of a teacher preparation program. Finally, researchers encouraged teachers to share the survey with other teachers if they were so inclined.

Our sample included 798 PK-12 teachers across the United States ($N = 49$ states). Participants' average age was 40 ($M = 40.51$, $SD = 10.38$), had 13 years of teaching experience ($M = 13.36$, $SD = 8.99$), were overwhelmingly White (87.6%), female (88.1%), and taught at the elementary level (PK-5; $n = 469$, 58.9%). More than half of participants (62.2%) taught in a Title 1 school, and more than four in five (82.8%) taught in a traditional public school. Approximately half of the participants (48.1%) taught in a suburban school, about a quarter taught in an urban setting (25.1%), and the rest taught in either a rural or small-town setting. See Table 1 for descriptive statistics for the study sample,

Table 1. Descriptive statistics for sample.

Variable	N	%	M	SD
Teaching Experience			13.36	8.99
Age			40.51	10.38
Race/Ethnicity				
African American/Black	30	3.8		
Asian American	14	1.8		
Hispanic	26	3.3		
Pacific Islander/Native Hawaiian	5	0.6		
White or Caucasian	695	87.1		
More than one race	21	2.6		
Other	7	0.8		
Gender				
Female	702	88.0		
Male	87	10.9		
Other	9	1.1		
SPED	77	9.7		
Title 1	496	62.2		
Elementary	469	58.9		
School Type				
Traditional Public School	661	82.8		
Magnet School	34	4.3		
Charter School	56	7.0		
Private School	47	5.9		
Geographic Location				
Rural	117	14.7		
Suburban	385	48.3		
Urban	200	25.1		
Small Town	96	12.0		

Note: N = 798.

The use of voluntary and convenience samples in social science research can lead to samples that are not reflective of the larger population of interest. As such, we compare our sample to national teacher demographics. This study's sample is reflective of the national teacher workforce in terms of teaching experience, the number of years taught at their current school, and teacher age. The sample is more female and White, and less Hispanic than national figures. Suburban teachers are also overrepresented in the sample. See Table 2 for a comparison of this study's sample with national demographics.

Survey

We considered several factors in the development of the survey. For instance, we balanced what we already knew about teachers' heavy workloads, as previously noted in earlier school year reports, while ensuring it was not burdensome (Jotkoff, 2022). The survey included questions that asked about teacher and school demographics. We measured teacher burnout with a brief three-item scale. Although it yielded a strong reliability metric (α=.89), some will view this as a limited approach to measuring the construct, especially since validated scales exist (e.g., Maslach Burnout Inventory). This was done intentionally to limit the length of time teachers needed to dedicate to participate in the study. In studies conducted throughout the pandemic, teachers reported

Table 2. Comparing current study's sample with national teacher demographics.

Variable	Current Study (N = 798) %	M	National Demographics %	M
Teaching Experience[a]		13.4		14.5
Years at Current School[a]		9.0		8.2
Age[a]		40.5		43.2
Gender[a]				
Female	88.0		76.6	
Male	10.9		23.4	
Race/Ethnicity[a]				
African American/Black	3.8		5.8	
Asian American	1.8		2.4	
Hispanic	3.3	.3	9.3	
Pacific Islander/Native Hawaiian	0.6		0.2	
White or Caucasian	87.1		80.3	
More than one race	2.6		1.7	
School Type[b]				
Traditional Public Schools*	87.1		82.2	
Charter Schools	7.0		5.1	
Private Schools	5.9		12.7	
Geographic Location[c]				
Rural	14.7		11.5	
Suburban	48.3		39.1	
Urban	25.1		43.8	
Small Town	12.0		5.7	

Note: Figures in the two right-hand columns represent national teacher demographics per the National Center for Education Statistics; [a] NCES (2016); [b] NCES (2021a); [c] NCES (2021b); * includes magnet school teachers.

increased workloads and elevated levels of stress, anxiety, and burnout (Carver-Thomas, Leung, & Burns, 2021; Kaden, 2020; Răducu & Stănculescu, 2022; Sokal, Trudel, & Babb, 2020; Westphal, Kalinowski, Hoferichter, & Vock, 2022), which further supported our decision to use a short burnout scale to limit the time and work required of teachers at the end of the school year. Additionally, we included scales that measured teacher job satisfaction (Skaalvik & Skaalvik, 2011), administrative support (Seidman & Zager, 1986), teacher autonomy (Virginia Department of Education, 2021), all using 6-point Likert scales ranging from *strongly disagree* to *strongly agree*. See Table 3 for means, standard deviation, and reliability coefficients for each scale in the model. See Appendix A for the full Teacher Burnout, Job Satisfaction, Teacher Leadership and Autonomy, and Administrative Support Scales.

Table 3. Means, Standard Deviations, and Alphas for scales included in models.

Scale	No. of Items	M	SD	α
Job Satisfaction	4	14.32	4.30	.86
Teacher Burnout	3	15.28	3.27	.89
Administrative Support	6	21.39	7.56	.91
Teacher Autonomy	9	3.39	.97	.85

Table 4. Correlation matrix of outcome variables, administrative support, and teacher autonomy.

Variable	I	II	III	IV	V
(I) Job Satisfaction	1				
(II) Teacher Burnout	−.587***	1			
(III) Teacher Morale	.600***	−.603***	1		
(IV) Administrative Support	.404***	−.421***	.437***	1	
(V) Teacher Autonomy	.394***	−.438***	.426***	.575***	1

Note: *** p < .001; ** p < .01; * p < .05.

To measure teacher morale, participants were asked to rate their current level of mental health on a 0 (*very bad*) to 10-point (*very good*) scale, similar to Senechal et al. (2016). Participants in this study reported low to medium-low levels of morale ($M = 3.74$, SD = 2.32). See Table 4 for a correlation matrix.

Models tested

We tested three separate regression models – one for each dependent variable of interest. Teacher job satisfaction was the dependent variable in the first regression model, teacher burnout was the dependent variable in the second model, and teacher morale was the dependent variable in the third model. Each regression model contained the same set of predictor variables. The two individual teacher demographic variables included were dummy variables for (1) nonwhite teachers and (2) female teachers. Six school-level dummy variables were included in the model as well to account for poverty, geography, and school type. A dummy variable for a school's Title I status was included as an approximation of the poverty level of the students who attended the school. Dummy variables were included for teaching in rural and urban schools. Three additional dummy variables were included for teaching in schools of choice: (1) magnet schools within a traditional public school system; (2) charter schools; and (3) private schools. Finally, two scales (described above) were included to measure teacher autonomy and administrative support.

Data analysis

All models were tested using linear regression analysis (Darlington & Hayes, 2017), and all analyses were conducted in Stata version 17. The alpha significance level was set a priori at .05. Prior to analyses being conducted, the data were screened to ensure that the requisite assumptions were met for linear regression analysis. Given the range of responses to the pandemic that happened across state contexts (e.g., Marshall & Bradley-Dorsey, 2020), robust standard errors were clustered at the state level. The full sample included 830 participants. Fewer than one percent of participants had missing data for any of the variables included in the model with two exceptions. These records were removed before analysis. Twenty participants were missing data for the state in which they taught. Given the importance of this variable, these records were deleted listwise. A final sample of 798 participants was included for the job satisfaction and teacher burnout models. An additional 49 participants did not respond to the teacher morale item. As such, the third model included 749 participants. Collinearity diagnostics were run for each model, and variance inflation factor values were found to be acceptable for all models. Models were evaluated in terms of the amount of variance explained (R^2).

Results

Job satisfaction

The first model explored the predictors of job satisfaction. The model was significant $F(10,49) = 47.17$, $p < .001$, with approximately 22% of the variance explained by these variables ($R^2 = .219$). Four variables were found to be significant predictors of job satisfaction. Female teachers ($\beta = 1.437$) and those who taught in private schools ($\beta = 1.010$) reported greater job satisfaction than their peers. Magnet and charter school teachers reported levels of job satisfaction similar to their TPS peers. Teachers reporting greater levels of teacher autonomy ($\beta = 1.088$) and administrative support ($\beta = .145$) also reported increased levels of job satisfaction.

Teacher burnout

The second model explored the predictors of teacher burnout. The model was significant $F(10,49) = 22.92$, $p < .001$, with approximately 24% of the variance explained by these variables ($R^2 = .245$). No demographic or school-related variables were found to be significant. Teachers in schools of choice (any type) reported levels of burnout similar to their TPS peers. Teachers reporting greater levels of teacher autonomy ($\beta = 1.088$) and administrative support ($\beta = .145$) reported decreased levels of teacher burnout.

Teacher morale

The third model explored the predictors of teacher morale. The model was significant $F(10,49) = 49.24$, $p < .001$, with approximately 26% of the variance ($R^2 = .261$) explained by these variables. All but two predictor variables were found to be significant. Female ($\beta = .564$) and nonwhite ($\beta = .445$) teachers reported increased levels of morale. Teaching in Title I schools ($\beta = -.384$) and urban schools ($\beta = -.290$) was associated with lower levels of morale. Private ($\beta = .759$) and charter school ($\beta = .606$) teachers reported greater levels of morale than their TPS peers. Teachers reporting greater levels of teacher autonomy ($\beta = .613$) and administrative support ($\beta = .089$) also reported

Table 5. Regression findings – predictors of job satisfaction, teacher burnout, and teacher morale.

	Dependent Variable		
	Job Satisfaction	Burnout	Morale
Predictor Variable	β(SE)	β(SE)	β(SE)
Nonwhite	−.174(.383)	−.319(.271)	.445(.152)**
Female	1.437(.456)**	.306(.308)	.564(.189)**
Title 1	−.316(.241)	.268(.232)	−.384(.132)**
Urban	−.526(.393)	.379(.212)	−.290(.128)*
Rural	−.351(.339)	.274(.263)	.161(.201)
Charter	.439(.641)	−.527(.371)	.606(.247)*
Private	1.010(.463)*	−.765(.421)	.759(.313)*
Magnet	.827(.482)	−.755(.473)	.361(.267)
Teacher Autonomy	1.088(.142)***	−.935(.145)***	.613(.076)***
Administrative Support	.145(.019)***	−.112(.013)***	.089(.316)***
N	798	798	749
R^2	.219	.245	.261

*** $p < .001$; ** $p < .01$; * $p < .05$; Robust standard errors clustered at the state level.

increased levels of morale. See Table 5 for beta coefficients and robust standard errors for all three models.

Teacher autonomy and administrative support in schools of choice

Teacher autonomy and administrative support were significant predictors in each of the three models tested. As such, it was of interest to learn whether these variables presented differently in traditional public schools and schools of choice. To test this, two one-way analysis of variance (ANOVA) tests were conducted. Results demonstrate that teachers received a similar amount of support from their administrators, regardless of school type $F(3,794) = 1.35$, $p > .05$. However, significant differences were found in terms of the level of autonomy teachers experienced across school type $F(3,794) = 11.89$, $p < .001$., $\omega^2 = .04$. Bonferroni post hoc tests revealed that participants who taught in charter schools and private schools reported experiencing greater levels of autonomy than teachers who worked in traditional public schools.

Discussion

The purpose of this study was to explore teacher experiences at the conclusion of the 2021–2022 school year. We sought to understand what predicted teacher job satisfaction, burnout, and morale, and we were specifically interested in learning if these experiences varied by school sector. Compared to their TPS peers, teachers in private schools reported greater levels of job satisfaction and morale. This finding is in line with previous literature (e.g., Lopes & Oliveira, 2020). Charter school teachers reported greater levels of morale, but similar levels of job satisfaction to TPS teachers. Teaching in a magnet school was not a significant predictor of any of the three outcome variables we studied. This is likely because while magnet schools certainly represent additional options for families to select for their children's education, they are still overseen by traditional public school districts and their school leaders have less autonomy to make decisions on average than private and charter school leaders. Teacher autonomy and administrative support were significant predictors in all three models. This is important since both are within a school's locus of control.

Torres (2014) has described teacher autonomy as "a cornerstone of the charter school movement" (p. 3). The literature on teacher autonomy in charter schools is mixed with some studies suggesting that charter school teachers experience greater autonomy than TPS teachers, but others suggest that there may be limits to this within larger CMOs (e.g., Waychunas, 2022). Conversely, Oberfield (2017) found some evidence that charter school teachers had more autonomy than teachers who work in TPS. He also found that charter school teachers were 30% less likely to report that completing paperwork and other mundane aspects of their job interfered with their ability to be successful in the classroom, an indication that charter school teachers experienced less "red tape" than what one would find in TPS. In a separate analysis, Oberfield (2016) examined the 2011–2012 Schools and Staffing Survey and found that charter school teachers in standalone charter schools felt as if they had more autonomy than those working in a school run by an EMO or CMO. Here, we found that private and charter school leaders reported greater levels of autonomy than TPS peers. In this study, we did not discern between those teaching in a school that was part of a CMO or not. Future research should continue exploring this, focusing on within-sector variation. Future research should also explore teacher autonomy, morale, and job satisfaction in U.S. private schools, given that most recent literature exploring this was conducted abroad.

Our findings suggest that teachers experienced burnout similarly across sectors. Similar to studies conducted earlier in the pandemic, the current findings suggest the critical role of administrative support for teachers (Love & Marshall, 2022; Sokal, Trudel, & Babb, 2020, 2021). These results also align with previous literature conducted before COVID-19, suggesting the importance of administrative support and its influence on teacher burnout (Ingersoll, 2001; Margolis & Nagel, 2006). As such, school leaders may try to incorporate more formative feedback on instruction and management, provide needed materials for instruction, support teacher mental health, and be aware of teacher workloads before asking teachers to add another task to their schedules (Carver-Thomas, Leung, & Burns, 2021; Walter & Fox, 2021).

Limitations and future directions

It is important to note some of the current study's limitations that others may look to address in future work. At first glance, the sample appears to lack diversity given that it is overwhelmingly White (87.1%) and female (88.0%). These figures are indeed elevated from national figures (79% White and 76% female; National Center for Education Statistics, 2016); however, they are broadly reflective of the demographics of the profession. Researchers should work to have more robust and diverse samples that may lead to more generalizable findings. Second, the sampling procedure also represents a limitation. Data collection occurred at one point during the school year. The anonymous link to the survey was posted in several places across multiple social media platforms to reach a large number of teachers. However, it should be acknowledged that teachers who elected to participate in this research and complete the survey may differ in important ways from those who never encountered the social media posts or did so and elected not to participate. Specifically, those who self-select to complete the survey may be more interested in the topic of the study and have more extreme (i.e., very negative or very positive) views about teaching during the pandemic and how it affected their mental health. Research suggests that voluntary samples can be prone to voluntary response bias, where those who elect to participate tend to overrepresent extremes rather than the general population (Chigerwe et al., 2020; Nield & Nordstrom, 2016). Future research would benefit from a more randomized selection of teachers and a longitudinal design that examines changes in teacher burnout throughout the school year.

This study's findings suggest that private school teachers had greater autonomy than their peers in other sectors. However, it is unclear if those findings are uniform across all private school teachers. Microschools and "pandemic pods" became an increasingly popular alternative to traditional public schools during the COVID-19 pandemic (Watson, 2022). However, participants were not given the option to indicate that they taught in one of these arrangements in lieu of a more traditional private school setting. By their very nature, teachers in microschools and pandemic pods have wide discretion to make decisions that make the most sense for the students they teach. It is possible that some of the private school teachers in our sample were microschool or pandemic pod teachers.

Additionally, the current study measured teacher burnout with a limited three-item scale. Although it yielded a strong reliability metric ($\alpha=.89$), some will view this as a limited approach to measuring the construct. This was done intentionally to limit the length of time teachers needed to dedicate to participate in the study. Future studies might consider more robust measures of teacher burnout, but also explore other predictor variables that may have a relationship with teacher burnout. Finally, future research needs to go beyond survey research of teachers. Future studies must consider specific interventions to support teacher well-being and limit teacher burnout. This will require more advanced research designs including quasi-experimental designs and true experiments.

Note

1. IRB approval was obtained from Auburn University (22–210 Ex 2204) and Christopher Newport University (1906155–1).

Disclosure statement

No potential conflict of interest was reported by the authors.

Funding

This research received no specific grant funding from any funding agency in the public, commercial, or not-for-profit sectors.

ORCID

David T. Marshall (iD) http://orcid.org/0000-0003-1467-7656
Natalie M. Neugebauer (iD) http://orcid.org/0000-0003-3293-4994
Tim Pressley (iD) http://orcid.org/0000-0003-3670-9751
Katrina Brown-Aliffi (iD) http://orcid.org/0000-0002-6233-2727

References

Agyapong, B., Obuobi-Donkor, G., Burback, L., & Wei, Y. (2022). Stress, burnout, anxiety and depression among teachers: A scoping review. *International Journal of Environmental Research and Public Health*, *19*(17), 10706. doi:10.3390/ijerph191710706

Allen, R., Jerrim, J., & Sims, S. (2020). How did the early stages of the COVID-19 pandemic affect teacher wellbeing. *Centre for Education Policy and Equalising Opportunities (CEPEO) Working Paper*, *1*, 15–20.

Bastian, K. C., & Fuller, S. C. (2022). Teacher and principal attrition during the COVID-19 pandemic in North Carolina: Updated analyses for the 2021-22 school year. *Education Policy Initiative at Carolina*. https://epic.unc.edu/wp-content/uploads/sites/1268/2022/09/Teacher-and-Principal-Attrition-During-COVID-19.pdf

Billett, P., Turner, K., & Li, X. (2022). Australian teacher stress, well-being, self-efficacy, and safety during the COVID-19 pandemic. *Psychology in the Schools*. doi:10.1002/pits.22713

Bourne, R. A. (2021). *Economics in one virus: An introduction to economic reasoning through COVID-19*. Washington, DC: Cato Institute.

Camp, A., Zamarro, G., & McGee, J. B. (2022). Changes in teachers' mobility and attrition in Arkansas during the first two years of the COVID-19 pandemic. EdWorkingpapers.com. https://www.edworkingpapers.com/ai22-589

Camp, A., Zamarro, G., & McGee, J. B. (2023). Movers, switchers, and exiters: Teacher turnover during COVID-19. *EDRE Research Brief, 1*(1–9). https://edre.uark.edu/_resources/pdf/2022-23_turnover-research-brief.pdf

Carver-Thomas, D., Leung, M., & Burns, D. (2021). California teachers and COVID-19: How the pandemic is impacting the teacher workforce. *Learning Policy Institute*. https://files.eric.ed.gov/fulltext/ED614374.pdf

Chan, M., Sharkey, J. D., Lawrie, S. I., Arch, D. A. N., & Nylund-Gibson, K. (2021). Elementary school teacher well-being and supportive measures amid COVID-19: An exploratory study. *School Psychology, 36*(6), 533–545. doi:10.1037/spq0000441

Chigerwe, M., Holm, D. E., Mostert, E. -M., May, K., Boudreaux, K. A., & Annunziato, R. A. (2020). Exploring issues surrounding mental health and wellbeing across two continents: A preliminary cross-sectional collaborative study between the University of California, Davis, and University of Pretoria. *PLoS One, 15*(10), e0241302. doi:10.1371/journal.pone.0241302

Darlington, R. B., & Hayes, A. F. (2017). *Regression analysis and linear models: Concepts, applications, and implementation.* New York: Guilford Press.

DeAngelis, C. A., & Makridis, C. A. (2021). Are school reopening decisions related to union influence? *Social Science Quarterly, 102*(5), 2266–2284. doi:10.1111/ssqu.12955

DeAngelis, C. A., & Makridis, C. A. (2022). Are school reopening decisions related to funding? Evidence from over 12,000 districts during the COVID-19 pandemic. *Journal of School Choice, 16*(3), 454–476. doi:10.1080/15582159.2022.2077164

Erichsen, K., & Reynolds, J. (2020). Public school accountability, workplace culture, and teacher morale. *Social Science Research, 85*, 102347. doi:10.1016/j.ssresearch.2019.102347

Fusco, M. (2017). Burnout factors: The challenge of retaining great teachers in charter schools. *Phi Delta Kappan, 98*(8), 26–30. doi:10.1177/0031721717708291

Goldhaber, D., & Theobald, R. (2022). Teacher attrition and mobility over time. *Educational Researcher, 51*(3), 235–237. doi:10.3102/0013189X211060840

Grossmann, M., Reckhow, S., Strunk, K. O., & Turner, M. (2021). All states close but red districts reopen: The politics of in-person schooling during the COVID-19 pandemic. *Educational Researcher, 50*(9), 637–648. doi:10.3102/0013189X211048840

Halloran, C., Jack, R., Okun, J. C., & Oster, E. (2021). *Pandemic schooling mode and student test scores: Evidence from US states* (No. w29497). National Bureau of Economic Research. https://nber.org/papers/w29497

Hartney, M. T., & Finger, L. K. (2021). Politics, markets, and pandemics: Public education's response to Covid-19. In Eds., M. Bernhard & D. J. O'Neill *Perspectives on Politics* (pp. 457–473). doi:10.1017/S1537592721000955

Houchard, M. A. (2005). *Principal leadership, teacher morale, and student achievement in seven schools in Mitchell County, North Carolina.* East Tennessee State University.

Hutchison, S. M., Watts, A., Gadermann, A., Oberle, E., Oberlander, T. F., Lavoie, P. M., & Mâsse, L. C. (2022). School staff and teachers during the second year of COVID-19: Higher anxiety symptoms, higher psychological distress, and poorer mental health compared to the general population. *Journal of Affective Disorders Reports, 8*, 100335. doi:10.1016/j.jadr.2022.100335

Huysman, J. (2008). Rural teacher satisfaction: An analysis of beliefs and attitudes of rural teachers' job satisfaction . *The Rural Educator, 29*, (2), 31–38. 10.35608/ruraled.v29i2.471.

Ingersoll, R. M. (2001). Teacher turnover and teacher shortages: An organizational analysis. *American Educational Research Journal, 38*(3), 499–534. doi:10.3102/00028312038003499

Ingersoll, R., Merril, L., May, H., Barton, J. A., Pittiglio, R., Ingersoll, R., & Jabs, E. W. (2014). What are the effects of teacher education and preparation on beginning teacher attrition? *JAMA Ophthalmology, 132*, (10) 1215–1220. 10.12698/cpre.2014.rr82. Philadelphia, PA Consortium for Policy Research in Education

Jones, A. L., & Kessler, M. A. (2020). Teachers' emotion and identity work during a pandemic. *Frontiers in Education, 5*, 583775. doi:10.3389/feduc.2020.583775

Jotkoff, E. (2022). NEA survey: Massive staff shortages in schools leading to educator burnout: Alarming number of educators indicating they plan to leave profession. *National Education Association.* https://www.nea.org/about-nea/media-center/press-releases/nea-survey-massive-staff-shortages-schools-leading-educator

Kaden, U. (2020). COVID-19 school closure-related changes to the professional life of a K–12 teacher. *Educational Sciences, 10*(6), 1–13. doi:10.3390/edusci10060165

Kotowski, S. E., Davis, K. G., Barratt, C. L., Davis, K., & Kotowski, S. (2022). Teachers feeling the burden of COVID-19: Impact on well-being, stress, and burnout. *Work, 71*(2), 407–415. doi:10.3233/WOR-210994

Kraft, M. A., Simon, N. S., & Lyon, M. A. (2021). Sustaining a sense of success: The protective role of teacher working conditions during the COVID-19 pandemic. *Journal of Research on Educational Effectiveness, 14*(4), 727–769. doi:10.1080/19345747.2021.1938314

Kush, J. M., Badillo-Goicoechea, E., Musci, R. J., & Stuart, E. A. (2021). Teachers' Mental Health During the COVID-19 Pandemic. *Educational Researcher, 51*(9), 593–597. *arXiv.* doi:10.48550/arXiv.2109.01547

Lopes, J., & Oliveira, C. (2020). Teacher and school determinants of teacher job satisfaction: A multilevel analysis. *School Effectiveness and School Improvement, 31*(4), 641–659. doi:10.1080/09243453.2020.1764593

Love, S. M., & Marshall, D. T. (2022). Teacher experiences during COVID-19. In D. T. Marshall (Ed.), *COVID-19 and the classroom: How schools navigated the great disruption* (pp. 21–65). Lexington Books.

Lumsden, L., Huitinga, I., Lumsden, L., & Dijkstra, C. D. (1998).Marrow-derived activated macrophages are required during the effector phase of experimental autoimmune uveoretinitis in rats. *Current Eye Research, 17,* (4) 426–437. 10.1080/02713689808951224. ERIC DigestNumber 120

Ma, K., Liang, L., Chutiyami, M., Nicoll, S., Khaerudin, T., & Van Ha, X. (2022). COVID-19 pandemic-related anxiety, stress, and depression among teachers: A systematic review and meta-analysis. *Work, 73*(1), 3–27. doi:10.3233/WOR-220062

Malik, M. (2021). A phenomenological study regarding the effects of leadership styles on perceived teacher morale and work performance at a charter school [Doctoral dissertation]. Lamar University.

Malloy, C., & Wohlstetter, P. (2003). Working conditions in charter schools. *Education and Urban Society, 35*(2), 219–241. doi:10.1177/0013124502239393

Margolis, J., & Nagel, L. (2006). Education reform and the role of administrators in mediating teacher stress. *Teacher Education Quarterly, 33*(4), 143–159. https://www.jstor.org/stable/23478876

Marshall, D. T. (2022). *COVID-19 and the classroom: How schools navigated the great disruption.* Lexington Books.

Marshall, D. T., & Bradley-Dorsey, M. (2020). Reopening America's schools: A descriptive look at how states and large school districts are navigating fall 2020. *Journal of School Choice, 14* (4), 534–566. doi:10.1080/15582159.2020.1822731

Marshall, D. T., & Bradley-Dorsey, M. (2022). Reopening schools in the United States. In D. T. Marshall (Ed.), *COVID-19 and the classroom: How schools navigated the great disruption* (pp. 147–164). Lexington Books.

Marshall, D. T., Love, S. M., Neugebauer, N. M., & Smith, N. E. (in press). *How additional professional time benefitted teachers during COVID-19*How additional professional time benefitted teachers during COVID-19 (S. M. McCarther & D. M. Davis Eds.). Information Age Publishing.

Marshall, D. T., Love, S. M., Shannon, D. M., & Neugebauer, N. M. (2022d). *Burnout, workload, and morale: Describing teacher experiences at the conclusion of a pandemic year.* SocArXiv. doi:10.31235/osf.io/cnxp6

Marshall, D. T., Pressley, T., & Love, S. M. (2022c). The times they are a-changin': Teaching and learning beyond COVID-19. *Journal of Educational Change, 23*(4), 549–557. doi:10.1007/s10833-022-09469-z

Marshall, D. T., Pressley, T., Neugebauer, N. M., & Shannon, D. M. (2022b). Why teachers are leaving and what we can do about it. *Phi Delta Kappan, 104*(1), 6–11. doi:10.1177/00317217221123642

Marshall, D. T., Shannon, D. M., Love, S. M., & Neugebauer, N. M. (2022a). Factors related to teacher resilience during COVID-19. Advance. doi:10.31124/advance.19799821.v2

McCarthy, C. J., Blaydes, M., Weppner, C. H., & Lambert, R. G. (2022). Teacher stress and COVID-19: Where do we go from here? *Phi Delta Kappan, 104*(1), 12–17. doi:10.1177/00317217221123643

Menter, K. (2022). Locus of control, burnout, and work engagement among K-12 teachers during COVID-19 remote learning. In *M.A.* Northern Illinois University. https://www.proquest.com/docview/2676590823/abstract/89BDF35BECB4469BPQ/1

Merseth, K. (2009). *Inside urban charter schools: Promising practices and strategies in five high-performing schools.* Cambridge, MA: Harvard Education Press.

Minihan, E., Adamis, D., Dunleavy, M., Martin, A., Gavin, B., & McNicholas, F. (2022). COVID-19 related occupational stress in teachers in Ireland. *International Journal of Educational Research Open, 3*, 100114. doi:10.1016/j.ijedro.2021.100114

Miraj, S., Reba, A., & Din, J. U. (2018). A comparative study regarding teachers' morale among public and private schools at secondary level in Peshawar. *Bulletin of Education and Research, 40*(2), 27–40.

Musaddiq, T., Stange, K., Bacher-Hicks, A., & Goodman, J. (2022). The pandemic's effect on demand for public schools, homeschooling, and private schools. *Journal of Public Economics, 212*, 104710. doi:10.1016/j.jpubeco.2022.104710

National Center for Education Statistics. 2021b, September. Table 208.20. Public and private elementary and secondary teachers, enrollment, pupil/teacher ratios, and new teacher hirs: Selected years, fall 1955 through fall 2030 [Data table. In *Digest of education statistics,* U.S. Department of Education, Institute of Education Sciences https://nces.ed.gov/programs/digest/d21/tables/dt21_208.20.asp

National Center for Education StatisticsCenter for Education Statistics. (2016). *Teacher turnover: Stayers, movers, and leavers.* Condition of education*Characteristics of public and private elementary and secondary school teachers in the United States: Results from the 2017-18 National Teacher and Principal Survey.* U.S. Department of Education, Institute of Education SciencesUnited States Department of Education. Retrieved [date], from2020 https://nces.ed.gov/programs/coe/indicator/slc.Nationalhttps://nces.ed.gov/pubs2020/2020142rev.pdf

National Center for Education Statistics. (2021a). *Number and percentage distribution of private elementary and secondary students, teachers, and schools, by orientation of school and selected characteristics: Fall 2009, fall 2017, and fall 2019.* United States Department of Education, Institute of Education Sciences. https://nces.ed.gov/programs/digest/d21/tables/dt21_205.40.asp

Ndoye, A., Imig, S. R., & Parker, M. A. (2010). Empowerment, leadership, and teachers' intentions to stay in or leave their profession or their schools in North Carolina charter schools. *Journal of School Choice, 4*(2), 174–190. doi:10.1080/15582159.2010.483920

Nguyen, T. D., Bettini, E., Redding, C., & Gilmour, A. F. (2022). Comparing turnover intentions and actual turnover in the public sector workforce: Evidence from public school teachers. *EdWorkingPaper* (No. 22–537). https://www.edworkingpapers.com/sites/default/files/ai22-537.pdf

Nield, K., & Nordstrom, A. T. (2016). *Response bias in voluntary surveys: An empirical analysis of the Canadian census* (No. 16-10). Ottawa, Ontario, Canada: Carleton University, Department of Economics.

Oberfield, Z. (2016). A bargain half fulfilled: Teacher autonomy and accountability in traditional public schools and public charter schools. *American Educational Research Journal, 53*(2), 296–323. doi:10.3102/0002831216634843

Oberfield, Z. (2017). *Are charters different? Public education, teachers, and the charter school debate.* Cambridge, MA: Harvard Education Press.

Pondiscio, R. (2019). *How the other half learns: Equality, excellence, and the battle over school choice.* New York: Avery.

Pressley, T. (2021). Factors contributing to teacher burnout during COVID-19. *Educational Researcher, 50*(5), 325–327. doi:10.3102/0013189X211004138

Pressley, T., Ha, C., & Learn, E. (2021). Teacher stress and anxiety during COVID-19: An empirical study. *School Psychology, 36*(5), 367–376. doi:10.1037/spq0000468

Răducu, C. M., & Stănculescu, E. (2022). Teachers' burnout risk during the COVID-19 pandemic: Relationships with socio-contextual stress—A latent profile analysis. *Frontiers in Psychiatry, 13*, 1–10. doi:10.3389/fpsyt.2022.870098

Remple, A. M., & Bentley, R. R. (1970). Teacher morale: Relationship with selected factors. *Journal of Teacher Education, 21*(4), 534–539. doi:10.1177/002248717002100414

Robinson, L. E., Valido, A., Drescher, A., Woolweaver, A. B., Espelage, D. L., LoMurray, S., Dailey, M. M. (2022). Teachers, stress, and the COVID-19 pandemic: A qualitative analysis. *School Mental Health, 15*(1), 1–12. doi:10.1007/s12310-022-09533-2

Roch, C. H., & Sai, N. (2016). Charter school teacher job satisfaction. *Educational Policy, 31*(7), 951–991. doi:10.1177/0895904815625281

Rogowska, A. M., & Meres, H. (2022). The mediating role of job satisfaction in the relationship between emotional intelligence and life satisfaction among teachers during the COVID-19 pandemic. *European Journal Investigating Health Psychology in Education, 12*(7), 666–676. doi:10.3390/ejihpe12070050

Rosenberg, D., & Anderson, T. (2021). Teacher Turnover before, during, & after COVID. *Education resource strategies.* https://files.eric.ed.gov/fulltext/ED614496.pdf

Ryan, S. V., Nathaniel, P., Pendergast, L. L., Saeki, E., Segool, N., & Schwing, S. (2017). Leaving the teaching profession: The role of teacher stress and educational accountability policies on turnover intent. *Teaching and Teacher Education, 66*, 1–11. doi:10.1016/j.tate.2017.03.016

Savas, A. C., Bozgeyik, Y., & Eser, I. (2014). A study on the relationship between teacher self efficacy and burnout. *European Journal of Educational Research, 3*(4), 159–166. doi:10.12973/eu-jer.3.4.159

Scafidi, B., Tutterow, R., & Kavanagh, D. (2021). "This time really is different": The effect of COVID-19 on independent K-12 school enrollments. *Journal of School Choice, 15*(3), 305–330. doi:10.1080/15582159.2021.1944722

Seidman, S. A., & Zager, J. (1986). The Teacher Burnout Scale. *Educational Research Quarterly, 11*(1), 26–33.

Senechal, J., Sober, T., Hope, S., Johnson, T., Burkhalter, F., Castelow, T., & Gilfillan, D. (2016). *Understanding teacher morale.* Richmond, VA: Metropolitan Educational Research Consortium. https://scholarscompass.vcu.edu/merc_pubs/56

Skaalvik, E., & Skaalvik, S. (2010). Teacher self-efficacy and teacher burnout: A study of relations. *Teaching and Teacher Education, 26*(4), 1059–1069. doi:10.1016/j.tate.2009.11.001

Skaalvik, E. M., & Skaalvik, S. (2011). Teacher job satisfaction and motivation to leave the teaching profession: Relations with school context, feeling of belonging, and emotional exhaustion. *Teaching and Teacher Education, 27*(6), 1029–1038. doi:10.1016/j.tate.2011.04.001

Slavin, R. E., & Storey, N. (2020). The US educational response to the COVID-19 pandemic. *Best Evidence of Chinese Education, 5*(2), 617–633. doi:10.15354/bece.20.or027

Sokal, L., Trudel, L. E., & Babb, J. (2020). Canadian teachers' attitudes toward change, efficacy, and burnout during the COVID-19 pandemic. *International Journal of Educational Research Open, 1*, 100016. doi:10.1016/j.ijedro.2020.100016

Sokal, L., Trudel, L. E., & Babb, J. (2021). I've had it! Factors associated with burnout and low organizational commitment in Canadian teachers during the second wave of the COVID-19 pandemic. *International Journal of Educational Research Open, 2*(2), 1–9. doi:10.1016/j.ijedro.2020.100023

Steiner, E. D., & Woo, A.(2021).Job-Related stress threatens the teacher supply: Key findings from the 2021 state of the U.S. teacher survey.*RAND Corporation.* 10.7249/RRA1108-1

Torres, A. C. (2014). "Are we architects or construction workers?" Re-examining teacher autonomy and turnover in charter schools. *Education Policy Analysis Archives, 22*, 124. doi:10.14507/epaa.v22.1614

Torres, A. C. (2016). The uncertainty of high expectations: How principals influence relational trust and teacher turnover in no excuses charter schools. *Journal of School Leadership, 26*(1), 61–91. doi:10.1177/105268461602600103

Veney, D., & Jacobs, D. 2021, September, *Voting with their feet: A state-level analysis of public charter school and district public school trends* Washington, DC National Alliance for Public Charter Schools https://www.publiccharters.org/sites/default/files/documents/2021-09/napcs_voting_feet_rd6.pdf

Virginia Department of Education. (2021). *Review copy 2021 Virginia school survey: Classroom instructors.* https://doe.virginia.gov/support/201-va-school-survey-classroom-instructors

Walter, H. L., & Fox, H. B. (2021). Understanding Teacher Well-Being During the Covid-19 Pandemic Over Time: A Qualitative Longitudinal Study. *Journal of Organizational Psychology, 27*(5), 36–50.

Watson, A. R. (2022). Pandemic pods and alternative modes of education. In D. T. Marshall (Ed.), *COVID-19 and the classroom: How schools navigated the great disruption* (pp. 197–210). Lanham, MD: Lexington Books.

Waychunas, W. (2022). Through the eyes of novice teachers: Experiences with professional cultures within and outside of neoliberal "no excuses" charter schools. *Research in Educational Policy and Management, 4*(2), 56–79. doi:10.46303/repam.2022.7

Westphal, A., Kalinowski, E., Hoferichter, C. J., & Vock, M. (2022). K-12 teachers' stress and burnout during the COVID-19 pandemic: A systematic review. *Frontiers in Psychology, 13*, 920326. doi:10.3389/fpsyg.2022.920326

Zamarro, G., Camp, A., Fuchsman, D., & McGee, J. B. (2022). Understanding how Covid-19 has changed teachers' chances of remaining in the classroom. Working Paper, Department of Education Reform, University of Arkansas. https://scholarworks.uark.edu/edrepub/132

Appendix A

Teacher Burnout Scale[a]

To what extent do you agree with the following statements?

Participants answer on a 6-point scale: (1) strongly disagree; (2) disagree; (3) somewhat disagree; (4) somewhat agree; (5) agree; (6) strongly agree

(1) I feel emotionally drained from my work.
(2) I feel burned out from my work.
(3) I feel frustrated with my job.

[a] Created for this study.

Job Satisfaction Scale (Skaalvik & Skaalvik, 2011)

To what extent do you agree with the following statements?

Participants answer on a 6-point scale: (1) strongly disagree; (2) disagree; (3) somewhat disagree; (4) somewhat agree; (5) agree; (6) strongly agree

(1) I enjoy working as a teacher.
(2) I look forward to going to work every day.
(3) Working as a teacher is extremely rewarding.
(4) When I get up in the morning, I look forward to going to work.

Teacher Leadership and Autonomy Scale (Virginia Department of Education, 2021)

To what extent do you agree with the following statements?

Participants answer on a 6-point scale: (1) strongly disagree; (2) disagree; (3) somewhat disagree; (4) somewhat agree; (5) agree; (6) strongly agree

(1) I am trusted to make sound professional decisions about instruction.
(2) I contribute to decisions about educational issues at my school.
(3) I am free to be creative in my teaching approach.
(4) I control how I use my scheduled class time.
(5) I set the grading and student assessment practices in my classroom.
(6) My role as an educator is respected under current policies.
(7) Current policies are improving our educational system.
(8) My scheduled work day includes sufficient planning time.
(9) My scheduled work day includes sufficient instructional time to meet the needs of my students.

Administrative Support Scale (Seidman & Zager, 1986)

To what extent do you agree with the following statements?

Participants answer on a 6-point scale: (1) strongly disagree; (2) disagree; (3) somewhat disagree; (4) somewhat agree; (5) agree; (6) strongly agree

(1) I get adequate praise from my administrators for a job well done.
(2) I feel the administrators are willing to help me with classroom problems, should they arise.

(3) I believe my efforts in the classroom are unappreciated by the administrators[a]
(4) My supervisors give me more criticism than praise[a]
(5) I feel that the administrators will not help me with classroom difficulties[a]
(6) The administration blames me for classroom problems[a]

[a] Reverse score these items.

Index

Note: Page numbers followed by "n" denote endnotes.

adolescents 3, 121–125
adults 16, 44, 110, 111, 121, 209
Allen, D. W. 111
Allison, P. D. 157n38
America's schools, reopening 50–63
assignments 14, 15, 23, 25, 32, 167
attendance 15, 25, 139, 164
attrition 238, 241
Auger, K. A. 1, 122

Bacher-Hicks, A. 96
Badura, P. 124
Baker, D. P. 137
Barratt, C. L. 242
Berends, M. 155n14
Berger, E. L. 125
Black student enrollment 149, 151, 154
Boniel-Nissim, M. 124
Branch, G. F. 148
brick-and-mortar schools 34, 153
Brooks, S. K. 124
Bryk, A. 205
burnout 3, 238, 239, 242, 243, 245, 247, 248, 251

Cameron, A. C. 157n32
Camp, A. 241
Carpenter, D. 208
Carter-Rau, R. 107
Catholic schools 171, 180, 205
Chan, T. H. 86
charter schools 3, 11, 20, 22, 23, 28, 133–135, 208, 216, 220, 230–232, 240; enrollments 4, 209, 239
child/children 3, 4, 16, 18–20, 25, 26, 32–33, 41–42, 44, 51, 62, 123, 137, 165, 166, 190, 191, 205–206, 210–211, 213, 215, 231, 233; characteristics 211, 212, 220, 229, 231
Childs, J. 233
Christakis, D. 96, 123
Christensen, C. 15
communication 19, 23, 24, 26, 28
compensatory education 113

continuity 6–11
control variables 88, 109, 111, 193, 194
Cordes, S. 155n10
core business statistical area (CBSA) 91, 93
Cosma, A. 124
Courtemanche, C. J. 84
Cowan, K. C. 125
Crain, T. P. 18

Dahl, R. E. 125
Davis, K. G. 242
DeAngelis, C. A. 94, 170–171, 179, 191
dependent variable 149, 174, 175, 177, 186, 193, 213, 246
disruption 6–11, 55, 62, 121, 202
district reopening modalities 56–58
Dorn, E. 191
Dornoff, S. E. 125
Duan, L. 124
Dumas, T. M. 124
dummy variable 246
Dunn, J. 208

economic variables 173, 176, 180, 185–187
education 41, 43, 44, 51–58, 131, 168–170
educational renaissance 34
elementary schools 57, 60
elementary students 52, 53, 59
Ellis, W. E. 124
e-mail 26, 33, 140
emergency remote-learning systems 106, 114
empirical approach 165, 168, 174, 175
empirical models 174
empirical specification 85, 90, 185–187
engagement 6, 19, 26
enrollments: changes 132, 142, 144, 149, 165, 168, 175–177, 180, 186, 193, 194; trends 138, 153, 189–197
equity 6–11, 41
ethnicity 134, 148, 153
explanatory variables 174, 175

260 INDEX

fall sports 55
Fazlul, I. 156n21
Ferrare, J. J. 155n14
Finger, L. K. 86, 170, 171, 179, 180, 191, 207
Fitzpatrick, B. R. 155n14
Flanders, W. 171, 191, 208
Forbes, L. M. 124
Frankenberg, E. 135
Fuller, E. J. 135
full-time virtual schools 18, 138
funding 2, 36, 45, 46, 83–85, 87, 90, 93–94, 99
Furman-Darby, J. 125
Fusco, M. 241

Garet, M. 86
Gelbach, J. B. 157n32
Gemin, B. 154n1
Goldhaber, D. 209
Goodman, J. 96
Great Recession 163, 164
Grissom, J. A. 152
Gross, B. 167
Gulosino, C. 134
Gys, C. 125

Haidt, J. 121
Hailey, C. A. 153
Halloran, C. 209
Hancock, B. 191
Hanushek, E. A. 148, 191
Harris, D. N. 137, 170
Hartney, M. T. 86, 170–171, 179–180, 191, 207
Hassig, S. 170
Hawrilenko, M. 96, 123
health safety 207, 216, 220, 224, 230–233
Henderson, D. R. 18
Hess, F. M. 8
heterogeneity 91, 137, 144, 230
homeschooling 4, 10, 18, 34–36, 43, 44, 180, 181, 192, 210, 233
Horn, M. B. 34
Hudde, A. 109
human life expectancy 7
hybrid instruction 52, 53, 57, 213, 220, 229–232

Imig, S. R. 240
independent k-12 school enrollments 163–181
independent schools 164–171, 173, 174, 178–180, 185, 186; enrollments 164, 165, 167, 168, 172–174, 178–181, 185, 186
in-person instruction 50, 51, 53, 56, 57, 59, 60, 84–86, 99, 207, 213, 220, 231
in-person learning 121, 122, 203–207, 215, 216, 220, 224, 231, 238, 239
instructional modes 202–205, 207–209, 211–213, 220, 224, 230–233
instrumental variables (IVs) 112
Internet speeds 144, 147, 148, 151, 152

Jack, R. 209
job postings 85, 96, 98, 99
job satisfaction 3, 238, 240–242, 245, 247–249

k-12 education 3, 4, 84, 85, 189
k-12 school closures 83
Kain, J. F. 148
Keane, R. 33
Kearney, C. A. 233
Koedel, C. 156n21
Kotok, S. 135
Kotowski, S. E. 242
Kroshus, E. 96, 123

Lake, R. 167
Larsen, M. 137
Laurito, A. 155n10
Le, A. H. 84
learning 52, 55, 84, 85, 106, 107, 113, 114, 125, 169, 170, 190, 191, 209, 243; losses 2, 3, 106–109, 112–114, 190, 191; modalities 2, 3, 51, 52, 165, 168–172, 176–180; outcomes 83, 84, 95, 99, 107, 109, 111, 114; pods 4, 11, 41–46, 233, 239; spaces 45
Lessler, J. 206
loneliness 123–125
Lopes, J. 241
Love, S. M. 50

Magis-Weinburg, L. 125
Makridis, C. A. 84, 94, 96, 170, 171, 179, 191
Malik, M. 242
Malkus, N. 15
Malloy, C. 240
Mann, B. A. 135, 137, 155n8
Marshall, D. T. 50
masks 3, 10, 52–55, 59, 151; wearing 3, 53–55
Mathis, W. J. 135
McCluskey, N. 164, 180
McDonald, K. 18
McGee, J. B. 241
McKinsey & Company 84
McNab, B. 84
media stories 22, 41
mental health 95, 96, 98, 99, 122–126, 246, 249, 250; outcomes 85, 98, 123
Merseth, K. 242
Miller, D. L. 157n32
Milwaukee Parental Choice Program (MPCP) 196
Miron, G. 134, 135
multinomial logit (MNL) 174–175, 187
Murnane, R. J. 137
Musaddiq, T. 96, 208

Naff, D. 125
Ndoye, A. 240
neighborhood schools 13, 18, 132–137, 148, 149
Newsome, U. W. 152

INDEX

Ng, K. 124
Nguyen, T. D. 241
Nitsche, N. 109

Oberfield, Z. 249
Okun, J. C. 209
Oliveira, C. 241
online education 132, 138, 144, 147, 148, 151–154, 192
online enrollment 4, 132, 133, 147, 148, 151–153
online learning 8, 23, 154, 230–232
online public education 131–154
online schooling 8, 10, 134, 137, 151, 152
online schools 10, 11, 147, 151–154
Opalka, A. 8, 167
Oster, E. 209

parental assessments 28
parental safety 203–206
parent-created schools 41–46
parents 3, 4, 13, 14, 16, 18, 19, 22, 26, 28, 32, 33, 42, 62, 203, 206, 210, 211, 230, 233; characteristics 211, 216, 229, 231; and students 19, 22, 153
Parker, M. A. 240
Parsons, E. 156n21
Patrick, S. K. 152
Patrinos, H. 107
pediatric mental health impacts 121–126
poverty 51, 57–60, 123, 126, 239, 246
private schools 10, 17, 20, 26, 28, 35, 42, 44, 45, 86, 107, 134, 208, 216, 220, 230–232, 248; enrollments 4, 185, 208, 209; parents 3, 8, 25, 26, 28, 30, 205, 230, 231; students 17, 83, 207; universe survey 185
public charter schools 209, 213, 239
public education 4, 62
public school: choice 192; funding 87, 89; shutdowns 189–197; students 17, 131, 134

quality 3, 6, 33, 34, 132, 136, 138, 210, 213, 230–232

race 20, 21, 56, 57, 59, 60, 91, 134, 136, 137, 144, 145, 148, 149, 153
racial composition 132, 136, 144, 148, 149, 151
Reardon, S. F. 137
regression models 149, 180, 212, 246
remote districts 89, 96, 98, 99
remote instruction 15, 50, 53, 56, 59, 60, 85, 91–95, 98, 99, 202
remote learning 2–4, 13, 16–19, 21–26, 33; options 56, 62
reopening guidance 51, 61
reopening schools 51, 52, 61, 84, 85, 87, 88, 189
Ritter, G. W. 135
Rivkin, S. G. 148
Rossen, E. 125
Roza, M. 94

Sarakatsannis, J. 191
Schafft, K. A. 135
Schneider, B. 205
school closures 2, 3, 84, 95, 106–114, 121–126, 204; duration of 106, 107, 109–112
school governance models (SGMs) 202–205, 207–208, 211–213, 216–220, 224, 230, 231, 233
school quality 111, 203, 204, 206–209, 211–213, 224, 229–232
school reopening decisions 83–100, 193
school segregation 134, 135, 153
schools of choice 239, 240, 243, 246, 248
Schurz, J. 15
Senechal, J. 246
Shannon, D. M. 50
Sherman, J. D. 86
Slavin, Robert 44
social closure 205, 230
social distancing 10, 59, 95
social welfare 99
sports 52, 55, 59, 61, 62
Staker, H. 34
Stange, K. M. 96
state reopening plans and guidance 52
Stride school 133, 139–145, 147–149, 151
stringency index 112
student achievement 132, 137, 153, 207, 242
student enrollment 89, 92, 93, 96, 132, 134, 144, 164, 194
Svacina, K. 124

Talkington, B. 8
Tan, W. 124
Tandon, P. 96, 123
teachers: autonomy 245, 247, 249; burnout 240–242, 245–247, 249, 250 (see also burnout); morale 238, 240, 242, 246, 247; and students 24, 122
Tornquist, E. 135
Torres, A. C. 249
traditional public schools (TPS) 3, 4, 8, 9, 20, 23, 24, 26, 28, 30, 34–36, 41, 207, 208, 213, 216, 240, 243, 248–250
tutors 19, 42, 44, 45

unionization 91, 93, 108
Urschel, J. 135

vaccination rate 107, 108, 111, 112
Valant, J. 170, 171, 179, 191
Vegas, E. 107
virtual charters 134, 192, 196; schools 44, 192
virtual education 190, 191, 193, 196
virtual public schools 133, 192
virtual school enrollments 132, 133, 135–140, 143, 147, 149
virtual schooling 34, 43, 44, 131, 133, 134, 136, 138, 152, 168

Viruleg, E. 191
vulnerable populations 52, 54

Waddington, R. J. 155n14
Waychunas, W. 241
Wicks, M. 154n2
Williams, S. 125
Woessmann, L. 191
Wohlstetter, P. 240
Woods, S. C. 152
working parents 22

work responsibilities 22, 26
worst global pandemic 7
Wu, C. 96

Yelowitz, A. 84
Yeong, M. 125

Zamarro, G. 241
Zhang, L. 95
Ziedan, E. 170
Zimmer, R. 84